P9-EDZ-128

INVASION OF THE MIND SNATCHERS

INVASION OF THE
MIND SNATCHERS

Television's Conquest of
America in the Fifties

ERIC BURNS

TEMPLE UNIVERSITY PRESS PHILADELPHIA

Eric Burns is a cultural historian and former television journalist. He was named by the *Washington Journalism Review* as one of the best writers in the history of broadcast journalism. His books include *The Spirits of America: A Social History of Alcohol* and *The Smoke of the Gods: A Social History of Tobacco* (both Temple), which were named the "Best of the Best from University Presses" by the American Library Association. He is also the author of *Broadcast Blues, The Joy of Books,* and *Infamous Scribblers: The Founding Fathers and the Rowdy Beginnings of American Journalism.*

TEMPLE UNIVERSITY PRESS
Philadelphia, Pennsylvania 19122
www.temple.edu/tempress

All attempts were made to locate the copyright holders for the images published in this book. If you believe you may be one of them, please contact Temple University Press (*www.temple.edu/tempress*). The publisher will be sure to include appropriate acknowledgment in subsequent editions of this book.

Library of Congress Cataloging-in-Publication Data

Burns, Eric.
  Invasion of the mind snatchers : television's conquest of America
in the fifties / by Eric Burns.
      p. cm.
  Includes bibliographical references and index.
  ISBN 978-1-4399-0288-2 (cloth : alk. paper) — ISBN 978-1-4399-0290-5
(electronic) 1. Television broadcasting—Social aspects—United States.
2. Television broadcasting—United States—History—20th century. I. Title.
  PN1992.3.U5.B85 2010
  302.23'45'0973—dc22

                                                     2009052963

⊗ The paper used in this publication meets the requirements of the
American National Standard for Information Sciences—Permanence of Paper
for Printed Library Materials, ANSI Z39.48-1992

Printed in the United States of America
2 4 6 8 9 7 5 3 1

This book is dedicated to

Lydia Yacovoni Burns
Henrietta Yacovoni
Jack Vincent Burns

with whom I watched so much television in the fifties.

Contents

A Note to Readers

NVASION OF THE MIND SNATCHERS: *Television's Conquest of America in the Fifties* is about the way Americans reacted to TV in the decade when we reacted most strongly—which is to say, when the new medium was at its most powerful, its most preoccupying, its most life-altering. The book has little to do with technology, much to do with the men, women and children who so willingly yielded to the spell that the technology cast in their homes.

I was one of them. Since I was born midway through the forties, I am not only the author of this volume but one of its sources, as are a number of friends and acquaintances whose birthdays are within a few years of mine. All of us were not only sentient during the fifties, but attentive. We watched television daily, played our own versions of the shows that were our favorites, purchased the merchandise they promoted, and observed the behavior of the adults around us who were just as deeply under the medium's spell as we were. But since they tuned into different programs than we did, they revealed their subservience in different ways.

Invasion of the Mind Snatchers, though, is a history, not a memoir. The first person singular pronoun is used sparingly. Sources for the book other than the author and his playmates, and these make up the vast majority, are listed in both the notes and the bibliography.

Eric Burns
Westport, Connecticut
January 3, 2010

Introduction

Philo T. Farnsworth's Discontent

N 1880, long before the story of this book officially begins, Jesse James and his gang tried to rob the First National Bank of Northfield, Minnesota. They failed. They were chased out of town by an enraged citizenry. Back to the drawing board. In the same year, Wyatt Earp spent a few months as deputy sheriff of Tombstone, Arizona, and 14-year-old Butch Cassidy, born Robert LeRoy Parker, committed what was probably the first crime of his life, stealing a pair of blue jeans and, out of either naïveté, braggadocio or some perversely twisted sense of honor, leaving behind an IOU that led to his capture.

In more cultured circles, Peter Tchaikovsky, Johannes Brahms, Franz Liszt, and Gilbert and Sullivan were still writing music, and Robert Louis Stevenson, Thomas Hardy, Henry James and Mark Twain were still turning out novels, although the latter had not yet gotten around to his masterpiece, *Huckleberry Finn*. Oscar Wilde and Henrik Ibsen were alive and well and writing plays, and William Butler Yeats and Robert Browning were still calling upon their muses for elegantly crafted poems. Van Gogh and John Singer Sargent painted; Rodin sculpted; and at the other extreme of artistic expression, P. T. Barnum staged circuses and freak shows for the less cultured sorts whom he believed were born every minute.

The first canned fruits and meats had just begun to appear on the shelves of grocery stores, but the country's first skyscraper, all of ten stories, was still three years away from looming over Chicago's business district. An act of Congress permitted female attorneys to argue before the Supreme Court, but there were so few such creatures at the time that it hardly mattered. The president of the United States was Rutherford B. Hayes, and there were thirty-eight stars on the flag. The principal means of employment for Americans was farming, the principal means of attire a shirt or skirt or pair of pants made by the womenfolk in the family, and the principal means of transportation the foot.

And yet in 1880, four years after he patented the telephone, Alexander Graham Bell took out the first patents for the device that would eventually become television. He thought of it, however, less as the medium we know today than as an improvement on his previous invention—a telephone that allowed a person not just to speak to another but to look at him in the process. Bell called his new brainchild a *photophone,* and it excited him so much that he would sometimes work on it all night, unable to sleep. "I have my periods of restlessness," his wife-to-be quoted him as saying, "when my brain is crowded with ideas tingling in my fingertips when I am excited and cannot stop for anybody."

And he did not stop, not until he had actually built a photophone, a clumsy looking machine that did not work, functioning neither as photo nor phone. But Bell did not expect it to; he knew the time was not yet right, the science not yet sufficiently advanced. The photophone would one day revolutionize the way people communicated with one another, of that he was certain, so certain that he donated his prototype to the Smithsonian Institution, wanting credit for the concept if not the execution. The Smithsonian accepted the gift. But it hung no banners to boast of the acquisition, and the device did not attract either publicity or crowds once it was displayed.

THE TELEPHONE, as it turned out, was indispensable to the development of television. It laid some of the conceptual groundwork for the later medium but, more importantly, it inspired men to imagine that if voices could travel across wires, so could pictures. They had not thought of such a thing before; they were thrilled, as was Bell, to think of it now.

In 1877, not long after Bell had begun discussing and writing about his photophone fantasies, a government official in Boston named George Carey made sketches for something he referred to as a *selenium camera,* which would enable people to "see by electricity." Other visionaries were doodling their own sketches for electrical sight, and were giving them such names as *telectroscopes* and *iconoscopes* and *electric telescopes* and *electric eyes* and *picture radios* and *radio visions.*

Also in 1877, the *New York Sun* published a letter to the editor that made the following claim:

> An eminent scientist of this city . . . is said to be on the point of publishing a series of important discoveries, and exhibiting an instrument invented by him by means of which objects or persons standing or moving in any part of the world may be instantaneously seen anywhere and by anybody.

The report was premature. It was also startling, the stuff of fiction, the kind being written by the wildly imaginative Jules Verne, another of the era's notable authors. But could it ever be the stuff of fact? Some of those who read the letter in the *Sun* that day in 1877 did so in the glow of a candle, others in the noxious fumes of gaslight. If they lived in the cities, horses clattered by their windows, pulling carriages and wagons along roads that were not paved. And yet one day pictures were to ride invisibly on the breezes until they landed on a screen of some sort, and in that instant become visible a thousand miles away from their origin?

It hardly seemed possible.

THE WORD "TELEVISION" does not seem to have been used until 1900, when a Russian scientist uttered it at the First International Congress of Electricity, part of the Paris World's Fair. In 1907, it appeared in this country in *Scientific American.* Three years later, the *Kansas City Times,* as premature as the *New York Sun* had been, announced that "television [is] on the way." Shortly afterward, other publications, for both scholarly and general audiences, began to employ the term, as did most of the men who were trying to make the gadget a reality.

Not, however, Philo T. Farnsworth. To him, television was an image dissector, and he had begun thinking about it as a freckle-faced, tousle-haired teenager. He was thinking other fantastic thoughts too, and despite his youth, had been doing so for several years. "At an age when most children are still playing with building blocks," wrote a journalist some time later, "[Farnsworth's] special delights were a toy dynamo and a toy electric motor. He hooked up the dynamo to the flywheel of his mother's sewing machine, thus generating enough current to run the motor, and by frequently taking apart and putting together all his apparatus he learned a good deal about the theory and practice of electrical machinery."

He learned so much, in fact, that at the age of fourteen he figured out how to attach a battery to the family's washing machine and convert it from a manual to an electric, the only one of its kind in Beaver, Utah, in 1920. His mother's washday burden was lightened, as her sewing burden had previously been lightened. Neighbors came to see the new appliance, as they had previously come to see the sewing machine, and gaped as if it were one of those famed rural legends, the two-headed calf. Young Philo stood to the side and accepted congratulations modestly.

Then he turned his attention to more challenging matters, perhaps memorizing Einstein's theory of photoelectrics, which he did at about this time. Like Einstein, Farnsworth wanted to be known for the brilliance of his ideas when he grew up—but even more, he wanted those ideas to have practical applications, to result in products that would cause the whole world to gape, making the marvelous a daily occurrence. Einstein was a hero to Farnsworth, but he had other heroes too, heroes of a more utilitarian bent: Edison and Morse and the Wright Brothers and, at the top of his list, Alexander Graham Bell.

Although no one person can be said to have invented television, Farnsworth comes the closest. In 1922, when he was sixteen, his chemistry teacher, Justin Tolman,

> found the study-hall blackboard chalked from border to border with electrical circuit diagrams, on which Farnsworth was feverishly scrawling the finishing touches.
>
> "What's this got to do with chemistry?" Tolman asked.
>
> "I told you I wanted to be an inventor, and this is my invention," Farnsworth said. "I've got to tell you about it. You're the only person I can make sense to."

The electrical circuit diagrams were Farnsworth's first sketches of an image dissector.

IN 1924, Farnsworth's father died, and Philo dropped out of college to support his mother and younger siblings. He would do so, he hoped, by forming his own company to manufacture image dissectors, although by this time, according to biographer George Everson, he too was using the term *television*, at least on occasion. Everson, who would eventually become Farnsworth's business partner as well as his chronicler, was, when the two of them met, the head of the local office of the Community Chest. Farnsworth had come to see him, and his partner Leslie Gorrell, in the hope of finding a job that would bankroll his dreams. Everson recalls:

> I asked Phil [sic] if he planned to go on to school. "No," he said, "I can't afford it. I've been trying to find a way to finance an invention of mine but it's pretty tough. In fact, I'm so discouraged that I think I'll write up my idea for *Popular Science*. I imagine I could get a hundred dollars if I worked it right."
>
> "What is your idea?" asked Gorrell.
>
> "It's a television system."
>
> "A television system! What's that?" I asked.
>
> "Oh, it's a way of sending pictures through the air the same as we do sound," said Phil.
>
> "Where did you get that idea?" I inquired.
>
> "I thought of it when I was in high school. . . . Then when . . . I went to Brigham Young University I told a couple of the professors about it. They encouraged me and let me try out some things in the lab to prove it would work."

And work they did. Or soon would. A year later, Farnsworth, having finally built a working model of his image dissector, dissected two images, the first time anyone had ever accomplished such a feat. Since the images consisted of 54 horizontal lines, compared to the 480-plus lines that make up today's television pictures, or more than twice that number on high-definition sets, the images were not very clear. But the banker to whom Farnsworth showed them, applying for a loan to support further research, had no trouble making out what they were. The first was a horse that had been painted on a piece of glass. The second, more fittingly and more discernibly, was a dollar sign.

A few days afterward, Farnsworth impressed the banker even more by showing him a different kind of image, one that moved; a burning cigarette with trails of smoke flattening against the screen. The problem, as Michael Ritchie describes it in *Please Stand By*, his account of TV's beginnings, "was that the smoker had to stick his face so close to the transmitter tube that he blistered his nose on its hot lights."

Still, the banker gave Farnsworth the money he wanted. He could keep on dissecting images. There would be no more burn victims in the process.

MORE THAN TWO DECADES would pass before a dollar sign was an appropriate symbol of television's success. But that the medium could be more than a gimmick, that it could be an effective, if one-sided, means of communication, would be established quickly.

In fact, within weeks of Farnsworth's initial broadcasts in 1927, the American Telephone and Telegraph Company arranged for Secretary of Commerce Herbert Hoover to appear on the small screen. Very small. It measured two inches by three inches, about the same height, though not as long, as one of today's credit cards. But Hoover was the first government official ever to be captured within such boundaries. Positioning himself before a televisor, or transmitter tube, he began speaking in that stiff-collared way of his, which was even stiffer when the setting was a formal one.

"It is a matter of just pride to have a part in this historic occasion," Hoover said. "We have long been familiar with the electrical transmission of sound. Today we have, in a sense, the transmission of sight. . . .Human genius has now destroyed the impediment of distance in a new respect, and in a manner hitherto unknown." Hoover spoke in Washington, D.C. He was seen and heard more than 200 miles away in New York City.

When he finished his remarks, J. J. Carty, vice president of A.T.&T., sat before the televisor and said a few words about the communications breakthrough in equally stiff-collared fashion.

Then, as suddenly as if a switch had been thrown, which is precisely what had happened, the platitudes ended and the levity began. The engineers at A.T.&T. flipped off Washington and turned on their studio in Whippany, New Jersey—and in that instant, the *New York Times* reported, there materialized on the screen a fellow named A. Dolan, "a comedian, [who] first appeared before the audience as a stage Irishman, with side whiskers and a broken pipe, and did a monologue in brogue. Then he made a quick change and came back in blackface with a new line of quips in Negro dialect."

The *Times* was charmed. It thought Dolan "went over very well." It also thought Hoover performed acceptably. With the technology, however, the *Times* was positively enraptured. It not only published a front-page story on what amounted to TV's first variety show, but introduced the article with so many headlines that they piled up almost to the fold.

FAR-OFF SPEAKERS SEEN
AS WELL AS HEARD HERE
IN A TEST OF TELEVISION

And . . .

LIKE A PHOTO COME TO LIFE

And . . .

HOOVER'S FACE PLAINLY
IMAGED AS HE SPEAKS
IN WASHINGTON

And . . .

THE FIRST TIME IN HISTORY

And . . .

PICTURES ARE FLASHED BY WIRE
AND RADIO SYNCHRONIZING
WITH SPEAKER'S VOICE

And . . .

COMMERCIAL USE IN DOUBT

And . . .

BUT A.T. & T. HEAD SEES A NEW
STEP IN CONQUEST OF NATURE
AFTER YEARS OF RESEARCH

The story spilled from page one onto page twenty, where it appeared under yet another headline, the blackest, boldest yet:

**TELEVISION TRIUMPHS IN ITS FIRST DEMONSTRATION
BETWEEN NEW YORK AND WASHINGTON**

It is not known whether Philo T. Farnsworth saw the *New York Times* on April 8, 1927, the day of the eight headlines and the voluminous article under them. If he did, he would have wondered why his own accomplishments had not received similar attention, and might have begun to fear they never would. In fact, they never did, partly because after Hoover's appearance on TV, the medium began to grow so rapidly, with so many people now conducting experiments in so many different places and in so many different ways, that it became impossible to separate one individual's contributions from those of anyone else.

PHILO FARNSWORTH did not age gracefully. Neither circumstances nor his disposition would permit it. The older he got, the more time he spent with lawyers, the less with his image dissectors and vacuum tubes and electrical scanners and cathode-rays, all of which he invented and all of which helped improve the quality of both the picture and the sound of television. In fact, Farnsworth eventually would hold more than 160 patents relating to the medium, but they did not come easily; he had to fight off challengers for many of them, which is to say that he had to fight for his role as one of television's principal creators, both in the public eye and among his fellow scientists.

One of the men who wanted to deny him that role was Vladimir Zworykin, a Soviet physicist who came to the United States after the revolution of 1917 and, despite never losing his comically thick Russian accent, became the leading engineer for the Radio Corporation of America. Zworykin was himself responsible for a number of advances in television's development, including the use of an electron microscope and infrared image tubes.

But he could be as deceitful as he was ingenious, and on one occasion took his deceit to a scandalous extreme, visiting Farnsworth's lab, claiming to be an admirer when his real mission was espionage. Farnsworth, who had never heard of Zworykin, and was far too innocent for his own good, welcomed his guest, took him on a tour of the facilities, and showed him his image dissector. Zworykin picked it up and looked at it admiringly, examining it from all angles. He asked questions. What is this for? What does that do? Farnsworth answered Zworykin, expert to expert. "This is a beautiful instrument," the Russian said. "I wish I had invented it myself."

Whereupon he promptly started trying. He committed to memory as much of the dissector's design as possible while holding it in his hands. Then, after bidding Farnsworth farewell, took notes on the device and made drawings and, back in the RCA lab, worked with his staff to come up with his own version of an image dissector, which he would later try to pass off as his own work.

Farnsworth's principal adversary, however, was David Sarnoff, for whom Zworykin acted as henchman as well as chief engineer. Sarnoff wanted Farnsworth's patents, and he did not care whether he bought them, stole them, or simply got permission from a court to make use of them—although the latter two options, being cheaper, were his preference. Sarnoff and Farnsworth were at odds for many years, each suing the other, each accusing the other of all manner of duplicitous behavior, erroneous claims, and financial skullduggery.

It was Farnsworth who had the stronger case. Sarnoff, however, had more lawyers, and when the legal combat between the two men finally ended, it was quantity that mattered, not quality. Sarnoff got almost everything he desired, which, in simplest terms, meant the right to make a fortune from ideas and labors that were largely another's. Farnsworth amassed a smaller fortune of his own, as the court ruled that RCA had to pay him a variety of licensing fees and royalties. But it was Sarnoff's name that would henceforth be synonymous with television, not Farnsworth's. It was Sarnoff who founded an empire, Farnsworth a series of companies, some of which proved more of a burden than a boon.

And to make sure the general public knew of Sarnoff's court-appointed eminence, he took the extraordinary step of petitioning the Radio and Television Manufacturers Association to proclaim him "the Father of Television." It did. Also at Sarnoff's request, the group designated Zworykin "the Inventor of Television." Farnsworth was as hurt as he was enraged. He believed that he had been cheated out of both money and renown. He was right on both counts, and never got over his bitterness.

FARNSWORTH had personal problems to contend with as well, more than any man should have to bear and more than any man could bear well. One of his children, a son, died of a throat infection before reaching his second birthday, and, in his sorrow, Farnsworth began to withdraw from his wife, sometimes not even talking to her or looking at her when they passed in the house or sat for a meal. She believed that he blamed her for their boy's death, although there is no record of his ever having said such a thing, and the two of them would never again be as close as they had been before the tragedy.

Some years later, Farnsworth's brother was killed in a private-plane crash. This time he *did* assign blame—to himself; it was Farnsworth who had encouraged his brother to take up aviation, cheering him when he got his pilot's license, delighting in the increasing amounts of time he spent in the skies, the same skies through which, in completely different form, Farnsworth's dissected-television images so effortlessly glided into their receivers.

For most of his adult life, Farnsworth was subject to a variety of maladies, most brought on by nervousness, fatigue, too much alcohol, and too much worrying about money. The latter was exacerbated shortly after his brother's death by a forest fire that destroyed some property he owned in Maine; he had planned, just two days later, to meet with his insurance agent to take out extra coverage on the land. Not long afterward, Farnsworth suffered a nervous breakdown; his weight dropped to a mere 105 pounds and he had to be hospitalized. As a result of his treatment, he developed a drug addiction, and was able to rid himself of it only after several years of tribulation.

FARNSWORTH DID NOT THINK that TV was aging gracefully, either. His wife told a newspaper reporter that there was a time when "he wouldn't even allow the word 'television' to be used in our home. When the *Encyclopedia Americana* asked him to do the article on television, he just threw the letter in the waste basket."

The problem with dissected images, Farnsworth believed, was not just that he had been denied the starring role in their inception. He also thought the programs weren't very good. Nor were they sufficiently varied. There were too many cowboy shows being broadcast at the dinner hour, he told his family early in the fifties, and he did not want them wasting their time on such fare. Nor did he want them wasting their time on other kinds of shows at other hours on the device he had done so much to bring into being. "There's nothing on it worthwhile," his sons reported him as announcing to the family on one occasion, "and we're not going to watch it in this household, and I don't want it in your intellectual diet."

Farnsworth was not alone in proclaiming a lack of intellectual nutrition on television, which he thought of as yet another of his offspring. In fact, his was but one voice in a multitude that seemed to be growing as fast as the medium it denigrated.

Part 1

THE MEDIUM

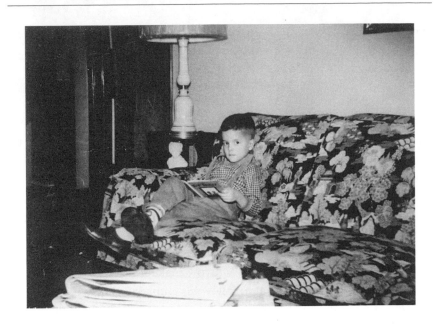

Chapter 1

Damning the "Theenk"

THE "INVENTOR" OF TELEVISION, according to the Radio and Television Manufacturers Association, had also become disenchanted. Asked on one occasion what it was about TV that made him most proud, Vladimir Zworykin replied, "Da svitch." His interviewer did not understand. "Da svitch," Zworykin repeated angrily, "so I can turn the damn theenk off!" He, too, worried about the effects of his electronic progeny on his genetic progeny. "I hate what they've done to my child. . . .I would never let my own children watch it."

Like Farnsworth, Zworykin was upset with both the similarity of the programs and their lack of quality. The two men did not like each other; Farnsworth thought Zworykin a thief, and to Zworykin, Farnsworth was a bumpkin, far more lucky than skilled. But each was passionate about the medium he thought of as his own, convinced of its potential for enlightenment, insistent that its content be worthy of its marvelous technological heritage.

David Sarnoff, however, disagreed. Despite being perhaps the most powerful man in television as the fifties began, he seemed to abdicate responsibility for everything but the profits, and chose a curious analogy to explain himself. "We're in the same position of a plumber laying a pipe," Sarnoff said. "We're not responsible for what goes through the pipe."

Who, then, one could not help but ask?

THE JOURNALIST Edward R. Murrow had made his name as a radio reporter for CBS in Europe during World War II. Of the new medium he was wary, even before he first showed up on it. In fact, despite his striking appearance—sternly handsome face, slicked back hair, and bespoke London suits—he wanted nothing to do with the small screen. When William S. Paley, the president of CBS, told him to give up radio and turn his attention to TV, he objected, saying that he had no confidence in either the merit or the staying power of television.

But Paley did. He insisted that Murrow make the move, and of course the employee had no choice but to follow his employer's dictate—which he did with such ease, and to such acclaim, that he surprised even himself.

Still, Murrow remained ambivalent. "The instrument can teach," he would memorably say of TV some years later, "it can illuminate; yes, and it can even inspire. But it can do so only to the extent that humans are determined to use it to these ends. Otherwise it is merely lights and wires in a box."

Norman Cousins, editor of the prestigious magazine *Saturday Review*, did not believe humans were using it to the proper ends. Nor was he confident they ever would. To Cousins, there was about television the unmistakable scent of commerce, which made it a "billion dollar blunder" even before it was a billion dollar industry. He believed TV was being "murdered in the cradle" by executives who were hoping to profit in a manner that he considered illicit, by catering to the basest of viewer instincts.

It was a common complaint of the time, expressed most often by intellectuals who, on the one hand, had a point; nothing about television at this nascent stage suggested that it would promote high cultural standards. On the other hand, and more selfishly, these same intellectuals feared a loss of personal influence that they had almost surely exaggerated in the first place. Used to thinking of themselves as societal arbiters, they saw in television a purveyor of amusement so readily available in American homes, so varied in its offerings, and so easily comprehensible to all, that it would bypass the intellectuals' authority, making their censure irrelevant.

To Frank Stanton, Paley's second-in-command at CBS, that censure was already irrelevant. He believed television's foes were "not really reconciled to some basic features" of life in the United States—for instance, that people ought to be able to decide for themselves what to do with their time. In other words, Stanton cast the foes of the medium as something more insidious than opponents of a new form of entertainment; they were, at base, foes of democracy itself.

NBC chairman Robert W. Sarnoff, son of David, was not nearly so grandiloquent in his thinking, but it was he who spoke for the majority of televisions's lords and masters: "if we listened to the eggheads," he complained, after having already listened to them longer than he wanted to, "we'd be out of business in six months."

The battle lines, then, were drawn at the beginning of the fifties. On one side were the executives who regarded television as a business like any other, a venture that would bring profits to them to the extent that it brought pleasure to their customers, and they would not consider the possibility that, in matters unrelated to the bottom line, it might in some ways cause harm to those who watched it, that it would diminish and exploit men and women and children in ways of which they were not even aware.

On the other side were the dissenters, those for whom only the harm was apparent, people who could not admit the likelihood that so ingenious a tool of technology as television would at times benefit the society to which it communicated, even if inadvertently.

THE POET T. S. ELIOT, one of the twentieth century's reigning eggheads, might have thought that six months was *too* long for Robert W. Sarnoff to be in business. But the danger he saw in television was different from that of other early naysayers. It wasn't so much the mediocrity of the programs that bothered him; rather, it was the circumstances in which the programs were viewed. TV, he said, is "a medium of entertainment which permits millions of people to listen to the same joke at the same time, and yet remain lonesome."

It was a prospect that also troubled Paley. As the overseer of both radio and television for CBS, its comedies and dramas in addition to its journalism, he did not have much time for poetry, and might not even have known of Eliot's comment. But despite hoping for the largest possible audience for all his ventures, he was apprehensive about the audience being made up of individuals or small groups of family members. "It is hard to tell just how television will be handled," he said, even though he was already one of its principal handlers. Most likely, he thought, people would in time watch it "in movie theatres, because of the size of the theatre screen which would make television more enjoyable. Man is a social creature; he likes to rub shoulders with his fellows."

It would not be until the early sixties that Newton Minow, chairman of the Federal Communications Commission, the government agency charged with regulating TV, borrowed the title of T. S. Eliot's most famous poem and referred to the medium as "a vast wasteland." But well before that, Robert Hutchins saw it as something similar: alien terrain. In his farewell address to students, Hutchins, a highly respected philosopher who had spent twenty-two years as president and then chancellor of the University of Chicago, went to extremes both vitriolic and comical in discussing the effects of the small screen.

> The horrible prospect that television opens before us, with nobody speaking and nobody reading, suggests that a bleak and torpid epic may lie ahead which, if it lasts long enough, will gradually, according to the principles of evolution, produce a population indistinguishable from the lower forms of plant life.
>
> Astronomers at the University of Chicago have detected something that looks like moss growing on Mars. I am convinced that Mars was once inhabited by rational human beings like ourselves, who had the misfortune, some thousands of years ago, to invent television.

In his own way, Raymond Chandler agreed with Hutchins. Thought by many to have created the modern private-eye novel, or at least the hard-boiled variety thereof, Chandler sampled the new medium and found it wanting. "[T]elevision's perfect," he said after watching a few shows, then went on to explain why it wasn't. "You turn a few knobs . . . and lean back and drain your mind of all thought. And there you are watching the bubbles in primeval ooze. You don't have to concentrate. You don't have to react. You don't have to remember. You don't miss your brain because you don't need it."

You are, in other words, sedentary, almost inanimate, and this is what troubled a number of observers, among them the child psychologist Bruno Bettelheim. "Thus being seduced into passivity and discouraged about facing life actively on one's own is the real danger of TV."

Many years later, the authors of the book *Going Negative: How Political Advertisements Shrink & Polarize the Electorate*, cited a study that would not have surprised either Chandler or Bettelheim. As reported in the *Boston Globe* in 1990, the study found that "watching television takes less concentration than eating a bowl of cereal."

BUT PEOPLE WERE INACTIVE physically as well as mentally when they sat before their sets, and this too seemed cause for concern, especially in the case of youngsters. Some parents complained that boys and girls who once took to the outdoors willingly now had to be ordered to leave the house, and even then would sometimes refuse, or at least delay their departures until their favorite shows had ended. In fact, according to a survey taken in the mid-fifties, three out of every five American children spent more time in the house after the family bought a TV set than before, meaning that they were not playing sports as much as they used to, not engaging in as many physical games like tag or hide and seek as they used to, not even running through their neighborhoods for no reason other than the sheer exhilaration of movement.

Among those troubled by a nation of increasingly sedentary children was the occupant of the White House. In the summer of 1956, Dwight Eisenhower created the President's Council on Youth Fitness, giving the group Cabinet-level status and hoping through its pronouncements to inspire young Americans to make better use of their bodies. News stories announcing the Council appeared in papers all over the country; posters urging children to exercise more were taped to store windows and thumb-tacked to public bulletin boards; famous athletes and even movie stars appeared on some of the posters touting the benefits of a robust physique. In schools, gym teachers emphasized the need for students to concentrate on their bodies as well as their minds. Physical-education classes at my high school in Ambridge, Pennsylvania, suddenly became more rigorous, and to be excused from them now we students had to present a note from a doctor rather than one with a parent's name forged at the bottom.

It was all to no avail. The following year, a study of more than eight-thousand boys and girls between the ages of five and twelve found so many of them panting after only minimal exertion that the Council decided it had to do more than merely urge. It had to demand. The president announced that gym classes would henceforth require more of their students than they ever had before, and he authorized a national-testing program in the schools to see that the requirements were met. But Eisenhower's new steps only confirmed the results of the previous study: minimal exercise was maximum effort for all too many boys and girls. Something more would have to be done.

Ike's successor in the White House, John F. Kennedy, did it. Or tried. The greatest advocate of the strenuous life to hold the presidency since Theodore Roosevelt, Kennedy continued the fitness program, but with a difference. Students were no longer just to be tested, they were to meet Council-established guidelines: to perform a certain number of sit-ups and push-ups and chin-ups, to climb a rope or run half-a-mile in a certain amount of time, to throw a softball a certain distance. Those who did were awarded medals or certificates. Those who didn't were embarrassed in front of their classmates, all the more so when physical-education teachers posted the results of the tests where all could see them, making a point of commending those who had achieved passing scores. The goals remained in place for several years, and even up to the present the federal government, as well as various state agencies, encourages boys and girls to achieve certain standards of physical well-being.

There were a number of reasons for the lessening vigor of young Americans during the fifties. It was, for example, the decade when fast-food restaurants, to cite the subtitle of this book, began their own conquest of America, the result of which was that burgers, fries, and shakes became a staple of the teen diet. It was also the decade when automobiles replaced bicycles and walking among more affluent teenagers, occasionally for journeys of a few blocks or even less. But another reason for increasing flabbiness among adolescents, and a significant one, was the lure of television, and it seemed to many an impediment to fitness that would only increase with the years.

ULTIMATELY, THOUGH, it was the medium's effects on the mind that seemed more ominous. It was these that drew most of the attention and led to most of the research and polling. "Adults spend 29.1% less time reading books than they did before TV came into the living room," reported *Time* magazine in February, 1950, which went on to state that "magazine reading is down 22.6%, newspapers 4.7%." If Communism was perceived as the great external threat to the United States as the fifties began, television, some people believed, was an equal menace within our borders.

The following month, March of 1950, we boys and girls were discovered to be spending more time watching television than we were doing homework, and almost as much time in front of the tube as in the classroom: 27 hours a week in school, 28 within range of the screen. As the fifties wore on, we would watch even more TV, surpassing 30 hours, then 31, and constantly, if more gradually, climbing.

And as both parents and educators could attest, when we young ones settled ourselves in front of the tube, we watched it with uncommon devotion. We would not miss our favorite programs. We would not shift our eyes from the screen when the programs were on. We were reluctant to converse with others who were watching, even during commercials, which were as fascinating to us in their way as the rest of the medium's offerings. We might not have smoked cigarettes or mastered the finer points of grammar, but we knew that Winston tasted good like a cigarette should. Speedy Alka-Seltzer became one of our favorite cartoon characters. Dinah Shore's peppy rendering of "See the USA in a Chevrolet" might not have been one of our favorite songs, but we heard it so many times we could not get it out of our minds—and in some families Mom and Dad and the older siblings were joining Dinah, singing along like carolers at a Christmas celebration.

"I have frequently gone into the homes of my friends with young children," said Orville Prescott, the esteemed literary critic of the *New York Times*, "and it is an alarming sight to see those kids, particularly on a Sunday afternoon from about three-thirty until about eight, sit with a glazed stare in their eyes and look at that television screen. There is no intelligent reaction at all, and if you go into the room this little child of five who has been taught manners for five days a week, says, 'Shut the door or get out!' It is not only corrupting their minds, I think, but ruining their manners."

Prescott was one of the few to complain about bad manners. But many were the complaints about corrupted minds.

In Cincinnati, Walter J. Clarke of Xavier University supervised a series of interviews with almost one thousand seventh and eighth graders in sixteen Cincinnati schools. "It would be a gross misinterpretation of the data," Clarke declared upon finishing his interviews, although not very lucidly, "to hold that in the case of a given child his habits of watching television could not affect his school achievement. The data gathered in this study reveals [sic] that poorer television habits [watching a lot of TV] and lower IQs, [less] parental control and poorer school achievement tend to be found in the same child."

Back to comprehensible English: we youngsters were not only getting dumber, it was said; we were getting tired, staying awake longer than we used to. In 1949, Charles M. Sheehan, the principal of an elementary school in Clifton, New Jersey, noticed "the nodding heads and drooping eyelids" of many of his students, and decided to do some investigating.

> Of the 562 students [in his school], 279 had television receivers at home, twice as many as had sets a year ago. Then, 9 per cent of the student body was doing unsatisfactory work. Last week, when Sheehan handed out second-period report cards, 30 per cent were under par. Almost all the failures had television sets in their homes. Ironically, none of the below-average students behaved badly. They were too tired to be rambunctious.

This lack of rambunctiousness, according to a woman who had been teaching school in Melrose, Massachusetts, for more than twenty years, was far more troubling than it might at first seem.

> The children are tired nervously, physically, emotionally, and mentally; they show the effects of eye-strain; they have acquired erroneous ideas; and their minds are so completely engrossed by television, that they have no capacity for learning.
>
> They have no sense of values, no feeling of wonder, no sustained interest. Their shallowness of thought and feeling is markedly apparent, and they display a lack of co-operation and inability to finish a task. Could this be the result of passively sitting and watching? Or are minds and bodies alike, too tired?

THE PRINTED PAGE had never been more imperiled. It suddenly seemed old-fashioned, inert, a relic of the pre-technological culture that had not been able to leap the gap to the present. The page's virtues—that it appealed to the intellect more than the viscera, and that it required the reader to picture for himself what could not actually be seen—had somehow turned into liabilities.

Betsy Rath felt threatened. In Sloan Wilson's novel *The Man in the Gray Flannel Suit*, which may be the most emblematic tale of the fifties, Betsy, the title character's wife, decides at one point that her family will no longer give

into the threat. She announces to her husband Tom that the family is going
to make some changes.

> "No more television."
> "What?" [Tom says.]
> "No more television. I'm going to give the damn set away."
> "What for?"
> "Bad for the kids," she said. "Instead of shooing them off to the
> television set, we're going to sit in a family group and read aloud.
> And you ought to get your mandolin fixed up. We could have friends
> in and sing—we've been having too much passive entertainment."

It did not happen. Tom did not start playing the mandolin again. Betsy
did not give away the TV. The two of them did not sit together every night
and read aloud to their three young children. Not even in fiction, it seems,
could television plausibly be so disregarded.

MANY REAL-LIFE PARENTS were disturbed, too. Many educators were disturbed. Many social critics were disturbed. The American Television Dealers and Manufacturers' Association, on the other hand, was adjusting quite
nicely, thank you. In 1950, it took out a series of ads trying to persuade
adults that the infatuation of young people with TV was not only to be in-
dulged, but encouraged. "There are some things a son or daughter won't tell
you," one of the ads began. "Do you expect him to blurt out the truth—that
he's really ashamed to be with the gang—because he doesn't see the same
shows they see? . . . How can a little girl describe the bruise deep inside? . . .
Can you deny television to your children any longer? Youngsters today need
television for their morals as much as they need fresh air and sunshine for
their health."

The *New York Times* did not go nearly so far. But it was much more
sanguine in its view of the tube than many. It thought that foes of the small
screen, despite their data and observations, were overreacting, and it did
not come to that conclusion casually. On June 24, 1951, it began to publish
a seven-part series called "What TV Is Doing to Us." Written by radio and
TV editor Jack Gould, by far the most influential media commentator in the
country at the time, and researched by more than a hundred members of
the *Times* staff from one end of the country to the other, the articles were an

overview of all facets of television: the cultural, the technical, the financial, the political, the academic—so much news about TV that it could barely fit into print. And this at a time when there were no more than a hundred stations in the country sending out signals to fewer than eleven-million households, meaning that there was one television in the United States for every fourteen or fifteen persons.

Books, the *Times* found, were not an extinct species, nor was there any danger they soon would be. Sales in most major cities had dropped in the past year, but television did not seem to be the main reason. "More likely causes," Gould wrote, "were the high cost of books, the general increased cost of living, competition from magazines which digest books, competition from 25-cent editions and reduced prices offered by book clubs."

Doubleday & Company, one of the largest publishers in the United States, reported that its loss in sales, compared to the previous year, had been "negligible." Other publishers issued similar statements. They did not yet know what to make of television; they were wary more than pessimistic.

In a few more years, however, publishers would understand the new medium better and, as a result, bemoan it more. In 1954, Americans would spend thirteen-million fewer dollars for books than they had in 1953, even though the population had increased by almost three million in that time. "To put it another way: Americans spent about $500 million last year for books," according to a 1955 study in *U.S. News & World Report*. "They spent $600 million just to keep their radio and TV sets repaired, in the same period."

The *Times* reporters were writing in 1951. They did not know what was coming. Neither did some of the libraries contacted by the paper, where officials were encouraged by the advent of television. They said that book borrowing had increased in the past two years, especially among children. It was true in San Antonio and San Diego, in Tulsa and Nashville, in Buffalo and Syracuse, in Dallas and Jacksonville, in Memphis and Wilmington, Delaware, and in such Pennsylvania cities as Erie and Lancaster.

However, many librarians noticed a different kind of borrowing, as more and more young people were signing out volumes on the same subject matter as their favorite TV shows: westerns and cop dramas and sagas of outerspace exploration. When ABC's *The Mickey Mouse Club* began to televise the exploits of youthful detectives Frank and Joe Hardy, for instance, Hardy Boys books went flying off library shelves as if magnetically repelled. The same was true of volumes featuring the young female sleuth Nancy Drew.

When the adventures of Tarzan made their way to the small screen, Edgar Rice Burroughs found a new generation of admirers, as did the authors of similar kinds of books, like the Bomba the Jungle Boy series, written by a number of men under the pseudonym Roy Rockwood.

"There is something in television," believed Frances Clarke Sayers, of the New York Public Library, "which is natural for the stimulation of reading and for children's guidance."

But not only were different kinds of books being read by America's children, patterns of library use were changing. Students were now less likely to drop in on weeknights, when our favorite shows were on TV, than on Saturday afternoons and early Sunday afternoons, when the programming did not appeal as much. Many libraries told the *Times* that boys and girls did not check out fewer books during a given visit; we simply checked them out at different times of day, and perhaps took longer to get through them than we had in the past.

BUT LIBRARIES WERE NOT faring well in all cities. The *Times* reported that attendance was down among young people in Boston, Cleveland, Phoenix, and Pittsburgh, to name but a few. In my hometown, not far from Pittsburgh, boys and girls who once dropped into the library as a matter of routine now paid a visit only when term papers and other school projects required it. In Wayne County, Michigan, people of all ages were visiting the library less. According to the results of a study published by *Library Journal* on February 15, 1951, only 4.3 percent of the county's adults were reading more since television entered their lives, while 42 percent were reading less. Among those of my age group, 13.7 percent were spending more time with the printed page, 35 percent less. In New Orleans, where library facilities were being similarly underutilized, a spokesman thought the decline would be temporary. "TV as novelty was a greater deterrent to reading," he predicted, "than TV as an established medium."

He was wrong. The *Times* was wrong. Again, 1951 was far too early to be making pronouncements about the long-range impact of television on literature. And after many years had passed and it was no longer too early, after television had become that established medium, reading, as a consequence, became a less-established habit for most Americans. And it would remain a less-established habit for the rest of their lives. At present, the United States ranks somewhere in the mid-twenties among the nations of the world in the annual number of books read per capita. The majority of people in our country allow twelve months to pass without opening so much as a single book, and many who do open one are likely to choose a romance novel or a volume that tells how to lose weight, consolidate debt, release one's inner child or behave more ruthlessly in business.

The earliest American generations would not have thought it possible.

IN SEVENTEENTH CENTURY NEW ENGLAND, there was no higher priority than reading since there was no higher priority than salvation, and only by studying the Bible and other books of a religious nature could salvation be achieved. There was as well a strong relationship between literacy and liberty, for only by reading books of a philosophical and political nature, especially Locke and Hume, Rousseau and Kant, could the New World colonists lay the foundation for the country that would one day be the United States. The late social critic Neil Postman wrote that "between 1640 and 1700, the literacy rate for men in Massachusetts and Connecticut was somewhere between 89 percent and 95 percent." The rate for women in the same colonies, he has reckoned, was "as high as 62 percent in the years 1681–1697."

In the following century, it is estimated that as many as three-quarters of the adult white males in all thirteen colonies read books and, further, that they had begun to expand their repertoires—not just religion and philosophy anymore, but science, husbandry, poetry, and works of fiction, the majority of which were imported from booksellers in London. The percentage of readers was especially high in urban centers like Boston, where, according to John Adams, one was as likely to encounter a comet in the heavens as an illiterate man on the streets. But, says historian Joseph J. Ellis: "Even in the back-country counties of Pennsylvania . . . the male literacy rate had reached 65 percent by mid-century."

Literacy rates in all parts of the nation are thought to have climbed even higher by the midway point of the nineteenth century, and to have remained at that level for several decades. Americans might have toiled in their fields or shops all day, but many of them found an hour or so after supper to read by candlelight, sometimes doing so aloud to the children in the family who had not yet learned to read for themselves. In the following century, specifically in 1920, when Americans were asked to name the ten greatest human beings in all of history, four were authors: Shakespeare, Dickens, Tennyson, and Longfellow.

And then Americans began to read even more. "The only thing that boomed during the Depression was the libraries," writes Page Smith in *Redeeming the Time: A People's History of the 1920s and the New Deal.* "In Muncie, Indiana, Helen and Robert Lynd's Middletown, the circulation of books rose 145 percent between 1929 and 1933. 'Big things were happening that were upsetting us, our business and a lot of our ideas, and we wanted to try to understand them,' a businessman told the Lynds."

That it all began to change with television, that the consumption of books declined 18 to 20 percent the moment people obtained a television set, should surprise no one. More than half a century after TV's boom decade, in 2007, ProLiteracy Worldwide, one of the largest, most active groups of its kind, would conclude as follows: "Higher literacy proficiencies are related to less television viewing among older persons." And further: "Adults who watched [fewer] than four hours of television a day outperformed [in literacy tests] those who watched more."

THE *NEW YORK TIMES* remained in the dark. It found no evidence of diminished performance in the schools in the fifties. Or of diminished eagerness for learning. Or even "the nodding heads and drooping eyelids" that elementary-school principal Charles M. Sheehan observed in Clifton, New Jersey. In fact, some schools claimed improvement. Gould notes: "Use of television to introduce children to many personalities, events and topics to which they otherwise might not be exposed, a large number of school officials said, actually was contributing to the education of the younger generation." Continuing, he reports that many school officials told him "[i]mproved vocabularies for children in the primary grades apparently was one benefit of TV."

Sometimes teachers would assign a program for homework. They would tell their students to watch an episode of *Dragnet* and write a paper on police investigative techniques, or of *The Millionaire* and analyze the effects of sudden wealth on an unexpecting recipient. The most commonly assigned show of the fifties was probably *Watch Mr. Wizard*, on which Don Herbert, as the title character, conducted simple scientific experiments and explained to a young assistant and viewers why things turned out as they did. It was physics and chemistry come to television, a class particularly prized by the majority of American high schools that could not afford their own laboratories.

Teachers were also fond of the occasional TV show based on a literary classic, a few of which are discussed in chapter 5. They believed these programs to be an easier way to introduce David Copperfield, Tom Sawyer, or Captain Nemo to their students than to insist on their reading the book. Easier, yes; more efficacious, no.

As later research would reveal, students that watched a television version of a literary work ended up knowing less of the story and retaining it for a shorter period of time than those who did the reading. They did not understand the characters' motivations as well, nor did they seem to have as firm a grasp of the author's intent. To come upon David Copperfield as presented by television was to make a casual acquaintance; to come upon him as presented by Charles Dickens was to know him intimately, and thus benefit all the more from the author's perceptions of the boy's life and times.

Soon educators began to demand a greater number of programs for strictly educational purposes, like *Mr. Wizard*. In fact, some educators wanted entire channels to be devoted to the classroom. So did at least one of the commissioners of the Federal Communications Commission (FCC), the government agency in charge of regulating television. Frieda Hennock, a former trial lawyer, asked her fellow commissioners to allocate twenty-five percent of all U.S. television stations not yet assigned to commercial owners for use in schools.

Hearings held by the FCC in 1950 on both her proposal and similar ones attracted the support of "62 representatives from colleges, universities, the United States Office of Education, the National Education Association and other groups that are not easily pushed aside." All of them expressed the hope that the TV set would be more than a device to which students would flock after school to cleanse the palate of learning.

But it did not seem likely to happen. As Gould writes, "Several officials of institutions foresaw serious difficulty . . . in financing and producing educational programs, and there were a number of appeals for a comprehensive study of the whole field of educational TV, including active cooperation with stations supported by advertising revenue."

By *active cooperation,* Gould meant financial assistance, which in turn meant that commercial television would donate a portion of its profits to support programming that would instruct rather than simply wile away a few hours of a boy or girl's evening; that it would produce courses for the edification of students from kindergarten through college; that, through its resources and good will, it would play an active role in improving academic performance in all American schools.

It sounded noble. Which was, of course, the problem. The National Association of Broadcasters (NAB) was not interested. It had no intention of cooperating in such a venture, actively or otherwise, claiming that advocates of educational TV did not have a clear idea of their financial needs. The NAB further charged that they did not have any experience in TV production or distribution. And it claimed that they had not even determined what kinds of programs would best serve their stated goals.

The NAB was careful, however, in phrasing its demurrals. It did so in such a way that it seemed to be objecting to particular flaws in the educators' proposals, not to financial aid to noncommercial television as a general principle. But the NAB *did* object in principle; broadcasters were not about to take money out of their own pockets to finance a competing venture, no matter how feeble the competition might turn out to be. Was General Motors supposed to subsidize mopeds?

The year after the *New York Times* ran its epic series, however, the Federal government decided that it should be the agency to finance television that supplemented curricula; and in 1952, National Educational Television (NET), which would in 1970 become the Public Broadcasting Service, went on the air and into American homes and classrooms. In fact, many of the early programs were actually filmed in classrooms, as teachers stood in front of blackboards presenting lectures and demonstrations, and broiling under lights that felt like the surface of the sun. They wrote with a piece of chalk in one hand and wiped the sweat from their foreheads with the other. Most of the teachers were less than dynamic: they tended to be more nervous in front of a television camera than they were in front of an assembly of students familiar to them.

IN THE MEANTIME, several organizations had developed, and would continue to develop, closed-circuit television systems for their own purposes. Rather than relying on NET, a number of school districts, like the one in Schenectady, New York, produced programs to complement its own courses. So did more than a hundred other schools in New York State, which formed the Mohawk–Hudson Council on Educational Television and turned out daily offerings to complement their textbooks. In Philadelphia, as the fifties began, *U.S. News & World Report* found that

93,000 pupils view the school system's own TV program. [The city] started in-school telecasts in 1947, and now has 300 sets in public schools and 1,200 others in suburban, private and parochial schools.

San Diego public schools have an in-school TV system; Chicago schools are planning to use a new educational TV station for both grade and high schools. Pittsburgh is about to launch the biggest experiment yet, with $140,000 in Ford Foundation funds. Here the schools will teach fifth-grade reading and arithmetic and a fifth-grade course in French.

To encourage the use of television as an electronic textbook, so-called listeners' councils were formed all over the country—in Cleveland and Southern California; in San Francisco and Madison, Wisconsin; among other places. Their goals were to pressure television stations to provide suitable programming, to pressure educators to make use of such programs, and to impose penalties when the previous two conditions were not met.

But it was not just schools that went into the television business as the fifties began. So did private enterprise, with firms of all sorts, those that specialized in both goods and services, setting up their own studios and producing seminars for new employees and refresher courses for veterans, instructing them on company procedures and goals. The United States Navy was the first of the armed services to make use of TV, introducing its men to military strategy and the proper use of weapons, especially those that had been newly developed and about to enter the trial stage.

It was the medical profession, however, that made the most frequent use of closed-circuit television at the time. As *Life* magazine reported before the fact, the 15,000 members of the American Medical Association attending the group's 1949 convention in Atlantic City "will watch the first large-scale demonstration of television in full color. On 20 specially built receivers, 1,000 doctors at a time will see a Caesarean, an appendectomy, a bone graft and other operations as up to now only the operating surgeon and his assistants could see them."

Two years later, a hospital in Kansas City, Missouri, began using color TV to instruct its physicians and nurses, and soon other medical facilities—not only hospitals but universities that offered pre-med courses—were following their lead.

Psychiatric institutions also found television to be helpful, although rather than creating their own programs they were usually content with those already on the air. In 1956, *TV Guide* informed its readers of a study revealing that mental patients who watched such programs as *Tales of Wells Fargo, The Mayor of Hollywood,* and *My Little Margie* improved by 16.2 percent over those who did not watch television. The study did not explain why this was so, nor did it define the word *improve.* But the magazine went on to quote a doctor who believed that the tube "might well rank with tranquilizing drugs" in the treatment of people who were emotionally distressed.

Had they known about the study, Robert Hutchins, Raymond Chandler, and other early opponents of TV would have been ruefully amused. One imagines them concluding that, although they knew television could make you crazy, they did not realize that if you kept watching it after the point at which you lost your mind, you might be able to regain roughly one-sixth of the sanity that had departed before you started staring so reverently at the screen in the first place.

Chapter 2

The New American Family

A S THE FIFTIES BEGAN, it was not certain that television deserved all the criticism it got—if for no other reason than it was not certain it deserved all the attention. One could still believe, if one tried hard enough, that people would lose interest in the medium as it became more ubiquitous. Or that it would demand more programming than could profitably be produced and therefore would not be a viable business in the long run. Or that it would be used primarily for educational purposes after all, and men and women and boys and girls would watch it to better themselves, thereby contributing not only to their own welfare but to the more efficient functioning of the democratic process, in which they would now be more capable participants. Or that it would remain an expensive purchase and consumers would not be able to afford it, and they would have to continue to find the radio and a weekly movie more than enough to satisfy their entertainment needs.

It was not to be, not any of it. Yes, a TV set was a luxury early in the fifties, but no sooner had it been hauled out of its box and plopped down in the living room than people began to think of it as a necessity. If you walked along a street in a typical American town one night you might notice lamps turned on in living rooms and see the silhouettes of people engaged in conversation or playing board games or perhaps reading books or catching up on the afternoon newspapers. If you walked along the same street a few weeks later you might see that the rooms were dark except for cold, gray, rectangular glares coming out of newly arrived sets. On your first trip down the street the rooms would have been quiet; on the next there was the faint hum of music and dialogue from the speakers, audible in some cases out on the sidewalk.

In some places it was happening just that quickly.

In other places it was happening more slowly.

In virtually all places it was happening inevitably.

In my place, a neighborhood at the foot of a huge hill that overlooked some of the steel mills of Western Pennsylvania, the Burnses were one of the first families to get a television. We were the envy of some, a curiosity to others.

The boy across the street from us, who did not have a TV, was the most curious of all. Almost every night, he would peek through our living-room window after dark as my mother, father, and I browsed through the new programs. One night my mother noticed his reflection in the screen, and turned around quickly enough to see his face framed against the glass with his hands. She smiled and got up to invite him inside. He ran away, embarrassed.

But the next night he came back, although this time he stood on the other side of the window. My mother turned again, her instincts entirely hospitable; he, however, would drop below the sill. Which he did the following night too, and one or two nights after that, his head popping up and down like that of a jack-in-the-box, his fascination with our television overcoming his shame in peeking. At this point my mother stopped looking, pretending she did not know he was there. She told my father and me not to look either, and emphasized to me that I was never to mention the subject when the boy and I played together.

A few weeks later, though, the boy's world righted itself. His parents got a TV set of their own, and I stood on the inside of our living-room window, looking out as a large truck pulled into his driveway and the precious cargo was unloaded onto a hand truck. The boy saw me and smiled up to his ears, signaling me to join him. In a matter of seconds I was positioned at his shoulder, and the two of us, like altar boys trailing a priest, followed the deliverymen into the house as the new set was given its place of honor. It was the ritual in which I had partaken less than a year earlier, and I was pleased to be a part of it again, if only as a witness this time. The television would be for my companion, as it was for me, a secular blessing.

YET IN 1950, it was a blessing only for the few. There were TVs in only a small minority of American homes, and the stations transmitting to them were still part-time ventures; like most of the people who watched them, they retired overnight. In fact, in some of the smaller markets the stations also went off the air for a few hours in the afternoon, as if they as well as their viewers needed a few hours to catch their breaths before settling into the programming rigors of the evening.

In the largest market, New York City, both WNBT and WABD began broadcasting at 9:30 A.M. WJZ did not join them until 11:30, and WOR and WPIX at noon. Among the daytime offerings on these channels were *Beauty Forum, Television Shopper, Household Hints, Kitchen Kapers, Kitchen Fare, Homemaker's Exchange, TV Telephone Game, Lucky Pup, Happy Felton's Knot Hole Gang*, which provided baseball instruction for young players; *Paddy Pelican*, a puppet show; and *Life with Snarky Parker*, another puppet show, this one set in the Old West and featuring, in addition to the title character, bad guys with names like Ronald Rodent and Blackie McGoo, and a femme fatale known as *Cuda Barra*. In retrospect, however, *Life with Snarky Parker* is best known for its director, a young man named Yul Brynner, who would go on to distinguish himself on the other side of the camera with less hair and more adult formats.

The postprandial hours in New York featured more prestigious fare, such as NBC's *Star-spangled Revue*, which one night presented Lucille Ball, Bob Hope and Dinah Shore; and, immediately following it on the same network, *Star Revue*, with Jack Haley, Basil Rathbone, Patrice Munsel and Dorothy Sarnoff, who was not only the boss's wife but a witty actress who once gave the following advice to a fellow thespian: "Make sure you have finished speaking before your audience has finished listening."

Other night-time choices in New York included talk shows and game shows, such as *Truth or Consequences*, the long-running radio hit that was proving just as popular on television; public-affairs programs on such topics as the use of unclaimed animals in medical research; a drama called *Mr. Keen, Tracer of Lost Persons*; and *The Original Amateur Hour*, a distant forebear of *American Idol*. There were a few situation comedies, like *The Life of*

Riley, which for one year starred Jackie Gleason, but at this stage the sitcom was a rarity, and no one could have predicted either the success or longevity such programs would begin to enjoy when the fifties gathered steam.

Just as the New York stations started their broadcast days at different times, so did they end them at different times. Many of them had an 11 P.M. newscast or talk show; the latter, on WNBT, was called *Broadway Open House* and was hosted by an actor and comedian named Jerry Lester. It would in time evolve into the *Tonight* show, first with Steve Allen, then Jack Paar, Johnny Carson, Jay Leno, Conan O'Brien, and then a few seconds later, Leno again.

After the late news on WPIX it was time for *Romantic Rendezvous*, an intriguing title for a program, but one whose content I have not been able to discover. It was followed by *Night Owl Theatre* and then more news at 12:35. By this time, the other stations in New York had gone off the air. There were seven stations altogether in 1950, and the final show of the day on most of them was *Sermonette*, a brief homily by a local cleric urging peace and brotherhood in the name of the Almighty. The last picture of the day, however, was not a man of the cloth but an American flag blowing in nature's breeze with a squadron of fighter jets soaring overhead and a recording of "The Star Spangled Banner" as accompaniment. When the final notes faded away, so did the flag and the planes. The screen then filled with electronic snow, a crackling mixture of black-and-white dots that would pop frantically until morning if the set were left on. And sometimes, apparently, it was.

A cartoon from the period shows a man lying on the living-room sofa in his pajamas, sound asleep in front of his snowy screen. His wife, in bathrobe and curlers, stands behind him, lips scowling and arms folded across her chest. She can't believe that her family has spent so much money on a nightlight.

EVEN THOUGH there were televisions in fewer than one of every ten American homes as the fifties dawned, Americans were now buying them at a rate of 20,000 a day, and nowhere were they buying as many as in New York, where sales were so great that firefighters, of all people, began to complain. The problem was there were so many antennas on rooftops. As *Time* reported, "Firemen not only trip over the wires, they also have their hats knocked off by the dipoles [the rods extending in opposite directions from the lead-in wires], thus 'leaving them in danger from falling debris if they have to work bareheaded.'"

People had problems on the ground too, and not just in New York. Most stores that sold televisions put samples of their wares in display windows, and they invariably attracted crowds. According to newspaper accounts in several cities, the crowds were sometimes so large that they clogged the sidewalks, and pedestrians wanting to get by had to step into the streets to pass. The managers of the stores were delighted, especially when the gawkers came inside to shop.

But most did not, and in fact some of them showed up to do their gawking every day at the same time, occasionally for periods of an hour or more. They might bring food and beverages with them, perhaps a companion or two, in a few instances even folding chairs, which they set up as close to the TV sets in the store window as they could. These were people who enjoyed the free shows so much that they were willing to put up with the considerable inconvenience of not being able to hear a single word of them. It was like watching a silent movie without the benefit of subtitles, an experience that they nonetheless seemed to find entrancing.

In California it was not just sidewalks that were crowded. So, too, was some public transit, at least for a while. A bus company running between Los Angeles and San Francisco increased ridership by installing TV sets in what they called *deluxe vehicles,* and the passengers "just love it," the company president declared. He went on to announce plans to wire up his entire fleet, every bus, no matter how short the run.

The plans were not, however, carried out. Riders stopped loving the televisions once they got over their initial enthusiasm and noticed that the quality of the picture in a moving vehicle was a lot like the overnight snow on their sets at home. Before long the TVs were removed from the deluxe buses; the passengers went back to reading the papers and staring out the windows.

Or perhaps they did something else. Perhaps they turned to their seatmates and made a comment about last night's episode of *Candid Camera,* the first of the medium's reality shows; or *The Morey Amsterdam Show,* another early sitcom; or the quiz show *Break the Bank* with the bombastically cordial Bert Parks. For that was another of the changes brought about by television in the fifties—never before had so many people been able to watch the same entertainment in the same circumstances at the same time. They might have been lonesome in the process, as T. S. Eliot declared, but they had virtually the same things on their minds the next day when they were not alone, when they were joined by others on buses or commuter trains, in offices or in factories, in stores or schools, and could not wait to share their enthusiasm for the televised pleasures they had so recently experienced.

There was, in other words, not just an entirely new dimension to the culture because of TV, but an entirely new basis for conversation among the men and women who were exposed to it. Often they were strangers before the conversation began, but it didn't matter; if they had seen the program that their seatmate or coworker or customer or fellow student had seen the previous evening, they were off and chatting, new friends with a new, if in many cases only momentary, bond.

But tonight there would be another TV show—tomorrow, perhaps, another bond.

IN DECEMBER, 1953, there were 360 TV stations in the United States, with 231 of them having begun operations within the past year. In Hawaii, not yet a state, television had arrived at the end of 1952. "No doubt your invention will be one of the greatest of all time," wrote a resident of Honolulu to Philo T. Farnsworth. "We in the islands are enjoying life more with the coming of television in December." There is no record of Farnsworth's replying.

The broadcast day now started earlier in most parts of the country, with NBC's *Today* starring Dave Garroway signing on at seven; and it ended later, with a number of stations running old movies that did not begin until twelve-thirty or one the next morning.

Most of the country's major newspapers, not just the *New York Times* and a few others, now had a man on the television beat, a specialist such as the crime reporter or local government reporter or the society editor. Usually he wrote a column every day and never ran short of material. He provided biographical sketches of this new breed of individual: the TV star, who was in most cases an old breed of movie or radio star. Or he previewed upcoming programs on the networks, sometimes reviewing them if the network had provided an advance copy, or he told about the new programs and personalities in his own city.

On occasion, he chuckled at the jealousy of his fellow journalists. "They used to come up to me," explained Win Fanning of the *Pittsburgh Post–Gazette*, long after his beat had been established, "and they'd say, 'You lucky bum, you get to sit around on your duff and watch TV all day while we're out trying to get the lowdown on liquor store holdups and purse-snatchings. You've got it made.'"

"Do you?" I asked him.

The response was a wink.

Fanning's coworkers had another reason to be jealous of him. His column became one of the most widely read in the paper shortly after it first appeared, and stayed that way throughout the duration.

TWO YEARS LATER, by the decade's mid-point, most of those who had hoped the small screen would be a passing fancy finally gave up. More than half the homes in the country now had television sets, and some families were buying more than one—a set for the adults, another set for the kids. In the Farnsworth household, there were for a time eight sets. Not one of them, however, worked. "One day," according to biographer Evan I. Schwartz, "[Farnsworth's] son Kent came home from school crying, telling his parents that no one in school would believe his father invented television because he was the only one who didn't watch. So Farnsworth hooked up a set for his son and then turned into one of TV's earliest critics."

People were buying televisions not just in the large cities but in small ones, rural areas that were hundreds of miles from urbanity. In 1955, more than thirteen percent of Americans still lived on farms, and for them TV had a special importance.

> Weather reports are more complete, more understandable [compared to newspapers and radio], as given on TV.
>
> Surveys show that farmers and their families tend to buy TV sets as soon as broadcasts are available in their areas. They watch TV more than city people, especially in the earlier evening hours. One obvious reason is that fewer attractions are available than in cities. But farm housewives watch TV in the daytime, too. They like the demonstrations of cooking and sewing.
>
> County agricultural agents are heavy users of TV. They've found that, on nights when popular TV programs are on the air, attendance at farm meetings falls off. Demonstrations of new farm techniques can't compete with TV's entertainment. So the county agents, more and more, are putting on their own TV programs, with the help of local stations.

Institutional sales for television also shot up: more sets for schools, for businesses, for military bases, and far more for hospitals, although they were now being used as much for the solace of patients as for the training of staff, and for the physically ailing instead of the mentally incapacitated. "Hospitals," it was reported, "have found that TV is a morale builder and a good weapon against boredom. TV proves especially helpful in keeping convalescents occupied after they become well enough to take an interest in life, but are still too sick to go home. TV 'gets them out of themselves, turns their minds away from their illness.'"

According to a study at the time, Americans spent $15 billion buying and repairing television sets between the end of World War II and the mid-fifties, and that "is 15 per cent more than the country spent for new school and college buildings. About a billion more has gone into TV stations and equipment."

AND PEOPLE COULD NOW WATCH television without being interrupted by anything so mundane as a meal. Although frozen food had been available for several years, in 1953 the poultry packer C. A. Swanson & Sons came up with a new idea for selling it. Faced with a surplus of some 520,000 pounds of frozen turkeys after Thanksgiving and having no means of storing it for any length of time, the company decided to leave the meat in its cryogenic state, but hack it into dinner-size portions and package it with mashed potatoes and peas in an aluminum serving tray with ridges in it that kept the various items separate. A piece of foil covered the top to prevent burning in the oven. The meals were not cheap; Swanson sold them for ninety-eight cents, which is more than seven-and-a-half dollars today.

But it was the company's stroke of genius to attach just the right name to its new product. It did not call the meal, say, Frosted Fowl Remnants, or Unsold Chicken Chunks. Rather, Swanson called it a *TV Dinner*, and offered it to the public in a cardboard box that actually looked like a television set, with a picture of the turkey and mashed potatoes and peas filling the screen. Around the screen were brown and black vertical lines, simulating a wood-grain finish; a picture of a small tuning knob appeared in the lower-right corner of the package.

All a housewife had to do was slide the tray out of its container, plop it in the preheated oven, then situate herself in front of the television with the rest of her family while it cooked. "The busy Mrs. America," writes American

Studies professor Karal Ann Marling, "could even throw away the dirty dishes after her family had dined in the company of their favorite TV stars!"

But they did not dine elegantly. "The freezing process was slow by modern standards," according to journalist Andre Mouchard, "which led to big ice crystals. Big crystals are the bane of tasty frozen food." In fact, as far as historian J. Ronald Oakley was concerned, the whole notion of TV Dinners was a bane. He has referred to them as a "dietary loss [that] was also a social one, for family conversation, already relegated to commercial breaks during the evening hours, was reduced even more now that the need to gather in the dining room was eliminated."

That's a lot of people writing about a little product.

But the words didn't matter. Swanson reported that by the time TV Dinners had been on the market for a single year, Americans had consumed more than 25 million of them, at least a few, it has been reported, by the occupants of the White House, Dwight and Mamie Eisenhower. No one claimed that the food was particularly tasty, but it was certainly convenient, and there was something about the tray, the simplicity and practicality of the design, that caught the eye—and the trained eye, at that. In 1986, the Swanson TV Dinner tray was "inducted" into the Smithsonian Institute, "solidifying the TV Dinner's role in American history."

That's a lot of glory for a little product.

Which, in turn, led to other products. People did not have to eat their meals by balancing them on their laps or placing them on the coffee table and constantly bending over for a mouthful. Instead, they could set them on little folding tables, the tops of which were shaped like television screens— rectangular with rounded corners. Cal-Dak, one of the principal manufacturers of these tables, called them *TV trays*. "Perfect for TV dining, buffets, bedside stand," read one of its ads. "Choice of 8 colorful trays. Fits over the knees. Folds for storage." They were available at fine stores everywhere for a mere $2.95.

Actually, for a few months in 1953, as part of a promotional campaign in grocery stores, they were available for only a dollar, assuming that you sent it to the company that made Niblets corn with a label from one of their cans.

And there was more. The TV tray "joined a whole family of home furnishing designed exclusively to be moved into positions close to the set: Servel's Electric Wonderbar, a 'refrigerette' on casters, 'so handy while watching TV!'; a roll-around 'television plastic dinette set' from Virginia

House in a choice of three woodgrain finishes; electrified serving carts of every description."

If viewers wanted a desert, or perhaps a snack before the main course, they could enjoy "TV Time Popcorn's tubes of kernels and hardened cooking oil [which] afforded a glimpse of the contents through a window shaped like a picture tube."

Television in the fifties was a new experience for the taste buds as well as for the eyes. Although he never spoke publicly about them, Philo Farnsworth surely found them as lacking in nourishment as the TV.

A FEW FAMILIES, very few, were eating their dinners in front of color screens. The technology had been in place for some time; the legalities had not.

The first color program seems to have been CBS's *Premiere*, a variety show starring, among others, newspaper columnist-turned variety show host Ed Sullivan and former radio chatterer-turned TV chatterer Arthur Godfrey. It aired on June 25, 1951. But the CBS show was possible mainly because of hardware developed by NBC parent RCA, and David Sarnoff, who apparently never wearied of litigation, had gone to court well before June 25 to prevent CBS's initial color broadcast. After several decisions and reversals in lower courts, the case went to the highest, the United States Supreme Court, which sifted through the various complications and ruled against Sarnoff. CBS could go ahead with *Premiere* as planned.

Not used to losing, Sarnoff was outraged. He was also undeterred. He ordered NBC to begin airing color shows of its own as soon as possible, and would in fact produce more of them in the next few years than CBS and the barely existent American Broadcasting Company and Dumont Network put together. All that remained was the official sanctioning of color television by the FCC, a foregone conclusion which became fact in December 1955.

Still, the networks proceeded cautiously. The cost of color sets was prohibitive; not many people could afford them in the early fifties. In 1954, Westinghouse tried to increase sales by lowering the price on its twelve-and-a-half-inch model from $1,295 to $1,110, but it was too small a reduction to matter to most people. In fact, the month before the price cut, Westinghouse reported selling only thirty sets in the entire United States. By the end of the decade, there were 500,000 color TVs in American homes, slightly more than one percent of the total televisions. The pace of sales was increasing, but slowly. More and more programs were being broadcast in color, but the vast majority of Americans was content, for the time being, to watch them in black-and-white.

Also continuing to increase was the length of the broadcast day. It now began even before *Today,* with such educational offerings as *Sunrise Semester* and *Continental Classroom* starting at 6 and 6:30 A.M. in many markets, time periods that must have made the critics slap their foreheads in chagrin. Finally television was providing programs designed for the betterment of young minds—but when were they on? At a time when most children could not watch them because they were either sleeping or getting ready for their real-life classrooms!

Television also was ending the day later, with movies running into the early hours of the morning, often a double feature starting after midnight.

As for the number of sets, there was at least one in ninety percent of all American homes by the end of the fifties, an almost inconceivable ten-fold increase from the decade's beginning. Opposition to TV proved to be a movable object. The medium was an irresistible force.

BUT WHAT KIND OF FORCE? How were people to think of television? As an appliance? A piece of furniture? A sort of player piano with more to offer than merely aural gratification?

Actually, it made less sense to think of TV as something mechanical than it did as something almost human. New neighbors perhaps, a few of whom had moved in next door and a few of whom had settled across the street and a few of whom had commandeered the next block—and all of whom were constantly dropping by to visit. They might have been, as the *New York Times* magazine put it in the late fifties, "loud-mouthed, sometimes delightful, often shocking, thoroughly unpredictable." But they were also astonishingly versatile.

Some of them could sing and dance and make us laugh, and if we did not laugh they could at least make the laugh track laugh. Lawrence Welk had a band and played his music conventionally; Liberace had a piano and played his music flamboyantly. Others were athletes and journalists and public figures who recited speeches on current events that the newspapers reprinted the next day. Still others—for the television set comprised not just a few neighbors but a whole neighborhood in itself—gave away money and prizes to contestants in the studio. In the case of Godfrey and Peter Lind

Hayes and Art Linkletter, to name a few, they just gabbed, bantered, shot the breeze—to movie stars and singers about their latest films and records, to kids who, on Linkletter's program, said the darnedest things. And then there was *Ding Dong School*, which brought education to the afternoon hours and was presided over by Miss Frances, a "matronly schoolmistress [who] read and sang, taught basic reading, writing, and 'rithmetic, and conducted playtimes in coloring and finger-painting, an activity that must have delighted mothers at home."

But most of all what they did, these new neighbors, these new *kinds* of neighbors, these beings who appeared on our television screens as two-dimensional agents of their three-dimensional selves—most of all what they did was what all of us had done as children: they pretended, acted out parts, frolicked through games, although they did it so much more elaborately than we ever could, with so many more refinements. They made believe they were committing crimes and arresting criminals and conducting trials and fighting Indians and rounding up cattle and waging war and wielding their swords against knights from other kingdoms and giving chase to pirates and exploring outer space and, on the sitcoms, trying to cope with stubborn husbands and confused wives and mischievous children while, on the increasingly popular afternoon soap operas, they were divorcing their husbands and cheating on their wives and trying to disinherit their children for offenses real and imagined. There was so much of life on television that never made it into life as most of us lived it.

And it all looked so real, in large part because it looked so instantaneous. Karal Ann Marling quotes the social critic Gilbert Seldes, whom she identifies as "the most persuasive apologist for early television":

> "The novel says: 'He walked,' Seldes wrote, while "television says: 'Look, I am walking.' Perhaps the movies say: 'He was walking.'" The presentness of television was a function of its location, in the home: events witnessed there became part of the continuum of daily life, making it almost impossible to believe, for example, that what was happening on screen might have occurred before the viewer saw it.

The sword-wielding, the Indian fighting, the argument that would lead to the divorce—all of them seeming to take place in the very moments we saw them on the screen. We were not just viewers but eyewitnesses to life as it was actually being . . . well, dramatized.

But paradoxical as it seems, even if the behavior of those we were watching often left something to be desired, the behavior of viewers seemed to be improving. According to at least a few early surveys, television was the greatest boon to the nuclear family since a house in the suburbs with a picket fence surrounding a newly mown lawn. "Television is keeping families together at home," the Charles Alldredge public-relations firm determined in 1950, and then reinforced the generality with specifics: "husbands spend 42.8 percent more of their leisure time at home than they did before; wives 39.7 percent more; children 41.3 percent more."

If other surveys are to be believed, TV was not just bringing families together, but strengthening their ties, especially those between husband and wife. One woman, who had apparently been denied sufficient quantities of her mate's affection prior to the purchase of a television, now said that the programs provided "something we can share," and going even further, claimed that the instrument "saved our marriage." Another woman, no less grateful, is quoted as saying that "until we got that TV set, I thought my husband had forgotten how to neck." Still another found her husband returning home earlier from work in the evening to watch his favorite shows, which he did with an arm around his spouse's shoulder and a tender word in her ear during station breaks and commercials for products in which he was not interested.

Even a morning program might contribute to wedded bliss, or at least to wedded coexistence. So thought the recently divorced host of such a program. "God knows that a lot of husbands watching the [*Today*] show aren't arguing with their wives," Dave Garroway said. "Why, a show like this might have saved my own marriage."

FOR SOME REASON, family life had become especially Edenic in the environs of Baltimore. *Time* reported on a survey conducted by Joseph Barlow, a high-school principal in Essex, Maryland, which "seemed to show that TV has knit families more closely; reduced street accidents to children; improved adolescent behavior; [and] sped up housework by wives eager to get at their sets."

Other sources, such as a 1955 article in *Better Homes and Gardens*, claimed that the tube reduced accidents to children because it reduced the amount of time they spent outside.

A number of parents approved of TV because it keeps the child quiet and at home. This would seem to be of benefit more to the parents than to the child. Children need to make noise at times, just as they need other interests than just staying home watching television. . . .

Parents felt that TV teaches liking for music to their children under 5 years of age and develops imagination for these youngest children. For the pre-teens and teen-agers, parents felt that it informs them of current events. (Editor's note: Though few of the youngsters expressed interest in news or similar programs.) . . .

Significantly, in answer to the question, "How has television affected your children's moral standards?" 23 percent of the parents felt that television viewing has improved the moral standards of their children, only 3 percent that it tends to tear down moral standards, while 54 percent of parents answering said that TV has had no effect either way.

Television might have been turning children into couch potatoes long before the term came into use, but it was also said to be making them feel closer to their parents than they used to, in part because they were spending more time under the same roof, often in front of the same screen. No less important, the generation gap was supposedly closing because many of the programs on that screen were teaching boys and girls the arcane rituals of adulthood. In the words of Robert Lewis Shayon, a former colleague of Murrow's at CBS Radio, television "is the shortest cut yet devised, the most accessible back door to the grownup world."

At the least, television provided frequent and dependable service as a baby-sitter. In 1947, the show-business newspaper *Variety* reviewed a new program called *Puppet Television Theater*, which starred Buffalo Bob Smith and a marionette endowed with 72 freckles and called Howdy Doody. It was a program that would, in the fifties, as *The Howdy Doody Show*, become the most influential and fondly remembered half-hour for kids in the history of TV.

On the basis of the premiere episode, *Variety* found *Puppet Television Theater* to be the kind of show "that could be responsible for the sale of lots of sets. In the middle class homes there is perhaps nothing as welcome to the mother as something that will keep the small fry intently absorbed, and out of possible mischief, for an hour. This program, at least the one that was broadcast last weekend, can almost be guaranteed to pin down the squirmi-est of the brood."

Apparently it did. According to a newspaper report less than three years later, a young woman was pushing her toddler through a supermarket in his stroller. "'What's your name, Sonny?' asked an amiable clerk. 'Howdy Doody,' piped up the tot. His mother tittered: 'He can't say his own name yet.'"

AS FOR KIDS who were worse than squirmy, who were troubled and fret-ful and suffered from the injustices of a malfunctioning family, television could also provide relief. Rick Mitz, a child of the fifties who would write *The Great TV Sitcom Book* in the eighties, says that the small screen dis-tracted him from his parents' unsavory marriage, helping him to remain ignorant of its details. "I know more about Lucy's relationship with Ricky than I know about anything else—except, possibly, Harriet's relationship with Ozzie."

Television allowed Mitz not just to visualize a different kind of family from his own, but to imagine being a part of it.

> The sitcom community was my family, my private people, my dear-est friends. I was a displaced baby, hatched from a twenty-four inch Sylvania and fostered out to my parents until the day when Rob-ert Young [*Father Knows Best*] and Donna Reed [*The Donna Reed Show*]—my *true* parents—would come to claim me. . . .While my parents were across the hall yelling at each other, I hid away in my room, watching my portable black-and-white, playing voyeur to a neighborhood of television families that got along better than we did. When Paul Petersen had a problem, his mother, Donna Reed, and his father, Carl Betz, dealt with him respectfully and lovingly. Donna Reed didn't scream at her kids to clean up their room.

There were, of course, those who saw peril to the family from TV. Among them, as strange as it seems, was an NBC executive, Robert P. Mc-Dongh, who sounded one of the loudest alarms. "With television," he said, "the appeal is to the eye as well as to the ear. . . . [T]he audience must watch a television play in order to receive full enjoyment. And if the housewife does that for too many days each week, the divorce rate may skyrocket, as irate husbands and neglected children begin to register protest."

It is true that the divorce rate in the United States increased in the 1950s. There is no evidence, however, that television had anything to do with it. It was the children who were more likely to neglect the parents because of the tube than the other way around.

ROBERT YOUNG, Donna Reed, Carl Betz, Paul Petersen, and all the rest of the electronically generated humans who appeared in our homes did so in miniaturized form, having been squeezed into frames more suited to photographs of them than to their actual, life-sized personages. But this did not lessen their impact on us. To the contrary, it made them more compelling, as if they had been scaled down for the express purpose of making us feel at ease with them, and thus allowing them to fit comfortably into, and ultimately to provide new contours for, the daily pattern of household activities around them. The little TV stars who were now such a big part of our lives "create[d] the illusion of intimacy," as Richard Schickel writes in his important book *Intimate Strangers,* "breaking down the barriers that formerly existed between the well-known and the unknown."

Consider the previous barriers. Before the small screen, the presence of celebrities was a special occasion in our lives. We put ourselves out, literally and figuratively, to partake of their company. We drove to the movie theaters or concert halls where they were appearing and paid for tickets, paying as well for a babysitter if we had children too small to take with us or tend to themselves or hand over to Howdy Doody. We had dinner early or left home even earlier to eat at a restaurant before the movie or concert, which was another expense, as was gas for the car, perhaps even parking.

Then with show time nearly upon us, we took our seats and awaited the curtain, having gathered in a dark and voluminous room with people who were little more than outlines in black to us, but with whom we shared a devotion to the famous men and women who were about to present themselves for our diversion.

Moments later the curtain rose, and if we were watching a movie as opposed to a stage performance, the celebrities appeared on the screen not as the dwarves whose images Farnsworth and Zworykin were still working on in their labs, but as giants, larger-than-life beings, filling our consciousness as they filled our fields of vision, their shoulders wider than our front stoops and their smiles longer than our sofas. We might have become used to their enormity over the years, but it was still an eerie sensation to be exposed to such an unnatural disproportion for a couple of hours, one that left us feeling lightheaded and a little unsteady on our feet as we weaved our way up the aisle and out of the theater when the movie was over.

Writing of his earliest days as a filmgoer in the forties, Shickel says that

the tone of the relationship between the admired and their admirers was quite different from that with which we are familiar today. It was not based on an imagined intimacy fostered by the media [meaning television]. On the contrary, it was based on a palpable reality, namely, the vast gulf that ordinarily separated the favored from the ill-favored, or the merely unfavored.

The key phrase in the preceding is *imagined intimacy,* just as Schickel earlier referred to *the illusion of intimacy.* Television not only permitted such a feeling; it encouraged it, made it virtually inevitable. It was still possible for us to appreciate the skill and renown and even the glamour of celebrities on the small screen, but what we could not do anymore, as we could with movie stars, was regard our TV neighbors with a distant veneration, with awe, which is, after all, an admission of inferiority on the part of the person who feels it. When the setting is as casual and emotionally manageable as our own living rooms, so is our response to others within that setting, even when those others are the electronically-generated presences on television.

As a result, Americans of the fifties found themselves dividing their celebrities into two classes, something they had never done before. They did not feel about *Beat the Clock*'s Bud Collyer as they did about *An Affair to Remember*'s Cary Grant; or about *Strike It Rich*'s Warren Hull as they did about *Soldier of Fortune*'s Clark Gable; or about *The Colgate Comedy Hour*'s large-breasted Dagmar as they did about *The Seven Year Itch*'s Marilyn Monroe. In each case, although it was the latter for whom they felt something akin to worship, it was the former with whom they could more easily fantasize an intimacy.

And so, little by little, the small-screen performer became important to us in a way that the big screen performer had never been. We began to write fan letters to our favorite TV stars as much as, and in many cases more than, we did to our movie idols, and our tones were more familiar, although still adoring. In addition, we revealed our imagined intimacy in other ways. As early as 1943, a station in Los Angeles began to broadcast what might have been television's first talk show, hosted by a young man named Franklin Lacey. Sometimes, when the show was over, there would be phone calls waiting for Lacey and his guests from viewers who wanted to invite them over for dinner. We never thought to invite Humphrey Bogart or Rita Hayworth to sup with us. Four years later, at the same Los Angeles station, as Michael Ritchie tells us, "When newscaster Stan Chambers broadcast the news with a sniffle, viewers came to the studio with their personal cold remedies." We never thought to go to the sound stages with medicine for Gary Cooper and Greer Garson.

As the fifties wore on, we talked about television personalities more and more with our friends, wondering about their romances and their hobbies, their newest ideas and their next projects, their wardrobes and the glittering events to which they wore them; after all, they were far more visible in our lives, far more frequent in their appearances, than were the men and women in films. Bud Collyer made a TV show every day; it took Gary Cooper several months to make a movie.

These new priorities were especially apparent in Hollywood, the long-time home of big-screen celebrities, even at its most famous restaurant.

> The Brown Derby now buzzes with talk of TV, and Gus, its maitre d'hotel, gives his best tables to the TV stars. Tourists who once paid to ogle the movie stars' homes now want to see the live TV shows and ogle the homes of Jack Webb, Lawrence Welk and Liberace. Such film gossipists as Hedda Hopper find themselves devoting increasing space to TV personalities. When the famed old Cocoanut Grove [night club] reopened a fortnight ago, the society columns listed as guests George Gobel, Hugh (Wyatt Earp) O'Brien, Art Linkletter, even Milton Berle.

It is just as true today. Think of the celebrities, the tiny percentage of them, who, in the past decade, were interviewed on television either seldom or not at all: Robert Redford, Jack Nicholson, Al Pacino, Robert De Niro. Their inaccessibility would have made them objects of fascination in a different age, enchantingly mysterious, like Cooper and Bogart and Hayworth. It is no longer the case. Now, because of their lower altitude, it is the less Olympian figures, the TV personalities, whom we truly revere. We find them more accessible. We seem to get more in return from them, if only, as Schickel says, in our imaginations.

Before 1950, we learned about our show-business favorites from magazines such as *Photoplay, Silver Screen, Modern Screen, Screenland,* and *Movie Star Parade* among others. But none of these forums had the impact of today's vehicles of runamuck celebrity adulation. It is because of television that *People* magazine not only exists but thrives. It is because of television that *Entertainment Tonight,* which made its debut in 1981, is as of this writing still on the air even though it often has nothing to say about singers and comedians and movie stars other than that they are alighting from their limousines to attend a premiere and are, at heart, really private people with hearts, as well as glittering accoutrements, of gold.

The relationship that exists today between Americans who are not famous and those who are, a series of hallucinations that began more than half-a-century ago and was created by the presence and persistence and size of the images on TV sets, is the reason that our culture is so riddled with the indiscriminate adoration of big-name nonentities. Many of them became stars without our even knowing it, just sneaking onto our screens to fill in some of the countless hours on some of the countless networks. In fact, many of them seem to have no talent more discernible than that they fit so easily within the user-friendly dimensions of the screen.

Then again, they are neighbors, almost family; we do not judge them as harshly as we do others. Television is the place where, when you show up, we have to take you in.

SOME PUNDITS IN THE FIFTIES, in addition to analyzing television's impact on society, began to compare it to that of the automobile a few decades earlier. It was *that* consequential, they argued, *that* far-reaching, long-lasting, and decisive. The effects of the car and the television set were also completely dissimilar, but for precisely that reason, contemplating them made for interesting mental exercise.

The automobile gave people a physical mobility they had never known before; television made us sedentary at the same time that it gave us a vicarious mobility far beyond the reach of four wheels.

The automobile allowed the members of a family to scatter; television brought us together, although in a curious and unconventional manner.

The automobile enabled men and women to travel greater distances for livelihood and leisure, encouraging the dispersal of the workplace and the growth of suburbs; television encouraged a different kind of spread, with the variety of its programs making it possible for us to indulge our own interests to an extent that had never been possible before, and in fact to be persuaded that we were interested in subjects that had never previously caught our attention.

The automobile required extraordinary alertness and rapid decision-making; television enabled a viewer to relax to the point of somnolence and still feel that he or she had had a rewarding, or at least relaxing, experience.

The automobile offered so many models that a person could define one-self for all to see by the one chosen and in which he or she was publicly displayed driving around town; television offered so many models of programming that we Americans could define ourselves in even more varied ways, revealing to others the nuances of our personalities by the manner in which we selected and discussed our favorite shows and stars.

What the two inventions had in common, believes Karal Ann Marling, was that they "allowed the family to escape the pressures of modern times," providing freedom and choice, and as a result they disrupted previous life-styles at the same time that they set about introducing and formalizing new ones. They were agents of the future, but the present made them warmly and pervasively welcome.

Chapter 3

The Hula Hoop and the Bomb

IT WAS NOT JUST THE TECHNOLOGY that permitted television to dominate the leisure hours of Americans in the fifties; it was the fabric of the years themselves. They were a unique time in history, a fulcrum that tipped from yesterday to tomorrow with unprecedented speed and astonishing range—swinging from Perry Como to the Beatles; from Doris Day to Faye Dunaway; from Norman Rockwell to Jackson Pollock; from William J. Levitt to I. M. Pei; from Graham Greene's rumination on Catholicism *The Heart of the Matter* to Ken Kesey's nuthouse epic *One Flew Over the Cuckoo's Nest*; from *South Pacific* to *Hair*; from the *Saturday Evening Post* to *Playboy*; from boxy Hudson Hornets to tail-finned Chevy Impalas; from Sloan Wilson's gray-flannelled brigades to Allen Ginsberg's beat poets; from baseball's supremacy on the sporting scene to the rise of the N.F.L.; from the daily injustice inflicted on black Americans to the first stirrings of rebellion and progress; from main streets to shopping centers; from restaurants as we had always known them to McDonald's and other fast-food eateries where haste made profit; from the land age, which had always been, to the space age, which would never end.

From black-and-white television sets to color.

It is doubtful that so much cultural change had ever compressed itself into so short a period of time before. Once television had solved its initial problems of size and image quality, Americans would have yielded to its invasion no matter when it happened—but the time was especially right in the fifties. To a significant extent, though, it was right because of events that preceded those years, when the United States went through three difficult, but very distinct, periods of upheaval.

FIRST WAS THE GREAT DEPRESSION, the most wrenching and longest-lasting financial disaster this country has ever known. It began with the stock-market crash at the end of the twenties, which, as I wrote in a previous book, "was so complete, so cataclysmic, so far-reaching in its consequences that the very act of plummeting took several days to happen, starting on Black Thursday, October 24, 1929, and not reaching its nadir until Tuesday, October 29, with the unprecedented sell-off of 16 million shares of stock and the similar forfeiting of at least as many dreams."

To one degree or another, the depression lasted throughout the thirties. Stores and factories shut down, as did restaurants and entertainment venues, some never to reopen. Even the banks had to close, although most unlocked their doors again after a few days or weeks. Between 1930 and 1933, the value of industrial stocks in the United States dropped eight percent, and in the latter year a quarter of the nation's work force, some thirteen million people, was unemployed, no longer a work force at all.

Many Americans lost not only their jobs but their savings and, as a result, their homes. Some moved in with relatives or found cheaper, more crowded lodgings than their old ones. There was the occasional report of a person taking temporary shelter under a bridge or highway overpass, or even spending his nights in a large cardboard box, the kind that had once held a refrigerator, a washing machine, or maybe even a large, console TV.

Ultimately, the Great Depression was as damaging emotionally as it was monetarily.

The unofficial end of the hard times was World War II, the second period of upheaval, which provided economic recovery in the worst way possible. Suddenly the steel mills and other palaces of industry were opening again, and those that had stayed open through the thirties were retooling to manufacture war materiel and related goods. Men and women who had not held steady jobs for years now had several among which to choose; they were welcomed in offices and on assembly lines and at the cash registers and counters of new stores that were opening with remarkable suddenness. Old stores added to their inventories and expanded their floor space, servicing the hordes of newly employed with all manner of products and services.

Others found their employment far from home. In some cases, it did not last long. Although a minority of America's uniformed soldiers were actually dispatched to the battlefields of Europe and various Pacific outposts, more than 400,000 of them were killed in combat. As for those who survived, having seen so much death and dismemberment around them, the horror which was their first reaction turned almost immediately to numbness, a numbness that was at once a self-protective shell and a kind of emotional death. Some of them suffered injuries that would not only cut their lives short but torment them while they continued.

Their angst, and that of their families, was the third of the upheavals preceding the fifties. Americans might have won the war, but the first years of peace were yet another front for them, and the battles here did not go nearly as well, at least not at the start. Millions of men were mustered out of the armed forces and back into civilian life between 1945 and 1948, and a redeployment of that magnitude could not help but create more problems than it immediately solved. Husbands and sons and brothers went to war; in some cases, strangers returned.

One of those problems, especially for disabled soldiers, was employment, and to no one was it more important than to Don Weiss, the head of the New York office of the Veterans Administration. What frustrated him most was the perception that an injured man was, ipso facto, a less productive one. Weiss did not believe it. In fact, he knew that in many cases the opposite was true; an injured man, especially one whose wounds were war-related, was often a more productive worker because he had greater incentive, more discipline, more to prove. If the Nazis or Japanese could not stop him, neither could the demands of civilian workplaces.

But how to change the minds of those who were hiring? Weiss simply could not think of a way—until one night, relaxing and watching TV, it came to him. Don Weiss, who had never thought of himself as an especially creative sort, and certainly not a media executive, had suddenly come up with an idea for a brand new kind of television show.

The next morning he arranged a meeting with the manager of New York station WABD. He pleaded with the man to turn over half-an-hour a day for a program on which disabled soldiers would, in effect, audition for work. The station manager was dubious. He had never heard of such a thing before: television as a kind of want ad. It did not sound like much of an incentive to viewers.

But there were so many hours to fill on the new medium and so few kinds of shows as yet available—and perhaps so much favorable publicity for WABD to reap if a program as patriotically intended as this proved a success. The station manager told Weiss he would give it try.

On the first episode,

one set [in the studio] was a practical cabinetmaker's shop, in another set an electrical wiring job was set up, and a third was a radio repair shop. Taking each set in turn, the screen showed actual disabled vets working at their specialties. After each shot, the scene shifted to the desk of a VA doctor, who produced the man's records and described his war service and the exact nature of his disability. Then the veteran demonstrated the completed job and, at a cue from the announcer, stepped up before the camera and made his personal pitch to employers. "If you have a place for this man," says the announcer, "pick up your phone and call. . . . " And a slide gave the number.

In the course of the series, men have operated lathes; repaired watches, shoes and typewriters; laid brick; set linoleum tiles, and drawn posters. Once they moved in a car so a vet could fix a brake drum. Often they time an operation to sow the man's competence. Employers who know these operations can pretty well judge a man's skill. They see him move around and forget the word "cripple," and also get an idea of the man's personality.

According to the Veterans Administration, between fifty and a hundred employers called in after the program and after succeeding programs in the series—and many of those who had plied their trades on it, pariahs in their job quests only a few days before, now found themselves with a number of offers awaiting them. They also found themselves insisting to the kids in their neighborhoods who had never paid attention to them before that they were not the TV stars they seemed, not really. They were just ordinary guys who had fought for their country and were about to go to work now, like other ordinary guys.

DISABLED OR NOT, returning GIs needed time to get adjusted to their new vocations. After all, their previous employment in the trenches had made them edgy and fearful, quick-tempered and sometimes sullen. They struggled to adapt to duties of a more conventional, less menacing nature. A number of them found that ennui had replaced the ambition they felt when younger. After the war, Tom Rath, *the* gray-flannelled man, found a position with the Schanenhauser Foundation, which financed both scientific research and the arts. He had killed seventeen men as a soldier—one of them, accidentally, a fellow American.

And now, as a civilian? Rath was living a life so absurdly different from the one he had lived abroad that he did not know what to make of it. "You've worked hard," his wife says to him at one point, after he had been at Schanenhauser for a while but still seemed adrift, "but at heart you've never been really trying." He did not argue. He knew she was right. What he did not know was what to do about it.

Neither did many of the other men who had returned from battle with him. In 1945 and for the remainder of the decade, the divorce rate was twice that of the prewar period, with about one out of every three married couples ending their unions. And there were other signs of societal dislocation: more calls to the police about domestic disturbances, more visits to doctors and psychiatrists, more absenteeism on the job, increased consumption of alcohol and arrests for drunkenness, and a higher crime rate among the children of GIs, who would come to be known as juvenile delinquents.

These were events of sweeping magnitude, leading up to and into the fifties, and it is important not to make unprovable generalizations about them. But it is safe to say that the men who had served in the military, and the people with whom they shared their homes upon returning, needed to get their minds off the past. Sometimes just a little break, a few minutes, would be enough to refresh them—half-an-hour, say, while Groucho Marx hosted the game show *You Bet Your Life*, jiggling those fake eyebrows of his, leering at the female guests and promising guests of both genders that if they uttered the secret word a duck that also had fake eyebrows would drop down from the ceiling and present them with a hundred-dollar bill.

Or Americans needed to take some time off from anxiety and watch Bert Parks host another game show called *Stop the Music*, on which contestants signaled an orchestra into silence as soon as they could identify the song it was playing.

Or people would sit back in their favorite chairs and grin as Stu Erwin, a hammy comedian, was grinning himself into a state approaching rictus. What else could he do? His wife and two daughters ignored his advice every time he opened his mouth to give it, proceeding on their merry ways on the sitcom first known as *Life with the Erwins* and *The Trouble with Father,* then later as *The Stu Erwin Show.* The poor namesake was a buck private in a family of female sergeants.

Programs like these gave a listless man a chance to divert himself, a bruised man a few minutes of mindlessness, which at times was a passable imitation of peace. It also gave him a form of justice. As Jeff Greenfield writes, television seemed to some ex-GIs "a kind of spoil of war, a down payment on the wondrous world promised . . . in all those magazine ads they scanned in barracks and foxholes."

Gradually Americans began to find themselves again, to slip into new lives, which were often facsimiles of the old ones, adjusting to the changes the war had brought. They began to put aside mourning and fretfulness, to believe again in their families and their futures. Some did better than others. Most of them made at least a degree of progress. Television was one of the numerous steps in their recovery.

BUT THERE WERE REASONS to be troubled by the present as well as the past. The fifties were perilous and uncertain days in themselves, and considering their already-agitated state, a lot of Americans tended to see the decade as even more threatening than it really was.

In the decade's first year, it was impossible to walk into a drugstore anywhere in the United States and buy such a thing as a tranquilizer. On the eve of the sixties, Americans were swallowing more than a million pounds of the paranormal little pills a year, and occasionally washing them down with beverages that made for a mixture more volatile than sedating.

They did so, in some cases, as they wondered whether the mushroom clouds that had risen over Hiroshima and Nagasaki to end the war would someday hover over their own country. It was not an idle concern. The Soviets were now working on an atomic bomb, and had gone from being allies to enemies in but a few years, their brand of communism seeming to many a threat to everything for which the United States stood—a threat, in fact, to our very existence.

The Soviets were also developing a weapon potentially even more destructive than the atomic bomb, the hydrogen bomb. We Americans had tested one in 1952; the Soviets did it a year later, and one of the reasons they were so prompt in their response, or so the accusation went, was that spies were passing secrets to them, *our* secrets, passed by spies who were *our* people.

In 1953, Julius and Ethel Rosenberg were put to death for such treachery. Most Americans were stunned. We asked ourselves: How many more subversives are there that haven't been caught yet? How much do they know? How much can their knowledge hurt us? How soon will that knowledge reside in the arsenals of the enemy?

The questions seemed all the more pertinent in 1957, when the Soviets launched an artificial satellite called *Sputnik* into orbit around the earth. It remained there, circling and taunting, for three months, and for the first twenty-two days it sent back radio signals to earth. *Sputnik* spanned the globe at the previously incomprehensible speed of 18,000 miles per hour.

Americans had been working on a satellite too, and we expected ours to ascend before the Soviets'. To be second was bad enough, but worse was ahead. The U.S. satellite *Vanguard* blasted off its launching pad two months after *Sputnik*. Its flight lasted less than three seconds. It achieved an apogee of six feet. Then it exploded, the little satellite falling back to earth in more pieces than anyone could count.

Foreign newspapers ridiculed us. Instead of *Vanguard,* they called our spacecraft *Kaputnik, Stayputnik, Flopnik.* They said it was the most embarrassing moment in the history of American science, as it surely was, and made jokes about our ineptitude, our pretensions, our goals for the exploration of the heavens.

But at the same time, on television. . . .

Comedians such as Danny Thomas and Red Skelton were telling different kinds of jokes, and these did not come at the expense of our space program. Sitcoms such as *The Great Gildersleeve* and *The Bob Cummings Show* allowed us to laugh at the mishaps of others, to forget for a few minutes that so many other people in so many other places were laughing at us. And westerns such as *The Rifleman* and *The Restless Gun* reminded us that, at least in the fictionalized land of cowboys and Injuns, the good guys eventually won, no matter how much they had to suffer before the final credits rolled.

As consolation, it was not much. We Americans needed more, much more. We needed relief, encouragement, increased Federal spending on existing and yet-to-be-created projects that would restore both national and personal pride, result in a rededication to excellence, and help us justify the faith we felt in U.S. supremacy in matters ranging from the moral to the technical to the political.

Or, at the least, we needed to keep the drugstore shelves stocked with those little white pills.

In the meantime, we continued to hang out for a few hours each day with our neighbors, the new ones, the ones on TV, and they were making believe with all the earnest and blissful duplicity of their craft that *Sputnik* had never happened and the bombs on the testing grounds would never explode over a city. We took what comfort we could.

TV WAS NOT our only source of diversion in those days. There were others even less substantive. Perhaps more than any other decade in the century, with the possible exception of the twenties, the fifties were a time of frivolity in the United States. Armageddon threatened; fads ruled.

We slipped hula hoops over our heads and whirled them around our waists for as long as we could keep them going. We pulled Silly Putty out of its plastic eggshell and kneaded it into all sorts of improbable shapes. We tossed boomerangs at one another and wondered why they never came back.

There were musical fads, songs like "Purple People Eater," "Stranded in the Jungle," "My Boy Lollipop," "The Chipmunk Song," and Dickie Goodman's "Flying Saucer" records, with snippets of other songs, by stars ranging from Elvis Presley to Chuck Berry to the Platters, edited into an improbable story line.

There were dance fads, such as the Stroll and the Hand Jive.

There were clothing fads: pedal pushers, poodle skirts, pegged blue jeans, black-leather jackets.

There were footwear fads: saddle shoes, white bucks, penny loafers.

There were hairstyle fads: duck's ass hairdos for boys, ponytails fastened high on the head for girls, often with bangs drooping to the eyebrows.

And there were fads that defied categorization, like Pez dispensers, which enabled us to shoot little pellets of candy into our mouths, and spud guns, so we could shoot potatoes at others.

A society that embraces fads is a distracted society. A society that changes fads quickly is a restless society. A society that treats its fads seriously, spending more time and money on them than they deserve, writing so many newspaper and magazine articles about them that they seem major events, is a society that does not have the emotional wherewithal to treat its serious concerns seriously. What was silly about the fifties—and this was true of *You Bet Your Life* as well as of hula hoops—was, in large measure, a reaction to what was ominous.

WHAT COULD BE MORE OMINOUS than another war? We never officially called it that, but in 1950, only five years after the end of World War II, Americans returned to the battlefield, sending troops to Korea, which had recently been partitioned into two mutually antagonistic states. We took the side of the South, fighting the Communist North until 1953, when an inconclusive cease-fire ended most of the battles, if not the political rivalries that had led to them.

Hostilities of a different kind were underway at home. In our own South, blacks struggled for civil rights against angry white mobs that tried to deny them, in many cases by blocking the entrances to schools which, according to the U.S. Supreme Court, were now to be integrated. Some in the mobs threw stones at black children, boys and girls who were defenseless, well-dressed, and frightened out of their wits.

TV cameras took pictures of their actions. Microphones recorded their words, the vilest epithets that could come to the racists' riddled minds. The role of television in covering the domestic violence of the fifties is discussed in more detail later in this volume. Suffice it to say for now that millions of people all over the country, regardless of their attitudes toward desegregation, were stunned by the vicious behavior of their fellow Americans, which gave even further cause for trepidation.

But TV showed us more than just the racial conflagrations in the South and the more deadly battles a world away in Korea. It showed us the Rosenbergs as the date of their demise drew closer and the possibility of reprieve grew dimmer. It showed us the rantings of Senator Joseph McCarthy, who told us the Rosenbergs were but the tip of the iceberg, that there were Communists in high places throughout our government, our schools, our military—who knows, maybe even our nursery schools!

TV showed us artists' renderings of *Sputnik* and taunted us with reproductions of its beep. It showed us *Vanguard* bursting into flames. And it showed us hula hoop competitions and ads for Silly Putty and boys and girls dancing in those odd-looking but short-lived fashionable outfits of theirs.

Television showed us, in other words, the small pictures that made up the big picture of a uniquely vexing and eclectic decade, and we Americans turned to the tube when we needed information about our woes, just as we turned to it when what we needed was a way to escape from those woes. Never before had such a piece of machinery existed, one that was so versatile, so vivid, so close at hand.

Prior to television, we had seen moving pictures of the world's great events only in newsreels when we went to the theater; we had never known the immediacy, the sometimes terrifying proximity, of seeing such events in what we had always thought of as the safety of our homes. Newspapers could bring us the news in more detail, radio more quickly, but neither affected us the way television did. In our bewildered state, we tried to make sense of so unprecedented a visual assault as we sat in our favorite chairs in the most familiar of surroundings.

JUST AS THE TRANSITION from war to peace did not start out smoothly for returning soldiers and their families, neither did it begin well for the economy. The soldiers needed jobs, and there were not enough of them in the immediate aftermath of the war. Nor would there be enough until factories that manufactured armaments converted to the production of civilian goods and services. That was the biggest job of all.

The United States had shifted from peace to war a few years earlier, but the country could not simply reverse the process and attain the results it desired; a return to the pre–World War II economy, even if such a thing were possible, would have meant a return to the last days of the Depression, and no one could bear the thought of enduring conditions like those again. Something different was called for, something far more demanding; we had to establish the kind of solid fiscal foundation in our country that we had not known for more than twenty years.

We began by reducing defense spending, which allowed President Eisenhower to balance the budget, or come close to it, midway through his first term. The result, as is almost always the case when government spending is restrained, was a growth spurt in virtually all sectors of the civilian economy.

When growing companies hired ex-soldiers to fill new positions, they often found themselves with employees who were no less competent as civilians than they had been as warriors. Sometimes these men ended up in the executive suites. Tom Rath, whose experiences should not be discounted simply because he did not exist, decided to change jobs and take a position as one of the top officials at the United Broadcasting Corporation, the largest television network in the country. He could see where the times were headed. He wanted to be going in the same direction in that gray flannel suit of his.

What was happening in the United States was also happening abroad. By the autumn of 1953, virtually the entire world was at peace, and in some countries, traders proved more receptive to American products than they had been before the war. We, in turn, were more willing to do business with them than we used to be. We opened our markets; they opened theirs—it was, for America's fiscal well-being, the most un-vicious of cycles.

As a result, on the eve of Eisenhower's campaign for a second term in the White House, the United States had entered "a period of general prosperity," which was referred to by journalists fond of the president as the *Eisenhower prosperity*. Profits were climbing for almost all American companies; the stock market reached new highs and then surpassed them. The gross national product for the second quarter of 1956 soared to a record annual rate of $408,300,000,000. One-and-a-half million more Americans had jobs now than they did a year earlier, and personal income had also reached a record level while continuing to ascend. There was more money in savings accounts than there had ever been before, and stockbrokers and investment counselors reported that they had never been so confident, had never seen such confidence in their clients, had never handled more money in more transactions for the benefit of all involved.

What it meant, among other things, was that more and more Americans could buy television sets, especially since the prices for both black-and-white and color models dropped throughout the decade and into the next. A black-and-white General Electric tabletop model with a 17-inch screen cost $289 as the fifties began; at the start of the sixties, a black-and-white Philco tabletop with the same-size screen cost $249. In 1954, an Admiral color console, 15-inch screen, sold for $1,175; by 1968, the same company's color console with a 23-inch screen, went for a mere $349.

The comedian Ed Wynn had predicted it earlier. "In the beginning," he said, "a television set cost hundreds of dollars and you could see a few bad shows. In a couple of years, you'll be able to buy a television set for a few dollars and see hundreds of bad shows."

BUT THE EX-SOLDIERS were not making critical judgments. Neither were their families. Neither were millions of other Americans. Just as sales of tranquilizers soared between 1950 and 1960, so did sales of TVs, which, with the exceptions already cited, also seemed to have a calming effect on those who were exposed to them regularly.

Chapter 4

Invisible Doughnuts and Coonskin Caps

E VE ARDEN, born Eunice Quedens in Mill Valley, California, in 1908, was an actress known for brassy performances in supporting roles in the kinds of movies that needed all the support they could get, such filmed-to-be-forgotten follies as *Stage Door, Hollywood Romance, That Uncertain Feeling, My Dream Is Yours,* and the little-known Fred Astaire–Ginger Rogers vehicle *We're Not Married.* Cast as Joan Crawford's pal in *Mildred Pierce,* a more substantive part than usual for her, Arden earned an Academy Award nomination in 1946. But it did not give her career the boost she was hoping for. She remained a bridesmaid on the big screen, never a bride, all the way through 1951's *Goodbye, My Fancy,* also starring Joan Crawford.

The following year, however, Eve Arden found stardom in television. She became Connie Brooks, a high-school English teacher with a quick wit, warm heart, and an obvious passion for the welfare of her students. The program was the sitcom *Our Miss Brooks,* and so sympathetic was Arden's portrayal of the title character that the National Education Association made her an honorary member. Shortly afterward, the Alumni Association of the Teachers College of Connecticut cited her for "humanizing the American teacher."

Educators everywhere were delighted with their Miss Brooks and, pleased to be presented in so positive a manner on TV, they reciprocated by giving her additional awards, inviting her to speak at their conferences, even writing articles about her and her instructional techniques that were published in professional journals. Sometimes a teacher would see her on the street or in a restaurant or theater; the teacher would invariably tell her how much she meant not just to him or her but to the entire profession. She would always respond graciously.

But it is one thing to express gratitude, quite another to suggest a change of employment. After *Our Miss Brooks* had been on the air for little more than a year, Arden began to receive offers to teach real English courses in real American high schools, offers that came from people who should have known better: principals, superintendents, and presidents of school boards. Apparently the offers were based on the assumption that if someone could so admirably convey the successes and tribulations of a teacher on television, she could be equally admirable, and informed, in the classroom. Not only that, her fame would ensure both discipline among her students and publicity for the school. Besides, she had to do a lot of research to play her role, didn't she? Might that research not be the equivalent of a B.A., of a teaching certificate?

Arden expressed her own gratitude for the offers, pleased that so many people found her so convincing, which is the ultimate accolade for an actress. But privately she must have wondered whether the school officials were themselves in need of education. She never gave a serious thought to accepting any of the positions.

Other TV actors of the time were also assumed to be the characters they portrayed, or at least to have the same knowledge and abilities. When making personal appearances, Al Hodge and Don Hastings, who played Captain Video and the Video Ranger, were often asked about the perils of interplanetary travel. Clayton Moore and Jay Silverheels, otherwise known as the Lone Ranger and Tonto, were asked about the dangers of life in the Old West. Phil Silvers, Sergeant Ernie Bilko of *You'll Never Get Rich*, was asked what he found most upsetting about life in the military. *Dragnet*'s Jack Webb, with his flat-top haircut and chop-chop manner of speaking, was mistaken for a cop; *Highway Patrol*'s chubby and blustery Broderick Crawford for a state trooper; *Wagon Train*'s rugged Ward Bond for the master of a real caravan making its way across the prairie, despite the fact that no such procession had headed westward through America for more than half a century.

So rampant did this kind of confusion become, and so long did it last, that when a cough-medicine ad in the 1980s featured an actor wearing a white coat with a stethoscope draped around his neck, the FCC required him to begin his pitch as follows: "I'm not a doctor, but I play one on TV."

Much is remarkable about fifties' television, but nothing more so than the faith it inspired in viewers, their belief in the fundamental truth of what they were seeing and hearing. And, to a lesser extent, it continues today, with soap-opera actors—to give but one example—occasionally getting mail that condemns them either for their adulterous behavior or their poor choice in partners.

BOB ELLIOTT AND RAY GOULDING, known simply as Bob and Ray, played so many roles that people could not remember them all, much less believe that they actually *were* the members of the multitude they claimed to be. Two of early television's most sophisticated performers, they had been, a few years earlier, two of the most sophisticated performers on radio. They were satirists—their material inventive, their delivery deadpan, their list of targets extensive. One of Elliott's most famous characters was Tex Blaisdell, a cowboy singer who claimed to be doing rope tricks on the radio while he warbled. It was, of course, hard to prove.

Also on their show, the two of them would mention the names of fictitious advertisers. One was a company that made "chocolate cookies with white stuff in-between." They also claimed to be sponsored by the Monongahela Metal Foundry, which prided itself on "casting steel ingots with the housewife in mind," and by the makers of Einbinder Flypaper, "the brand you've gradually grown to trust over the course of three generations." Their listeners seemed to know they were kidding.

But when Bob and Ray moved to television in 1951 for a fifteen-minute show on NBC, they increased their repertoire from mere tag lines to entire commercials. To say they were not prepared for the response is to say that a sunbather is not prepared for a snowstorm.

On one program, they offered their viewers a chance to buy cracked phonograph records; they had received a shipment that had "dropped just a few inches off the delivery truck," the two men said, and as a result were available at a surprisingly reasonable price. On another program, they sold invisible doughnuts, "all gone but the hole." On another, the two men pitched TV antennas without sets attached to them "to fool the neighbors into thinking you watch television." On yet another, the products in question were sweaters with the letter O stitched on them, "just right for people whose last names begin with O; if yours doesn't, why not change it?" And on still another episode, Bob and Ray advertised chocolate bunnies that were supposedly left over from the previous Easter. "We make this offer," Bob said, "because our bunnies were near a radiator and they kind of melted down a bit. Now, however, they're moldable into any shape you want."

Surely there were people who laughed. Surely there were people who knew that cracked records would not play, no matter how short their descent to pavement. Or that a doughnut hole without a doughnut around it equals zero.

But there were also people, a surprising number of them, who did not think things through quite that far. They called the studio, demanding to know where they could buy these products and asking how much they cost. Some of the would-be purchasers complained, wondering why Bob and Ray hadn't provided the relevant information as part of the commercials so they could rush right out and buy the goods as soon as the show was over. By the time they went through all the trouble of finding out how and where to order the merchandise, it might be out of stock.

Bob and Ray were dumbfounded. So were their telephone operators who tried to deal with calls from hundreds upon hundreds of zealous bargain hunters, as the lights on the switchboard in front of them remained solid and unblinking for more than an hour.

No less dumbfounded was Dave Garroway on NBC, who read about the lust for fictitious products in Bob and Ray's audience and, not able to make himself believe it, decided to try something similar on *Today*. In the drollest manner he could summon, Garroway told people they could purchase, for their very own, a dead tube from one of the actual studio cameras that brought his program into their homes. He held one up, shook it. It was dead, all right.

But no matter—people ordered the tubes, or tried to order them, by the thousands. Garroway was as puzzled as Bob and Ray had been. He had no idea how to get his hands on so many burned-out TV tubes. The medium had not been in existence long enough to have exhausted enough of the little glass cylinders to fill all the requests for them. What were people thinking?

The previous summer, Orson Bean preceded all three of the other TV personalities in befuddlement. A comic actor who was considerably funnier onstage than his second cousin, Calvin Coolidge, had been in the White House, Bean served as host of a program called *Blue Angel*. One day, displaying either his wit or his boredom, he said "Just write in, folks, and we'll send you $5000 worth of secondhand sneakers, six miles of dental floss, an all-expense paid trip to Youngstown, Ohio, and a screen door equipped with 200 flies."

The response was overwhelming. Tuning in to *Blue Angel* for nothing more than a little amusement, people found themselves rewarded with unimaginable largesse—or so they thought. The sneakers seemed to be the most popular item, although a farmer in Pennsylvania confessed that what he wanted was the floss; six miles of it, he thought, ought to be more than enough to construct a fence around his land. As *TV Guide* put it: "Neither Bean nor *Blue Angel* ever recovered from the shock. Within a few weeks, the show was off the air—temporarily, anyhow—and Bean was looking for work."

It should go without saying that the farmer who wanted the floss is the one who ought to have searched for new employment.

AND THEN THERE WAS THE CASE of Soupy Sales, slapstick comedian and inadvertent criminal mastermind. The incident to be related did not occur until 1965, but it is included here for two reasons: first, because it is such a startling example of people's willingness to obey those who speak to them on television that I found it irresistible; and second, because the groundwork for the incident was so firmly laid in the fifties. What Sales did, and what his audience did upon hearing him, would not have been possible had Americans not developed the trust that we did in TV in the first full decade of its eminence.

Known before his show-biz days as Milton Supman, Soupy got his start in television in Detroit in 1953. He was an entertainer whose jokes were broad, witless, obvious, and more often than not meant to be. When he finished telling them, the worst of them at least, he would be hit in the face with a cream pie flung at him by someone off-camera. Whereupon he would grin sheepishly, wipe the cream from his eyes, lick a little of it from his fingers, and make some sort of vacant remark, usually about how tasty the pie was. That was the *real* punch line, and it was just as unfunny as the one that had preceded it. Sales is to Bob and Ray as the Three Stooges are to Mort Sahl.

In 1964 Sales moved to New York, where he hosted an early morning program for children on WNEW-TV that became so successful it was televised to other cities as well. He enjoyed the show, seemed to take as much pleasure in his youthful fans as they did in him; children, he may have concluded, were the natural audience for his kind of humor. But, planning a long night of adult revelry on New Year's Eve, Sales did not want to drag himself into the studio for a program early on January 1, 1965. He asked for the day off. His bosses refused. *Show up for work or look for work elsewhere,* they told him, in what he thought was an unwarranted display of ill will for the season and disrespect for his stature. But show up he did.

He was not, however, happy about it. Nor, he thought, did the show go particularly well that day. And when it turned out that it had been mistimed as well, that there was a minute or more to spare after the last commercial, Sales was forced to ad-lib. Usually he enjoyed something like this, a few moments of spontaneity, a chance to show off his real self, his flair for unrehearsed jollity.

Today, though, he was not in the mood. In his own words, albeit written in a memoir more than three-and-a-half decades later, this is what he said that day to his youthful audience:

Hey, kids, last night was New Year's Eve and your mom and dad were out having a good time and it's only right, since they work hard all year long. And they're probably still in the bedroom asleep. Now, what I want you to do is tiptoe into the bedroom and don't wake them up and you'll probably see your mom's pocket-book on the floor along with your dad's pants. Now, be real careful, because we don't want to wake them up, but I want you to go into your mom's pocket-book and your dad's pants and you'll find some little green pieces of paper with pictures of guys with beards on them. Now, what I want you to do is take those little pieces of green paper and put them into an envelope, and on the envelope I want you to write, Soupy Sales, Channel 5, New York, New York, and you know what I'm going to send *you* in return? A postcard from Puerto Rico.

Sales claimed that the kids "knew I was fooling around." The mailman whose route included WNEW-TV thought otherwise. Over the next few days he delivered thousands of extra envelopes to the station, enough to fill several more bags than usual. By the end of his shift he must have felt as if his shoulders had drooped to his kneecaps.

Inside the envelopes were those little green pieces of paper Sales had asked for. According to one account, he received almost $80,000 from those who fell victim to his Fagin-like charms; "but," he said, "except for a few actual dollar bills—which, by the way, we put into the Jerry Lewis canister for muscular dystrophy—all of it was Monopoly money." Other versions of the story put Sales's total take at slightly higher than $80,000 and as low as $20,000. At this late date, no one will ever know the truth.

Regardless, both Sales and his employers were embarrassed—at the deed, the response, and the excoriating publicity it received. Perhaps most of the slips of paper *had* been manufactured by Parker Brothers rather than the U.S. mint—but Monopoly money is seldom found in adult wallets, and as popular as it was, Monopoly games were not to be found in the majority of American homes.

As for the legal tender, perhaps most of it actually *was* donated to charity, but if it had been mailed to Sales in an envelope with a return address, it was returned to the sender with a brief note of apology. The station mimeographed hundreds of such notes.

Sales did not go to Puerto Rico, but was given ample time to do so, as the general manager of the station told him to stay away from the studio until further notice. "I was very depressed about the whole thing," he writes. "No one likes to be suspended, especially for something that was so innocuous and, when you think about it, ridiculous."

But when Sales did not appear on his next show, the station enlisting someone else to fill in for him, the mail deliverer again became a beast of burden. Thousands of people, adults and children alike, wrote to demand that their man Soupy be reinstated. Thousands more called. *We want Soupy, we want Soupy.*

Sales was back on the air, his usual ebullient self, after a mere two weeks.

Like Eve Arden, Bob and Ray, and other performers before him, Soupy Sales did not realize that the power of television was so great as to transcend common sense.

IT IS NO SURPRISE that adolescents were willing to chip in for Sales's Puerto Rican idyll. By now they were as accustomed to obeying adults on television as they were at home. In the fifties, Captain Kangaroo had told boys and girls to behave kindly toward one another and many of us did, or at least considered the notion. Uncle Johnny Coons had told us to eat food that was good for us and some of us obeyed—occasionally, if not at all meals. Miss Frances had told us to get our homework done on time and the kind of children who watched her show, *Ding Dong School,* had probably already finished. Jon Gnagy of *You Are an Artist* had shown us how to draw realistic animals, and those of us who were tired of our childish scrawls emulated him as best we could. A decade later, when Soupy Sales told our younger brothers and sisters to send in money, it was understandable that they would not hear the jest in his voice, assuming a jest was actually there.

But how to explain the job offers for Eve Arden, the demand for Bob and Ray merchandise? Surely there is more to it than gullibility. Surely most Americans could distinguish between actress and role, between legitimate product and spoof. Surely part of the reason we did not do so in these early cases was our assumption that since the television was such a miracle of engineering, the messages it relayed were to be taken seriously, especially when those who delivered the messages were so impressive in their presentations. They looked right at us as if they could see us across the room. They talked to us as if they knew how carefully we were listening, as if they, too, imagined an intimacy. They were like politicians whose campaign promises sound credible to us not because they actually were, but because the people making them had such an inherent appeal.

And maybe, just maybe, records *could* play if the crack was slight enough. Certainly melted chocolate could be reconfigured if you left it next to your own radiator for a while; after all, it was heat that had altered its form in the first place. Even though a dead television tube was of no practical value to a person, might it not make an interesting souvenir? What, after all, was so practical about one of those four-inch tin replicas of the Empire State Building that a tourist could buy on Manhattan street corners?

REAL ADS, of course, were another matter entirely. People could actually go to a store and buy Ajax, the foaming cleanser, which cleaned the dirt right down the drain; or they could buy Geritol, with a blend of twenty-six different vitamins and minerals guaranteed to make you look and feel younger; or they could buy Serutan, the vegetable laxative that is "Natures spelled backward." Lucky Strike cigarettes—whose slogan *L.S.M.F.T.* was known by one and all to stand for *Lucky Strike Means Fine Tobacco,* tobacco that was *so free and easy on the draw*—were available at newsstands and restaurants and in vending machines everywhere.

At the start, television viewers might have been skeptical about the claims that were made for these and other items. But once we started cleaning our sinks or gulping down our supplements or inhaling our cigarettes, the power of suggestion, of *televised* suggestion, made the claims seem true. Brand A might have been the same as Brand B, but the one that was advertised on TV somehow seemed to clean better, energize us more, taste smoother as we inhaled.

Americans did not complain about commercials then as much as we do now. In fact, in the words of a report by the NBC Research Department in 1960, "The viewer watches commercials in the same way that he watches programs—in fact he looks for the same things in commercials that he seeks in programming. He does *not* think of commercials as something different apart from programs. The viewer not only watches commercials and is influenced by them, but he feels *obligated* to watch and be influenced."

Sometimes what the viewer felt was appreciation, because the ads provided advice about household chores or personal hygiene or automotive maintenance, advice that was hard to find elsewhere. At other times he might have felt enjoyment, because the ads were little shows of their own—the Ajax jingle was sung by a cute little trio of cartoon elves; "Lucky Strike cigarettes jumped out of the pack, square danced, did close-order drills."

Still other viewers looked forward to commercials because they provided biologically necessary breaks in the programs. What author Eric Goldman found out about Toledo in 1954 was true of many American cities of the time. Goldman noted that "the Water Commissioner of Toledo, puzzled why water consumption rose so startlingly during certain three-minute periods, checked and rechecked his charts, theorized and retheorized, finally hit on the answer: Toledo was flushing the toilets during the commercials."

But not everyone was flushing a toilet during every commercial; in fact enough of us were staying in our seats to make television the most prized advertising medium in the history of American business. The same NBC

Research Department report also indicates that TV surpassed radio in ad dollars in 1952, and overtook magazines and newspapers three years later. It has not been surpassed since, although television executives of the early twenty-first century wonder whether the Internet will one day be a threat.

It was not just because the commercials were abbreviated programs that they were popular among so many. Of greater significance was the fact that they were the means by which those of us watching television could best initiate ourselves into the consumer culture that was so important a by-product of the Eisenhower prosperity. More people could now afford to buy more things than ever before, and TV ads helped us decide which things were most deserving of our dollars, not only because they performed the best and lasted the longest and were the most economical, but because they conferred the most status. It was during the fifties that the phrase "keeping up with the Joneses" entered the American vocabulary; and the best way to keep up with them was to watch the ads on television, the same ones the Joneses were watching, and to make the same buying decisions they did. The fact that we never knew who the Joneses were did not deter us. The point is that we were engaged in identical pursuits, and television commercials quickly established themselves as the guides to our material goals.

Advertisers knew this. They researched their customers as thoroughly as they did their products, and put no less care into their commercials than the networks did into their programs. They also put in money. "While ad spending in general increased 258 percent in the fifties," write Douglas T. Miller and Marion Nowak, "TV ad expenditures rose 1,000 percent. Commercials brought the networks incredible profits. In 1953, CBS earned a profit of $8.9 million. The next year that network became the single largest advertising medium in the world. Its profits reached $11.4 million. By 1957, CBS profits totaled $22.2 million."

In 1950, Proctor & Gamble devoted less than two percent of its advertising budget to television. Ten years later, the figure was ninety-two percent. In 1956, it and its fellow American corporations spent $488 million to produce and broadcast television commercials, an amount they had never even approached before. The next year they would exceed that total, and in 1958 would exceed *that* total; they would keep exceeding totals for most of the years to follow.

One of the reasons that companies spent so much money on advertising was that the networks kept raising their rates as their audiences grew larger. Another reason was that the costs of producing commercials soared during the decade. According to CBS, in a study reported in the April 19, 1958 issue of *Business Week*, the average sponsor in 1951 spent $10,150 to buy time on a half-hour evening TV show and another $10,400 to pay the actors, directors, and other people that brought the ad to life. In 1957, the time cost $44,200 and the personnel $33,900.

Television was an enormous investment for advertisers. Not once in the fifties would they have cause to regret it.

IN 1955, the CBS quiz show *The $64,000 Question* made its debut. It was the right show, the right time, the right time slot—Tuesday nights at ten. No previous program of its kind had ever given contestants a chance to win so much money, and thus no program had ever created so much tension among contestants and viewers alike—not the artificially contrived tension of *Racket Squad* or *Man behind the Badge*, tension from which the end-of-the-episode outcome was known to viewers in advance, but the real-life tension of human beings playing the most high-stakes game of their lives. It was, like *Candid Camera*, on which viewers were humiliated rather than interrogated, reality TV well before the term came into being. Those of us who watched *The $64,000 Question* at home were captivated, identifying with the contestants in this case as if they truly *were* neighbors, men and women who might have been smarter than we were—at least in the areas in which they chose to be questioned—but were drawn from the same ordinary walks of life.

Our favorite contestant was probably Dr. Joyce Brothers, a pretty blond psychologist, twenty-eight years of age, with a degree from Columbia and a knowledge of boxing that was as remarkable as it was incongruous. Over the course of several weeks, Brothers won the entire $64,000, answering an astonishing variety of questions. Among other things, the *New York Times* reported, she

> named the cestus as the special gloves gladiators wore in ancient Rome; Daniel Mendoza as the first of the scientific boxers to become champion of England; in 1791; Gentleman John Jackson as the English champion who taught boxing to Lord Byron; William Hazlitt as the essayist who wrote "The Fight" after having seen Bill Neat defeat Thomas Hickman in England in 1821, and "Hickman the Gasman" as the boxer's nickname.

She also knew that Jack Dempsey sent Luis Firpo to the canvas nine times in their 1923 fight and that the fight lasted three minutes and fifty-seven seconds.

Yet she was so petite, so precise and soft-spoken, so dainty in her step— it seemed unlikely that she would ever watch a boxing match, much less be a scholar of the sport. Brothers was able to parlay the publicity that resulted from her unlikely knowledge into a career as a dime-store celebrity for the rest of her days.

Others who held us in their thrall for a time were Gino Prato, a shoe-maker from the Bronx, who seemed to know all there was to know about opera; Catherine Kreitzer, a Pennsylvanian so familiar with the works of Shakespeare that she might have been his co-author; and Robert Strom, an eleven-year-old boy who won $192,000 on *The $64,000 Question* and its later spin-off, *The $64,000 Challenge*. Prato and Kreitzer appeared only on the former program, and both stopped at the $32,000 plateau, with Kreitzer confident she could have gone on to win the full amount; she stopped, she explained, because she was a diligent reader of the Bible as well as Shake-speare, and the Good Book said, "Let your moderation be known unto all men."

The $64,000 Question was human drama at its most engaging. It was financial wheeling and dealing at its most lucrative. It was television at its most riveting. It was also advertising at its most effective. After but a few weeks, *The $64,000 Question* became one of the top five shows on the air; more than 47 million people watched an average episode, and on some nights that was more than 80 percent of the total viewing audience in its time period. President Eisenhower, it was said, tuned in whenever he could and did not like to be disturbed when he did. Perhaps he was watching the night that Marine captain Richard S. McCutcheon was a contestant, making his third or fourth appearance. The whole country seemed to be watching that night, and "[a] convention of wholesale druggists in White Sulphur Springs, West Virginia, was halted for the announcement: 'The Marine has answered the question!' The druggists cheered wildly before going on with their business."

The program's sponsor, Revlon, which liked to proclaim itself "the greatest name in cosmetics," quickly became the nation's greatest seller of cosmetics. As David Halberstam wrote in his history of the fifties, "Some Revlon products sold out overnight, and the show's master of ceremonies had to beg the public to be more patient until more Revlon Living Lipstick was available. The head of Hazel Bishop, a rival cosmetics company, subsequently blamed his company's disappointing year on the fact that 'a new television program sponsored by your company's principal competitor captured the imagination of the public.' It was the most primal lesson yet on the commercial power of television."

And an effective one. In 1955, Revlon's sales were up 66 percent over 1954. A few years earlier, Bonomo Turkish Taffy was among several companies to have had a similar, if less extreme, experience. According to Ray Morgan, Bonomo's TV spokesman, the company had been sponsoring a kids' show called *Magic Clown* for less than a month when they "had to put on two extra shifts at the Bonomo factory, and they're still six or seven weeks behind on their orders."

ACTUALLY, there was more than one primal lesson to be learned about the commercial power of television, and American businesses not only learned them but wasted no time in putting them into effect. For example: companies that advertised on popular shows sold more products than companies advertising on not-so-popular shows; companies that advertised on not-so-popular shows sold more than companies ignoring TV altogether. And a corollary: companies that managed to include their own names in the titles of the programs they sponsored sold the most of all. Milton Berle's weekly hour, the most-watched show in America for several years, was actually called *Texaco Star Theater.* "You can trust your car to the man who wears the star," sang the actors who pretended to be service station attendants at the start of the program and during the commercials, "the big, bright Texaco star!"

There were also *The Voice of Firestone*, a weekly concert of classical music, and such dramatic series as *Lux Video Theatre, The Ford Television Theater, Armstrong Circle Theatre, Your Lucky Strike Theatre, Kraft Television Theatre, General Electric Theatre, Ponds Theater, The Revlon Mirror Theatre, The RCA Victor Show, Goodyear TV Playhouse, The Philco TV Playhouse, Plymouth Playhouse, The Buick Electra Playhouse, Schlitz Playhouse of Stars, Pepsi Cola Playhouse, The United States Steel Hour, The Kaiser Aluminum Hour, The Motorola TV Hour, The Bell Telephone Hour,* and the *Hallmark Hall of Fame.*

Other programs, more miscellaneous in nature, included *Gillette Cavalcade of Sports, Gillette Cavalcade of Stars, Disneyland, Pabst Blue Ribbon*

Bouts, *Chesterfield Sound off Time*, and *The Colgate Comedy Hour*, with entertainers such as Fred Allen, Eddie Cantor, and the comedy team of Dean Martin and Jerry Lewis taking turns as hosts.

The most outrageous attempt by a company to promote itself in this manner came from Kaiser-Frazer automobiles, which insisted on calling their weekly show *Your Kaiser-Frazer Dealer Presents "Kaiser-Frazer Adventures in Mystery" Starring Betty Furness in "By-Line."* Newspapers, however, saved their ink and space, just listing the program as *By-Line*.

Today, major American corporations want naming rights for the stadiums of professional sports teams; half-a-century ago, naming rights for a TV show seemed the height of self-aggrandizing glory.

THE OCCASIONAL TRIP to the bathroom notwithstanding, we Americans were so enamored of commercials in the early days of television that we not only bought the products they featured, but developed an unusual fondness for the people who smooth-talked us into handing over our money. Rex Marshall, the handsome spokesman for Reynolds Aluminum, is not remembered today. But in the fifties he was one of the most recognized of all small-screen faces, and as a result was offered the starring role in a short-lived program in New York called *Date with Rex Marshall*, with female contestants competing against one another to win the title prize.

Other stars of commercials, like the stars of the shows, got fan mail, requests for autographed pictures and personal appearances, and the occasional request for a tryst or marriage. Unlike Eve Arden, though, Marshall was not offered new employment; no one at Reynolds tried to sign him up for a management position in the aluminum industry.

There was also the similarly long-forgotten Julia Meade, who appeared regularly on Ed Sullivan's variety show and, always stylishly dressed and coiffed, urged people to buy Lincolns and Mercurys. As a result, she was the subject of a flattering article in *Look* magazine, which told us of "her behind-the-scenes aspirations to a Hollywood contract, her years of study at Yale's drama school, and even her annual salary for walk-ons and commercials ($16,000)."

The era's most notable example of fame through product endorsement, though, was Betty Furness who, before attracting the attention of Kaiser-Frazer, was a movie actress and "a model who opened and closed

Westinghouse refrigerator doors at the 1952 national nominating conventions." Following in Marshall's footsteps, she was rewarded for her exposure with her own show, *Meet Betty Furness*, and after that with the aforementioned longest-titled program in TV history.

Then she went further. Furness parlayed her television exposure into federal office, being named a Special Assistant for Consumer Affairs to President Lyndon Johnson, and distinguishing herself as an energetic and effective advocate for the American spender. Afterward, she returned to television as a consumer reporter for WNBC-TV in New York and finally, in 1976, became a regular on *Today*, also on the consumer-affairs beat. In the latter role she was, for a time, a coworker of mine, and a crisply efficient one.

Later TV personalities, as famous as Furness in commercials but unable to capitalize on their renown as she did, included Jane Withers as Josephine the Plumber, who recommended Comet cleanser for bathroom and kitchen stains; Gunilla Knutson, who stroked her cheek with a can of Noxzema shaving cream and urged men to "take it off, take it all off"; and Jesse White, the Maytag repairman pining away in loneliness because his company's products never broke down and he never got to leave the shop. These people, who assumed their roles primarily in the sixties, provided even more examples of television's fifties-nurtured influence. They demonstrated that the medium could make celebrities out of those who appeared for only a few seconds at a time. Or, as was the case with Dr. Brothers and her fellow quiz-show contestants, it could make celebrities out of people who appeared for longer than a few seconds but only a few times. All one had to do was be seen on television—the viewers would remember, and their memories would do the rest.

LYNDON JOHNSON'S PREDECESSOR in the White House, so savvy about the image he wanted to project, was for that reason especially savvy about television. Not only did John F. Kennedy use the small screen to outperform Richard Nixon in the debates that helped him win the 1960 presidential election, and not only did he use it in a series of campaign ads that made his youth appear a form of vitality that qualified him to deal with the dangers of the cold war much more competently than old man Ike; he continued to make use of the medium throughout his all-too-brief stay in the Oval Office. It was in front of a camera that he most effectively established his credentials as a leader, promoted his visions for the American future, and flashed his charm and erudition to the journalists who attended him. The historian Arthur Schlesinger Jr., an aide to Kennedy, remembers his press conferences as being "a superb show, always gay, often exciting, relished by the reporters and by the television audience."

Then came the administration's task of imposing its standards for physical fitness on the schools, trying to entice boys and girls to stop watching so much television and get outside and flex their muscles. In its own way, it must have seemed a challenge as great as the one posed by the Soviets. How did the White House meet it? In the most practical yet paradoxical way possible. It took out ads on TV. The kids might not have done what the ads urged them to do but, as Kennedy well knew, there was no more effective way to be sure that they got the message. Kennedy probably accomplished the extraordinary feat of achieving success and failure at the same time, through the same means.

NO ONE, HOWEVER, was more impressed by the effectiveness of television advertising than the advertisers themselves. Nor was anyone more surprised, at least at the outset. Never before had companies been able to reach so many potential customers at a single time. Never before had they been able to appeal to them in so innovative a manner. Never before had potential customers reacted so positively. It was crucial, then, that sponsors not do anything to diminish the effectiveness of this wondrous new tool of financial persuasion.

The risks were great, the margin for error small. People who made a purchasing decision as a result of a commercial could just as easily buy a different manufacturer's product if the commercial put them off; or, no less important, if the show on which the commercial appeared was one that the audience found offensive. In other words, at the same time that advertisers were basking in success, they were wallowing in caution, an attitude that, if taken to its extreme, leads to paranoia. Some advertisers managed to achieve paranoia before caution was even a reasonable response. Such was the regard for the new medium in corporate America. Such was the awe felt by those who thought the medium could make them rich beyond their wildest projections.

It all seems to have started in the early forties, when only the most optimistic of ad executives could have foreseen what television would eventually become. Michael Ritchie tells of a program called *When a Girl Marries*, in which, according to an early script, "Mary Jane Higby, one of the show's star characters, loaned a mink coat to her fictional maid. The sponsors, Prudential Life Insurance, panicked that this would start a stampede of servants borrowing valuable furs—causing personal property insurance rates to rise dramatically. Prudential exercised its veto rights. The script was changed; the maid didn't get the coat."

It takes a certain kind of individual to overreact like this. That the episode of *When a Girl Marries*, as originally written, would have led to throngs of servants borrowing valuable coats, that the coats would somehow have been less safe as a result, and that insurance rates for personal property would have risen dramatically as a further result—this is the kind of perversely creative thinking one more usually associates with those who write scripts, and farcical scripts at that, than those who sit in judgment of them.

It was also creative thinking on the part of the Ford Motor Company to agree, on another occasion, to sponsor a program only if the Chrysler Building were painted out of a backdrop of the New York skyline. No less creative was it to "automatically and arbitrarily delete from the English language any words that suggests a competitive product. You can't 'ford' a river if it's sponsored by Chevy; you can't offer someone a 'match' if it's sponsored by Ronson lighters." In fact, "[i]n some cases, you can't even use the word *American*. It might be in the name of a rival tobacco company," such as the American Tobacco Company, which manufactured Lucky Strike.

When General Electric, a sponsor of the dramatic anthology *Studio One*, learned that one of its episodes would be based on Rudyard Kipling's novel *The Light that Failed*, it was horrified. General Electric could not be associated with failing light. The program ended up being called *The Gathering Night*.

This kind of thinking would become more and more prevalent, and devious, as television moved through the fifties. Some people were upset about it. Mort Weiner, NBC's vice president of programming, was not. In fact, in testimony before the FCC, he claimed the sponsors' wariness made perfect sense.

[A]n automobile manufacturer doesn't want an automobile accident in the story; a manufacturer of bathroom fixtures sold through plumbing supply dealers specifies that no jokes about plumbers are to be used. These requirements do not really interfere with the entertainment objectives of the program or with their creative integrity. We have learned to accommodate our operations to this type of request.

Learned to accommodate? Yes.
No loss of integrity? Read on.

"JUDGMENT AT NUREMBERG," a play originally written for television that went on to become an Academy Award–winning movie, was one of the shining moments of television in the fifties. Based on the Nuremberg war trials, the play looks into the minds and motives of Nazi judges who, believing that they were simply enforcing the law, as opposed to committing crimes against humanity, upheld the execution of Jews ordered by Adolf Hitler. Abby Mann's script was powerful, unflinching, tragic; and the production's occasional use of documentary footage gave it a realism that made its emotional impact all the greater.

As for the unintentional comic moments, they were provided by the sponsor.

When officials of the American Gas Association first learned of plans for a dramatization of the trial, they decided it would be a perfect use of their advertising dollars. They were a little-known trade group whose executives wanted it to be better known, and more respected; affiliating themselves with a program of social and historical significance seemed an ideal way to achieve their goal. The Association agreed to finance the *Playhouse 90* presentation of "Judgment at Nuremberg," and, given the seriousness of the subject matter, also agreed to keep commercial interruptions to a minimum. Cast and crew were hired; rehearsals began; an air date was scheduled. All seemed to be proceeding on schedule.

Then it occurred to at least a few of the members of the American Gas Association that their product was the means by which Jews had been put to death in Hitler's extermination camps. This, they decided, would never do. The Nazis did not use American Gas Association gas, of course, or even American gas—but it was gas nonetheless. Why, they must have asked themselves, did those scoundrels have to decide on *gas*! The Association considered backing out of the deal, but it was too late. It was not too late, however, for a little editing—and that is precisely, and preposterously, what happened.

As an official of the Association later explained,

[W]e get paid for going through the script. In going through the scripts, we noticed gas referred to in half a dozen places that had to do with death chambers. This was just an oversight on somebody's part. We deal with a lot of artistic people on the creative end, and sometimes they do not have the commercial judgment or see things as we are paid to see, and we raised the point with CBS and they said they would remove the word "gas," and we thought they would, and they did in some cases, and at the last minute, we found that there were some still left in. As a result—and this was just, I think, stupidity—the show went on the air where the word "gas" was deleted by the engineer rather than rehearsing the talent.

"Deleted," meaning this: when the American television audience of 1959 saw "Judgment at Nuremberg" on television the night of April 16, 1959, and one of the judges or other characters mentioned that Jews were to be exterminated, it was simply said that the Jews had been sentenced to (pause) ovens. Not gas ovens: just (pause) ovens. There was some lip movement during the pause, the lips moving in the shape of the word "gas," but there was no sound.

It was as if the judges had consigned their victims to be baked, as if their precedent were Hansel and Gretel rather than the unspeakable anti-Semitism of the Third Reich. So engrossed in the play were most viewers that they did not notice the omissions, or the occasional syllable of silence before the word "ovens," and in fact so engrossed were they that they never would have made a connection between the sponsor and a brief mention of the use to which gas had been put by a different kind of society at a different time. The American Gas Association, to say the least, overreacted. Nonetheless, it had its way and history had its rewrite.

It would happen again. In fact, it had happened before. Midway through the fifties, perhaps the most famous television author of the time, Rod Serling, who would go on to create and write most of the scripts for *The Twilight Zone,* had an idea for *The U.S. Steel Hour,* based on an appalling incident of racial violence in the South.

One day in the summer of 1955, a fourteen-year-old black boy named Emmett Till went to a grocery store in a small town in the Mississippi Delta. Till did not live in the area; a Chicagoan, he was visiting relatives nearby and had been sent to buy some food for them. One of two things happened next: either Till whistled at the white woman who was a clerk at the store, then suggested that he had had sex with white women before, an unlikely boast; or, a chronic stutterer, he made a sound that was a wolf whistle, or could somehow be construed as one. No one is sure which, but when the woman's husband heard about the incident, he was not in the mood to make distinctions.

He did not hear about it immediately, however, not until he returned from a business trip a few days later, but he raged at the news, just as he raged at the fact that local law enforcers had not arrested Till for his behavior. There was only one choice, he decided: he would have to take matters into his own hands.

Enlisting the help of his half-brother, the man kidnapped Till from his great-uncle's house, despite the old man's tears and pleas and futile clutchings. They took the boy to a deserted plantation, where what seems to have happened is that the man and his half-brother beat the boy senseless, cut off one of his ears, poked out an eye, and shot him to death with a pistol. Then they tied a 75-pound weight around Till's neck, fastening it with barbed wire, and dragged the body to a nearby river and threw it in.

The murderers were arrested the next day. They admitted the kidnapping, but nothing else, claiming they had let Till go after warning him about proper behavior around a white woman. They had no idea what happened next, they said; the last time they saw the victim the boy was alive and well and heading back to his family—better educated in the ways of the South, but as untouched as he had been before the kidnapping.

Few people believed them, but neither did anyone raise a voice in protest. Especially not in the courtroom, where even the prosecutor, racist to the core himself, found little of an objectionable nature in the defendants' story. The case went to the jury quickly. The jury returned with a verdict even more quickly, barely more than an hour, and it would not have taken that long, one of the jurors later told a reporter, if they had not taken a break for a soft drink. The defendants were found not guilty. Cheers echoed through the halls of justice. The cause of Emmett Till's death was not addressed. Neither was his present whereabouts.

Serling intended to write about the crime itself, but explained he was also drawn to the story by the motivations of the jurors who set the killers free. Why would they do such a thing? How could human beings react to the taking of another human being's life by refusing to punish the deed in some manner? Exactly how *un*-human was a young black boy thought to be, regardless of what he might have said to a woman of a different race?

Serling wanted to go further, writing about the town in which the crime had occurred and the area surrounding it, where almost the entire white citizenry had not only welcomed the verdict but accepted the killers back into their midst with bear hugs and hearty handshakes and round after round of free drinks, toasting them for their acquittal. Serling was bewildered. As much as condemning such behavior, he sought to understand it.

In broad terms, very broad, *The U.S. Steel Hour* approved the idea for Serling's script, which he called "Noon on Doomsday." In a sense the producers and sponsors had no choice, since the murder of Emmett Till had received so much publicity that high ratings for a fictionalized version of the tale were virtually guaranteed.

Also guaranteed was an eruption of disapproval.

Several "Southern White Citizens Councils"—collections of empty-headed bigots and former Ku Klux Klansmen—became outraged and threatened a major boycott of United States Steel. Serling joked, "Does that mean from now on everybody below the Mason–Dixon line is going to build with aluminum?" Actually, United States Steel feared the Ford Motor plant would pull its sheet-metal orders. Ford was having an "industrial public relations" problem with white and African-American workers on its Southern assembly lines. Air this show in the South, Ford warned, and race relations would be set back five years. CBS-TV was even asked to block the show in the Southern markets—which, to its credit, it refused to do.

No credit, however, could be claimed by U.S. Steel. Serling could go ahead and write his screenplay, executives told him, but it could not be situated in the Mississippi Delta. It could not even be located in the southern half of the United States. The reason was obvious. It would upset the people who lived there.

But the incident had *occurred* in the South, Serling replied; everyone who watched the program would know it was based on the Emmett Till case and therefore that the kidnapping and trial and celebration of the verdict had happened in Mississippi. Further, they would know the reason it happened there was that the crime reflected the racial attitudes on the part of all too many people who lived in that part of the country.

No matter. "The southern location had to be changed," Eric Barnouw writes in the third of his three-volume history of broadcasting in America. He goes on to say that even "[a]n unspecified location was not good enough; it had to be New England; to *prove* it was New England, [the program] had to open with a shot of a white church spire. Anything that might conceivably suggest the South had to be changed. Once this sleuthing began, almost anything seemed southern. A Coca-Cola bottle had to be removed from the set. An executive busied himself restoring the missing g's in present participles. Plot details were changed every day, and the final show was an absurdity in a total vacuum."

There were more absurdities. Till was no longer a boy; he was a man. And he was no longer from Chicago; he was from a foreign country. And, as if the truth and Serling's vision of it had not already been sufficiently sabotaged, preposterized and shredded, Till was no longer black; he was white.

The South was placated. It would not rise again, against *The U.S. Steel Hour*, at least.

Serling, however, was disconsolate. After deliberating for a while, he went ahead and wrote the script, struggling to make the points he wanted to make but for the most part failing, unable to overcome the ineptitude forced upon him. In retrospect, he wished that he had given up on the idea. "I was destroyed by this show professionally, I think, for about eleven or twelve months. People kept referring to me as 'that guy who wrote that thing.' It also struck me that I was now a controversial writer, so-called."

It was not what one wanted to be called in those days when, as will be seen, Senator Joe McCarthy's influence may have been waning, but was still felt in darker corners.

"Another incident," Barnouw reports, referring to yet further corporate intrusion into the realms of both broadcasting and life as it is actually lived, "caused international repercussions."

> General Motors sponsored the anthology series *General Motors Theatre*, seen over the Canadian Broadcasting Corporation network [as well as in the United States]; it sometimes re-used scripts from the United States anthology series and sometimes used Canadian originals. In 1954 it scheduled a script titled *The Legend of the Baskets*, by Canadian writer Ted Allan, about a Mexican peasant who turned out beautiful baskets at a leisurely pace, at low price. Approached by American industrialists with a plan to mass-produce the baskets (he would supervise and get rich), he turned it down because it would destroy his artistic satisfaction. The script had caused no alarm at lower echelons but during rehearsals an executive, representing the sponsor, decided the script was an attack on the capitalist system

and had to be canceled. An earlier script was repeated. The censorship of Canadian television by an American sponsor caused something of an uproar in the Canadian press.

In this country General Motors instituted a new policy to avoid uproars of any kind. It announced that it "has elected to avoid being concerned with matters that are controversial"—as simple, and final, as that. General Foods explained it had a "feeling that eating is a pleasant experience," and for that reason had "definitely gone in for the light entertainment shows" around the dinner hour. And a Proctor & Gamble memo to advertising agencies told them that under no circumstances would the company sponsor "material that may give offense, either directly or by inference, to any commercial organization of any sort." Then, continuing in a remarkably straight-faced manner, the announcement stated that nothing "could in any way further the concept of business as cold, ruthless, or lacking sentimental or spiritual motivation."

NO INDUSTRY, HOWEVER, was more sensitive about the programs on which its advertising appeared than tobacco. The fifties was the decade when it first began to fear for its life. In 1952, *Reader's Digest*, the most widely read magazine in the world, reprinted an article originally published in the *Christian Herald*, the most thorough indictment of cigarettes ever presented in the mainstream press. The *Christian Herald* piece was called "Smokers Are Getting Scared." The headline for the *Reader's Digest* version, read by millions of people, was "Cancer by the Carton."

The following year, the Associated Press, International Press, and United Press, the three largest wire services in the country, reported on a study by the *Journal of American Geriatrics* that found that "the tremendous and unprecedented increase of bronchogenic carcinoma in recent years is due to the carcinogenic effect of tobacco." Newspapers and radio and TV stations all over the country picked up the story: and just so there would be no misunderstanding, they did not accuse tobacco of causing something misleadingly polysyllabic like bronchogenic carcinoma—they accused it of causing *cancer*. Coldly, bluntly: cancer.

And in 1955, the U.S. Bureau of the Census revealed that one-and-a-half million Americans had quit smoking in the past eighteen months, the largest number ever recorded for such a period of time. It was a startling loss for the tobacco companies—of both revenue and credibility. They had to do something. Presenting exculpatory evidence would have been ideal, but since there wasn't any, the companies decided to do the next best thing: lie. They began to take out ads, on TV and in print, claiming their product was safe.

And according to the ads, it was about to be even safer, as they were now developing filters, magical little accessories stuck onto one end of the cigarette that blocked out the evil ingredients the companies swore didn't exist in tobacco in the first place. At the same time, they said, filters allowed the wonderful flavor of burning vegetation to get through the protective device to the smoker's taste buds.

But that was not enough. In addition to producing commercials for television, tobacco companies began, for all practical purposes, to produce entire shows. For example:

> When a guest on the quiz program *Do You Trust Your Wife?* was asked his mate's astrological sign, he said Cancer. The host thought nothing of it. The producer thought nothing of it. The studio audience, as far as anyone knows, made no untoward associations. But the tobacco barons who paid the bills for the show gulped in resounding unison. Cancer? they said. What the hell kind of sign is *that?* They ordered the episode to be re-shot; in the new version, the spouse was an Aries.

On *Men Against Crime*, sponsored by Camel, a memo was circulated to writers, telling them what to do before they even rolled a sheet of paper into their typewriters. They were not to call for thugs or miscreants or any other kind of undesirable characters to smoke a cigarette. They were not to allow characters of any sort to make a disparaging remark about a cigarette. Furthermore, "no one was to be given a cigarette to calm his nerves, since this would imply that nicotine was a narcotic; fire or arson were not to be shown, for this might remind people that cigarettes caused fires; and never, ever, was anyone to cough on a show."

Camel also sponsored *Camel News Caravan*, anchored by John Cameron Swayze, who was "short, silky and nasal, often sporting a boutonniere as he hit the airwaves." His newscast, on NBC, was introduced by an announcer who said, "Sit back, light up a Camel, and be witness to the latest happenings."

Swayze was under orders not to include stories about the tobacco-cancer link in the program, despite the fact that almost every other journalistic outlet in the country was reporting it, with increasing frequency. The program was also not permitted to present film in which a NO SMOKING sign appeared, although that was an easy enough restriction, since few such signs existed in the fifties. Nor, since Camel was a brand of cigarette, was Swayze allowed to show a clip of anyone smoking anything *but* a cigarette, with the single exception of Winston Churchill, who was often in the news and so commonly known to be a cigar smoker that he transcended the prohibition.

Swayze did not object to any of this, at least not publicly. A heavy smoker himself, he kept a Camel lit during the entire fifteen-minutes of his nightly program and puffed away during breaks and film clips. He sat back, lit up, witnessed the latest happenings.

Sometimes when he was on the air reading his script, the viewer could make out wisps of smoke curling over his shoulder and wafting around his head. It was as if there were a fire in the wastebasket under his desk and Swayze was determined to ignore it. The program was live, however; when John Cameron coughed, there was nothing anyone could do about it.

Over at CBS, Edward R. Murrow refused to be cowed. His *See It Now* program devoted several episodes to the case against tobacco. Murrow smoked like a chimney, as the expression goes, through all of his anti-tobacco presentations, and through all of his other on-air appearances. A three-packs-a-day man, Murrow said he could not go more than half an hour without a cigarette. But one cannot help wonder what went through his mind as he exhaled, introduced a damning film clip about the effects of smoking to an audience of millions, then, off camera now, inhaled.

Murrow died in 1965. Cause of death: lung cancer.

WHAT ALL OF THESE SPONSORS had in common—the insurance company and the gas association and the steel manufacturer and the tobacco firms and the rest of the advertisers in TV's early days—was a mistrust of reality. It was too hard to predict, too undependable; reality was sure to be offensive to someone, sure to be confusing to someone else, and for that reason sure to distract from the impact of the sponsor's message in one way or another. In later decades, it might have been the audience that insisted on a simple and sanitized version of American life on the tube; but it was the sponsors that introduced the notion, who got people used to it. It was sponsors who created an almost totally distorted picture of life in the fifties, which was brought into homes from New York to California, from Minnesota to Texas.

IN 1954, the noted playwright Elmer Rice wanted to bring a different kind of picture to TV. Specifically, he wanted to adapt his 1929 Pulitzer–Prize-winning drama, *Street Scene,* for the small screen. But according to the advertising agency he approached with the project, *Street Scene* did not have the proper tone for the tube, was insufficiently uplifting. After all, as one of the reviews of the original Broadway production had pointed out, the play takes place in "an average New York tenement house on the grimier edge of the middle class." TV was not in the market for grimy edges. The ad agency was candid in telling Rice of its objections to the play.

> Foremost among these objections is the squalor of the setting, the lower class social level of all the chief characters, and the utterly depressing circumstances which they all find themselves in. . . .
>
> We know of no advertiser or advertising agency of any importance in this country who would knowingly allow the products which he is trying to advertise to the public to become associated with the . . . general "down" character . . . of *Street Scene.*
>
> On the contrary, it is the general policy of advertisers to glamorize their products, the people who buy them, and the whole American social and economic scene. . . . The American consuming public as presented by the advertising industry today is middle class, not lower class; happy in general, not miserable and frustrated, and optimistic, not depressed.

And advertisers would do their best to keep audiences happy in general, or at least to keep them from feeling ill-disposed toward the products that they made not only through the fifties but beyond. As James Twitchell writes in his book *Carnival Culture,* "A scene in which wild dogs chase a girl on an episode of *Little House on the Prairie* [1974–83] was cut because one of the sponsors was Puppy Chow. No cat food commercials appeared on *Alf* [1986–90] because the alien threatens to eat the family cat."

AMERICANS DID NOT BUY only what was seen in commercials; Americans also bought what was seen in the programs, and this was something the networks and producers had never expected. It had never occurred to them that the sitcoms and westerns and cop shows themselves might be showcases for selling products—but television, it seemed, was so powerful a means of moving merchandise that it could do so without even trying. A character wore a certain kind of clothing on the air and his fans wanted to wear it, too. We wanted to drive the car he drove, eat the food he ate, drink the beverages he drank, tote the briefcase or purse that he or she toted, copy his or her hairstyle and perhaps dye our hair the same color. Depending on our age, gender, and taste, we wanted hairdos like Mamie Eisenhower or Jack Webb; attire like Julia Meade or Edward R. Murrow; pizzazz like Eve Arden or Bert Parks; breasts like Dagmar, no matter how artificially contrived.

Or, if for some reason we could not emulate our favorite TV star in one of the preceding ways, we wanted at least to associate ourselves with him, adorn ourselves with his image or name, which is to say that, in a manner of speaking, we wanted to become advertisements for our idol as we went about our daily activities. If a person cannot be a celebrity himself, he can at least have the satisfaction of being a billboard for one, and in the process, at some level of consciousness, believe that some of the luster is transferred. Long before Americans were wearing Tommy Hilfiger shirts, we were tramping off to school with Hopalong Cassidy lunch boxes.

For those of school age, owning such a product was the most gratifying way to take part in the consumer culture. We might have enjoyed the visual displays of TV commercials, but for the most part the ads themselves did not address our desires. Boys and girls did not buy cars, toothpaste, mouthwash, shampoo, hair tonic, deodorant, laxatives, vitamin supplements, makeup, medicines, household cleaners, aluminum foil, waxed paper, insect sprays, pet food, cigarettes, razor blades, insurance policies, or most of the other goods and services that sponsored our favorite shows on weekday evenings. For us to decide how to spend our allowances according to the dictates of television in post-Depression, postwar America, we had to look someplace other than commercials for our cues. Hopalong Cassidy provided the first of them.

From the vantage point of the present, it does not seem that he could have failed. Hoppy, as he was known to his young admirers, was a brand name of long-standing, created in a short story by Clarence E. Mulford in

1904 and since then having been featured in hundreds more short stories as well as comic books and novels and, in time, more than sixty feature-length films.

In 1949, when NBC chose a barely-known actor named William Boyd to play Hopalong Cassidy, the program became the first western ever to appear on a network, and the genre that would so dominate television through the fifties and sixties was successfully underway. We children now had a hero of our own in the home, one with rugged good looks, a sense of derring-do, and a determination to triumph over every obstacle that villains put in his way. I can still see Hoppy ducking from a hail of bullets that missed him from point-blank range. I can still see him smiling back at a villain, pulling the trigger of his gun, and dropping the miscreant to the dust with a single shot. Then he would hold the business end of the weapon up to his mouth and blow away the smoke. God, what a man!

In 1950, Hoppy triumphed in a different manner. He became the first television character ever to be memorialized on a lunch box. At the time, it did not seem like much of an achievement, and in truth the company that made the lunch boxes, Aladdin Industries, was not expecting much. The year before Boyd's character was featured on its product, Aladdin sold 50,000 units. The next year—the plastic container having now been emblazoned with a silver-haired, black-hatted, black-clothed cowboy astride a rearing white horse and firing a six-shooter at unseen desperadoes— Aladdin sold 600,000 units.

Hopalong Cassidy products were rushed to stores like medical supplies to a disaster scene. In addition to lunch boxes, they included cowboy hats, kerchiefs, soap, wristwatches, roller skates, badges, knives, guns, holsters, dinnerware, cups and plastic plates. Children bought them all and demanded more. When an elementary-school teacher in Bergenfield, New Jersey, was asked why she had resigned her position in 1950, she complained that all her students wanted to talk about was William Boyd's alter ego. "Over and over," she said. "Just cowboys and Indians and Hopalong Cassidy. It's no wonder they are bored by school. How can I compete with Hopalong Cassidy?"

Soon there were other cowboy shows to compete with, and other cowboy merchandise on the shelves of stores and the wish lists of young Americans. Our goal was to keep up with the Joneses' kids, who were in turn keeping up not just with Hoppy, but with other heroes of the Wild West such as Roy Rogers and Dale Evans and Pat Brady; Wild Bill Hickok and Jingles; the

Cisco Kid and Pancho; the Lone Ranger; Lash Larue, Johnny Mack Brown, Hoot Gibson, the Range Rider, and my favorite, the three Mesquiteers, who were the equivalent of one of the later rock supergroups, but none of whose names I can remember now.

And the way we kept up with the young Joneses was by stockpiling even more products bearing our idols' likenesses than they did: cowboy shirts with ornate piping, cowboy wallets with thick stitching and cowboy ID cards inside, chaps, spurs, gun belts, rain gear, notebooks, pencil sets, tool kits, walkie-talkies, and on and on, even if the items had nothing to do with the life on the prairie in the nineteenth century.

In fact, even characters who had nothing to do with the prairie could be stars at merchandising, just as long as enough kids watched their exploits. There was a Captain Midnight decoder badge and a Captain Video space game and a Space Cadet insignia ring and a Rocky Jones, Space Ranger, badge and a Captain Gallant Junior Legionnaires membership certificate and a Super Circus baton-twirler doll and a Coca-Cola finger puppet from *Rootie Kazootie* and a Howdy Doody shake-up mug into which one was to pour Ovaltine and milk and then jiggle them together into a tasty yet nutritious chocolate beverage.

BUT THE GREATEST HERO OF ALL for children in the fifties, and perhaps the greatest hero of all time as far as television marketers were concerned, was Davy Crockett. In real life, Crockett, a nineteenth-century woodsman, was a figure of few admirable traits. He ran away from home at the age of thirteen, no longer able to abide his parents any more than they were able to abide him. He became an Indian fighter, a U.S. Congressman, and a soldier who died battling the Mexicans at the Alamo. He cussed, drank, smelled even worse than the average nineteenth-century horseman, and flirted with any lady who could stand his proximity.

Along the way Crockett got married, but the arrangement was too civilized for him. He has been described as "a dirty, lazy, drunken cowardly loser who abandoned his wife and children to lead a drifter's life." He has also been described as a liar. "When he claimed he had shot 105 bear [sic] in nine months," it was said, "his fellow tipplers refused to believe a word of it on the sensible grounds that Davy couldn't count that high."

On television, however, the man was transformed into something else altogether: a rescuer of damsels, thwarter of criminals, defier of nature's excesses and, if the cause was just, slayer of man and beast alike—even if not 105 of the latter in a mere nine months. In all likelihood, he wore deodorant and cologne, and his well-tailored buckskin was always nicely pressed. The small-screen version of Davy Crockett was introduced by Walt Disney on his ABC program *Disneyland* in December, 1954.

By the following May, Crockett merchandise had grossed more than $100 million, an astonishing figure, one more in keeping with a small country's gross national product than a large company's bottom line, and this even though there were only five episodes of *Davy Crockett* in the entire series—so small a number for such a seismic impact. When the episodes were repeated, the impact was even greater; the series drew a larger audience the second time around than it did the first.

The program's theme song, "The Ballad of Davy Crockett," was so ubiquitously played that it seemed for a time like the national anthem. It sold seven-million copies in six months, becoming one of the biggest-selling records of the entire decade. Disney executives were startled; they had no idea a tune that was little more sophisticated than a commercial jingle could be such a success. They tried to repeat that success. They brought out a mambo version of the song: "Davy, Davy Crockett, King of the Wild Frontier, cha-cha-cha."

The mambo version was not even one of the biggest-selling songs of the day it was released.

The most successful Crockett product, though, and probably the most valued item ever promoted through a television program, was the coonskin cap, Davy's trademark headgear, a furry little item shaped like an upside-down cereal bowl and pointlessly adorned with a tail hanging down one side, usually worn so that the tail ended up in the crook of the neck, tickling the cheek.

The cap was the second piece of Davy Crockett merchandise I owned, the first being a guitar that, having been strung with pieces of plastic instead of silver-plated copper wound around nylon, was incapable of playing a tune. I strummed it anyhow. I did not, however, wear my cap as often as my friends wore theirs. I did not like the feel of the tail flapping against me as I ran, and I seem to recall a peculiar smell, especially after I wore the cap once in the rain.

But for some youngsters at the time, a coonskin cap was mandatory. As an adult, Steven Spielberg remembered what it was like to be a boy without one, even for a few days:

I was in third grade at the time. Suddenly the next day, everybody in my class but me was Davy Crockett. And because I didn't have my coonskin cap and my powder horn, or Old Betsy, my rifle, and the chaps, I was deemed the Mexican leader, Santa Anna. And they chased me home from school until I got my parents to buy me a coonskin cap.

The only individual I ever encountered who was not enraptured by coonskin caps and other Davy Crockett paraphernalia was Charlie Brown, the star of Charles Schulz's comic strip *Peanuts,* which I read every afternoon in the long-since defunct *Pittsburgh Press.* One day, Charlie decided he had had enough of the entire marketing campaign.

First panel: Linus watches as Charlie digs a hole with a shovel and throws a familiar furry object into it. "Don't tell me you're burying your coonskin cap?" Linus says, amazed.

Second panel: Charlie replies. "Uh huh. . . . I got up this morning from my Davy Crockett bed, put on my Davy Crockett slippers, and went to eat my Davy Crockett cereal."

Third panel: Charlie continues. "I'm sitting there in a Davy Crockett chair eating with a Davy Crockett spoon out of a Davy Crockett bowl . . . *Suddenly it hits me. . . .*"

Fourth panel: Charlie looks bleakly at Linus, the shovel standing next to him. "Where will it all end?"

ALL TOLD, more than ten-million Davy Crockett coonskin caps were sold in the United States, and to one particular business, the best days of which had seemed forever behind it, the sales were the most unexpected of windfalls. "The wholesale price of raccoon skins," revealed Landon Y. Jones, "jumped from 25 cents a pound to $8 a pound." Jones puts the total number of Davy Crockett products at an incredible 3,000. In addition to those about which Charlie Brown complained (some of which did not really exist), they included T- shirts, sweaters, sweatshirts, gym shorts, boots, slippers, pajamas, underwear, belts, bandannas, jackets, dolls, knapsacks, books, sleds, blankets, snowsuits, hairbrushes, toothbrushes, phonographs, souvenir photos and posters and postcards, picture frames—and of course lunch boxes.

But none of these products would have been successful had it not been for Davy Crockett, and Crockett would not have been successful had it not been for Fess Parker, and Parker would not have been successful had he not been visible, and appealing, to the majority of people who watched him. Which is to say that television could not have sold its goods had it not first sold its personalities. And it was the latter, the stars of the shows, the men and women providing the gold for television's Golden Age, who, more than any other factor, established television as the ruling cultural medium of the American fifties.

Chapter 5

"Really Big Shows"

I T WAS NOT A GOLDEN AGE, though—not really. With few exceptions, what made television glitter in the early days was its newness more than the excellence of its programs. If people of my approximate age remember those programs with a special fondness, it is in part because they coincide with the very beginning of our memories, memories that were produced in part by the most formative instrument in our lives at the most formative time in our lives.

But the quality of some of the programs was undeniable. Among the best were episodes of dramatic anthology series like *Studio One* and *Playhouse 90* and a number of the programs listed earlier that were named after sponsors. Other anthologies included TV's first such series, *Fireside Theatre*, and offerings such as *Armchair Theatre*, *NBC Television Playhouse*, *Four Star Playhouse*, *Actors Studio*, and *Robert Montgomery Presents*, in which the actor would introduce each week's program, as Alistair Cooke and Russell Baker would later introduce *Masterpiece Theatre*.

The names of the shows stayed the same from week to week, but only the names. The stories changed, the casts changed, the settings changed, the writers and directors changed—each episode of a dramatic anthology series was like going to a different theater to see a different play. Never before had television turned out so many good programs so often. Never before had it varied content and style to such enriching effect. And never before had it been forced into so grand a display of innovation. As medium historian Rick Marschall explains,

> Writers and producers had to forego the spectacular dimensions of the movie screen, and even shrink, in effect, the dimensions of the theatrical stage, heretofore drama's most intimate mode. Hence television dramas were those of personality rather than action; the focus was on characters, conflict and emotion. It can be argued that Golden Age television drama cannot be classified solely by the calendar and by the medium—a particular sort of play emerged, fashioned not only by television's limits, but by its potentialities.

Still, the critic Harriet Van Horne, although snippy, was also accurate when she wrote in 1951: "If you study the week's television log in the Sunday papers, you'll find about twenty-five dramatic shows regularly scheduled. Of these twenty-five, fewer than ten are careful, show-wise dramatic productions aimed at an adult, theatre-going audience. The rest, claptrap." But what wasn't claptrap, what wasn't twisted out of recognizable shape by spineless advertisers, was a seam of rare and valuable ore running through the caverns of 1950s television.

ON OCCASION, the anthology series produced new versions of tales already known to the audience, like adaptations of Academy Award–nominated movies and plays that became award-winners or nominees of one sort or another in their TV incarnations. Other early fare included TV versions of novels or short stories, always of literary merit; or of events in the news, always of social or political merit, such as "Judgment at Nuremberg" and "Noon on Doomsday." Virtually all the dramatic anthology series of the fifties were broadcast live, an unthinkable feat today. Among the highlights, in addition to the preceding, were these:

The Barretts of Wimpole Street, based on a 1934 film about the romance between the poets Elizabeth Barrett and Robert Browning. The movie was one of the candidates for Best Picture that year; the television version was most notable for the performance of Katherine Cornell, one of the regal stage figures of the era, who played Barrett with touching elegance.

The Moon and Sixpence, based on Somerset Maugham's novel about the life of the French painter Paul Gauguin and starring another regal figure of the acting world, Laurence Olivier. In Maugham's rendering Gauguin is a London stockbroker named Charles Strickland who, like the similarly impassioned Gauguin, abandons his family to pursue his art—and the less civilized side of his nature—in Tahiti.

Wuthering Heights, the only novel Emily Brontë ever wrote, but in terms of quality, a virtual lifetime's oeuvre. Set in England's most desolate moors, it is an emotionally wrenching tale of desolation both physical and psychological, of sorrow and illness and love letters that express obsession as much as love. In the TV version, Richard Burton played the doomed Healthcliff in even more tormented fashion than Brontë had written him, and Rosemary Harris was Catherine, his object of desire whose fate was to lie in a grave adjoining Heathcliff's. Like *The Barretts of Wimpole Street*, it too had won a Best Picture nomination on the big screen.

Cyrano, a play by Edmond Rostand, a fictionalized treatment of the life of French author Cyrano de Bergerac who, in addition to writing comedy, tragedy, and science fiction, was one of the preeminent swordsmen of his age. Unfortunately, he also possessed one of the age's preeminent noses, and it was his attempt to find love despite his comical appearance that was the gist of the play. José Ferrer, with padded proboscis, played Cyrano both on TV and in the later movie version.

Our Town, the Thornton Wilder play that won the Pulitzer Prize for drama in 1938, and that has probably found more poignancy in the quotidian than any other drama in American history. Frank Sinatra was the stage manager on TV and Paul Newman and Eva Marie Saint played the other leading roles.

Newman also starred in *The Eighty-Yard Run*, based on an Irwin Shaw short story about a man who visits a football stadium "in the spring twilight," with "the sky green behind the stadium," and dreams not only of the glory that he had once attained in that stadium, but of the glory that has not been his, in any facet of his life, ever since.

A two-part version of Ernest Hemingway's novel of love and duty in the Spanish Civil War, *For Whom the Bell Tolls* was one of the most expensive TV productions of the fifties, the cost estimated at more than $300,000. But *A Night to Remember* might have surpassed that amount. Taken from

Walter Lord's nonfiction account of the sinking of the *Titanic*, a best-seller in 1955, *A Night to Remember* was brought to television, we are told, with the assistance of "107 actors, 31 sets, and 7 cameras." To repeat, it was presented live: no edits, no second takes, no stopping to change sets. To make sure that *A Night to Remember* could not be forgotten, it was repeated a few weeks later, as were several dramas of the period—so engaged was the audience, so insistent that they be allowed to relive the experience again promptly.

Also brought to live television in the fifties were adaptations of Sinclair Lewis's *Dodsworth*, F. Scott Fitzgerald's *The Great Gatsby*, Anthony Hope's *The Prisoner of Zenda*, Dostoevsky's *Crime and Punishment*, Stephen Vincent Benet's *The Devil and Daniel Webster*, Henry James's *The Turn of the Screw*, and Shakespeare's *Romeo and Juliet*.

CBS attempted to bring George Orwell's *1984* to live television, but could not find anyone capable of fashioning a workable script. In 1953, the network gave up and resorted to film, turning Orwell's futuristic masterpiece into perhaps the first made-for-TV movie.

Also presented on film was *Peter Pan*, Sir James M. Barrie's ode to perpetual childhood, which aired a number of times during the fifties and sixties, each showing an event more than a rerun, a chance for the audience to sing along with familiar songs, whimper at familiar partings and reunions, hiss at familiar pirates, and revisit the ever-enchanting Never Never Land. Mary Martin had played the boy who wouldn't grow up in the Broadway version of the play. She repeated the role, with equally androgynous charm, on TV.

NO LESS IMPRESSIVE than the classic stories brought to the small screen by anthology series in the fifties was the number of original dramas that they commissioned. Some went on to even greater acclaim as feature films and one of them, *Marty*, would win the Oscar as Best Movie of 1955. Ernest Borgnine, in the title role, was named Best Actor. On television, it was Rod Steiger who played the part of a lonely man who meets a similarly lonely woman at a dance one night and falls awkwardly and poignantly in love with her.

The TV version of "The Miracle Worker," broadcast in 1957, starred Patty McCormack as the deaf and blind child Helen Keller and Teresa Wright as her teacher, Anne Sullivan. "The final dramatic scene," it has been written, "in which Sullivan broke through and communicated with

Helen, combined the best in dramatic tension and honest sentimentality (a major factor in Hollywood's decision to turn it into a movie, starring Patty Duke)." Duke won an Academy Award for her performance as Keller, as did Anne Bancroft, who had assumed Teresa Wright's role.

Another play written for television and superbly adapted by Hollywood was 1958's "Days of Wine and Roses," starring Cliff Robertson as an alcoholic who marries Piper Laurie and turns her to drink as well. He is Joe, she is Kirsten, and side by side they sink into a boozy abyss, out of which Joe begins to climb only after he hits bottom and decides he needs to sober up not just for his own sake, but for that of their daughter.

Kirsten is not so determined, not at first; she moves out on her family, living alone for a time with her demons, then begs Joe to take her back. She also begs him to break open a bottle with her—not now and not often, just once in a while, on special occasions; that way, she says, things between them will be just as they were before. It is the last thing Joe wants to hear.

> "You remember how things were, do you remember? *Do* you remember? It was a threesome, you, me, and booze, right? Right, remember? Don't get me wrong, it was great while it lasted."
>
> "We can have it back, Joe."
>
> "If I'll drink with you. If I'll—Well, I won't, that's finished, that's through. . . . You and I were a couple of bums on a sea of booze in a leaky boat and it sank, only I got something to keep me from going under. I'm not going to let it go for you or anybody else. If you want to grab hold, grab hold, Kirs. But there's only room for you and me, no threesome.

Jack Lemmon played Robertson's part in the movie version and was nominated for Best Actor of 1962.

There was even a made-for-TV opera in the fifties, Gian Carlo Menotti's *Amahl and the Night Visitors*, the tale of a disabled boy with a marvelously abled spirit and the remarkable things that happen to him on the night of Christ's birth. The program premiered in 1951 and became a Christmas tradition throughout the fifties and well into the following decade.

Bizet's *Carmen* also found its way to the small screen, with such numbers as the "Toreador Song" wafting into American homes through speakers not nearly up to the standards of such grand music.

But viewers eagerly forgave the hollow audio, just as they forgave the occasional botched line or out-of-focus close-up in the programs. They had never seen operas in their living rooms before. They had never seen plays starring the biggest names in theater and movies before. "In the 1950's everything seemed new, original, and fresh," said Paul Newman many years later.

As a result, the audience was too captivated to complain about the occasional mistake, too enchanted with what Jeff Greenfield has called "the intangible magic of a live, this-is-it performance." *Hallmark Hall of Fame* producer George Schaefer also believed that programs like these were able to do something magical for their audiences: "to catch the glowing, growing kind of performance you might see on the stage if you were a bumblebee buzzing around everywhere you wanted to be. This is a distinct contribution of television. In this unique way, the medium does something beyond the living stage, and something film can't do at all."

JUST AS TELEVISION DRAMAS of the fifties were able to attract the most accomplished performers of the time, so did they attract the most gifted people behind the cameras. Rod Serling, winner of three Emmys, was but one of the extraordinary writers who was drawn to the small screen. Another was Paddy Chayefsky, whose credits, in addition to *Marty*, included screenplays for the movies *Paint Your Wagon*, *The Americanization of Emily*, and *The Hospital*. His best-known big-screen opus, voted one of the top-ten movie scripts of all time by the Writers Guild of America, was *Network*, in which Peter Finch, as a crazily sane anchorman no longer able to tolerate the world about which he reports, invites his viewers to raise their windows, stick out their heads, and join him in screaming at all within distance, "I'm mad as hell, and I'm not going to take this anymore!"

Also writing for television at mid-century were Robert Sherwood, who won three Pulitzer Prizes for his stage plays, including the still-resonant *Abe Lincoln in Illinois*; Gore Vidal, not only an accomplished playwright but a prolific one, who was said to have turned out seventy TV dramas in two years, and who would later become much better known for his novels; and Horton Foote, an even more accomplished playwright, who would win two Academy Awards for his screenplays.

Among the movie directors who got their starts in TV-anthology series were George Roy Hill (*Butch Cassidy and the Sundance Kid*, *The Sting*, *The*

World According to Garp, and *Thoroughly Modern Millie); *Sidney Lumet *(Serpico, Dog Day Afternoon,* and the film versions of *12 Angry Men* and *Network);* Delbert Mann (the film version of *Marty,* for which he won an Academy Award, and *Lover Come Back, That Touch of Mink, The Dark at the Top of the Stairs,* and *Desire Under the Elms);* Robert Mulligan *(Fear Strikes Out, To Kill a Mockingbird, Love with the Proper Stranger, Inside Daisy Clover,* and *Summer of '42);* and John Frankenheimer *(Birdman of Alcatraz, The Manchurian Candidate,* and *Seven Days in May).*

The strain on them, on all of them—actors, writers, directors and others—was immense. "One study," Greenfield writes, "estimated that between 1950 and 1955, for just *three* weekly series, more than three hundred original hour-long plays were written and produced." The people responsible for the series found themselves in the extraordinary position of complaining about workloads more intense than anything they had ever known before at the same time that they were delighted to be able to do the kind of work that was a source of both profit and pride.

But it could not last and they knew it. They could not maintain the pace without sacrificing the quality that was the most distinguishing characteristic of their efforts. By the time the decade had ended, so, with few exceptions, had the dramatic-anthology series. *Playhouse 90* had closed its doors; *Fireside Theatre* had torn down its marquee; *Studio One* had dropped its curtain and struck its sets.

IRONICALLY, ONLY AT THE START of the fifties were the anthology series as successful commercially as they were artistically. In the decade's first full season, from October 1950 to April 1951, *Fireside Theatre* and *Philco TV Playhouse* were the second- and third highest-rated programs on the air, with *Robert Montgomery Presents* finishing eleventh. Two years later, only *Fireside Theatre* made the top ten, and it sneaked in at the very bottom. Two years after that, *Ford Theatre* was the top-ranked dramatic series in the country at number eleven. For the rest of the decade, not a single one of the anthologies finished in the top twenty for an entire year.

It could hardly have been otherwise, and not just because of the demands of mass production on superior stagecraft. The dramas were not lighthearted fare, and Americans liked their television best when it was taking their minds off their troubles. The dramas did not feature actors and actresses in recurring roles, and Americans liked their television best when, in true neighborly fashion, they could get acquainted with the characters, learn their habits and idiosyncrasies, and look forward to seeing them again next week. The dramas were constantly changing locales, and Americans liked their television best when they could enter homes and workplaces and various other surroundings that they already knew, that were in some ways as comfortable to them as their own abodes. It was, in fact, remarkable that the anthology series lasted as long as they did. With the exception of a brief and ill-fated craze for quiz shows inspired by *The $64,000 Question*, the fifties were a decade of comedies and westerns.

October, 1952–April 1953: four of the top-ten programs were either sitcoms or variety shows featuring comedians, with the guest lists of the latter including other comedians who performed in skits and humorous dialogues with the stars.

October 1954–April 1955: seven of the top-ten shows were comedies of one sort or another.

October 1956–April 1957: three of the top four and six of the top-ten shows were westerns. Five of the top fifteen were comedies.

October 1958–April 1959: the top four shows were westerns, as were nine of the top fifteen. Four of the top fifteen were comedies.

The following year: five of the top-fifteen shows, including the top three, were westerns; another five were comedies.

Television was settling into its routines, and Americans were happy to settle in with them.

IN THE BEGINNING, few people thought the program was a good idea, so few it is surprising that CBS executives discussed it as often as they did, much less that the show eventually got on the air. Lucille Ball was a reasonably well-known movie actress in the forties, but far from being a headliner, at most a step above Eve Arden in big-screen stature. As for her husband, Desiderio Alberto Arnaz y de Acha III, he was a bit, well . . . ethnically diverse for the time.

But Ball *did* think the show was a good idea; in fact, she insisted on it, and when CBS agreed to a sitcom for her under the condition that someone else play her husband, someone with a name like Tom or Bob or Mickey, she was all the more insistent in refusing. She was married to Desi Arnaz in real life; she would be married to him on the air. Besides, as Ball well knew, Arnaz's accent and his occasional struggles with the English language would make the show even funnier.

Finally CBS gave in. It had long wanted to do some kind of program with Lucille Ball, believing her comedy ideally suited to television, and Ball managed to persuade the network that the ideal format was a weekly sitcom about a Cuban bandleader named Ricky Ricardo and a ditzy American redhead named Lucille McGillicuddy, who had somehow ended up married to him. They lived in a New York apartment building whose landlords and unlikely best friends were the ingloriously named Fred and Ethel Mertz—he a short, bald curmudgeon, she a stumblingly indecisive accomplice to the redhead's misadventures, which were legion. CBS decided to call the show *I Love Lucy*.

Jeffrey Hart, in his optimistically titled volume *When the Going Was Good! American Life in the Fifties*, tells of the premiere episode, which was watched with nail-biting apprehension by both CBS executives and advertisers:

> The first show, in October, 1951, established the formula from which the show never deviated. It was called "The Girls Want to Go to a Nightclub." Two husbands, Fred and Ricky, plot to go to the boxing matches despite the fact that their wives have made plans to go to a nightclub for the Mertzes' anniversary. Lucy and Ethel refuse to go to the fights. Fred and Ricky arrange for a couple of blind dates, but Ethel and Lucy disguise themselves as hillbillies and substitute for the dates. The first show drew raves from the television critics and was an instant success with the television audience. Lucille Ball's groan of "E-u-u-u-u," whenever she—frequently—got into trouble became as familiar as "Yes, we have no bananas" had once been.

For the next six years, *I Love Lucy* was one of the top-three programs on television, as Ball proved herself skilled not only at telling jokes but at performing feats of almost Chaplinesque physical comedy. Among the more famous: her efforts to keep up with an assembly line in a candy factory that seemed hellbent on outdistancing her; and dressing up like Harpo Marx and then standing in front of him, facing him, aping to the best of her ability his every move, trying to persuade him that she was not an imposter but rather his reflection in a mirror.

Ball also proved herself skilled at choosing leading men. Seldom did an episode of *I Love Lucy* go by without her husband's accent getting a laugh or two. In one show, instead of admitting that he was teasing her, Arnaz says, "I was just tizzin' you, honey. You look beautiful to me all the time."

Ball replies, "You were not tizzin' me."

Arnaz substitutes *jintz* for *jinx, splane* for *explain,* and *thin'* for *thing.* "Never mind making fun of my English," he scolds her after she has chuckled at his expense.

"That's English?" she says.

The program was by far the most popular and influential of the decade's sitcoms. The writing was good, although not exceptional; the acting was flawless in its timing and small comedic touches; and the casting could not have been better, even down to the bit parts, like such occasional performers as Elizabeth Patterson, who played the crusty and easily confused babysitter, Mrs. Trumbull. *I Love Lucy* won two Emmys as Best Comedy and was nominated in that category, as well as several others, every one of its six years on the air. And it seems to have remained on the air, at some time of the day or night, on one station or cable network or another, somewhere in the world, every minute of every year since.

Other highly rated sitcoms of the period included *Father Knows Best* with Robert Young and Jane Wyatt; *Make Room for Daddy,* which later became *The Danny Thomas Show,* and *The Jack Benny Program,* with their eponymous leading men; and *The Gale Storm Show* with its eponymous leading woman. There was *The George Burns and Gracie Allen Show,* featuring George as the straightest of straight men and Gracie as the most addled of housewives, so much so that in one episode she mailed an empty envelope to her mother, explaining to George that she would be pleased to receive it because no news is good news. Almost as addled was Joan Davis in *I Married Joan.*

And there were *The Donna Reed Show; December Bride* with Spring Byington as an aging widow whose daughter and son-in-law were constantly trying to find a new man for her; *Dennis the Menace,* based on the comic strip and starring the impish Jay North; *The Many Loves of Dobie Gillis,* which introduced Bob Denver as TV's first beatnik; *Mr. Peepers,* in which Wally Cox raised timidity to new heights of mousiness; *The Adventures of Ozzie and Harriett,* although, despite the program's introduction of teen idol Ricky Nelson, "a milder set of adventures could not be imagined"; and *The Life of Riley* with William Bendix (originally Jackie Gleason) as an aircraft worker who could not spend nearly as much of his leisure time at leisure as he wanted to, and was known to exclaim, when more than usually frustrated, "What a revoltin' development *this* is!"

The Real McCoys, starring Walter Brennan, was, in its backwoods way, a predecessor to *The Beverly Hillbillies*, the most popular sitcom of the sixties, while another predecessor was *The Andy Griffith Show*, which later became *Mayberry RFD*. *The Goldbergs*, whose cast included the doomed actor Philip Loeb, added a touch of sentiment to the comic trials of a Jewish family trying to make it in New York, while *I Remember Mama* was *The Goldbergs* for Norwegians and *Life with Luigi* was *The Goldbergs* for Italians.

Most of these shows featured mother, father, a kid or two or more, and at least one complication per thirty minutes. They were set in the living rooms and kitchens of middle-class suburban homes, and all of them ended happily, if not ever after, at least until next week, when a complication very similar to that of the previous week would bedevil the cast yet again.

Comedians hosting top-rated shows in a variety format included Martin and Lewis, who delighted audiences until, no longer able to stand each other, much less prove mutual sources of delight, they split up; Red Skelton, whose repertoire of characters was extensive enough for an anthology series of his own; Sid Caesar and Imogene Coca, whose *Your Show of Shows* was written by such future luminaries as Mel Brooks, Neil Simon, Carl Reiner, and Larry Gelbart; Jackie Gleason, whose program's frequent high point was a skit about a bus driver named Ralph Kramden and his perpetually suffering wife Alice, a skit that would in time be expanded into a much-revered show of its own called *The Honeymooners*; and George Gobel, with his crew cut and uniquely low-keyed manner, who liked to say that he thought of the world as a blue suit and himself as a pair of brown shoes.

Among others starring in variety shows in the fifties were the bejeweled pianist Liberace, the actress June Allyson, the hayseed Tennessee Ernie Ford, country singers Jimmy Dean and Red Foley, and more mainstream warblers like Frank Sinatra, Perry Como, Eddie Fisher, Patti Page, Dinah Shore, Rosemary Clooney, and Kate Smith, who lives on half-a-century later through her oft-played version of "God Bless America."

BUT THE MOST POPULAR of the variety shows, and without question the most varied, was *Toast of the Town*, hosted by Ed Sullivan, which later had its name changed to *The Ed Sullivan Show*. "Right here, tonight on our stage, the entire Boer War! C'mon, let's hear it!" was one comedian's comment on Sullivan's eclectic list of guests—and he did not exaggerate by much.

"As a former newsman," writes Jeffrey Hart about the star, "he had a shrewd sense of the week's headlines. If a heroic fireman had made news by rescuing someone or talking a would-be suicide out of it, he might get a walk-on and introduction on the Sullivan show. If someone had made athletic news, he might come on for a brief exchange with the emcee. Sullivan had clowns, comics, plate spinners, and dog acts."

He also had tumblers and gymnasts and Elvis Presley, although, contrary to popular belief, Presley made his television debut not on Sullivan's program but on *Jimmy Dorsey's Stage Show*, hosted by bandleader Tommy's bandleader brother, in January 1956. Sullivan had jugglers and acrobats and Rudy Vallee; Oscar Hammerstein II and Gertrude Lawrence and Señor Wences, who made his fist into a puppet and engaged it in conversation. He had the Italian puppet Topo Gigio and the dazzlingly improbable tap dancer Clayton "Peg Leg" Bates. He had ventriloquist Paul Winchell and his dummy Jerry Mahoney and, at separate times, both Dorsey brothers leading their bands. He showcased Pearl Bailey, Louis Armstrong, and other black entertainers long before most other TV shows were receptive to minorities except in demeaning roles.

Sullivan's lineup of guests included other singers and musicians seldom seen on television, such as classical violinist Yehudi Menuhin and cellist Pablo Casals, and opera singers Robert Merrill and Roberta Peters. It included the West Point Glee Club and the New York City Ballet and the occasional yodeler whose name no one could possibly recall and whose act never resulted in an encore. And Sullivan featured the stars of many other shows, such as Perry Como, Steve Allen, and Bing Crosby. One night, Catherine Kreitzer, the $32,000 winner on *The $64,000 Question*, made an appearance reciting verses from Shakespeare.

Perhaps more than anything else, though, Sullivan was known for his animal acts, so many animal acts that the comedian Don Rickles once joked about the reason he did *not* make a scheduled appearance: "I was booked on the Sullivan show," Rickles said, "but my bear died."

Ed Sullivan was the unlikeliest television star of the decade, if not the medium's entire history. A man so lacking in charm, so devoid of even the rudiments of a performer's magnetism, so physically graceless that it seemed as if he would fall over his own feet when he stepped onto the stage—he appeared less the host of a TV program than someone who had sneaked into the studio when the cop at the stage door went out for a sandwich. People wondered about Sullivan throughout the fifties. How did a man like that get his own television show? How did he keep the show year after year? How did that show, one year, trail only *I Love Lucy* in the ratings? There seem to be four answers:

First, when the program began Sullivan was a gossip columnist for the New York *Daily News*, and such a powerful one that CBS executives thought his connections would ensure the biggest names in show business for his television guest list. The stars always wanted to appear in his column; why would they decline to appear on his TV show? In fact, they did not.

Second, Sullivan was so witless on camera that those stars could be sure he would never best them in repartee. They were like the beautiful girls in high school who always hung out with the losers so they would look even better by contrast.

Third, realizing his deficiencies on camera, Sullivan kept his small talk to a minimum, meaning that his guests had more time to sing and crack wise and spin their plates and make their dogs jump through hoops than they might have had with a host who had an act, or at least a personality, of his own.

Fourth, Sullivan's gravedigger demeanor turned into such a running gag in American life that Ed Sullivan impersonations became for a time virtually a new branch of show business. Always able to laugh at himself, which seemed to be one of Sullivan's few endearing qualities, he would even book some of the impersonators on his program—and they would shrug their shoulders up to their ears, scowl at the audience, and utter the signature Sullivan phrase, "We've got a really big show for you tonight." Or, in most cases, "We've got a really big *shew* for you," which was not really the way Sullivan pronounced the word, but it was close, and seemed more in keeping with the stiffness of his personality.

The radio comedian Fred Allen, who shared *The Colgate Comedy Hour* hosting duties for a time with Martin and Lewis, and who was a graduate of the Bob and Ray school of deadpan humor, was once asked the secret of Sullivan's success. "Ed Sullivan will be around," Allen replied, "as long as someone else has talent." As it turned out, he was around all the way until 1971, by which time improbable Ed had long since given up his newspaper column and been a TV star for twenty-three years.

WHAT I LOVE LUCY was to sitcoms and Ed Sullivan was to variety shows, *Gunsmoke* was to westerns. Starting out on radio in 1952, the program moved to television three years later and two years after that was the top-rated show on the small screen, a position it held without even a hint of faltering for the rest of the decade. It would go on to become the longest-running scripted series with continuing characters in the history of the medium, lasting a few weeks short of twenty years.

Gunsmoke starred James Arness as Marshal Matt Dillon of Dodge City, Kansas, and Dennis Weaver as his deputy, Chester Goode. When Weaver left the show for a program of his own, Ken Curtis took over as sidekick, playing the permanently disheveled and less-than-brilliant Festus Haggen. Milburn Stone was Doc Adams, and Amanda Blake the town's saloonkeeper and rare female presence, Miss Kitty Russell.

Gunsmoke is considered the first TV western for grownups, meaning, for one thing, that the acting was sophisticated and in many cases underplayed, which is to say realistic—this in contrast to the broad performances of the stars of the westerns aimed at children. A Matt Dillon lunch box would never have been a hit with the classroom crowd.

The program was well-written too, avoiding plot clichés as much as possible for its genre, and also avoiding clichéd dialogue. None of the characters on the show ever said anything like, "They went thataway," or "I'll git the varmint," or "Mount up, boys, we're a-headin' fer the Pecos." One episode featured a boy whose mother was a prostitute, working in a bordello that Marshal Dillon allowed to operate in Dodge City despite its being against the law. But it was a decision he agonized over, and with which he was never totally comfortable. A grownup kind of indecision about a grownup issue.

Perhaps the least adult thing about *Gunsmoke* was the Marshal's love life. He didn't have one. He wouldn't think of visiting the bordello, unless on business, not even at the loneliest of moments, and in twenty years of consorting with Miss Kitty, he never once held her in a passionate embrace, never once kissed her on the lips, never once suggested that they slip into a bunk in an unoccupied jail cell and lock the door behind them. Few were the viewers who thought Miss Kitty wouldn't have appreciated at least one of those signs of affection, and returned it rabidly.

Other top-rated westerns in the fifties included *The Life and Legend of Wyatt Earp* with Hugh O'Brian as the title character who was sometimes a lawman, sometimes a saloonkeeper, sometimes a buffalo hunter; *Have Gun, Will Travel,* with Richard Boone as a gunfighter who preferred to avoid violence whenever possible and presented a business card both to clients and victims; *Wagon Train* with Ward Bond in charge of getting passengers and cargo from Missouri to California; *The Rifleman* with Chuck Connors as a widowed rancher with a violent past now trying to rear his son in peace; and *Maverick* with James Garner as a gambler who had a sense of humor as well as a sense for cards.

Wanted: Dead or Alive starred Steve McQueen as a bounty hunter who always got his man; *Cheyenne* was Clint Walker, a large fellow who simply "wandered the West trying to avoid trouble but with little success"; Jock Mahoney played *Yancy Derringer*, dressed in white, who carried the title weapon in his hat and walked with a cane that was in reality a sheath for a sword. No less elegantly attired, although in black, was Gene Barry as Bat Masterson. Rin Tin Tin, a German shepherd, was not attired at all. On television, the dog lived in a fort in the Old West and was constantly rescuing its inhabitants from Injuns and other evildoers; in real life, Rinty, as he was known to his friends, was the only dog listed in the Los Angeles telephone directory.

One of *Rawhide*'s two leading men was a young buck named Clint Eastwood, playing a cattle driver trying to get his herds to market despite rustlers and bad weather and all manner of other difficulties. He would go on to demonstrate talents that no one knew he had, which resulted in some of the most influential movies ever made.

AND THERE WAS so much more on television in the fifties, despite the scarcity of networks and independent stations. There were cop shows like *Dragnet* with Jack Webb and Ben Alexander; private-eye shows like *77 Sunset Strip* with Efrem Zimbalist Jr., Roger Smith, and Edd "Kookie" Byrnes; lawyer shows like *Perry Mason* with Raymond Burr as the undefeated courtroom champion; help-the-needy shows such as *Queen for a Day* and *Strike It Rich*, in which woebegone women told the stories of their lives— the diseases and bankruptcies, the divorces and natural disasters—and the one with the saddest tale, the dimmest prospects for the future, was the winner.

There were kids' shows, such as *The Mickey Mouse Club, Captain Kangaroo, Winky Dink and You, Gerald McBoing-Boing, Rootie Kazootie, Howdy Doody,* and the gentler *Kukla, Fran, and Ollie,* with Fran being a human and the other title characters sweet-natured puppets. There were game shows like *The Price Is Right* with Bill Cullen, and big-money quiz shows including not only *The $64,000 Question* but *The $64,000 Challenge, The Big Surprise, Twenty-One, Tic Tac Dough, Dough-Re-Mi, Top Dollar, Dotto,* and *The $100,000 Surprise,* starring Mike Wallace. There were talk shows like *Arthur Godfrey and His Friends,* which shared the top ten for a few years with *Arthur Godfrey's Talent Scouts,* a daily double that has not been matched since.

In addition, fifties TV also served up different kinds of anthology series from those already mentioned, such as *Disneyland,* hosted by Walt Disney, on which Davy Crockett made his appearances; Rod Serling's *The Twilight Zone;* and the fiendishly horrifying *Alfred Hitchcock Presents,* in one memorable episode of which a wife clubs her husband to death with a frozen leg of lamb, then lets it thaw and serves it for dinner to the policeman who is trying to investigate the fellow's death but finds himself baffled about the murder weapon.

Some shows were hard to categorize. *This Is Your Life* was a kind of on-air memoir for celebrities. *Superman* was a comic strip brought to black-and-white life. On the *Good Morning* show, a woman once won a prize when her fox terrier said "Hello" and "All right," or yapped to that effect. And then there was *Today,* a potpourri of news, entertainment, and idle chatter which, after a rocky start, began to succeed around the time it too turned to animals, adding a chimpanzee named J. Fred Muggs to the cast.

The chimp quickly became popular. Too popular to suit host Dave Garroway, who just as quickly became jealous. In fact Garroway, in an especially vindictive fit of envy, was said to have spiked the chimp's orange juice with Benzedrine one morning to make him behave poorly, something Muggs did so seldom that he topped Garroway in the amount of fan mail received. This, of course, made the host even more jealous, especially since some of Muggs's mail contained proposals of marriage from humans, women who, Garroway must have been consoled to realize, would certainly have gotten cold feet as the big day approached.

That, in summary—a summary that does not even include *Arthur Murray's Dance Party, Zoo Parade, The Big Top,* or such soap operas as *The Edge of Night* and *As the World Turns*—was American television between 1950 and 1959. So many hours of so many programs, so many stars and formats from which to choose, so many ads for so many products, so much publicity in so many newspapers and magazines, such a clamorous block party it all was—a neighbor here, a neighbor there, scores of neighbors everywhere, hour after hour after hour. The electronic snow that signaled the end of the day's festivities kept starting later at night and ending earlier in the morning, becoming shorter and shorter. Fall asleep and you might miss it.

It is no wonder that the rest of the entertainment business was afraid it might soon be out of business.

Chapter 6

The Competition

I T WAS NOT JUST BOOKS that found themselves overwhelmed by the appeal of the small screen in the fifties; for a time, the big screen also became a victim. *The Greatest Show on Earth*, the circus epic directed by Cecil B. DeMille and starring Charlton Heston, Jimmy Stewart, and Betty Hutton, might have been playing at the Rialto on a Saturday night early in 1953, but playing at home were *Talent Patrol*, yet another forerunner of *American Idol*, this one sponsored by the U.S. Army as an aid to recruiting; *The Jackie Gleason Show*; *Saturday Night Fights*; and *My Favorite Husband*, a sitcom in which Joan Caulfield's character was virtually indistinguishable from Lucy Ricardo. In fact Lucille Ball had played the Caulfield role in the radio version of *My Favorite Husband*, which inspired much of the *I Love Lucy* lunacy.

In truth, *The Greatest Show on Earth* was not *that* great, but it was better than the TV shows that opposed it. TV, however, had too many advantages to overcome. The programs were free, easily accessible, diverse in content, and liberally sprinkled with commercial breaks for even more diversity, as well as for occasional trips to the bathroom or refrigerator. A person could watch television in his underwear or pajamas, spread out on the sofa rather than squeezed into a theater seat, and enjoy a TV Dinner on a TV tray while partaking of the entertainment. More and more, Americans were taking these factors into account as we mapped out the hours of our leisure. After all, convenience was one of the requisites of spare time for most; the more convenient the performance, the less demanding we could be about its quality.

THE SIGNS OF HOLLYWOOD'S DEMISE were obvious even before the fifties. By the summer of 1948, educators at Hofstra College (now University) on Long Island had become so convinced of television's coming impact that it formed a TV research bureau, headed by Dr. Thomas E. Coffin. He and his assistants conducted "depth interviews" of 137 families in the area who owned televisions, and what he discovered was that

> movie attendance among his TV viewers had fallen off 20 per cent, and a follow-up not yet completed indicates that this figure has climbed to 30 per cent. These people not only go to movies less, but when they do, they don't like them as much, and the longer they have TV sets, the less they like movies. Eight per cent of "new owners" reported slipping movie yens, while 17 per cent of those with sets six months old showed the same symptoms.

In 1949, the *New York Times* revealed similar findings in more general terms. Many people stopped going to the movies as often as they used to as soon as they got their televisions, and a few told the paper that they no longer went at all. The *Times* wasn't sure about the total extent of the decline but, after weighing the results of several different surveys, guessed that as much as one-third of the movie audience had been lost to the new medium even before the fifties began, "which, if true, would spell an economic upheaval for Hollywood in the near future." And that is precisely what happened—in the *very* near future.

In fact, less than a year later, *Time* magazine released figures of a far more foreboding nature: "Among TV set owners, adult attendance at movies has dropped 72% (from an average of 4.51 times a month to 1.27 times). But children's attendance has declined only 46%." *Only* 46 percent? Surely film producers were not consoled by the fact that almost half the children in

America whose families owned televisions had now stopped showing up at their local movie theaters.

A few months after the *Time* report, plans for a huge new motion-picture emporium in Union, New Jersey, were canceled; instead, the developers would build a supermarket. Americans might not be going to the theater as much as before, but people still needed something to eat; if nothing else, we needed a place to buy our TV Dinners.

In locations other than Union, plans for movie theaters were also scrapped or, more commonly, not drawn up in the first place; and in a number of places existing theaters went out of business. New York: 55 movie houses closed in 1951. The same year in Los Angeles and environs: 130 screens went blank.

Other theaters became enterprises of a different kind: flea markets, churches, department stores, meeting halls for social groups of one sort or another, perhaps storage space for different kinds of retail business. Or, most haunting of all, as was the case in Rochester, Pennsylvania, a town about ten miles from my Ambridge, the grand old Oriental Theatre withered into an unoccupied shell. Whether it was later torn down or vandalized into a similar state, I cannot remember. I only remember how it stood proudly in the town's modest skyline throughout my teenage years, and how nearby businesses began to crumble in the fading presence of both the movie house and the stell industry.

In Ambridge, which had a population of about 20,000, we had four theaters early in the fifties, and each of them offered a weekend double feature of first-run movies for a quarter. Sometimes, one or two of them would try to entice children to drop in even earlier by filling the morning hours with a program of seventeen cartoons for an additional quarter. On Saturdays, we could spend virtually every sunlit hour in the darkness for a mere four bits.

But as the decade drew to a close, so did the cartoon jamborees— and only two of the theaters remained, both of them having seen better days. Their screens were stained, their seats ripped, and the carpets on the aisles worn through so that the cement floor showed underneath. By the time the evening shows started, the floors were littered with popcorn boxes and candy wrappers; since the managers could not afford anyone to sweep up, they did the cleaning themselves, once a day, before the theaters opened.

After another year, Ambridge had one theater. Two years later, none at all.

And in a fictitious place called Thalia, Texas, one night, Lois Farrow "took her bourbon into the den and switched TV on. A Claudette Colbert movie was just starting." Lois curled up in her favorite chair, started draining her glass. People like her weren't going to the movies much anymore in Thalia. People not like her weren't going, either. It was too far to walk even if it had not been too far before she got a TV; it was too long a drive even if it took only a few minutes. And it was hard to sneak a bottle of bourbon into a movie theater, harder still to empty it without others noticing, curling their noses at the fumes. As a result, Larry McMurtry called his novel about the Thalia *The Last Picture Show*. By the ending of the book, it had closed.

ACROSS THE COUNTRY IN 1955, *U.S. News & World Report* discovered, "weekly attendance in movie theaters was at the rate of 50 million, little more than half the size of the movie audience in 1946, the movies' best year and also the year that TV came generally on the scene." It was a startling drop. A boom time for much of America, the Eisenhower prosperity was proving to be a bust for an industry perceived as the most glamorous.

Even theaters that survived the diminished audiences and stayed in business, and there were many, had fewer films to show. "Output of major feature films for theaters dropped sharply," *U.S. News & World Report* also learned, "from 432 in 1951 to a total of 354 in 1953. Then came another drop, to 303, in 1954."

And there were times when it was not feasible to show a feature film at all, times like Tuesday nights, when Milton Berle's phenomenally popular program took over the country by taking over the airwaves. "Movie theaters could not run shows at 8 P.M.," remembers Jeff Greenfield; "stores gave up late hours on Tuesday nights; bars, often the only establishment with a television set, found business leaping at 8 P.M. on Tuesdays, with crowds packing every square inch of space."

The movie industry did not just lose customers; it lost employees. Directors, actors, camera operators, set designers, lighting technicians, audio engineers, makeup people, hairstylists, grips, gaffers, film editors—a lot of them, no longer able to find steady employment in feature films, stopped trying and instead offered their services to the television networks. Here, such professionals were eagerly welcomed, given steady work that was getting steadier, and more lucrative, all the time.

BUT HOLLYWOOD'S FUTURE, the post-television variety thereof, would be even brighter than its past. It would not happen immediately, and would require that several steps be taken by several studios over a period of several years. All in all, though, the movie industry would recover from the sudden assault of TV sooner than most people initially thought. The reports of its death, as reasonable as they seemed at the beginning, turned out to be exaggerated.

The industry's new life began in February 1953, when, after much internal debate, 20th Century–Fox announced that it would convert its entire filmmaking operation to Cinemascope, a new system for showing movies that utilized not just a wider screen, but one that curved in front of the viewer at a 145-degree angle, making people feel as if they were not merely watching the film but enveloped in it. Television, Fox hoped, would now seem *so* small a screen as to leave the audience disengaged.

But considering the falling fortunes of movies at the time, it was a gamble for the studio, an enormous one, and Fox executives knew it. One skeptic compared it to purchasing the grandest, most state of the art ocean liner in the days after the *Titanic* had dropped to the bottom of the Atlantic. Fox invested $25 million—more than three times what the *Titanic* had cost four decades earlier—on eleven Cinemascope features and the specialized cameras and other equipment needed to produce them.

The first of the films to be released was *The Robe*, based on Lloyd C. Douglas's novel about the Roman soldier in charge of the brigade that had crucified Jesus, a novel that had spent parts of three years on the best-seller list, winning popular, if not critical, acclaim. The movie starred Richard Burton, Jean Simmons, and a strapping young brute named Victor Mature, whose well-muscled, well-oiled body was there primarily for window dressing. "I'm not an actor," Mature said near the end of his career, "and I've got 67 films to prove it!"

The Robe was a best-seller for 20th Century–Fox, too. Although it was released late in 1953, it became the second biggest-grossing movie of the year, and the other ten films in the original Cinemascope package were also money-makers for the company. The movies were not dead yet.

That was step one on Hollywood's road back to financial well-being.

Step two, 1955: several studios decided that they should join the competition rather than try to beat it. RKO led the way. Again, after a great deal of back and forth within the company, it decided to sell its entire library of motion pictures to television. The price was $15 million. TV stations had been running movies prior to the mid-fifties, mostly late at night, but they were largely inferior productions that had been obtained on an individual basis or in small lots from second-rate studios; viewers had seldom heard of them and there were few big stars in the cast.

The RKO deal was the first bulk sale to television from a major distributor, and the studio did not release the films until they had exhausted their runs in theaters, which is to say, until they had made as much money for RKO as they were likely to make in their originally intended venues. Other movie producers, though not all, were quick to conclude that they too should sell their products to the opposition, that when the movies reached the point at which there was no further market for them in the theaters, the TV sale was free money. In this sense, television was not a competitor at all; it was, rather, a subsidiary.

"In July 1956," wrote William Boddy, "[the trade journal] *Television* reported that 2,500 feature films had been released to television in the previous thirteen months as studios scrambled to license their feature libraries in order to avoid a feared buyer's market. In 1956, Columbia reported an income of $9,700,000 on its feature sales to television; Warner Brothers earned $15 million in television sales that year."

Early in 1958, Paramount, one of the last holdouts, also made a deal with the networks, selling to TV all the movies it had produced before 1948 for a price of $50 million.

Step three, also 1955, initially taken by Warner Brothers alone: in addition to dealing most of its movies to television, the studio began to produce original programs for the new medium, the first of which were hour-long westerns such as *Cheyenne* and *Sugarfoot*. Next came hour-long adventure shows, including *77 Sunset Strip*, *Bourbon Street Beat*, and *Hawaiian Eye*.

The studio also came up with a short-lived anthology called *Warner Brothers Presents*, "originally including a 10-minute segment about upcoming theatrical releases as a sop to theater owners. Called *Behind the Scenes* and hosted by Gig Young, it was soon discovered that TV audiences just wanted the television episode, not a documentary commercial for movie houses."

The idea of motion-picture companies rolling TV shows off their assembly lines soon caught on, and other studios began to turn out series of their own, shows that were like the little brothers of movies: same kinds of stories, same kinds of action, same kinds of characters—but diminished in scope and half the length. As a result, almost overnight, "43 per cent of Hollywood's film-making capacity" was employed by television.

It was a percentage that would continue to climb for several years.

A single Hollywood TV show, NBC's daily *Matinee Theater,* hires 2,400 actors a year for speaking parts—50% more than the players used by Warner and Paramount combined in all their 1956 movies. The show uses as many scripts—250 a year—as all the studios put together.

A single TV film producer, Desi Arnaz' and Lucille Ball's Desilu, which turns out *I Love Lucy* and 14 other shows, spends $21 million a year, employs up to 1,000 at peak periods, and produces more film footage than the combined output of the five major movie studios.

The two biggest talent agencies in U.S. show business, William Morris and the Music Corp. of America, now get $9 in fees from TV deals to every $1 they earn from the movies.

In the ranks of the movies' own guilds, fully half of the actors (plus Mickey Mouse, Rin-Tin-Tin and Lassie), cameramen and cutters earn their living in TV.

It was all good news for the film studios. But it was bad news for theater owners, as the number of feature films that the studios produced continued to drop throughout the decade. A movie that would have made a profit in theaters had it run for only two weeks now had to run for a month, and the second two weeks emptied the till of the proceeds from the first two. Said an official from one theater chain, "When you take into consideration the fact that in New York City alone 175 films are available weekly on television, in addition to many other live television programs, principally between the hours of 7 P.M. and 10 P.M., which is the best playing time for theaters, it is crystal clear that the competition the industry faces is of heartbreaking proportions."

Theater ownership would not be a truly lucrative business again until well after the fifties, when Hollywood started making more movies and corporate entities took control of the theaters, playing several films at once on several screens in the same building, the screens smaller than they used to be, the number of seats per screen smaller than it used to be, the walls so thin between the screens that during the tender, moonlit kiss in your particular cubicle you could hear the bomb exploding in the cubicle next door.

The movie palace of the past was gone. The plasterboard condo known as *the multiplex* had taken its place.

IN THE LONG RUN, though, the key to Hollywood's meeting the challenge of television was its decision, made at different times by different studios, and sometimes, it seemed, not even made consciously at all, to turn out movies that were different from TV shows, very different, movies not appropriate for the small screen because, in the words of the Proctor & Gamble memo cited earlier, they contained "material that may give offense"; movies that, as the memo to playwright Elmer Rice stated, were not "happy in general," had "a general 'down' character"; movies more mature in theme than most TV programs, so that they would bring the viewer—the more mature viewer, at least—a different and often more thoughtful kind of experience than small screen opuses provided.

In my opinion, most of the films on the following list were made, at least in part, to compete with television, offering entertainment of a kind that the television networks would not even consider transmitting into the home—because it was too sexy or violent, too accepting in its attitudes toward sex and violence, too accepting of homosexuality, too accepting of racial harmony for some, too foul in its language for others, too frightening or gruesome, too critical of government or religion or the legal system or other institutions of authority, too dependent on audio of a high quality to convey the richness of its music, or perhaps, in the case of epics like those made by director David Lean, too sweeping visually to be appreciated on a small screen: Cinemascope was required to achieve their full impact.

Regardless of the reason, these are some of the movies that, to some degree, were produced by American studios, or in a few cases imported and released to acclaim in the United States, due to the enormous popularity of television.

THE 1960S

The Collector
The Apartment
Sons and Lovers
The Sound of Music

Elmer Gantry
Never on Sunday
Butterfield 8
Who's Afraid of Virginia Woolf?
The Hustler
Midnight Cowboy
Alfie
Blowup
Dr. Zhivago
Lawrence of Arabia
Irma la Douce
Bonnie and Clyde
The Graduate
In the Heat of the Night
Hush . . . Hush, Sweet Charlotte
What Ever Happened to Baby Jane

THE 1970S

Five Easy Pieces
M*A*S*H
A Clockwork Orange
The French Connection
The Last Picture Show
The Godfather, Part 1 and Part 2
Deliverance
The Exorcist
Chinatown
One Flew Over the Cuckoo's Nest
Jaws
Dog Day Afternoon
Taxi Driver
The Deer Hunter
Coming Home
Apocalypse Now

Of course, movies like these only led television into more-adult content of its own, and that in turn encouraged movies to become more adult still, which is to say, in many cases, more lascivious and violent and antisocial. It also led them to become more childish, with pyrotechnical displays of special effects overwhelming the plot and the few traces of logic that the plot had contained in the first place.

And then the cable networks like HBO and Showtime entered the competition with their own excesses, to which the movies responded by exceeding *their* previous excesses. And so it went and continues to go into the twenty-first century: in the past a gunshot wound to the arm that drew no blood, now a bullet to the brain exploding the eyeball and shattering the cranium into a hundred bloody pieces; once the titillation of a woman beginning to unbutton her blouse, now full frontal nudity and explicit sex accompanied by language of an equally graphic nature.

That, however, is a subject for a book other than this.

RADIO'S PROBLEMS were even more immediate, although David Sarnoff, of all people, was caught unawares. Asked to compare the two media in 1938, he seemed to favor radio over the newer one. "Television reception," he said,

> is not, cannot be, like sound reception. Today, radio is used as a background for other entertainments, or by the housewife who . . . listens to the music, while she goes on with her work. Television can never be that, because not only will it require close attention on the part of the onlooker, but it will also be necessary for the room to be somewhat darkened. . . . [L]isteners . . . instead of roaming around as they do now while enjoying a program, will have to sit tight and pay close attention to whatever is being thrown on their screen. But will they want to do this? . . . I don't know.

Others did know. They wanted to do it, could not wait to do it. Early in the fifties there were reports that a few Americans, perhaps believing they would rather intimidate the Joneses than imitate them, were throwing their favorite listening devices into the trash the day their televisions were delivered, making a ceremony of it, wanting the neighbors to see: conspicuous consumption giving way to conspicuous rejection.

Less ostentatiously, and just as infrequently, some people would wrap the cords around their radios and take them up to the attic or down to the basement and hide them away on a cobwebbed shelf, not certain they would ever have use for them again. Invariably they would.

In most cases, though, Americans simply left their radios where they had always been—on the kitchen counter, on an end table in the living room, on the nightstand in the bedroom. And they continued to listen, although not nearly as much. "An overwhelming majority of television owners," the *New York Times* declared, "between 75 and 90 per cent—report that they listen less to the radio." And the longer someone owned a TV, the shorter the periods of time he or she tended to devote to its predecessor.

When men and women did turn on the radio, at least in the first few months of its joint tenancy in the home with television, they did it more out of habit than genuine interest in a program, or so they reported to pollsters. They were, it seemed, gradually weaning themselves away from their old reliance, gradually becoming disenchanted with radio's shortcomings.

Fred Allen, one of radio's most successful humorists before moving to TV, thought it was inevitable. "Even without the coming of television," he wrote, "the survey figures showed a gradual shrinking in the mass audience. The audience and the medium were both getting tired. The same programs, the same comedians, the same commercials—even the sameness was starting to look the same."

BUT THERE WERE DIFFERENCES too, and they made the prospects for radio seem even dimmer. The medium lost its stars to the tube—among them Milton Berle, Jack Benny, Bing Crosby, Groucho Marx, Arthur Godfrey and Bob Hope, with the latter's radio ratings having plummeted so quickly that he could not wait to escape to TV. In 1949, Hope attracted 23.8 percent of the potential radio audience; two years later, a mere four percent. Although he never did a regular series for television, he began to host specials, which he did, albeit with decreasing frequency, all the way until 1996.

And radio was losing its programs to TV—among them *Amos 'n' Andy, Gunsmoke, The Lone Ranger, Superman, Captain Midnight,* and *Meet the Press.*

The listening box, then, had to find new stars, new programs, new *kinds* of programs, new ways for a medium that had nothing to offer the eye to make itself appealing to people who now thought of themselves as viewers more than listeners. It sounded impossible.

A few stations tried simulcasts. *The Ed Sullivan Show, Philco TV Playhouse* and *Arthur Godfrey and His Friends* were among the programs broadcast on radio and TV at the same time for a while. But the experiment did not work. Too many families owned both devices; all of them preferred the televised version of the show to the audio only, unless for some reason they could not position themselves in front of the TV at the appropriate time.

NBC owned both radio and television outlets, and wanting to figure out how best to allocate its manpower and resources between the two mediums, commissioned a study of people in Fort Wayne, Indiana. "Before buying a TV set," the study found, "the average person spent 2 hours and 2 minutes a day listening to radio. . . . After getting the set, the same person spent 52 minutes listening to the radio, or less than half the time he formerly spent."

The study was seconded by research that considered the radio and television audiences as a single entity. In January 1949, 81 percent of Americans on the receiving end of broadcasts were listening to the radio. By the end of the year, the percentage had dropped to 59, with TV making up the difference. By the end of the following year, an even more significant drop had been registered.

In places other than Fort Wayne, people who had tuned into their radios for an average of three hours and forty-two minutes a day in 1949 were tuning in for less than half-an-hour in 1950. That same year, Baltimore became the first city in the United States whose citizens spent more time over the course of a week watching television than listening to the tinier box that had so long been their companion. Before the year was out, the same would be true of several more cities.

The radio business was doomed—so said industry executives quoted in trade journals; so said editorials in those same publications; so said TV critics; so said a number of people who used to be frequent listeners. Employees were laid off and advertising revenues sank. In 1950, network radio stations made more than $130 million in profits. In 1955, the figure was slightly less than half that amount.

The suffering was not limited to the networks and individual stations that produced programs. Companies that manufactured radios, such as RCA, Atwater Kent, and Philco, were now manufacturing far fewer and being forced to sell them for lower prices. A few of these companies, which also made televisions, decided to concentrate on the latter. Smaller companies, producing radios only, simply went out of business.

BUT RADIO WOULD ADJUST to television even more quickly than the movies did, although, as has been suggested, "surrender" might be a better word, for the only way that radio could survive television's blitzkrieg in the fifties was by giving up virtually everything it had previously been and completely remaking itself.

Let us go back once more to 1949. A publication called *Nation's Business* analyzes the future of radio as the growing shadow of television falls over it.

> Many rural areas may never have television because of the nature of the beast, and factors like low cost, portability and freedom to work or relax while you listen will always provide a big market for sets. While TV steals the living room, more radio sets will appear in bedrooms, kitchens, dens and workshops, offering refuge to those who wish to use only their ears. As the big variety shows move into television, transcribed music, news broadcasts and daytime serials will take over more and more radio time. Many popular events, like political conventions and baseball games, probably will always be "simulcast" (a new word in advertising circles) over both media.

It is a surprisingly prescient paragraph. Of course, because of satellites, cable, and stronger broadcast signals than were available in the fifties, rural areas today are as saturated with television as is the rest of the country. But the author of the article, Harland Manchester, was right about almost everything else. When transistor radios went on sale midway through the fifties, gadgets that were a fraction the size of previous models and operated on batteries, they provided even more portability than existed when Manchester wrote; we could now listen to the radio while shopping, walking to school, lying on the beach. No longer was it necessary for us to position ourselves within a few feet of an electrical outlet to be entertained or informed through the ears.

As far as "freedom" was concerned, to use Manchester's word, the radio granted it not just to those who were working or relaxing, but to people driving or riding in cars, which many of us were doing several hours a day. We still are. In 2010, and certainly long before, driving an automobile was the activity in which people were most often engaged when listening to the radio. More than any other, it is probably the activity responsible for radio's continued success. No one has as yet figured out a way to watch both TV and oncoming traffic at the same time.

Although wrong about daytime serials, Manchester was also right about radio programming changing to music and news. As far as the former was concerned, television executives had made one of their few significant missteps of the fifties. With virtually the sole exception of Dick Clark's *American Bandstand* on ABC, the new medium ignored the decade's startlingly new songs, the social force called rock 'n' roll, which was proving to be almost as culturally significant as television, and certainly as transforming to the world of music as TV was to mass communication.

And television continued to ignore rock 'n' roll long after it became apparent that, with its raucous beats and racy lyrics, its long-haired and gaudily attired singers, it was changing the very patterns of American life: shaping attitudes, determining behavior, challenging values, influencing fashion, creating new vocabularies, and dominating conversations—not only among teenagers who were thrilled by what they were hearing, but by the adults who were appalled by its implications.

In cities all over the country, radio stations started playing Elvis, Little Richard, Chuck Berry, Fats Domino, Jerry Lee Lewis, Gene Vincent, and Ricky Nelson, not to mention such one-or two-or-a-few-more-hit wonders as the Marcels, the Del Vikings, the Five Satins, the Clovers, the G-Clefs, the Cadillacs, the Capris, the Dominoes, and the Fireflies. Result: the advertisers who had previously deserted the stations returned in droves. Or, if not precisely those advertisers, then others with products specifically aimed at a younger audience, one that seemed to have been sent from demographic heaven directly into the embrace of companies whose product lines consisted of soft drinks, snack foods, cigarettes, blue jeans, and acne-removal cream.

In other parts of the United States, areas with older populations, radio began to emphasize a different kind of music, the music that the men and women in their signal range had grown up with, the big bands of Glenn Miller and Benny Goodman, Duke Ellington and Count Basie, Artie Shaw and Kay Kyser, Bob Crosby and Mitch Miller, Harry James and Gene Krupa, Tommy and Jimmy Dorsey. The first oldies but goodies.

Or they continued to play the singers that the rock 'n' roll stars were displacing on other stations: Frank Sinatra, Tony Bennett, Vic Damone, Nat "King" Cole, Dean Martin, Steve Lawrence and Eydie Gorme, Patti Page, Teresa Brewer. Here, too, was an audience not being served by television, on which singers like these appeared infrequently at best, singing a song or two on a variety show, and then giving way to a comedian or dancer or juggler.

As for those people who wanted more news than the fifteen minutes that the TV networks provided each evening in the fifties, and more than the half-hour offered by the network affiliates in the nearest large city, they could find it every hour on the radio. And since there were so many more radio stations than television stations, there was almost surely a radio station closer to them than a television outlet, which meant that the news it broadcast was more relevant to the concerns of the listeners' community.

Radio also broadcast lengthy discussions of current affairs, both local and national, by informed people on both sides of an issue, something much less common on television. Eventually, there would be stations that provided discussions all day long, inviting those who were so inclined to call in and express their own opinions, first about current affairs, eventually about sports.

As a result, radio not only survived the initial onslaught of television but, after a period of adjustment, prospered. In 1948, there were 1,522 AM stations and 158 FM stations licensed to operate in the United States. A decade later, the numbers had shot up to 3,079 and 530. It was not radio as people had known it prior to TV, but it was radio nonetheless, a successful business with different kinds of audiences from those it had attracted before, audiences that were both growing and becoming increasingly loyal to the kinds of programming they now heard.

The listening box had not gone out of business; it had instead carved out a series of niches all its own.

FOR A FEW YEARS, attendance at live theaters also declined, and for the same reasons that attendance at movies had dropped off; many did not want to endure the trouble and expense of going out when an acceptable substitute was available at home. In fact, unless we lived within easy commuting distance of Broadway or the prominent theaters in another major city, the substitute was more than acceptable; it was superior. Why buy a ticket for the Elm Street Community Playhouse in the basement of the local Methodist Church to see the guy who owns the hardware store play Cyrano when we could sit in our living rooms and watch José Ferrer assume the role much more competently? Why squeeze into the splintery wooden seats of the local high-school auditorium for a rendering of *Our Town* when we could maintain our ease at home and watch a version that starred some of the most famous names in show business?

In fact, the whole notion of the family night out, regardless of destination, was affected by TV. Statistics showed that those Americans who owned televisions in the early fifties stayed within their four walls more often than those who did not. "While home, they do more entertaining, a new social event being the party that centers around the screen. Nearly half of the television owners acknowledge that their choice of an evening to go out is influenced by what programs are on. Political groups and social clubs are feeling the rivalry of television." And, making the point again: "Tuesday evening, the night when the top-ranking Milton Berle show is on, is avoided as a meeting night."

Middle-class men and women used to go to a restaurant once a week or slightly more or less. Now they were going once a month. On rarer occasions they used to go to nightclubs, or at least bars with live entertainment. Now they did so hardly at all. According to a magazine account of Dr. Coffin and those 137 families on Long Island he so carefully examined, "all forms of dining out and dancing have fallen off 42 percent among his guinea pigs. To sum up, all evening gadding, whether you spend money or only drive out to see Aunt Minnie, has declined about 30 per cent among these representative set owners. And competing home hobbies have taken a similar licking."

So did sporting events. Not only was it easier to watch a game on television, but, depending on the kind of seat a person could afford at the ballpark, he or she could often get a better view of the action on the sofa. And he could hear the announcers explaining strategy, analyzing the more complicated plays, sharing funny anecdotes about the players. As the fifties began, people in Washington, D.C., told *Time* "that they go to wrestling and boxing matches 44.7% less than before; football, 40% less; baseball, 36.7% less."

Only drinking establishments did not seem to suffer smaller turnouts, and that was because most of them had installed a TV behind the bar. They also had jukeboxes in a back corner of the joint, but people were not playing them nearly as much as they used to. Either they did not want to hear the music anymore or, more likely, the sots on the stools, transfixed by television, raised too much of a protest at the competing noise. The owners of some of these places finally had to get rid of the jukeboxes, making them yet another casualty of the rapidly growing dominance of television.

BUT IT WAS ALL TEMPORARY, aberration more than trend, nothing more than the initial reaction of Americans to the initial availability of the small screen. Just as movies and radio adapted to TV after a few years, so did other cultural venues and the people who frequented them.

Starting early in 1954 and continuing through the rest of the decade, attendance at live theaters increased in almost every city or town that had live venues. We might have been inspired to start showing up again by the anthology series on TV, or it might have been that the anthology series inspired people to form more local dramatic groups and that they began to present more skilled productions for which television had helped us develop a greater appetite. Regardless, as the fifties slipped by and there were fewer live dramas on TV, those who wanted to see stage plays had to do what they did before television: get out of the house and go to the theater. We seemed almost as willing as we had been in the old days.

But the theater was not the only destination to which Americans returned with renewed interest. We also went back to our club meetings, our political gatherings, our drop-ins at Aunt Minnie's.

There was, however, a difference. We were more selective now than we used to be, socializing primarily on nights when our favorite programs were not on, or possibly dining early at our favorite restaurants so we could be back home in time for Lucy or Groucho or Marshal Dillon or Ed Sullivan's latest really big show. Or perhaps, after a dinner at Aunt Minnie's, we just stayed there and watched TV with her and Uncle Max.

Nightclub owners, concert promoters, and others associated with live performances reported better business as well with the approach of the sixties. Having watched our favorite entertainers so often on TV, we seem to have decided it would be a treat to see them in person for a change, their television appearances making them all the more appealing, all the more real, as flesh-and-blood human beings. If we saw the stars in person, we could enjoy them for longer periods of time than they appeared on TV, and without commercial interruption. Television, in other words, had made the stars into even bigger stars, so big that it was no longer enough to see them merely in two dimensions.

The crowds at sporting events also began to increase. Just as a trailer for a movie piques interest in the movie, so did a baseball game on television seem to pique interest for an afternoon at the ballpark, part of the appeal being the company of fellow fans, not to mention the sunshine and warm breezes, the hot dogs and beer, the souvenirs—the real experience as opposed to the electronically filtered one. Then the fans could go home and see the highlights on a TV evening newscast, hearing some of the same anecdotes and analysis that the announcers had offered earlier, during the radio broadcast—experience the best of both worlds, a single game becoming a doubleheader of sorts.

In short, what we Americans learned to do as the fifties progressed was incorporate television into our lives rather than allow our lives to be controlled by it. The medium became a choice rather than a czar. Of course for years to come, and up to the present, TV would be the first choice for most of us. We would continue to schedule other activities around our favorite programs: *All in the Family* and *M*A*S*H*, *The Waltons* and *Laverne & Shirley*, *Cheers* and *The Cosby Show*, *Mork & Mindy* and *Hill Street Blues*, *Seinfeld* and *Murphy Brown*, *Touched by an Angel* and *Who Wants to Be a Millionaire?*, *Friends* and *American Idol*.

And when devices like VCRs and TiVO came onto the market and we were no longer chained to the times of our favorite shows as determined by the networks, it became even easier for us to go to the movies or the ballpark, the tavern or the concert. We simply recorded the TV shows we enjoyed most, watching them according to our own schedules.

Ultimately, it seemed, television proved not so much a threat to other media as a complement to them. We did not use the word in those days, but we were discovering there was something synergistic about the small screen. It promoted other forms of entertainment just as other forms of entertainment were promoting TV. We saw someone on the tube; we wanted to see him or her on the big screen or in the nightclub. We heard a song on the radio; we wanted to see the singer in our living rooms. We went to the theater to see a new movie; we wanted to see the star make a guest appearance with Ed Sullivan, or at present, on *Good Morning America* or *Oprah* or one of the late-night talk shows. The net result, although it would not be fully achieved until well after the fifties had disappeared from our rearview mirrors, was that we Americans, with so many choices for amusement, would spend more and more time amusing ourselves than we ever had before.

BUT TELEVISION DID MORE than amuse in the fifties. It reshaped governance, reconfigured campaigning, reinforced attitudes toward race, later redefined attitudes toward race, gave inadvertent birth to the women's rights movement, gave religion a place in the public arena that it had not enjoyed for more than a century, began a never-ending debate about portrayals of violence, and called into question its own integrity in a scandal the repercussions of which shaped the medium for decades to come.

It is to these topics that this volume now turns.

Part II

THE MESSAGES

Chapter 7

The First Senator

MAYBE ED SULLIVAN *wasn't* the most unlikely TV personality of the fifties. After all, he had started out as a gossip columnist, writing about celebrities in such an intimate way that he became something of a celebrity himself. He told about "Gloria Swanson's 'Sunset Boulevard' grossing a cool $1,000,000 in seven weeks at Radio City Music Hall." He informed his readers, tersely and ungrammatically, that "Noel Coward battling flu." He asked people to "consider the charm technique of Dinah Shore."

Sullivan did not have a charm technique of his own. Nor did he have any particular talents other than learning this kind of information and typing it onto a sheet of paper before deadline, but his job made him a star by association. His name was known to hundreds of thousands of New Yorkers, and scores of television executives were among them.

Estes Kefauver's name, on the other hand, was known primarily in Tennessee, and in his earliest days only to those in the small farming community of Madisonville, where he was born and reared. He was an obedient boy, strong for his age and diligent about his chores. But he was determined to put farm work behind for more prestigious employment as soon as he could.

He graduated from high school with honors, distinguished himself at the University of Tennessee, and went on to Yale Law School. Returning to the South, he practiced for several years at a firm in Chattanooga, then, at the age of thirty-three, ran for the state senate as a Democrat. He lost, but was not discouraged. He would try again, and next time aim higher.

Three years later Kefauver was elected to the first of five consecutive terms in the House of Representatives, and in 1948 won a seat in the U.S. Senate. Among his campaign promises was a vow to fight for the economic interests of the little man, especially against monopolies. There was too much wealth in too few hands in America, Kefauver believed; he would do what he could to bring about a more equitable distribution. He "came off as a sort of Southern Jimmy Stewart," one observer noted, "the citizen-politician who gets tired of the abuse of government and goes off on his own to do something about it."

But he did not attract much national attention as a legislator. The problem, some people believed, was his manner. Kefauver was "intelligent, shrewd, but also awkward and bumbling. No one would have accused Estes Kefauver of being, in the phrase that came to haunt many a television figure in the coming years, just another pretty face." Nor was he the possessor of a pretty body. He was tall and gangly, had big hands and feet; he could look dignified enough when standing still, but when he walked he shambled, and suddenly the dignity seemed an illusion. For a time he wore a pair of black-rimmed glasses that gave a severe aspect to his face even when he smiled, which he often did.

Neither was Kefauver just another glib talker, or on occasion even a comprehensible one. "Words escaped him" it has been said; "awkward pauses punctuated his sentences. Part of his success with ordinary people, thought his senatorial colleague Albert Gore [Sr.], came from the fact that he was so awkward and uncomfortable as a speaker that listeners felt a responsibility to help poor old Estes out."

In 1948, they might have helped him out by suggesting that he wear something different on his head for a while. Kefauver was making his bid for the Senate that year, running in the primary against a candidate supported by E. H. Crump, the mayor of Memphis and Democratic boss of Tennessee. For that reason, Crump had ordered Kefauver *not* to run. Kefauver defied him, however, and the relationship between the two men, never close, turned to acrimony. In one of several tirades he delivered against Kefauver, Crump accused his opponent of being untrustworthy, a scoundrel, as "cunning" as a coon.

Kefauver resented the charge, in part because he did not like being disparaged, in part because he thought highly of the creature in question. The coon was "the most American of all animals," he said. Furthermore, "[i]t is one of the cleanest of all animals, it is one of the most courageous. . . . A coon can lick a dog four times its size; he is somewhat of a 'giant-killer' among the animals. Yes, the coon is all American." For a time, Kefauver even campaigned with a live raccoon, but the animal did not take well to the cage in which he was transported, nor to the crowds at the various whistle stops through Tennessee, which scared him more than anything he had ever encountered in the wild. Eventually, the animal had to be set free. He swore he would never have anything to do with politics again.

But that did not mean Kefauver was done with his crusade on behalf of the creature. When he released the coon, he slipped on a coonskin cap. It was a full half-decade before Walt Disney's version of Davy Crockett hit the airwaves, but Estes Kefauver of Tennessee was already decked out for the craze.

However his wardrobe—now consisting of a business suit, a white shirt, a dark tie, and a fuzzy hat with a tail on it—made him look even sillier than he had previously looked with the live animal at his side. What he should have done was simply disassociate himself from nocturnal little carnivores altogether. That he could not bring himself to do so worked to his detriment in the campaign. Kefauver was elected to the Senate despite coons, not because of them.

In many ways, then, he was to politics what Sullivan was to show business. Neither man seemed to belong; both became celebrated to an extent that seems puzzling to later generations. Sullivan was the bigger and more enduring star, but for a time, a time that no one could have seen coming, Kefauver would shine more brightly, and would as a result provide some of the most gripping and important television that the fifties had to offer.

KEFAUVER'S SYMPATHY for the little guy included not just the poor and powerless, but those who were the victims of organized crime. There had been many of them in the thirties and forties, and there was no reason to think there would be fewer in the fifties: so many people in debt to loan sharks and gamblers, so many being swindled by prostitutes and their johns, so many being forced to pay "protection" so that their businesses would not be vandalized or destroyed. Gangland murders made headlines in several cities, most of them shootouts among members of rival factions—*turf wars*, as they were known—in which one group of thugs would fight another for control of various criminal activities in a certain part of town.

At times the police were powerless to stop the violence. At other times they were unwilling, having been bribed into passivity, receiving more money for looking in the "wrong" direction on one night than they would make looking in the "right" direction for the rest of the year.

Of course most Americans had nothing to do with criminal activity, organized or otherwise. They were not preyed upon by gangsters and did not know anyone who had been. But, as noted earlier, the fifties was a time of exaggerated, often unrealistic, fear—and the fear of organized crime was not only exacerbated by press coverage of the occasional outbreak of violence, but by movies that had been popular for decades and continued to attract crowds, both to theaters and to TV screens late at night.

Among them: *Angels with Dirty Faces*, starring James Cagney, Pat O'Brien, and Humphrey Bogart; *Little Caesar*, starring Edward G. Robinson and Douglas Fairbanks Jr.; *The Public Enemy*, starring Cagney and Joan Blondell; *White Heat*, starring Cagney and Edmond O'Brien; and *Scarface*, starring Paul Muni, with Cagney, for a change, nowhere to be seen.

These movies and othersfed the public fascination with the so-called underworld, and the belief that it was more of a menace than it really was. Mario Puzo wrote his novel *The Godfather* in 1969, but it was set in the period from 1945 to 1954, when organized crime was most on Americans' minds and most in the headlines of newspapers.

So it was that on January 5, 1950, first-term Senator Estes Kefauver introduced a bill to establish a committee that would investigate organized-criminal activity in the United States. He did so, in part, on the urging of a group called the American Municipal Association, which believed that "the matter is too big to be handled by local officials alone; the organized criminal element operates across state boundaries on a national scale." Kefauver agreed. He wanted to know the extent of underworld influence, its methods, its profitability, its cost to the national economy, its plans for future expansion, its effects on the innocent or unwitting.

Kefauver's bill passed easily, and was signed into law without reservation by President Truman. It called for the establishment of a Special Committee to Investigate Organized Crime in Interstate Commerce. To most people, though, especially reporters, the group was known simply as the Kefauver Committee, named after the man who not only fought for its creation but was unanimously elected its chairman at the first session.

IN 1950 AND 1951, the committee took to the road, holding hearings in a number of cities, in a few of which, such as New Orleans, St. Louis, and Los Angeles, the proceedings were televised locally. Today's legislators would have drooled over the coverage. Yesterday's did not. They realized that, because of the viewing audience, "they had to be more careful of their language, and they could not help being conscious that audience demand called for 'moving along' with the testimony and not getting bogged down in tortuous details."

But they got bogged down anyhow. To the extent that people enjoyed watching the hearings, it was because they were different more than dynamic. The committee seemed to be doing little more than gathering information that most people either already knew or did not care to know in such overwhelming detail.

But occasionally the Senators, and viewers at home, learned something surprising: the identity of criminals not publicized before, the names of supposedly reputable businesses and even civic organizations in league with hoodlums, the means by which large sums of illicitly gained money were being collected and dispersed, and the fate of people who tried to resist such enterprises.

And, most embarrassing to the members of Kefauver's party, the committee learned that in virtually every city it visited there were powerful ties between organized crime and local political machines, the majority of which were controlled by Democrats, like Memphis's Crump. Back in Washington the news created an uproar. Democrats were incensed. They urged Kefauver either to call off the hearings or to pull his punches when it came to the criminals' political affiliations. Kefauver refused. The decision would come back to haunt him less than twelve months later.

In March 1951, the committee set up shop in New York, where its hearings "turned out to be a landmark, not so much in the history of crime or crime fighting as in the history of television and the coming of a national political theater." For it was in New York that the hearings were first broadcast on a widespread basis, to an impromptu network of some twenty stations east of the Mississippi. Those who watched, who were used to *Kitchen Kapers* and *The Life of Riley* and *The Rifleman*, had never seen anything like it before.

The TV cameras, however, were not the committee's idea. In fact, Kefauver said, "I didn't know that they were going to televise the New York hearings until a day or so before the hearings started." And when he found out about them, he and his fellow committee members tried to have them banned. They were tired of the pressure that they believed television imposed on them, pressure that would be all the greater in New York. But they were told the cameras would stay. Deals had already been made, and contracts signed, with the twenty stations.

Which were not, by any means, confident that the hearings would attract a large audience. But it was still early enough in the medium's history that filling an entire day with programming of any sort was a challenge. The Kefauver show would take up time, would not be expensive, especially since the "stars" did not have to be paid, and they might even make news on occasion, get people talking. Granted, a lot of the Senators were still droning on with their questions, craving attention; a lot of witnesses lowered their heads and mumbled and dissembled when they answered, craving anonymity. But the subject matter was important and could at times be provocative; airing the hearings seemed worth the risk.

Especially since—again, this being New York—not all the witnesses were stiffs. Some of them, in fact, were positively Runyonesque, so perversely entertaining that they seemed to be auditioning for shows of their own—if, that is, they could manage to stay out of jail long enough to preside over them. On the witness stand in the nation's largest city, among others, were such characters as William O'Dwyer, who had resigned as New York's mayor the previous year because of a police-corruption scandal and then proceeded to perjure himself before Kefauver's Committee; Joe Adonis, a Brooklyn crime boss whose Cadillac dealership sold cars for $10,000 and then demanded another $10,000 "as 'insurance,' or else [the customer would] find their dog up the car's exhaust pipe"; and Jake "Greasy Thumb" Guzik, a financial adviser to the late Al Capone whose first words to the Committee were, "I'm gonna refuse to answer any questions on grounds of incrimination. It may incriminate me or tend to incriminate me or lead to incriminating me in some devious way." When asked whether a lawyer had told him to respond that way, Guzik said no. "I heard it on television," he explained.

Also testifying in New York was Virginia Hill Hauser, who had shared her charms with a number of criminal figures, most notably the late gambler, bootlegger, and murderer Bugsy Siegel. Hill strutted into the hearing room wearing a mink stole so flashy that it was said to have cost half as much as one of Adonis's cars, and she had no sooner sat before the committee than she delivered an unforgettable opening statement. "You bastards," she began. "I hope a goddamn atom bomb falls on every goddamn one of you." The Kefauver hearings were educational television of a very different sort from that imagined by the medium's earliest critics.

ALL THE WITNESSES were reluctant to appear. The most reluctant, born Francesco Castiglia and having long since rechristened himself Frank Costello, was probably the leading organized-crime figure on the East Coast. To some people in his line of work he was the king of kings, to others "the prime minister of the underworld." Americans could not wait to see him, to find out for the first time what criminal royalty in their country looked like. But it was not to be, not in the way they expected.

Known for his professionalism in virtually all matters related to illegal enterprise, Costello was strictly an amateur when it came to television. He told the Kefauver Committee he would testify, but only if his face was not shown on television. As one of Costello's lawyers put it, "Mr. Costello doesn't care to submit himself as a spectacle." The committee agreed, and the two sides worked out a compromise; the camera would shoot only Costello's hands. It is unlikely that either the committee or Costello realized that the thug's extremities would turn out to be the greatest spectacle of the entire hearings. As Jack Gould wrote about what a *New York Times* headline referred to as TV's FIRST HEADLESS STAR,

> When the questions got rough, Costello crumpled a handkerchief in his hands. Or he rubbed his palms together. Or he interlaced his fingers. Or he grasped a half-filled glass of water. Or he beat a silent tattoo on the table top. Or he rolled a little ball of paper between his thumb and index finger. Or he stroked the sidepieces of his glasses lying on the table. His was video's first ballet of the hands.

But pictures of more than the witness's hands were available, because Costello's lawyers were as ignorant about the visual arts as the man who had hired them. The lawyers had insisted only, except for the hands, that TV cameramen not shoot their man. They had neglected to impose the same restrictions on newsreel photographers, and their pictures of Costello sweating from forehead to chin and down both sides of his cheeks, frequently trying to remove the moisture with a handkerchief, were shown not only in theaters but, through a special arrangement, on the networks' evening newscasts—a few such scenes being made available nightly.

Costello was not able to provide much in the way of enlightenment to the committee. Asked on one occasion what he did in 1946 to earn a mere $15,000, which was what he had claimed on his income taxes and was in truth closer to what he earned in a single day, he said, "Practically nothing." When asked what he did the following year to make the same amount he said, "Nothing. I did the same thing I did the first year, and I don't think I did a damn thing."

Other Costello replies were similarly uninformative. There were some things he did not know. There were others he did not remember. There were others about which he hadn't the least idea or the foggiest idea or the faintest notion. And there were still others about which he could recall no details, try though he might. And making the scene all the eerier as Costello's fidgety hands filled the TV screen and he professed ignorance in virtually every phrase that could be used for such a purpose was his voice. It was "a raspy baritone" that "seemed to emanate from some mysterious place," the result of a childhood operation on his vocal cords.

Finally reaching the point at which his refusal to testify was becoming as damning as truthful responses would have been, he decided that he had had enough. Frank Costello was done claiming ignorance. It was not just that he was unable to answer the Senators' questions because he didn't know the answers, he claimed; it was that his throat hurt so much he could not have provided a response had one somehow popped into his head. In fact, he said, his throat was so sore that his doctor referred to his ailment by the more technical name of *acute laryngo-tracheitis*. Surely a man with an ailment sounding as impressive as that could not be expected to continue addressing so zealous a band of inquisitors about matters of which he knew so little.

KEFAUVER: You refuse to testify further? . . .
COSTELLO: Mr. Senator, I want to think of my health first. When I
    testify, I want to testify truthfully, and my mind don't function.

KEFAUVER: Your mind seems to be functioning pretty well.

COSTELLO: With all due respect to the Senators . . . I have a lot of respect for them, I am not going to answer another question. . . . I am going to walk out.

Walk out he did, despite being cited for contempt of Congress. His departure provided even more riveting television, if only for a few seconds, as the cameras caught the back of Frank Costello departing from the hearing room in the company of his lawyer with his shoulders hunched and his gait a defeated shuffle, his crisply pressed, perfectly tailored suit drooping now, seeming to hang from him like something off the rack at a closeout. The hearing room door squeaked open, Costello and his lawyer eased through, and then the door slapped shut behind them. The camera lingered on it for a few seconds as the room remained silent. An estimated 30 million people were watching on television.

The advertising agency Young & Rubicam was so impressed not only with the moment but with the hearings as a whole that it took out a full-page ad in several New York newspapers to commend their clients, *Time* magazine among them, for sponsoring such a public-spirited enterprise.

With staggering impact, the telecasts of the Kefauver investigation have brought a shocked awakening to millions of Americans.

Across their television tubes have paraded the honest and the dishonest, the frank and the furtive, the public servant and the public thief. Out of many pictures has come a broader picture of the sordid intermingling of crime and politics, of dishonor in public life.

And suddenly millions of Americans are asking:

What's happened to our ideals of right and wrong?

What's happened to our principles of honesty in government?

What's happened to public and private standards of morality?

ULTIMATELY, the Kefauver Committee did not accomplish as much as its chairman had hoped. It issued citations to forty-five people, but for their unwillingness to testify, not for criminal activity, and only three of those cited were convicted. Further: "The committee proposed nineteen bills to improve law enforcement," writes Stephen Fox in his history of organized crime; "only one passed Congress, the Wagering Stamp Act, which proved unenforceable." The legislators confirmed the existence of Murder Inc., the mob's brutal enforcement arm and in addition confirmed that it was under the control of Albert Anastasia, perhaps the most brutal thug in American history. But they could do nothing to stop it.

And the committee's final report offered few surprises. "Organized criminal gangs operating in interstate commerce are firmly entrenched in our large cities in the operation of many different gambling enterprises such as bookmaking, policy, slot machines, as well as in other rackets such as the sale and distribution of narcotics and commercialized prostitution."

Gambling, however, was "the principal support of big-time racketeering and gangsterism. These profits provide the financial resources whereby ordinary criminals are converted into big-time racketeers, political bosses, pseudo businessmen, and alleged philanthropists. Thus the $2 horse bettor and the 5-cent numbers player are not only suckers not only because they are gambling against hopeless odds, but because they provide the moneys which enable underworld characters to undermine our institutions."

The Committee also allocated a few words in support of itself, suggesting that it had inspired numerous other bodies at the state and local level to look into organized crime. "Nearly every section of the country is experiencing a wave of grand jury activity with ensuing disclosures and indictments which are a testimonial to the American system of justice and the ability of the people to rid themselves of the scourge of the underworld by judicial process. It is reasonable to forecast that venal politicians whose corruption has permitted the racketeers to become so firmly entrenched will in large measure be eliminated as aroused and awakened citizens go to the polls."

Actually, it was not a reasonable forecast at all; awakened citizens often fall back to sleep with the passage of time and did, for the most part, in this case.

But by shining a spotlight onto criminal activities, the hearings forced at least some of those activities into the small, dark corners, wherein they could operate neither as efficiently nor as profitably as they once had. The Internal Revenue Service "set up a special rackets squad," reports Stephen Fox, "that convicted 874 gangster tax delinquents in the next six years," and Frank Costello spent most of the next five years in prison.

There were reports from some cities that hoodlums who had once conducted their affairs openly had been run out of business or arrested or both.

There were reports that brothels and gambling dens had been shut down and their proprietors fined or sent to jail. There were also reports of fewer complaints being filed by honest businessmen that they were being intimidated by hoodlums threatening violence.

Probably the most significant accomplishment of the hearings, though, was that the spotlight they had turned on organized criminals shone so brightly even FBI head J. Edgar Hoover had to acknowledge the glare. Prior to the hearings, Hoover had not paid much attention to organized crime. In fact, for decades he had insisted "that a violent, subversive, left-wing conspiracy threatened the United States" far more than a league of hoodlums, in which he might not even have believed. Commies, not crooks, were the principal threat to the American way of life. Perhaps the Kefauver hearings had not changed his mind, but they do seem to have broadened his outlook.

As a result, in 1957, when an organized-crime convention took place at the Apalachin, New York, estate of mobster Joseph "Joe the Barber" Barbara, Hoover listened intently to the reports of an agency informer. The meeting, said the informer, would be the largest such gathering ever, including more than a hundred thugs from the United States, Canada, and Italy. It was all Hoover needed to hear. It was time, he decided, to act.

And act he did, quickly and efficiently. Dozens of FBI agents, as well as even more personnel from local police departments, headed for Apalachin. They positioned themselves in the woods around Barbara's mansion and peered at the comings and goings through binoculars, taking what photographs they could and jotting down names, license plate numbers, and times of arrival.

After a few days, deciding they had gathered enough information, the agents moved in, storming Barbara's fortress with guns in one hand and badges in the other. The result was chaos. The crime bosses panicked, tried to flee. Some of them jumped out of windows and ran through the woods, either hiding themselves in thickets or along the banks of streams until the coast was clear. Others arranged with accomplices to provide them with rides to safer, less bug-infested places.

Most of the mobsters, however, were not so lucky. The FBI and local police officers had entered so swiftly and stationed themselves in so many places that the majority of convention attendees had no chance either to run for cover or to draw their guns. More than half of them were arrested, the biggest and most successful raid ever made on organized crime in the history of the United States. Among those taken into custody were Vito Genovese, Carlo Gambino, and Joseph Bonanno, all of them major players in their field. In fact, if there had been such a thing as an organized crime hall of fame, the three of them would have been charter members.

Although Estes Kefauver had nothing directly to do with what happened at Apalachin, although he was back in the Senate by then and had turned his attention to matters other than large-scale criminal enterprise, it was his example and the publicity generated by his hearings that made the attack on Barbara's residence possible. Never before had law enforcement officials so effectively confronted organized criminal activity in the United States. Never before had the lords of the underworld had so much to fear from the judicial system that was about to march them into the courtroom and, in at least a few cases, put an end to their illicit livelihoods.

BUT THE APALACHIN ASSAULT had not been televised. The Kefauver hearings, on the other hand, were a broadcast marathon, and if they made fewer inroads into organized crime than they had set out to make, they still managed to become a landmark of American popular culture. Writes Kefauver biographer Joseph Bruce Gorman,

> The twelve months preceding the Kefauver Committee's hearings in New York City had seen the percentage of homes in the New York metropolitan area with TV sets rise sharply, from 29 to 51 per cent. Programs, however, were still fairly unsophisticated and the Kefauver hearings offered a dramatic contrast to typical television offerings. In the morning hours, the hearings created seventeen times the normal viewing audience (26.2 per cent of homes vs. the normal 1.5 per cent); in the afternoon there was also a dramatic increase in viewing (from 11.6 per cent of homes to 31.5 per cent). It was estimated that an average of 86.2 per cent of those viewing television watched the hearings, and that an average of 69.7 per cent of the TV sets in the New York area were on during the hearings, twice as many as during a weekday World Series game in October 1950.

One night, a *Tuesday*, the hearings ran late and attracted a larger audience than Milton Berle, an astonishing feat. Consolidated Edison, the New York utilities company, had to put an extra generator on line to provide power for all the television sets in use in its region. And for several days, the marquee on a New York movie theater proclaimed

FREE TO PUBLIC
KEVAUVER TV
SENATE CRIME HEARINGS

In Chicago, so many people were watching the hearings that profits suffered in stores that usually did good business during the day. Finally, in frustration, a department-store manager took out an ad in a local newspaper. "Ten percent Off," it read, "During Kefauver Hours."

To *Life* magazine the effects of the hearings were unprecedented:

The week of March 12, 1951, will occupy a special place in history. The U.S. and the world had never experienced anything like it. In Detroit the telephone company noticed that for hours at a time normally clogged lines went practically unused. . . . Thousands of people stayed away from their jobs. . . . Trolley cars in many cities carried half their normal loads. New York cab drivers wasted gas in a vain search for passengers. It became apparent that at least one fifth of the population had absented itself from normal pursuits. All along the television cable it had suddenly gone indoors—into living rooms, taverns and clubrooms, auditoriums, and back offices. There, in eerie half-light, looking at millions of small frosty screens, people sat as if charmed. For days on end and into the nights they watched with complete absorption. In Philadelphia one man, no more rapt than others, sat staring, unaware of a fire until it had destroyed a shed in his back yard and swept into the upper story of his home.

From elsewhere came accounts of housewives becoming so mesmerized by Kefauver and company that "electric irons burned through their ironing boards."

The Senate's Special Committee to Investigate Organized Crime in Interstate Commerce attracted the largest television audience ever assembled to that time. As a result, even the Committee's chief counsel, Rudolph Halley, frequently seen whispering into Kefauver's ear, made it big. "One day," wrote Robert Lewis Shayon in the *Saturday Review of Literature*, "it was 'Who is this horn-rimmed, razor-tongued quarterback calling the signals for Tennessee's Kefauver . . .?' The next it was Rudolph Halley granting press conferences, making speeches, narrating a network crime series ('Crime Syndicate,' CBS-TV, Tuesdays; to be reviewed in a coming issue), and accepting a triple-threat nomination for the principal office at stake in New York this fall [the mayoralty] from the Liberal, City Fusion, and Independent parties."

So influential, in fact, was the Kefauver investigation as a media phenomenon that it even led to a new publishing genre. Robert Harrison, already responsible for a number of so-called girlie magazines, was inspired to create *Confidential,* a scandal magazine to continue titillating the public with criminal misdeeds after the hearings had ended.

> *Confidential's* success in featuring scandal stories about stars and other famous people resulted in dozens of copycat magazines and hundreds of "one-shots" (magazines focused on one star or personality). In the midst of fierce competition Harrison and others, such as *Suppressed* editor Edythe Farrell, gave the public (the televised Kefauver hearings notwithstanding) "what they can't get on television"—exposés of star secrets, racketeering, consumer scams and politicians' peccadilloes.

BUT IT WAS THE SENATOR from Tennessee who left the most indelible imprint as a result of the hearings, the senator whose children, watching him at home, "smudged the screen" by patting their father, trying to get his attention. Kefauver appeared on the cover of *Time* and other magazines and as a guest on the TV game show *What's My Line?* He was asked to play a part in a Humphrey Bogart movie about organized crime. He decided not to, but did agree to portray himself in a movie about gangsters called *The Captive City,* starring John Forsythe. Kefauver wrote a series of four articles about organized crime, or more likely employed someone else to construct them under his name, for *Saturday Evening Post.* With the help of another ghostwriter, he produced a book on his campaign against crime that spent three months on the *New York Times* best-seller list. And perhaps most remarkably, he won an Emmy, the first and only American politician to be honored for his performance on television—or, as the inscription on the award read, for his special accomplishment of "bringing the workings of our government into the homes of the American people."

Kefauver was pleased by all the attention. But he was a thoughtful man—prescient, as it turned out—and could not help but be troubled by his means of achieving notice. He worried about the televising of future investigative hearings, worried that the presence of cameras might eventually convert the serious business of government into yet another branch of show business. "I did my best during the course of our proceedings," he said, "and I hope the record will show I succeeded, to maintain a calm and judicial attitude."

That, however, was a matter for future concern. For the present, Kefauver had something more personal in mind. He wanted to capitalize on his newly won fame to become the Democratic nominee for President in 1952, and for a time he appeared to be the front-runner. Ultimately, though, he did not have a chance; his Committee had alienated too many people in his party by pointing out the connections between big-city Democratic machines and organized crime.

One of those connections was especially troublesome for Kefauver. In his early days in politics, President Harry Truman's mentor was Tom Prendergast, the less-than-vigorously ethical boss of Kansas City. Truman never forgave Kefauver for calling attention to Prendergast, and, not running for another term himself, the president wholeheartedly threw his support for the nomination to former Illinois governor Adlai Stevenson. Stevenson was not as well known as Kefauver, not as heroically perceived, and certainly not as energetic a candidate as Kefauver had been in the primaries. He was, however, the eventual winner of the nomination.

The Republican candidate was Dwight Eisenhower. Ike, as he was familiarly known, and California Senator Richard Nixon defeated Stevenson and Alabama Senator John Sparkman in a landslide in that November's general election. Eisenhower's popularity was such, however, that the results probably would have been the same no matter who the Democrats ran.

Kefauver tried again for the nomination in 1956. He lost again, but this time Stevenson, winning his second chance at the White House, chose Kefauver as his running mate. The choice, alas, only meant another defeat for Kefauver, as the incumbents beat the Democrats by an even greater margin than they had four years earlier. Kefauver had campaigned in his coonskin cap in '52, pre–Fess Parker. He did it again for a few weeks in '56, post–Fess Parker, explaining that Davy Crockett and "all of our great men of that era in Tennessee History wore the familiar ring-tailed, coon-skin cap." But it was a gimmick, unbecoming a man running for the nation's second highest office. The electorate wasn't impressed. Only Parker, it seemed, could endear himself to large numbers of people with such mangy headgear.

IT IS COMMONLY SAID that television first demonstrated its power to bring Americans together in the horrible days after President Kennedy was assassinated in 1963. Not so. The first demonstration came more than a decade earlier, when an enormous number of us, at least those of us watching one of the twenty stations in what was referred to as *a national hookup*, sat before our TV sets as the U.S. Senate Special Committee to Investigate Organized Crime in Interstate Commerce went about its appointed tasks. It was "the first big broadcast of an affair of their government," *Life* pointed out, "the broadcast from which all future uses of television in public affairs must date. . . . Never before had the attention of the nation been riveted so completely on a single matter."

In the final analysis, then, it was television that mattered most about the Kefauver hearings, not the effect that they had on organized crime. The committee's work, it was accurately reported, had made "the public hearing more public than it ever was before. In this fact lies the true measure of the importance of television's coverage of the hearings. It has shown that it can arouse public interest to a degree which virtually beggars immediate description."

But just as government officials could use the small screen to publicize a matter of importance to the citizenry as a whole, so could they use it for more selfish ends, and it would prove every bit as effective for the individual's goals as it had been for the greater good of society.

Chapter 8

The Second Senator

THE NATIONAL POLITICAL CONVENTIONS of 1952 were not nearly as popular with TV viewers as the Kefauver hearings had been. The most watched moment of either party's gathering was Eisenhower's nomination by the Republicans, not because it was a surprise to anyone, but because people wanted to share in the anointing of so admired a figure. The rating for nomination night, however, according to the Hooper scale, which preceded the Nielsen system, was 36. By way of contrast, the most recent episode of *I Love Lucy* had scored a 62. "In their drearier stretches," of which there were many, the *New York Times* magazine reported that "the conventions naturally rated far worse [than 36], dropping to a low of 17."

It seemed reasonable to assume that the campaign would not be any more of an attraction. Eisenhower, who had gone on to become the president of Columbia University after his reign as the Supreme Commander of Allied forces in Europe during World War II, was certain to win. It was just as certain, with that inbred military reticence of his, that he would not say or do anything quotable until he did—if then.

Democratic nominee Adlai Stevenson spent much of the campaign trying to live down his reputation as a highbrow. He could not do it. He recited his speeches in such measured tones and loaded them with such lofty
phrases that it might have been he, not his opponent, who had served as a
college president.

Stevenson's choice for vice president, John Sparkman, had done little
to stand out from the crowd since 1946, when he first held national office
from Alabama. On the other hand, Eisenhower's running mate, California's
Nixon, was much better known, having already established a reputation for
zealousness, and in some cases underhanded behavior, in pursuit of Communist influence in government.

Actually, Nixon might have resembled Ed Sullivan even more than
Kefauver did: same stiff shoulders, same lock-jointed gait and mechanical
movements, same inability to convey sincerity in a smile, and the same
awkwardness at making small talk, even with friends, even for short periods of time. Richard Nixon seemed destined to be a figure in the background of the battle for the White House. Instead, he turned out to be the
reason that the campaign of 1952 finally got interesting, and would go on
to prove "that being telegenic is not the sole criterion for being a television
communicator."

ON SEPTEMBER 18, the *New York Post*, an avidly pro-Stevenson paper,
charged that the Republican vice-presidential candidate was in his own
way as unscrupulous as the Communists whose behavior he so decried.
The *Post* had uncovered, it declared in bold black ink, a SECRET NIXON
FUND. Beneath that accusation was a more detailed one: SECRET RICH
MAN'S TRUST FUND KEEPS NIXON IN STYLE FAR BEYOND HIS SALARY.

The *Post* headlines made headlines in other papers as well. Television
and radio newscasts also reported the story, and news magazines analyzed
it in as much detail as they could find or invent. The Eisenhower campaign
was bombarded with telegrams, and in the first few days after the story
broke, three out of every four expressed their displeasure with Nixon, some
even urging Ike to find a new partner for the ticket. Suddenly the outcome
of the 1952 election no longer seemed a foregone conclusion.

According to the *Post*'s account, Nixon had won his Senate seat in 1950
through financial chicanery. Many of his campaign expenses, the paper
stated, had been paid for out of a so-called slush fund made available to the

candidate by a group of wealthy California businessmen. The fund was said to have picked up the tab for at least some of Nixon's travel, including hotel rooms, cabs and airfare, and for his written pleas to voters, including stationery and postage. It was further said to have contained, at various times, between $16,000 and $18,000.

As it happened, the charges were true. Every one of them. They were also common practice at the time, and despite the *Post*'s insinuations to the contrary, entirely legal. The travel expenses and charges for letter-writing to constituents were legitimate costs of campaigning. The citizenry was entitled to contribute to them. Other politicians, either holding or seeking a variety of offices, had similar funds of their own. In fact, as was later revealed, Stevenson had collected a large sum of money as governor of Illinois, and some of those who provided it were people doing business with the state at the same time that they were making their contributions, a much-less-ethical arrangement than the Nixon fund.

Of course the *New York Post* knew this. Of course its editors could have published an incendiary article about the Democratic candidate's bankroll and its sources. But political allegiances being what they were, the *Post* editors chose to believe that, while Nixon's practices were shady, Stevenson had used his particular monies not for his own ends but, as the official explanation had it, "to supplement the salaries of state officials," which was not only a ludicrous defense but, if true, might also have been against the law.

Still, understanding what it did about campaign funds, how they worked, and how common they were, it was strange that the *Post* decided to make an issue out of Nixon's. Why not attack him on other grounds? Why not accuse him of being more of an alley fighter than a statesman in his campaigns for the House in 1946 and the Senate in 1948? Why not take issue with his positions on various issues? Like all politicians, Nixon had his vulnerabilities; the slush fund, however, was simply not one of them.

Stranger still was the fact that the fund had been reported previously. Nixon had talked to journalists about it more than once, without hesitation and on the record. He had even given one journalist the name of the fund's administrator, so that he could interview the man in charge of the finances himself. The journalist would find, Nixon told him, that the contributors were not rich men, at least not all of them; the donations, both large and small, had come from people of all means who were simply showing their support for Nixon in his campaign against Communists. He was pleased that he had been able to attract such support, he said, open in his acknowledgment of the entire matter and, for that reason, the fund had attracted almost no notice the first time around, which was well before Nixon had become the vice-presidential nominee.

As a result, when the *Post* gave the Stevenson–Sparkman ticket a boost by resurrecting the story and casting it in an entirely different light, it seemed to many Americans something new—and insidious. Politics as usual became politics as illicit activity. Cause: journalism as usual.

Nixon was incensed by the *Post*'s report. He was even more incensed when stories started to spread about the specific uses to which his fund had supposedly been put, like sprucing up the Nixons' Georgetown home. According to one account, Nixon's wife Pat paid as much as $10,000 in cash for a decorator's services. She bought new drapes, a new sofa; she and her husband were clearly on the take.

In fact, the house did have a different look than it had before, but not because of a decorator. As Mrs. Nixon told reporters, inviting them in for a tour of the residence, she and her husband had simply shipped some of their furniture from California to their new residence in the nation's capital. Anyone who came to the house could see that the drapes and sofa were not new, she said angrily, and had certainly not been chosen by someone with a professional eye. The drapes were clearly faded, the sofa obviously worn from years of use.

But Nixon knew from the outset that his battle against the fund story would be a bitter one, no matter what he or his wife did. In fact, the day after the *Post* broke the story, the vice-presidential candidate was making a speech from the back of a train in Marysville, California. As he finished, one of his listeners asked about the fund. The engineer had given the signal to pull away. Nixon told him to stop so he could respond.

> You folks know the work that I did investigating Communists in the United States. Ever since I have done that work the Communists and the left-wingers have been fighting me with every possible smear. . . . And believe me, you can expect that they will continue to do so. They started it yesterday. They have tried to say that I had taken $16,000 for my personal use.
>
> What they didn't point out is that rather than charging the American taxpayer with the expenses of my offices, which were in excess of the amounts which were allowed under the law, what I did was to have those expenses paid by the people back home who were

interested in seeing that information concerning what was going on in Washington was spread among the people of this state.

I will tell you what some of the others [members of the House and Senate] do. They put their wives on the payroll, taking your money and using it for that purpose. Pat Nixon has worked in my office night after night, and I can say this proudly—she has never been on the government payroll since I have been in Washington.

Do you want me to do what some others are doing? Take fat legal fees on the side? During the time I have been in Washington I have never taken a legal fee, although as a lawyer I could legally have done so, and I am never going to in the future.

The crowd roared its approval. But there were many others yet to be heard from.

AT THE SAME TIME that Nixon was defending himself against the *Post*'s charges, something was happening that made him even angrier than the paper's attack, which, after all, he could accurately attribute to his enemies. Now, he believed, his friends were turning against him—in particular Eisenhower and his inner circle of advisers. Nixon expected them to come to his aid and to do it immediately, explaining that there was nothing improper about the fund, that the money had been used for no purpose other than to help Senatorial aspirant Nixon get his message across to the people of California, which was precisely what his backers had intended and the law permitted.

But the Eisenhower campaign, at least in the first few days after the *Post* assault, was publicly silent about Nixon's troubles. No statements were released, no comments made to reporters. It was just as well, for privately, Ike and his staff were fuming. All along, the general had been preaching honesty, integrity, the end of scandal and corruption in government. It was the theme of his presidential quest. Under the Truman administration there had been a mess in Washington, the general charged time and time again, and it was his intention to clean things up and keep them clean. He was never very specific about what kind of mess there was, although it certainly involved Soviet influence in high places; nor was he specific about the steps he had in mind to restore fairness and decency. But he was adamant that something had to be done and that he was the man to do it.

And then what happens? From out of nowhere the *New York Post* publishes this article which—even though it is totally misleading, the obvious work of Democrats who might themselves have been under Soviet influence for all anybody knew—suddenly makes it seem, at least to those predisposed to believe such a canard, as if Eisenhower would bring his own mess to Washington. "Of what avail is it for us to carry on this crusade against this business of what has been going on in Washington," he said, "if we ourselves aren't clean as a hound's tooth?"

But they were, at least as far as Nixon's Senatorial money-raising efforts were concerned, and to establish the fact beyond doubt the Eisenhower people ordered an independent audit of the fund—conducted by Price Waterhouse & Company, then verified by Gibson, Dunn & Crutcher, one of the largest and most reputable law firms in Los Angeles. The audit revealed, to the surprise of no one with any experience in politics, that there was nothing inappropriate about the money. It had been collected properly, dispersed properly, accounted for properly. Nixon was relieved at the finding, although certainly not surprised, and now, finally, expected his endorsement from Eisenhower.

It still did not come. Eisenhower continued to avoid reporters, or to avoid the subject of the fund when reporters managed to track him down. He did call Nixon on one occasion. "You've been taking a lot of heat the last couple of days," Eisenhower said. "I imagine it has been pretty rough." Nixon agreed, but Eisenhower offered neither consolation nor a solution. He hung up after a few pointless minutes and in the days that followed conversed no further with his running mate.

To Nixon, Ike's silence was the noisiest of all possible rebukes, and it shot his blood pressure into the danger zone. What did the old man want from him? What was he supposed to do? And how was he even supposed to find out what to do? Not only was there no longer any communication between the two men at the top of the ticket, there was little between their staffs, virtually none of which could be called meaningful.

After a few more days, the general's advisers made a decision. They put their heads together and decided not to decide; they would turn the matter over to the American people and let them make the call. Nixon was told to take his case to the electorate on national television, to buy half an hour of time on the networks to explain the fund and reiterate his probity and give examples of it. The reaction of those who watched would determine his fate. If viewers found his performance convincing, the Eisenhower campaign would welcome him back with open arms, at least when the cameras were snapping. If not, or so the implication was, he would be replaced on the ticket by someone above reproach. For the first time in history, a TV show would be a referendum on Presidential politics.

Nixon did not like the idea. To him it was worse than unjust; it was humiliating, and it revealed a spinelessness on the part of Eisenhower and his staff for which he would not forgive them even as he paid for it with his own pride and self-respect. He had, he believed, no choice. He was an ambitious man, not an idler and certainly not a quitter. He stopped campaigning for a while, isolated himself, and began to work on his speech. They would be the most important words of his young political life.

BEFORE LONG, Nixon would feel even more shabbily treated by Eisenhower. On the very day that he was to speak to the nation, he got a phone call in his hotel room from one of the general's top aides, former presidential candidate Thomas Dewey.

"There has just been a meeting of all of Eisenhower's top advisers," Dewey told Nixon, "and they have asked me to tell you that it is their opinion that at the conclusion of the broadcast tonight you should submit your resignation to Eisenhower."

For several seconds, Nixon was too startled to reply. He held onto the phone, looked into the distance, nothing more. Had he heard correctly? He was to submit his resignation? For what possible reason? What had he done? And what was the point of making the speech in the first place if he were to end it by stepping down?

Finally, in a voice that was little more than a whisper, Nixon said, "It's kind of late for them to pass on this kind of recommendation to me now. I've already prepared my remarks, and it would be very difficult for me to change them now."

Dewey then stunned Nixon even further. "I've got another suggestion as to how you can follow this up and come out of all of it the hero rather than the goat," he said.

Nixon waited.

"What you might do is announce not only that you are resigning from the ticket, but that you're resigning from the Senate as well. Then, in the special election which will have to be called for the Senate, you can run again and vindicate yourself by winning the biggest plurality in history."

Nixon felt as if, rather than being on the other end of the phone line, he was on the other side of the looking glass that Lewis Carroll had created for Alice. It was, for the California Senator, the end of his conciliatory attitude toward Eisenhower and all those who surrounded him with their timidity, cold-heartedness, and short-sightedness. It was also the last straw, but he would not allow it to break his back.

"Just tell them," Nixon hissed at Dewey after a few seconds, "that I haven't the slightest idea what I am going to do, and if they want to find out they'd better listen to the broadcast." Before Dewey could reply, he continued. "And tell them I know something about politics, too." He slammed the receiver into the cradle and stormed out of his hotel room, where members of his inner circle had gathered and had been listening, in a haze of bewilderment, to Nixon's end of the conversation. None of them followed him. For a few minutes, none of them spoke to one another. They needed time to make sense of the situation, just as Nixon did.

His address, which history would come to know as the "Checkers" speech, was scheduled to begin in less than six hours.

"THERE HAD BEEN A BREATHLESS SILENCE as Nixon and his small party walked out of the quiet hotel lobby and took the twenty-minute ride from the Ambassador to the NBC studio, one block from the famed intersection of Hollywood and Vine." So wrote Nixon biographer Roger Morris. "The candidate sat in the front seat of the Cadillac limousine, nervously shuffling his notes. . . . A handful of cheering Young Republicans were at the studio to greet him."

But Nixon would need more than that, much more. He would need the whole nation to cheer. Or at least some older Republicans as well as young ones. He would do his best to earn their approval, and before the call from Dewey he had been certain of success. Now he was certain no longer. In fact, he had begun to lose heart. The timing, he knew, could not have been worse, and he wondered whether the real purpose of Dewey's call had been just that, to shake his confidence, throw him off his game, seal his fate by jangling his nerves.

Nixon's speech would be directed by John Claar, a television veteran who was currently the director of *Our Miss Brooks*. He hoped to help the candidate give as convincing a portrayal of a righteous man as Eve Arden gave of a schoolteacher. Mannerisms, Claar thought, were one of the keys, mannerisms that did not seem mannered. After Nixon had been made up and brought to the set, a Spartan assembly of furnishings that one observer described as "a GI bedroom den," Claar and an advertising executive who was assisting him for the occasion started rehearsing with the candidate. They told Nixon to sit at the table that was the centerpiece of the set, "then stand next to it, then to repeat the same movements and stances again and again. As they prompted, Nixon practiced posing with one hand on the table and, in another position, with a hand informally in his pants pockets. Under similar direction he smiled, and smiled again, cracking momentarily the frozen-lipped frown he had worn since leaving his hotel room."

When Claar and the ad man were done with him, Nixon thanked them for their suggestions and retreated to his dressing room. His wife Pat followed, the two of them alone now, the clock ticking away.

A few minutes before air time, after sitting for a while in a stony trance, he turned to Pat. "I just don't think I can go through with this," he told her.

"Of course you can," she said, and he did.

"MY FELLOW AMERICANS," Nixon began, as Pat sat across from him on a small divan, just out of camera range but almost as close to her husband as she had been in the dressing room, "I come before you tonight as a candidate for the Vice Presidency and a man whose honesty and integrity has [sic] been questioned."

Referring to those who had contributed to his fund, he said that it would be "morally wrong if any of those contributors got special favors for the contributions they made." But they had not, Nixon swore, and furthermore, "not a cent of the $18,000 or any other money of that type ever went to me for my personal use. Every penny of it was used to pay for political expenses that I did not think should be charged to the taxpayers of the United States."

Nixon went on to give a detailed explanation of campaign-financing procedures and followed with further details about the audit that had exonerated him. One cannot help imagining at this point his once again questioning the purpose of his words. If he had been exonerated, why in the name of reason was he going through such a drill?

He was about ten minutes into his speech now, and his tone of voice had been factual, his manner reserved, as if he were teaching a course in the practical realities of government—but no longer. Suddenly, as if he were afraid the dryness of his tone might be making his audience restless, he assumed a different role.

"And so now, what I am going to do—and incidentally this is unprecedented in the history of American politics—I am going at this time to give to this television and radio audience a complete financial history, everything I have earned, everything I have spent and everything I own, and I want you to know the facts."

And give them he did, all the facts, the figures, the particulars. Pat had not wanted him to reveal such personal information, had in fact begged him to omit this section of the speech. "Why do we have to tell people how little we have and how much we owe? Aren't we entitled to have at least some privacy?" Her husband would not listen. There was too much at stake for self-respect.

The house in Washington that he and Pat had been accused of redecorating from the fund cost $41,000. They still owed $20,000 on it.

They had another home in Whittier, California that cost $13,000. They owed $3,000 on that one, and Nixon's parents were now living in it.

They owed $4,000 to the Riggs Bank of Washington, D.C., which they were paying off monthly at a rate of four percent.

They had a car, one, a 1950 Oldsmobile.

He had a life-insurance policy on himself for $4,000.

But: "I have no life insurance on Pat," he said. "I have no life insurance on our two youngsters, Patricia and Julie. . . . We have no stocks or bonds of any type. We have no interest, direct or indirect, in any business. . . .

"I should say this, that Pat doesn't have a mink coat. But she does have a respectable Republican cloth coat, and I always tell her she would look good in anything."

Nixon knew he was taking a chance here. As biographer Jonathan Aitken has written, he was making "a descent into a style of folksy corniness which could either stick in the gullet or pluck at the heartstrings. Pitching his speech at the right emotional level was therefore his great challenge." He could not be sure, at this moment, that he was succeeding. It was certainly not his usual style.

Nixon then revealed that, on one occasion, he had received a gift from a supporter that was, strictly speaking, a violation of the law. It was "a little cocker spaniel dog . . . black and white, spotted, and our little girl, the six-year-old, named it Checkers.

"And you know, the kids, like all kids, loved the dog, and I just want to say this, right now, that regardless of what they say about it, we are going to keep it."

Then Nixon shifted tone again, his jaw strutting and his eyes seeming to narrow. Back to the broader picture. He said that since he had come clean about his finances, so should Stevenson. Stevenson, Nixon said, had had a fund or two himself in his days as a public servant, "and I think that what Mr. Stevenson should do should be to come before the American people, as I have, [and] give the names of the people that contributed to that fund."

Furthermore, Stevenson's running mate, John Sparkman, "had his wife on the [government] payroll. I don't condemn him for that, but I think that he should come before the American people and indicate what sources of income he has had."

Nixon began to wind down. He blasted President Truman, "under whose administration the mess was made," and then criticized Stevenson for being Truman's hand-picked successor and, by implication, complicit in the misdeeds. He praised Eisenhower for being "the only man who can lead us into this fight to rid the government of both those who are Communists and those who have corrupted this government."

Now came the moment to which everything he had previously said had been leading, which also turned out to be the moment when he thought all was lost. Nixon concluded his speech by saying: "I am submitting to the Republican National Committee tonight through this television broadcast the decision which it is theirs to make. Let them decide whether my position on the ticket will help or hurt. And I am going to ask you to help them decide. Wire and write the Republican National Committee whether you think I should stay on or whether I should get off. And whatever their decision, I will abide by it."

But then disaster—or so Nixon feared. He ran out of time before he could give the RNC's address. He was just about to tell people how to contact the party's power brokers when the red light on the camera went off. Seconds later the studio lights began to dim. The network was now in a station break, and when it was over the next program would begin. Those close to Nixon at the time, some of his staff standing to the side of the camera or, in Pat's case, still sitting on the divan, saw him shake his head in frustration. Then they saw the tears begin to run down his cheeks. He was certain he had lost his chance to remain on the ticket.

HE NEED NOT HAVE WORRIED. The speech was a triumph. True, some people found it maudlin. The journalist Richard Rovere wrote that Nixon "may aspire to the grace and nobility of Quakerism but if so he has yet to comprehend the core of the faith. It would be hard to think of anything more wildly at variance with the spirit of the Society of Friends than his appeal for the pity and sympathy of his countrymen . . . on the ground that his wife did not own a mink coat." Authors Harry Castleman and Walter J. Podrazik exclaimed, "What a scenario! All it needed was some organ music underneath and the nation would have been awash in bathos."

But a more important critic was impressed. "I have seen many brave men in tough situations," said Dwight Eisenhower to reporters immediately after the address. "I have never seen anyone come through in better fashion than Senator Nixon did tonight." This even though Eisenhower must surely have blanched when Nixon called for Stevenson and Sparkman to reveal their finances as thoroughly as he did, for in the process they might have insisted that Eisenhower reveal *his* finances, and he had a stash of his own, more than $600,000 in an advance on royalties for his memoir of World War II that had been published four years earlier. Like Nixon's fund, this money would also have withstood Price Waterhouse scrutiny, but it might not have withstood the headlines that the *New York Post* and other liberal papers certainly would have given it.

The call to make such information public, however, was not heeded by Democrats. What *was* heeded was Nixon's plea to remain on the ticket. His speech was watched by the largest number of people yet to tune into a television program, even larger than the largest of the audiences for the Kefauver hearings, and the outpouring of support for Nixon from people who would later be known as "the silent majority" was astounding. More than 200,000 Americans took it upon themselves to find the address for either the Republican National Committee or their local Eisenhower/ Nixon campaign offices and flooded them with letters, telegrams of support and money. According to historian J. Ronald Oakley, "Almost $60,000 in contributions came in, too, almost enough to cover the $75,000 cost of the broadcast."

Oakley continues: "From all across the country," he writes, "people wrote that they had been moved to tears by the speech, and many of them sent handwoven dog blankets, dog collars, a dog kennel, a year's supply of dog food, and dozens of other canine gifts."

The day after the speech Nixon and Eisenhower met at an airport in West Virginia, the first time they had seen each other since the so-called scandal began. Eisenhower grinned at him. "You're my boy," he famously and condescendingly said, throwing an arm over his running mate's shoulders, and with that Nixon was not only back in the campaign's good graces, but even more deeply embedded in the public's good graces.

IN THE OPINION of Monica Crowley, a research consultant for Nixon in his last days and the author of two books about the former president, the "Checkers" speech had much in common with the Kefauver hearings. In both cases, what was important in the long run was TV's effect on politics rather than the message's specific effect on viewers.

> For the first time, a candidate for national office went over the heads of the media elite and took his case directly to the American people. It helped that Nixon had the truth on his side, of course. But there was something else: he understood that in a new media age, perhaps the facts weren't enough. Perhaps you needed to reach out to the viewers in their living rooms and appeal to them on an entirely different level. He was the first to figure out that in a cool medium like television, you needed the pull of emotion. By invoking his daughters' love of the family dog, he couched his political appeal in a distinctly and unforgettably *personal* way. It was a political speech that in the end, wasn't political at all. It was about *relatability*.

Crowley's analysis is an astute one. But between the lines is a warning, a warning that, remarkably, was first issued in 1939, when NBC, as an experiment, televised the New York World's Fair to a limited number of sets in the city. It was Fair science director, Gerald Wendt, who sounded the alarm, and it is paraphrased by Yale University scholar David Gelernter.

> TV is apt to change, not necessarily for the better, the way public figures are evaluated. Its "greater intimacy" of presentation will give the audience "a more vivid presentation of personality." So don't be surprised if TV should "still further enhance the value of what is called personality in public figures." Because of TV "the cultivation of a personal 'public' will itself be a valuable art." Financial and

political rewards may accrue "quite out of proportion to the actual value of the performer in his real job, whether it be President or statesman, labor leader or minister of God." In short, democracy, under the influence of television, is likely to pay inordinate attention to the performer and interpreter rather than to the planner and thinker.

Television's ability to cultivate a personal public could not have been more apparent than during the "Checkers" speech. People watching Nixon in their homes had not seen a mere thirty-minute political address, but an ingeniously constructed three-act play. Nixon was as unemotional as an accountant in act 1, which simply provided the narrative background for what was to follow. In act 2, Nixon was almost as weepy as a contestant on *Queen for a Day*, playing a character that he hoped would be perceived as strong enough to admit to an emotional side. In act 3, Nixon mustered up manliness of a more conventional nature and showed himself to be not only a stalwart, but as committed a team player as Eisenhower could possibly want.

In broader terms, what the performance had demonstrated, and what scores of politicians and other public figures had learned from it and would turn to their own advantages when the need arose, was that television was as malleable as it was powerful; a person could bend it to whatever purpose he desired, and more often than not, at least in the early days, those who watched would themselves bend, precisely in the performer's direction.

Chapter 9

The Third Senator

TELEVISION MADE KEFAUVER A STAR. It made Nixon a viable and eventually victorious vice-presidential candidate. But it would be the unmaking of Joseph McCarthy, the Senator from Wisconsin, whose specialty was a brand of anti-Communism both virulent and irresponsible. McCarthy was as committed to his cause as Kefauver had been to his, but the former's cause was exaggerated and self-centered. Yes, there were Communists in government in those days. And there were Communists in big business, the military and academia; there were Communists in tailor's shops and bookstores and at corner delicatessens, Communists bussing tables and slicing meat and bagging orders to go.

But neither their numbers nor their influence were ever close to what McCarthy claimed they were. People like the Rosenbergs were exceptions, and it is not even clear that *they* made a significant contribution to the Communist movement in general and Soviet military might in particular.

As a result, McCarthy's bluster would eventually overwhelm the dimensions of the small screen on which he continually made his charges. He was as emotional as Nixon had been in act 2 of "Checkers," but his emotions were those of a bully, not a beseecher, and television emphasized his mean-spiritedness no less than it did Nixon's pathos.

It took time, however, for TV to reveal McCarthy as the tyrant he truly was, and before it did, he would accuse the medium itself of providing sanctuary and encouragement to Communists, and would urge his followers to uncover them, to subject those who worked in television to the same standards of overwrought loyalty that the Senator was demanding of people in other occupations. Many of those efforts would be successful, in one case fatally so.

IT ALL STARTED on February 9, 1950, in Wheeling, which was, coincidentally, the same West Virginia city in which Eisenhower and Nixon would publicly make their show of amends two-and-a-half years later. The Senator had been asked to address a women's club on any topic of his choice, and, tired of being ignored by the press since his election to the U.S. Senate in 1946, tired of being a "junior" Senator in the public eye as well as literally, McCarthy determined to make headlines. He chose a subject that was already in the headlines from time to time, and was ripe for more of them.

"While I cannot take the time to name all of the men in the State Department who have been named as members of the Communist Party and members of a spy ring," he told his female listeners, who were properly horrified, "I have here in my hand a list of two hundred and five that were known to the Secretary of State as being members of the Communist Party and who nevertheless are still working and shaping the policy of the State Department."

McCarthy might have said there were eighty-three pinkos in the State Department. He might have said fifty-seven. Or it might actually have been 205. No one recorded his Wheeling speech, and in the weeks and months to come McCarthy would use a variety of figures when he repeated his accusations. He was no more accurate than he was ethical.

Regardless of the total he gave in Wheeling, his speech got him all the media attention he had hoped for, and even more. *At last someone had had the courage to speak out,* his supporters crowed. At last someone had focused the nation's attention where it ought to be, on a threat as grave as any we had faced on foreign battlefields. At last someone had cried wolf as wolves were actually snarling in approach, and thereby alerted his countrymen to the danger that so many refused to see.

McCarthy's Wheeling speech also inspired the publication of a pamphlet called *Red Channels,* a chillingly nonsensical document identified as the work of a group called American Business Consultants. There were, as it turned out, but three of them, former FBI agents already responsible for *Counterattack, the Newsletter of Facts to Combat Communism.* In its wake, fellow McCarthyites suggested that the three men look into Communist infiltration of television. They responded promptly.

Red Channels was distributed to executives at all the networks and, in the words of the *New York Times*'s Jack Gould, it "set off the most shocking panic I've ever seen in my life." Hollywood already had its blacklist in response to the Communist threat; now television had a document of its own to which executives could react with similar cowardice and illogic.

Red Channels was a list of 151 men and women employed in the TV industry who were suspected of either being Communists now or having been Communists in the past or of knowing Communists or of publicly agreeing with at least some of Communism's goals or perhaps even of simply having learned how to spell Communism. Among them were actors, actresses, writers, directors, and producers.

A few examples, which I have abridged greatly from *Red Channels*, follow. The left column reveals the organization, supposedly Communist-inspired, to which the person belonged; the right column tells of the particular nature of his or her offense with regard to the organization, and the publication, not always a reliable one, that cited the offense.

LILLIAN HELLMAN
Playwright, Author

Reported as:

Progressive Citizens of America, National Arts, Sciences and Professions	Participant, Cultural Freedom Conference, 10/25, 26/47. *Daily Worker*, 10, 27, 47, p. 2
National [Henry] Wallace for President Committee	Member. *Daily Worker*, 3/26/48, p. 7.
Progressive Party	Attended three-day conference. *Daily Worker*, 11/16/48, p. 5.
American League for Peace and Democracy	Sponsor, Refugee Scholarship and Peace Campaign, 8/3/39. *House Un-Am. Acct. Com., Appendix 9*, p. 410.

BURL IVES
Folk Singer, Entertainer

	Reported as:
American Friends of the Chinese People	Entertainer. "Stars for China Today." *New Masses*, 11/4/41, p. 30.
People's Songs	Sponsor, *Bulletin of People's Songs*, 9/47. Sent greetings. *Bulletin of People's Songs*, Feb.–March, 1947, p. 19. Member, Advisory Committee and sponsor, *Bulletin of People's Songs*, 2/46; Letterhead, 1948.
Committee for the First Amendment	Speaker. "Hollywood Fights Back" broadcast, 11/2/47. *New York Times*, 11/3/47, p. 19.

GYPSY ROSE LEE
Strip Teaser

	Reported as:
Hollywood Anti-Nazi League	Speaker at meeting. *Red Decade*, Eugene Lyons, 1941, p. 287.
League of American Writers; International Labor Defense	Auctioneer. Benefit Books Auction Sale. *Daily Worker*, 3/8/42, p. 8.

ORSON WELLES
Actor

	Reported as:
American Committee for Protection of Foreign Born	Affiliated. *House Un-Am. Act. Com., Appendix 9*, p. 340.
Artists' Front to Win the War	Presided, meeting Carnegie Hall, 10/16/42. *House Un-Am. Act. Com., Appendix 9*, p. 575.

Joint Anti-fascist Refugee Committee	Sponsor, Dinner "The Century of the Common Man," 10/27/43, Hotel Astor, *House Un-Am. Act. Com.*, *Appendix 9*, p. 942.
Negro Cultural Committee	Member. *House Un-Am. Act. Com.*, *Appendix 9*, p. 1341.
Theatre Arts Committee	Member, Executive Board. *House Un.-Am. Act.Com.*, *Appendix 9*, p. 1539.

The implication of *Red Channels* was as clear as its title. If the TV networks continued to rely on the services of people whom the pamphlet had identified as subversives, no matter how flimsy "the evidence" presented against them, they would be publicly labeled as employers that endorsed the goals of Communism.

A FEW DAYS after *Red Channels* was published, its absurdities suddenly seemed prescient, as reality gave the pamphlet an inadvertent boost. The Korean conflict broke out, and to many it seemed Communist-inspired. Television was not yet able to cover such an event very well; most of its reports consisted of film provided by the military, which had already edited and sanitized it for family viewing, or statements from "talking heads" at the State Department or Pentagon.

Nonetheless, the fighting was a boon for the more zealous of the anti-Communists, as the threat against which they preached now seemed all the greater. Surely the war would lead to more domestic spying. Surely more vigilance than ever before would be required to thwart the traitors. Surely all Americans, in the public sector and private, would have to do their utmost to remain untainted by subversive ideology. How the television industry's hiring practices fit into all this and why the industry needed special guidance from the American Business Consultants was never made clear.

To the men who ran the networks and produced the programs, it did not need to be. They did not ask questions. They did not seek to make sense of the situation. They did not examine the motives of those who had created the situation. Having already honed their skills at obeisance with advertisers, it was second nature for TV executives to prostrate themselves before those with political motives. "Where there's Red smoke there's usually Communist fire," many of them believed, and almost overnight *Red Channels* became the operating bible for television throughout the United States.

CBS began to require a loyalty oath from all its employees. NBC already had one, and continued to enforce it. Only ABC, a distant third in the ratings back then, defied the zeitgeist, as it "refused to look for Reds under its bed, even after the entertainer Gypsy Rose Lee, who hosted her own ABC television show, was named as a Communist . . . After the network resisted demands that she be fired, it received a special Peabody Award in 1951 for 'resisting organized pressure and its reaffirmation of basic American principles.'"

ONE MAN LISTED IN RED CHANNELS, a highly regarded writer named Millard Lampell, suddenly found himself no longer highly regarded, or even employable. "Pal, you're dead," said a friend of his in explaining the sudden change in his fortunes. "I submitted your name for a show and they told me I couldn't touch you with a barge pole." Why? Because he had been a sponsor of the Congress on Civil Rights. Because he had been a sponsor of the Scientific and Cultural Conference for World Peace. Because he had been a member of the advisory council of the People's Radio Foundation. Such affiliations at such a time could not be forgiven.

In fact, Lampell was not dead. He went on to write for the movies under a pseudonym, then, resuming his own name after the Red smoke had been blown away by long-delayed drafts of common sense, he returned to television, winning an Emmy in 1966 and, a decade later, writing the immensely popular miniseries *Rich Man, Poor Man*, based on an Irwin Shaw novel. Lampell lived productively and profitably until 1997.

Others who appeared in *Red Channels* were not so fortunate. Unlike Lampell, they were not even told the reason they were suddenly unemployable. They simply found that their phone calls were not being returned, not even from agents and co-workers they had thought of as friends. Their letters were not being answered, their pleas not being heard; their careers were stalled, and in many cases at an end, for reasons they could only guess.

Or, when they did receive responses, they were told that they had suddenly become the wrong type. The writers did not write the kinds of stories TV was looking for; the actors were too short or tall, too earthy or aristocratic, too forceful or understated; the producers did not have the proper experience for the project at hand.

In the summer of 1950, a few days after the actress Jean Muir had been signed to star in an NBC sitcom called *The Aldrich Family*, she was told that her contract had been canceled. Her name had appeared in *Red Channels*. It could not, therefore, appear in the opening titles of *The Aldrich Family*; neither the network nor the sponsor, General Foods, could afford it. At the time, Muir had never even heard of *Red Channels*.

A woman from Greenwich, Connecticut, named Hester McCullough, a particularly zealous supporter of McCarthy who seemed to have committed the names and felonies listed in *Red Channels* to memory, was one of the first to demand that Muir's contract be invalidated. She called an executive at General Foods to make her position known.

The executive, who might not have been familiar with *Red Channels* yet either, thought the demand unreasonable. "But Mrs. McCullough," he said, "she's just an actress. What harm can she possibly do?"

We do not know Mrs. McCullough's reply, but it was probably something like this: Muir might not be able to do any harm in her role on *The Aldrich Family*, just as writers like Lampell might not be able to do any harm in their scripts for innocuous entertainment programs. That is not the point. The point is that people like Muir and Lampell are being highly paid for their services, and they are donating a portion of that money to further the aims of Communism. American salaries should not fund America's demise. This is why Communists and their sympathizers should not be employed in television, or in fact in any other occupation.

It was the way people like Hester McCullough thought in the early fifties.

What proof was there that Muir was of Communist leaning? According to *Red Channels*, she had once joined scores of other Americans in signing a telegram that congratulated the Moscow Art Theater on its fiftieth anniversary. She had served as vice president of the Congress of American Women. She had contributed money to a publication called the *Negro Quarterly*. Surely nothing more was needed to call Jean Muir's patriotism into question.

Finally, General Foods was forced to yield. In explaining its decision to fire Muir, the company, in effect, explained nothing. It admitted that it had made no attempt to investigate the charges in *Red Channels*. It had made no attempt to enquire into Muir's background and character and past behavior. The fact that the charges had been made was enough. The best role of Muir's career was no longer hers.

Another name that appeared in *Red Channels* was Philip Loeb, a long-time Broadway actor who also had a part in a program sponsored by General Foods. He was Jake, one of the title characters in the CBS sitcom *The Goldbergs*. But when not acting he had signed a press release for the Council for Pan-American Democracy, had spoken at a rally of the Stop Censorship Committee, had served as a member of the Executive Board of the Theatre Arts Committee, and had joined many others in donating time and money to the End Jim Crow in Baseball Committee.

General Foods wanted Loeb fired. CBS refused. Since the show was a successful one, General Foods did not insist, nor did it threaten to withdraw its support. But it was not happy, even though Sanka Coffee, a General Foods product, had seen its sales increase fifty-seven percent since it became *The Goldberg*'s primary sponsor.

Even less happy were the Hester McCulloughs of the world, who were breeding like bunnies. They could not believe that CBS would dare to defy them. The network was a virtual satellite of the Soviet Union, the Hesters claimed. The pressure mounted, the volume increased, both in terms of the number of complaints and their decibel level.

Finally it all became too much. CBS not only dismissed Loeb, but canceled the series, despite the fact that *The Goldbergs* was one of its top-rated shows.

To NBC, it was an unforeseen gift. The network immediately picked up *The Goldbergs* and began enjoying the ratings on its own bottom line. But NBC was not as courageous as it seemed. It no longer allowed General Foods to sponsor the program and no longer included Philip Loeb in the cast. His absence was lamented by the *New Republic*, which pointed out that viewers "may detect a note of sadness in the popular comedy program of Jewish humor—Philip Loeb, who so aptly played the part of soft-spoken Pa (Jake) Goldberg, has left the family."

Loeb tried to find work on other TV shows, but could not. He tried radio: no luck there, either. He auditioned for roles in theater. He was able to get a few jobs at first, but would on occasion be harassed by members of the audience during performances. They booed his appearance onstage, hissed at him, called him predictable names. Some people even made a show of standing up and walking out of the building as he started reciting his lines, and in fact had probably come to the theater for precisely that reason. Soon Loeb became an outcast here too, so much so that, not only did he not get roles anymore; he was not even permitted to audition.

Philip Loeb put up with the ostracism as long as he could. But he was struggling now to pay his rent, to afford three meals a day, to hang onto the vestiges not of his career, which was gone, but of his sanity. That, too, seemed destined to desert him. Eventually a few hopeful signs appeared on the horizon, hints of employment, of less acrimony for his views, but Loeb could not believe in them, especially since he was still unable to pay his bills.

One day, shortly after the last rejection he could abide, he poured himself a glass of water, emptied a bottle of sleeping pills into his mouth, and washed them down in a single gulp. He was found dead in his apartment the following morning. He did not leave a note. He did not have to.

ONLY A FEW PEOPLE accused of subversive activities were able to escape unharmed from the storm whose epicenter was *Red Channels*. One of them was Lucille Ball, who did not actually appear in the publication but who, like all performers of the time, was subject to the same mania. When it was learned that she had registered as a Communist in 1936, actually attached her name to the party's membership roster, the sponsor of her program, Philip Morris cigarettes, panicked. The company did not want to sever its relationship with *I Love Lucy*, but neither did it want to be tarred as an agent of the Soviet menace.

The company panicked all the more, as did CBS, when the dreaded and almost entirely unreliable House Committee on Un-American Activities (HUAC), referred to as a source in so many of the *Red Channels* accusations, took an interest in the matter and decided to investigate Ball.

But it did not investigate for long. Ball was cleared by HUAC (the anagram rearranged for easier pronunciation) after a few days when one of its members somehow determined that, although the charge was true and the comedienne really had declared herself a Communist, she had done so only to please her grandfather in the last days of his life. Ball's declaration did not represent her true political sympathies. Her grandfather having passed away many years earlier, Ball had promptly quit the Party. Just as promptly, HUAC declared the comedienne no longer under suspicion.

She never should have been. Since *I Love Lucy* was the top-rated show on television at the time and its star was making a fortune from it, and was in the process of making an even bigger fortune from Desilu, the company that she and her husband had formed to produce other programs, her capitalistic inclinations were beyond question.

In fact, before filming of one of the *I Love Lucy* shows, Lucy and Desi, as was their custom, came out on set to greet the studio audience, and Desi introduced his wife as "my favorite redhead." Then he said, "That's the only thing red about Lucy—and even that is not legitimate."

As far as I have been able to determine, Joe McCarthy never commented on the Lucille Ball case, nor on the cases of Lampell, Muir, Loeb, or any of the other victims of *Red Channels*. That he was, however, pleased with the publication, with the perseverance of those who sought to eliminate Communist influence from the television business, he made clear on several occasions, praising his partisans for their unceasing dedication to the truest of American ideals.

ON MARCH 9, 1954, McCarthy's fellow Republican, Vermont Senator Ralph Flanders, who could not by the stretch of anyone's imagination have been considered soft on Communism, and who would later introduce a resolution calling for the Senate to censure McCarthy for behavior unbecoming to the senior chamber, decided he had had enough of his colleague. He accused him of distracting the United States from "dangerous problems" abroad by concentrating on threats at home, which Flanders thought were much overstated. He also claimed that McCarthy was "doing his best to shatter the Republican Party" by his methods, and his mindless zeal in pursuing them.

It was a scathing indictment from one Republican to another, and enough, all by itself, to make March 9 a bad day for McCarthy. But it would get worse. A few hours after Flanders's denunciation, Edward R. Murrow would devote his entire CBS News program *See It Now* to McCarthy, a program, according to one source, that "demonstrated that the medium of television could serve as a powerful independent force with the ability to affect national politics even beyond a national election."

Murrow said little during the thirty minutes. Most of that night's *See It Now* consisted of film clips, with McCarthy doing the talking. In one of them he savaged the Democratic Party for "twenty years of treason." He continued: "The hard fact is—the hard fact is that those who wear the label, those who wear the label *Democrat*, wear it with the stain of a historic betrayal."

In another clip, McCarthy was shown in action before the Senate's Permanent Subcommittee for Investigations, which he headed and which was the forum for most of his anti-Soviet diatribes. His witness on this occasion was U.S. Army General Ralph Zwicker, whom McCarthy berated for having promoted to the rank of major an Army dentist named Irving Peress. Peress may or may not have been a Communist or a Communist sympathizer; there was little in the way of evidence one way or the other. But his military record was unblemished and, as far as anyone knew, his dentistry was above reproach.

Furthermore, it was not General Zwicker's idea to promote Peress; the promotion was automatic after the dentist had spent a certain amount of time in the service and Zwicker, in signing the promotion papers, was only following long-instituted procedures.

None of it mattered to the senator from Wisconsin. Zwicker was "not fit to wear that uniform," McCarthy charged, and Peress, who had since been honorably discharged from the Army, should be made to sign up again so that he could be court-martialed.

The *See It Now* clip continued:

MCCARTHY: Nothing is more serious than a traitor to this country [Peress] in the Communist conspiracy. Question: Do you think stealing $50 is more serious than being a traitor to the country and a part of the Communist conspiracy?

ZWICKER: That [the decision to promote Peress], sir, was not my decision.

MCCARTHY: Shall we go into that for a while? . . . I think it is a tremendous disgrace to the Army to bring these facts before the public but I intend to give it to the public, General. . . . And wait till you hear the bleeding hearts scream and cry about our methods of trying to drag the truth from those who know, or should know, who covered up a Fifth Amendment Communist Major. But they say, "Oh, it's all right to uncover them, but don't get rough doing it, McCarthy."

Murrow had introduced the *See It Now* segment about the controversy over Zwicker by playing a few words on the matter from Senator Flanders. "He dons war paint," Flanders said of McCarthy; "he goes into his war dance; he emits his war whoops; he goes forth to battle and proudly returns with the scalp of a pink Army dentist."

Other clips in the program included one of McCarthy accusing Adlai Stevenson of being a Communist, which he was not, and another of his asserting that the American Civil Liberties Union had officially been listed as a Communist front organization, which had never happened.

Murrow concluded that night's *See It Now* himself. "The actions of the junior Senator from Wisconsin," he said, "have caused alarm and dismay amongst our allies abroad, and given considerable comfort to our enemies. And whose fault is that? Not really his. He didn't create this situation of fear; he merely exploited it—and rather successfully. Cassius was right. 'The fault, dear Brutus, is not in our stars, but in ourselves.'

"Good night and good luck."

THE FOLLOWING WEEK'S EDITION of *See It Now* was again devoted to McCarthy's crusade against Communism, this time as allegedly practiced by a mild-mannered black woman named Annie Lee Moss, employed at the Pentagon as a communications clerk. In that position, according to McCarthy, Moss had access to top-secret documents. The Army corrected him; she had no such access, handling only encoded messages that she could not read.

Nonetheless, McCarthy called Moss before his subcommittee, accusing her of having been a member of the Communist party in the mid-1940s, and having subscribed to the party newspaper, the *Daily Worker*.

McCarthy left the interrogation of Moss to the subcommittee's chief counsel, Roy Cohn, who conducted it precisely as his boss had instructed him to. Cohn asked Moss about Karl Marx. She did not know who that was. What about her subscription to the *Daily Worker?* Cohn wanted to know. Moss said she never had one. And when Cohn stated that a well-known Communist named Rob Hall had come to see Moss at her home, the subcommittee's minority counsel, Robert F. Kennedy, had to correct him. It was a different Rob Hall who had visited her. The Communist by that name was white; Moss's guest one evening had been a black man named Rob Hall who worked as a union organizer and had never been formally accused of subversive activity.

There were several bursts of applause from those who attended the hearing in favor of Moss. There were none in favor of McCarthy and his henchmen.

MANY OF THE PEOPLE who watched the two Murrow programs had either seen the film excerpts before, when they appeared on news programs or in newsreels, or had read the quotes in newspapers. But there was something about the way that they had been edited together, one immediately following the other, that demonstrated more clearly than ever the unrelenting nature of McCarthy's vituperation, thus making the whole of his anti-Communist campaign seem greater, and more irrational, than the sum of its parts.

But it was not just what he said. It was not just how he said it. This was television, after all, and as McCarthy spoke he presented a picture as sinister as his words. He scowled almost constantly, and the few times he didn't he curled his lips up into a reluctant kind of smile that was cold and mirthless, revealing his zealousness no less than did the scowl. His cheeks, on occasion, sagged into the shadows of his jaw and chin. He did not, at moments like these, seem just an opponent of Communism; he seemed an opponent of humankind.

To some people it was a fair portrait of the man. But others, including several enemies of McCarthy, were troubled. Murrow was a respected journalist and McCarthy a damaging public figure. But what if, at some point in the future, a less responsible journalist than Murrow decided to present an unflattering program about a more responsible legislator than McCarthy? If the power of television could be used to uncover tyranny, couldn't it also be used by people with lower ethical standards than Murrow to further an unjust cause, to advance the personal agenda of the newsman to the detriment of truth and fairness? Could a reporter one day be a demagogue no less than an unscrupulous government official?

To thoughtful viewers of TV, the *See It Now* episodes on McCarthy were as troubling in principle as they were commendable in their specifics.

SEE IT NOW was sponsored by Alcoa, which had its reservations about the program's taking on McCarthy but decided to stand behind it regardless, without trying to influence its content. No one from Alcoa saw a script of the McCarthy sound bites in advance or sat in on the editing of the episodes.

CBS, however, had not been nearly so courageous. It made a deliberate attempt to lessen the impact of the shows by lessening their audiences, refusing to take ads in any newspapers, as it usually did for *See It Now*. As a result, Murrow and his producer, Fred Friendly, paid for ads out of their own pockets. It was, however, money well spent. The audiences for the two shows were large ones, and some of their members, most notably those with public forums of their own, were inspired to break their silence and express reservations about McCarthy.

There was, as historian Richard M. Fried writes, "Chicago Bishop Bernard Sheil's speech in April, excoriating his fellow Catholic [McCarthy]. In Wisconsin, a small-town Republican newspaper editor surprised his readers by launching a bold, but ultimately futile, 'Joe Must Go' movement to recall McCarthy from the Senate. The Senate Republican Policy Committee revealed its own concerns about McCarthy by undertaking a formal study of the rules of procedure for investigating committees."

Thousands of people wrote to CBS denouncing McCarthy, and print journalists other than just the editor in Wisconsin went on the attack, insinuating that McCarthy was a liar, a slanderer, a threat to the very American values that he claimed were being threatened by others. There would be, these reporters and columnists and editors knew, a firestorm of response from the Senator and his supporters. They told themselves they could withstand it.

It wasn't easy. The McCarthyites were inexhaustible in expressing their outrage. They wrote hate mail to newsmen, and in a few instances to their families, sometimes vowing to seek revenge. In a few cases, they issued the threats in person, a McCarthy supporter running into an anti-McCarthy journalist in a public place and the two of them almost coming to blows. The McCarthy supporters took out ads and issued press releases that labeled Murrow a paid Communist agent, claiming that they had proof of his affiliation although never revealing it. They tried to organize a boycott of CBS, which had now become to them, despite its loyalty oath, *the Communist Broadcasting System*. They vowed that henceforth they would watch only NBC, ABC, and the Dumont network, the latter of which would cease to exist in another two years.

As for McCarthy himself, he was so upset by the *See It Now* broadcast that he demanded time from the network for a rebuttal. CBS gave it to him in early April, an entire half-hour of his own, and McCarthy could not have used it more poorly. In that brash, thoughtless, and perhaps even alcohol-fueled manner of his, he only succeeded in stirring further resentment against himself, and making Americans wonder all the more about his veracity. Although he was reading from a script, there were a few times when he seemed mystified about what charge to make next; at virtually all times his comments were irrelevant to the Murrow program to which he was ostensibly responding.

"You know," he said at the beginning, "it's interesting to note that the viciousness of Murrow's attacks is in direct ratio to our success in digging out Communists. Now ordinarily, ordinarily, I would not take time out from the important work at hand to answer Murrow. However, in this case I feel justified in doing so because Murrow is a symbol, the leader, and the cleverest of the jackal pack which is always found at the throat of anyone who dares to expose individual Communists and traitors."

But for the most part, Murrow had not criticized McCarthy on his program, viciously or otherwise. He had merely let McCarthy speak for himself, with two or three clips, like the one from Flanders, playing in opposition. And although McCarthy might have exposed a few individual Communists and traitors in the early fifties, most of them known for their treachery long before being named by the Senator, few of the accusations he made could be verified, only measured in terms of the damage they did to innocent men and women.

Murrow once again granted himself the last word. He commented on McCarthy's charges on *See It Now* the following week, but briefly. "He proved again," the newsman said of the Senator, "that anyone who exposes him, anyone who does not share his hysterical disregard for decency and human dignity and the rights guaranteed by the Constitution must be either a Communist or a fellow traveler. I fully expected this treatment."

Then in the same month, April 1954, the most trying month in the Senator's life to date, television established another early landmark for itself, beginning to broadcast the Army–McCarthy hearings.

THE SENATE Permanent Subcommittee for Investigations would conduct the proceedings. Again, Cohn would serve as chief counsel. He was "a hazel-eyed dynamo type with deceptively sleepy eyelids, carefully slicked hair . . . a man of extraordinary talents." And a man who suited McCarthy's interests perfectly. He was a Jew, so that no one could accuse the Senator of anti-Semitism, as some had done in the past; and, like the Senator, he was tenaciously self-promoting in his anti-Communism.

The problem was that Cohn had a friend. His name was G. David Schine, and he was "the golden boy, laid-back and intellectually lazy, a son of privilege, content to coast on his lucky lineage." There were allegations of a homosexual relationship at the time, and there have been allegations since. There has never been any proof.

But when Schine was drafted into the Army, Cohn lost control of himself in a manner that suggested his feelings for Schine were stronger than mere fellowship. He cursed, pounded desktops, kicked waste baskets and furniture legs and radiators. He was incensed that he and his friend would now be separated, and threatened to "wreck the Army" if it dared to send Schine overseas.

Instead, Schine was assigned to Fort Dix, New Jersey, meaning that, with Cohn spending almost all of his time in New York and Washington, Schine had conveniently been situated right in the middle, as accessible as a soldier could be to a civilian desperate for his company. Cohn complained to McCarthy, who was fond of Schine in his own right. He had previously employed the young man as a member of his staff and allowed him, in Cohn's company, to make a number of unnecessary and expensive trips at taxpayers' expense to investigate alleged Communist influences in U.S. libraries both at home and abroad. The two young terrors enjoyed themselves immensely. They didn't find any Commie literature, but nonetheless ordered libraries to get rid of books by such authors as Mark Twain, Theodore Dreiser, Ernest Hemingway, John Steinbeck, and Sinclair Lewis. It was such a lark! The maliciousness of Cohn and Schine far exceeded their maturity.

McCarthy, too, was upset that Uncle Sam wanted Schine. He claimed the Army drafted the young man simply to spite him because he, McCarthy, had been so hard on General Zwicker in the Peress case.

The Army's counter charges were more restrained, not to mention more accurate. A spokesman for the top brass accused McCarthy and Cohn of trying—and succeeding—to obtain special treatment for Schine. As William Manchester pointed out, "Unlike other recruits, Schine was given a pass almost every weekend. His limousine was allowed inside the camp to pick him up and bring him back. He was released from drill for no fewer than 250 long-distance phone calls. One rainy day, when everybody else was on the rifle range, Company K's commander found Private Schine goldbricking. Schine threw a comradely arm over the captain's shoulder and explained that he had been studying logistics 'to remake the military along modern lines'—an excuse which actually was accepted."

But McCarthy and Cohn were still furious. They continued to insist that their boy was being mistreated at Fort Dix. His mattress was lumpy or his food inedible or his boots didn't fit and he had to polish them himself, which of course all soldiers did—something, anything, everything. They called

Schine's superiors, demanding his release from duty on a variety of occasions for thoroughly nonsensical reasons: he was needed for this, needed for that; he was the only person in the Western Hemisphere who could carry out a mission crucial to national security—a mission the details of which, of course, McCarthy and Cohn were not at liberty to reveal.

When their demands were not heeded, the two men accused Army officials of misusing their power and conducting a personal vendetta to the detriment of the security of the United States and all the citizens thereof.

At this point the Army declined further response.

Finally, McCarthy decided to act. He ordered his subcommittee to look into the Army's treatment of Schine. This would hardly have been reason enough for hearings, despite McCarthy's bile, but he went further, hinting at Communist shenanigans in the military that Schine, McCarthy claimed, would be rooting out if his superior officers were not sabotaging him. It was a serious charge, very serious. It was also the biggest mistake McCarthy ever made.

SINCE THE SENATOR was himself a principal in the case and would be a witness, he had to turn the chairmanship of the subcommittee over to someone else for the hearings. That someone was Karl Mundt, a Republican from South Dakota who had joined Richard Nixon in co-sponsoring a bill to require all Communists living in the United States to register with the government, and to forbid them from holding public office. No slouch he, when it came to keeping pinkos in their place.

Cohn, too, had to step aside so that he could be interrogated, and the committee's chief counsel for the hearings was a young attorney from Tennessee named Ray Jenkins, handpicked by Cohn and, like him, an angry young Turk eager to ride McCarthy's coattails to fame.

Representing the Army, from the prestigious Boston law firm of Hale and Dorr, was an older man of entirely different nature. Joseph Welch's courtroom costume never varied: "conservative suit, little bow tie, an inevitable vest." His manner never varied either. "He appeared at times almost sleepy and indifferent," according to McCarthy biographer Fred J. Cook, "and he spoke in tones deceptively dulcet. It was all a camouflage; it gave to what he said the effect of a delayed time fuse."

The hearings were televised live on both ABC and Dumont. "CBS," according to intellectual historian Susan Jacoby, "fearful of losing revenue through the preemption of its popular daytime soap operas, declined to cover the hearings at all. NBC opted out early on, when it became clear that there was no drama to be had in the initial sessions. In their fifteen-minute evening news programs, both CBS and NBC presented snippets of the hearings, edited from ABC's live broadcasts."

ABC and Dumont hoped for an audience as large as the one that the Kefauver hearings had gotten. They did not quite make it. But just as Frank Costello's folded hands had provided an exhibition that neither viewers nor the history books would ever forget, so would the Army–McCarthy hearings, and by the time it happened, the audience would be much larger than it had been at the outset.

That exhibition, however, was many days in coming. Although the hearings were supposed to focus on the whether or not the Army was harboring Soviet agents, and whether or not Private G. David Schine was being hindered in his attempts to probe the matter, they did not start out that way. McCarthy was the first person to testify and Jenkins the first to question him. The chief counsel began by ignoring the hearings' focus and giving McCarthy carte blanche for his ravings, just as he had been told to do by his boss.

"Now," Jenkins said to the Senator, "while you have an audience of perhaps twenty or thirty million Americans . . . I want you to tell what each individual American man, woman, and child can do . . . to do their bit to liquidate the Communist party."

And off went McCarthy as he so often did, finding Communists in all sorts of unlikely places and railing at those who allowed them to continue with their nefarious schemes, so few of which seemed to come to fruition, to endanger the United States. It was familiar material. Perhaps too familiar. For the first time it seemed as if McCarthy's charges were aging, turning over-ripe, and in various news reports it became obvious that at least some viewers were becoming impatient, even suspicious. They wanted McCarthy to get to the point. It was one thing for him to accuse the State Department of being infested with Communists; what better cover could there be for a spy, what better source of information? It was one thing to accuse academia; after all, it was filled with effete Harvard and Yale types who had been born on the far fringes of liberalism and only drifted further to the left in their Ivy League classrooms. It was one thing to accuse show business; it was filled with men and women who, having never grown up, lacked the substance to see Communism for the peril that it really was.

But the Army? Communist infiltration at the highest levels among the very men who had fought so valiantly and recently in World War II and Korea, men who had risked their lives to *protect* us from both totalitarianism and Communism? It didn't seem possible. In fact, some journalists, even those who had previously taken McCarthy's side, were now suggesting that the Senator might have gone too far this time, and as a result, that his entire credibility might well rest on the hearings now underway. If McCarthy was right about subversives riddling the Army, Americans were probably not safe no matter what they did or upon whom they depended. But if he was wrong about the Army, perhaps he had been wrong about his other accusations, and the Communist menace was hyperbole from the beginning. McCarthy, then, would turn out to have been not a guardian of true democratic ways but a pompous fraud.

After several weeks of testimony, McCarthy himself provided the cue for the unforgettable moment.

ATTORNEY JOSEPH WELCH had the floor. Attorney Roy Cohn was on the stand. The subject was the manner in which McCarthy's subcommittee normally went about its business of inquiring into treasonous activity.

> WELCH: Mr. Cohn, tell me once more: Every time you learn of a Communist, or a spy anywhere, is it your policy to get them out as fast as possible?
>
> COHN: Surely, we want them out as fast as possible, sir.
>
> WELCH: And whenever you learn of one from now on, Mr. Cohn, will you tell somebody about them quick?
>
> COHN: Mr. Welch, with great respect, I work for the committee here. . . . If they are displeased with the speed with which I and the group of men who work with me proceed . . . I am sure they will give me appropriate instructions along those lines, and I will follow any which they give me.
>
> WELCH: May I add my small voice, sir, and say whenever you know about a subversive or a Communist spy, please hurry. Will you remember those words?

At this point McCarthy interrupted. He did not like the approach Welch was taking. Although Cohn did not seem to realize it, Welch was toying with him, belittling the magnitude of the problems with which the subcommittee dealt. Soon, McCarthy feared, Welch would become even more overt, making jokes at the subcommittee's expense, poking fun at the rationale for its very existence. McCarthy decided not only to stop the old man from Boston, but to put him on the defensive.

> MCCARTHY: [I]n view of Mr. Welch's request that the information be given once we know of anyone who might be performing any work for the Communist Party, I think we should tell him that he has in his law firm a young man named Fisher . . . who has been for a number of years a member of an organization which was named, oh, years and years ago, as the legal bulwark of the Communist Party, an organization which always swings to the defense of anyone who dares to expose Communists.

Fred Fisher was the lawyer to whom McCarthy referred. The Lawyers Guild was the organization, and not only was McCarthy's characterization of it exaggerated, but Fisher no longer belonged to it, having quit the group when he learned of its reputation in right-wing circles. Fisher was a skilled and dedicated attorney, and Welch had originally intended for him to play a key role in these hearings. Then he changed his mind. He decided it would be better for Fisher not to be in the same room with McCarthy, that there was no telling what McCarthy would make of Fisher's former ties with the Guild, even though they had nothing to do with the matters at hand.

Cohn tried to get McCarthy's attention, to signal him to be quiet; he sensed there was danger down the path his mentor was taking, although he could not have said exactly why. McCarthy, however, was a locomotive under a full head of steam.

"Jim," the Senator said to an aide, "will you get the news story to the effect that this man [Fisher] belonged to this Communist-front organization? Will you get the citations showing that this was the legal arm of the Communist Party, and the length of time that he belonged, and the fact that he was recommended by Mr. Welch? I think that should be in the record."

Cohn shook his head. McCarthy either did not see or did not care.

Welch decided not to regain the floor, not immediately. He allowed McCarthy to continue to rant, although, "obviously desolate, [Welch] sat with his head in his hands" as he maintained his silence.

When McCarthy finally finished, there was the unmistakable smile of a victor on his face, even though his eyes flitted about the hearing room uncertainly. Welch allowed the smile to remain in place for several seconds, then sat in place and tented his fingers on the table in front of him. He stood. In an even quieter voice than usual, he began to speak, and so devastatingly effective was he that he "went on to a career in minor television acting roles and as host of a TV series." He was not, however, playing a part now.

"Until this moment, Senator, I think I never really gauged your cruelty or your recklessness. Fred Fisher is a young man who went to the Harvard Law School and came into my firm and is starting what looks to be a brilliant career with us. . . . Little did I dream that you could be so reckless and cruel as to do an injury to that lad. It is, I regret to say . . . true that I fear he shall always bear a scar needlessly inflicted by you. If it were in my power to forgive your reckless cruelty, I will do so. I like to think I am a gentleman, but your forgiveness will have to come from someone other than me."

At this point McCarthy, simply unable to read the moment, tried to start in on Fisher yet again, but Welch would not permit him. His patience had been exhausted, although he conveyed sadness more than anger.

WELCH: Senator, may we not drop this? We know he belonged to the Lawyers Guild, and Mr. Cohn nods his head at me. I did you, I think, no personal injury, Mr. Cohn.

COHN: No, sir.

WELCH: I meant to do you no personal injury, and if I did, beg your pardon. Let us not assassinate this lad further, Senator. You have done enough. Have you no sense of decency, sir, at long last? Have you no sense of decency?

It was, of course, a question the Senator could not answer. Nor was he meant to. Rather, the question was meant to hang in the air and, like a shroud of some sort, descend slowly over McCarthy's shoulders. And that is precisely what it did.

After a few moments, Welch wrapped up his interrogation of Cohn, but his final words were just a winding down. His remarks about McCarthy's decency were his real conclusion. He told Mundt he was finished with the witness and the chairman could call the next one.

But he did not. Most of the men and women in the hearing room were clapping and muttering their approval to one another, and Mundt was not about to ask another witness to follow Welch's act. More surprisingly, he did not gavel the proceedings to order. The commotion, with Mundt's tacit approval, continued. It has been reported that six policemen were in the courtroom, under instructions to evict anyone who disrupted the hearing. None of them moved.

After a few minutes, the room began to empty. Some reporters had already departed, rushing to make their deadlines; others, with hours yet before their accounts were due, proceeded slowly, discussing what they had just heard, certain that it was the lead story for the next edition of their respective papers, perhaps even the biggest news that McCarthy, however inadvertently, had yet made. Men and women who were not journalists brought up the rear of the initial wave of those exiting, some silently, some whispering to one another, all of them aware that they had been witnesses to an event of enduring significance.

The television technicians were the last to leave, unplugging their wires and winding them up and putting away their equipment for the day, seeming to be in no hurry.

McCarthy was still there as they did. He sat alone. No one talked to him, not Cohn or Mundt, who had already walked out of the room without acknowledging him, nor any of the TV people, who did not pay him any attention as they wrapped up their extension cords and stowed their gear in its cases. McCarthy's scowl was deeper than ever, but it was befuddlement that he showed now more than anger, dread more than malice. He held out his hands, palms up.

"What did I do?" he asked.

The TV people did not answer.

THERE WOULD BE another six days of testimony from a variety of witnesses, but for all practical purposes, the show was now over. It was estimated that eighty million Americans saw at least some of the Army–McCarthy hearings, and a great number of them no longer felt as warm and fuzzy about the Senator from Wisconsin as they once had.

Neither did his fellow legislators. Later that year, Flanders introduced his motion to censure McCarthy and the Senate passed it by a vote of 67 to 22. By that time, McCarthy, who had long been a heavy drinker, had turned into an alcoholic. The days, so hard to face, seemed easier with a drink in the morning, another after lunch, one or two with dinner, and a nightcap to blot out thoughts of what tomorrow might be like.

On April 28, 1957, McCarthy was admitted to Bethesda Naval Hospital with severe liver problems. On May 2, at the age of forty-eight, he died. The cause of death was listed as "hepatitis, acute, cause unknown," although *Time* reported "unequivocably" that the Senator had died of cirrhosis of the liver. As was the custom, flags on all government buildings, including the White House, were flown at half-mast, and some of the TV newscasts that night showed pictures of them waving on their poles while the anchormen read their obituaries.

As for newspaper coverage, most of it was as respectful and objective as the obit writers could make it: conventional biographies of the man and his career, laced with a few references, nonjudgmental in most cases, to the tumult he had created. To read between the lines, however, was to discern a much more negative message.

Only one newspaper varied wildly from the pattern, and it was to be expected. Like McCarthy himself on so many occasions, the editors of the preposterously right-wing *Manchester* [New Hampshire] *Union Leader* had decided to charge conspiracy. And *what* a conspiracy! The charge was revealed in bold-faced type, all capital letters, with the subject's name inexplicably misspelled. The headline of the editorial was MURDERED!

M'CARTHY WAS MURDERED BY THE COMMUNISTS BECAUSE HE WAS EXPOSING THEM. WHEN HE BEGAN TO AROUSE THE UNITED STATES TO THE EXTENT OF THE COMMUNIST CONSPIRACY IN OUR GOVERN-MENT, IN OUR SCHOOLS, IN OUR NEWSPAPERS, AND IN ALL BRANCH-ES OF AMERICAN LIFE. THE COMMUNIST PARTY REALIZED THAT IF IT WAS TO SURVIVE AND SUCCEED IN ITS CONSPIRACY TO SEIZE CONTROL OF THE UNITED STATES, IT HAD TO DESTROY M'CARTHY BEFORE HE DESTROYED THE PARTY.

THREE SENATORS. Three men who served their country at what was almost the highest level. One of them became famous accidentally because of TV. Another became vindicated, although many thought at the expense of his dignity, because of TV. The third became notorious, unaware of the impression he was making on TV until it was too late to do anything about it.

What the three men had in common was that they had brought television into politics in such a way that the two would never be separate again.

It was left to another person to bring the medium into the political process in an entirely different, and ultimately more important, manner. This person outranked the Senators, and although his relationship with TV would never be more than ambivalent at best, he became the intermediary between what politics had been when Philo T. Farnsworth invented the tube, and what it would become in the second half of the twentieth century and into the twenty-first because of his invention.

Chapter 10

Advertising for President

DWIGHT EISENHOWER wanted to be elected. He did not want to be sold. He wanted people to vote for him for president in 1952 because of what they already knew about him, and because of what they would learn during the campaign in carefully crafted speeches that he would deliver before large audiences of friendly Republicans at expensive venues. He did not want people to vote for him because of the impression he made in television commercials, which was how people decided what brand of hair oil to use or what detergent to wash their clothes in. He was a man, not a product; his strength was his character, his ideas, not his personality or packaging. He should appeal to the electorate as Truman and FDR and others before them had done. Dwight Eisenhower was a man of the past, born in Abilene, Kansas, in the previous century, and it was in the past, he believed, that virtue resided.

But Eisenhower was seeking the nation's highest office in the present, in some ways even the future, and as he would discover from his running mate's explanation of his slush fund, as well as from the counsel of staff members and various television executives of Republican leanings, the new medium was making politics into something it had never been before. It was changing the rules, changing the procedures, changing them in fundamental ways—and it was doing so because of its ability to change the minds of those who watched it. Before Nixon's speech that night in September 1952, hundreds of thousands of Americans thought him dishonest. After the speech, many of those same people wanted to vote for him for the second highest elective office in the land.

But even before that, Eisenhower knew what a force television had become. Or should have known. His name had not even appeared on the ballot for the nation's initial primary in New Hampshire, but he won it anyway, as a write-in candidate. He owed the victory, at least in part, to NBC and CBS, which televised much of the campaigning in New Hampshire, including that done on Eisenhower's behalf. It was the first time the New Hampshire primary had been exaggerated into a story of national importance, and the result was that Ike's victory there virtually ensured his victory in other primaries. He was on his way to the nomination despite his noncandidacy. Television had given him his send-off and he had not even actively sought its assistance.

But could he be himself on TV if he were doing advertisements for the election? That was the question he asked himself as the primaries marched along. Yes, he was assured by the members of his staff, he could still be Ike from Abilene on the tube, could still be the man he had always been. But to ensure victory in November he would have to make his peace, his compromises, with technology. "Television personalities are likely to be the politicians of the future," *New York Herald Tribune* TV critic John Crosby had written in 1951. Eisenhower's advisers told him he had no choice now but to make himself such a personality, especially after the first few campaign ads he filmed were rejected by the agency that had produced them. Eisenhower was too stiff, too formal, his appearance more that of a drillmaster than a candidate for public office. The challenge was to find someone who could mold the man into a television-friendly shape while still allowing himself to be true to the person he really was.

Enter Rosser Reeves, Madison Avenue mahatma and possessor of enough self-confidence for a score of selves. At first, he did not seem a likely choice for an Eisenhower confidante, and both Reeves and the Texas oilmen who introduced him to Ike were wary of the candidate's response. They were right to be. Eisenhower was polite to Reeves, but never particularly warmed to him, despite the latter's oft-pronounced veneration for Ike and his public denunciations of Communism.

In fact, most people in Reeves's field had not warmed to him. He was respected but not admired, someone who got results, not plaudits; a man who not only thought highly of himself but often denigrated those who dared to question him. Reeves had his way of doing things, and believed in it to the point of megalomania. The purpose of advertisements was not to "reassure, entertain, or educate"; rather, "he argued that they should exist only to communicate the slogan."

And Reeves was a master at slogans. He could reduce any idea, any impression, to a bite-size morsel. His most famous slogan, still in use today, was for M&M's candy-covered chocolates, which he claimed would "melt in your mouth, not in your hand." It was true, but only if you did not hold them too long or squeeze too tightly while standing in a well-heated place.

Reeves was also known for the commercials he created for Anacin, which contained "the pain reliever doctors recommend most." What the slogan did not say was that the pain reliever was aspirin, which was not only Anacin's primary ingredient but the product that was its main competitor.

Many people found the Anacin ads, repeated almost hourly it seemed, "grating and annoying." But they drove the message home, drove it relentlessly, with the result that sales of Anacin tripled while the Reeves ads were running. He also increased cigarette sales by producing commercials in which actors dressed up as doctors and assured viewers that the product smoked smoothly, that it drew easily, that it was beneficial to the consumer's health and well-being. "All the tars and nicotine trapped in the filter are guaranteed not to reach your throat," one of Reeves's actors recited.

And now for his toughest assignment yet—trying to persuade one of America's most beloved public figures and greatest military heroes, a man used to giving advice, not taking it, and a man who did not want any part of campaign ads in the first place, to put his trust in someone for whom advertising was an art form: communication, carefully controlled, at its most basic and effective level, if not necessarily its most honest.

Granted an audience with Eisenhower and the people he trusted most, Reeves outlined his plan. He believed that in keeping not only with his own ideas about influencing people, but with the reputation for efficiency that the general had developed as a man of war, the ads for his presidency should be short and to the point. Actually, he wanted them to be short and to a lot of points.

Reeves proposed doing several different kinds of endorsements for the candidate. One of them, of course, would emphasize Eisenhower's military record, using film clips from his most triumphant moments of World War II. Ben Shapiro writes about one such ad:

> The narrator informs us, "Now another crucial hour in our history—the big question. . . ." And we cut to a younger man asking Ike directly, "General, if war comes, is this country really ready?" Ike, looking dead into the camera, sternly and indignantly growls, "It is not. The [Truman] administration has spent many billions of dollars for national defense. Yet today we haven't enough tanks for the fighting in Korea. It is time for a change."

But for the most part, this kind of endorsement was too conventional for Reeves. He wanted to do something different, and decided that the keystone of the campaign should be a series of spots introduced by an announcer in basso profundo who says, "Eisenhower Answers America." Then an ordinary citizen appears on camera, looking upscreen to the left, and asks a question. Cut to Ike looking downscreen to the right and answering it. Simple as that: one question, one response—the ads would run ten, fifteen, maybe twenty seconds. Not enough time for viewers to get bored, not even long enough for an M&M to get soft, much less melt.

Reeves had originally wanted to produce fifty such ads, but because of time constraints had to settle for twenty-two. Time constraints was, in this case, a euphemism for Eisenhower's impatience; he had no idea how long it would take him to record the responses to fifty questions, but that it was more time than he wanted to spend he had no doubt. Even twenty-two struck him as too many.

Trust me, Reeves said, in effect.

Eisenhower did not.

But he agreed to the plan, primarily because Reeves told him he could film all his answers at once, one right after the other. He would walk into a studio, utter twenty-two sound bites based on excerpts from speeches he had previously made—hence being true to himself—and then be free to go: to a cabinet meeting, a fund-raiser, the golf course, his bedroom for a nap. You give me two or three hours some afternoon, Reeves said to the candidate, and I'll give you two or three months' worth of campaign advertising that will ensure your victory in November.

Efficient, Ike must have thought, admiringly if grudgingly, *very efficient*. Still, he would sigh, it was a "hell of a way to get elected."

As for the questions to which the general would respond, Reeves would take care of that later. He would, in other words, do the job backward. After Eisenhower had recorded his responses, the ad man and a camera crew would drive up to Radio City Music Hall in New York, drag some tourists out of the ticket line, and take them to a quieter, pre-arranged spot where they could query the candidate. They would be "real people," Reeves enthused, who would speak "in their own clothes, with wonderful native accents." They would ask about the Korean War and international diplomacy, employment and the economy, Social Security and medical care for the elderly—and then Reeves would take the film back to an editing room and splice the questions to the answers in such a way that it would appear Ike and his fellow American were standing side by side, discussing the nation's problems and prospects like a couple of peers.

It sounded good. It didn't turn out that way.

The first problem arose before Eisenhower even stepped into the studio, when the makeup people started powdering his forehead and hairless pate. It's shiny, they explained to him. There's a reflection, and a reflection will distract from what you're saying; to prevent that, the powderers kept powdering. "To think that an old soldier should come to this," Eisenhower said, and must have longed for something that made more sense to him, like a confrontation with an enemy battalion over well-mapped terrain.

The second problem was that Ike did not want to wear his glasses on TV, believing they made him look too old; his age, it seemed, was one of the Democrats' few effective arguments against him, one that hinted he might not be able to serve out his term, and Nixon, the maudlin, dog-loving red-baiter, would end up running the nation. Fine. But without his glasses Eisenhower could not read the cue cards on which his lines had been written. The solution, Reeves determined, was bigger writing on bigger cards.

But it took a long time—and a lot of cardboard posters—to copy the general's responses in letters large enough for him to see, and as the work was progressing Ike was fussing and fretting himself into a fine froth. In other words, he was beginning to sweat. In other words, he needed more powder, not only on the top of his head but on his cheeks and chin, to cut down the sheen.

Finally the oversized cards were finished, Ike's entire face had a nice matte finish, and the camera began to roll. Eisenhower recorded his answers. He said things like:

"Yes, my Mamie gets after me about the high cost of living. It's another reason why I say it's time for a change, time to get back to an honest dollar and an honest dollar's worth."

Which, in the editing room, would be preceded by the words of a woman at Radio City Music Hall: "You know what things cost today. High prices are just driving me crazy."

Ike also said to the camera: "Well, the Democrats are sinking deeper into a bottomless sea of debt and demanding more taxes to keep their confused heads above water. Let's put on a sturdy life boat in November."

Which would be preceded by the words of a man at Radio City: "General, I'd like to get married, but we can't live on the salary I get after taxes."

Eisenhower again: "Can that be true when Americans are billions in debit and prices have doubled, when prices break our backs and we're still fighting in Korea? It's tragic, and it's time for a change."

From Radio City again, a black man this time, the only minority to appear in any of the twenty-two ads, leads into Eisenhower's response with, "General, the Democrats are telling me I never had it so good."

Eisenhower was still unconvincing in his presentation. His boss, however, claimed to be impressed. "The man is very good," Rosser Reeves stated for the record. "He handled himself like a veteran actor." It was no more truthful than the statements Reeves had written about cigarettes.

A DAY OR TWO LATER the grafting began, answers onto questions. Except that they did not fit, not really, not as well as they should have. First of all, most of the questions were not really questions at all, but comments. Second, Eisenhower's answers were not really answers but comments of his own that did not address the sentiments he had just heard as directly as they should have.

Consider the second of the examples just given.

Q: "General, I'd like to get married, but we can't live on the salary I get after taxes."

A: "Well, the Democrats are sinking deeper into a bottomless sea of debt and demanding more taxes to keep their confused heads above water. Let's put ourselves on a sturdy lifeboat in November."

It does not work. There are loose edges, corners that do not meet. Eisenhower is metaphorical, not conversational, and his so-called answer is in fact so nonspecific as to be meaningless. Certainly a man who was worrying that he could not afford to marry his sweetheart would not be put at ease by a pat phrase about a sturdy lifeboat a few months hence.

Making the spots seem even more artificial was the fact that Ike was obviously, and awkwardly, reciting his lines. As for the people at Radio City, they were even worse, sounding rehearsed and insincere, in part because they were not used to talking on camera, and in part because Reeves kept butting in, telling them what to say and how to say it, and what kind of facial expressions would be most suitable; they seemed to be struggling to remember Reeves's instructions at the same time that they remembered his lines, and their discomfort was obvious in their performances.

A person who watches the ads today, which is possible because of an online exhibit of the Museum of the Moving Image called "The Living Room Candidate," chuckles at how primitive they are—and then, if he can manage to keep his wits about him, suddenly gasps—as he realizes how quickly the concept of political dialogue has been debased, how it has been reduced to the huckstering tone of a commercial, taking on the rhythms, if not the humor, of a vaudeville exchange. Were it not for the thousands upon thousands of equally vacuous ads that Americans have witnessed in the decades since, it would be impossible to believe that such microchips of nonsense could play a role in so important a matter as deciding who should be elected President of the United States in the important year of 1952.

David Schwartz, who curated "The Living Room Candidate," admits the "Eisenhower Answers America" ads look crude today, but points out that "the commercials showed a deep understanding of the two main principles of successful political advertising. First, [they] emphasize personality. The ads establish Ike as being folksy, likeable, and in touch with the ordinary voter. . . . Secondly, the commercials . . . brilliantly reduced the Eisenhower campaign to three simple, easy-to-digest issues: get out of the war in Korea, get rid of corruption in Washington, and lower the cost of living."

THE WORST WAS YET TO COME. At least the "Eisenhower Answers the Nation" ads paid lip service to the issues of the day, and those who did the paying were real human beings, whose presence automatically conferred a certain air of reality, however slight, to the proceedings. Another Reeves ad for the campaign of 1952 was a cartoon, a troop of Looney Tunes–type characters who were drawn to represent normal American citizens, and they marched in exaggerated fashion with the goofiest of facial expression: cowboys, farmers, painters, cops, chefs, firemen, businessmen, housewives. Some of them carried Ike balloons, some held signs proclaiming their choice. Leading the procession was Uncle Sam and behind him, providing the beat for the marchers, was an elephant smacking a big brass drum with his tail.

The cartoon characters sang a little ditty on behalf of their man:

Ike for President, Ike for President, Ike for President, Ike for President.
You like Ike,
I like Ike,
Everybody likes Ike—for President;
Hang out the banners, beat the drums,
We'll take Ike to Washington.

People who took their politics seriously were aghast. Surely Americans didn't crave entertainment so desperatetly that they would not set aside a few minutes a day for Presidential candidates to explain their positions on important topics in a more dignified manner than a cartoon parade accompanied by an advertising jingle. Surely they didn't crave entertainment so desperately that they expected the candidates to provide it for them. Surely they didn't prefer kiddie-TV-type hokum to carefully reasoned position papers.

The journalist and critic Marya Mannes, as aghast as anyone, thought the 1952 campaign ads would not determine the winner of the election, but instead make a loser of the whole notion of serious political discourse. Writing in the trade journal *Reporter*, she poked fun at Eisenhower's ads, coming up with her own version of one:

Eisenhower hits the spot,
One full General, that's a lot.
Feeling sluggish, feeling sick?
Take a dose of Ike and Dick.
Philip Morris, Lucky Strike,
Alka-Seltzer, I like Ike.

If Rosser Reeves had heard the preceding, he'd have hired Marya Mannes on the spot.

NO LESS APPALLED by the Eisenhower ads was his opponent, Adlai Stevenson. "This is the worst thing I've ever heard of," he told a member of his staff after seeing the cartoon parade, "selling the presidency like cereal. Merchandising the presidency. How can you talk seriously about issues with one-minute spots?"

A substantive man, intelligent and deliberative, Stevenson was so little concerned with appearances that he once allowed himself to be photographed with his feet up on his desk and a hole in the sole of his shoe. When the picture was published, a journalist asked him whether he was embarrassed. Stevenson said he was not; it was the kind of thing that happened to shoes when a person did a lot of walking in them, he pointed out, and not only did he keep wearing them, he did not repair the hole, not immediately at least. Substance—that was the impression Stevenson meant to convey, not style.

He did not watch much television. He did not even have one in the governor's mansion in Illinois when he held the office. "On the few occasions when he wanted to watch a football or baseball game," biographer Porter McKeever tells us, "he would go to [a friend's] home. For a man who was about to become a central figure in the first presidential campaign conducted mainly on television, he was uncharacteristically unprepared."

Actually he *was* prepared, but in the wrong way. Stevenson had his own ideas about how to campaign for the presidency. "Suppose," he suggested, "that every Monday evening at peak viewing time, for an hour and a half, from Labor Day until election eve, the two candidates aired their views. They might on each evening take up a single issue. Each in turn might discuss it for half an hour, followed by rebuttal of one another for the third half hour. There are other possibilities, including face-to-face debate. But the central idea is that, in some manner, the principal figures, the candidates for President, appear together at the same prime time for a serious presentation of views on public questions."

Eisenhower would probably have agreed with Stevenson's notions, at least the broad strokes of them, but he never debated his opponent, who went ahead and aired his views in a much more detailed manner than did the general. In fact, most of the Stevenson "ads" were actually speeches, which ranged in length from a few minutes to half-an-hour. The longer ones usually ran late at night, when a lot of people were asleep and most of those who stayed awake and watched were people who had already made up their minds to vote for the former Illinois governor and had tuned in as much to enjoy his wit and erudition as to take his measure as a candidate.

The shorter speeches ran during primetime, but were still too long for their time periods, as they interrupted the sitcoms and westerns that people really wanted to see, infuriating them and causing a backlash against Stevenson, not to mention a mass changing of channels to stations that *were* running sitcoms and westerns. It was something that the Democratic candidate and his advisers, who did not have a Rosser Reeves among them, had never considered. And it was more important than they could have imagined.

Reeves, of course, had considered it. He scheduled virtually all of the Eisenhower ads *between* the sitcoms and westerns, and kept them short enough to fit perfectly into the gaps, which made Ike seem not only unobtrusive but, perhaps even more subliminally important, a part of the star-studded roster of television personalities that the early fifties featured. Let us take a Wednesday night in October, 1952. What do we see? *The Perry Como Show*, Ike, *Arthur Godfrey and His Friends*. Thursday night: *The George Burns and Gracie Allen Show*, Ike, *Amos 'n' Andy*. Friday night: *The Stu Erwin Show*, Ike, *The Adventures of Ozzie and Harriet*.

"You get the audience built up at huge costs by other people," Reeves explained, and then, before the audience can even think of turning its attention elsewhere, the candidate's message is complete and the flow of programming has not been disturbed. In fact, the candidate has become part of the flow, a small-screen celebrity as well as a political star.

Actually, there was at least one Stevenson ad short enough to air between programs—although just barely—and the candidate must have been even more irate about it than Eisenhower was about his cartoon supporters. In fact, one cannot imagine Stevenson giving his consent.

The ad is a song, the singer unknown. The composer is also unknown. So is the lyricist. Surely all have gone to their graves thankful for the anonymity. The tune was called "I Love the Gov," and it is as hard to read with a straight face today as it was to listen to all those years ago:

> *I'd rather have a man with a hole in his shoe*
> *Than a hole in everything he says.*
> *I'd rather have a man who knows what to do*
> *When he gets to be the Prez.*
> *I love the Gov', the Governor of Illinois.*

He is the guy that brings the dove of peace and joy.
When Illinois the GOP double-crossed,
He is the one who told all the crooks, "Get lost."
Adlai, love you madly,
And what you did for your own great state,
You're gonna do for the rest of the 48.

It was a far cry from that "serious presentation of views on public questions" that Stevenson had so rationally, and sincerely, advocated.

THE OUTCOME of the 1952 presidential campaign was never in doubt, at least not after Nixon regained his standing with both the electorate and the Eisenhower campaign following the "Checkers" speech. It is likely, in other words, that Marya Mannes was right; advertising did not have any influence on the outcome. Stevenson's thoughtfulness was simply no match for Eisenhower's popularity. His wry sense of humor was no match for Ike's heartiness. His background in Illinois government was no match for Ike's record of accomplishment in the European Theater of Operations.

But what the ads lacked in efficaciousness, they made up for in expense. According to the calculations of historian Carl Solberg, the Republicans spent $7,374,900 to elect their man, and fully a quarter of that amount went to television. The Democrats, even then the party of more straitened means, spent only $2,046,000; the percentage devoted to TV pitches is not certain, although it was surely lower than the Republicans' figure.

This, however, was just the beginning. One of the conclusions at which both parties arrived in 1952 was that, in a closer race, advertising *could* have made a difference, and therefore almost certainly *would* make a difference at some point in the future. As a result, Republicans and Democrats alike would spend more and more on television in elections to come, the percentages climbing quadrennially until, in 2004, it was estimated that fully 55 percent of the money spent by the two parties during the presidential campaign went for television. The estimate is similar for 2008, when the campaign of the Democratic victor, Barack Obama, paid for 489 ads on the four major networks and more than half-a-million appeals on local stations. The losing campaign, that of Republican John McCain, took out 408 network ads and more than a quarter-of-a million locally.

ALTHOUGH TV DID NOT SEEM to have had an effect on the results in 1952, it is believed to have stirred interest in the campaign and, as a result, led more Americans to show up at the polls than had been expected. An analysis in the *New York Times* magazine put it this way: TV "should probably be given a good share of the credit for the unexpectedly high registration throughout the country. Not only did TV indirectly stimulate a big turnout by the political interest it aroused, but, along with radio, it very directly pounded away at the theme through spot announcements, 'Get Out the Vote' shows, and other devices."

EISENHOWER NEVER SAID MUCH about the role of television in his first political campaign, although he seems to have entered the White House with more respect for it than he had before. Or at least more tolerance. Perhaps, old military man that he was, he had begun to look at TV as a new kind of weapon, one just as capable of misfiring as it was of operating properly, but, when it did operate as it was supposed to, capable of inflicting great harm on the opposition.

To make sure it did not misfire, at least according to his own standards, Eisenhower dismissed Rosser Reeves immediately after the election and started to make his own decisions about the tube. Among other things, he authorized the televising of his inauguration, which Truman had done four years earlier, and later invited cameras to a press conference and a cabinet meeting, both of which were firsts for the small screen, the first glimpses the American public had ever had at either.

But in 1956, when he ran for reelection, Eisenhower did not appear in his campaign pitches. Instead, he relied on the endorsements of others, which had been scripted by advertising executives with whom Ike felt more comfortable than he did with Reeves.

A woman pushing a vacuum cleaner down a hallway: "To be happy, it's important to like your neighbors, and for them to like you. So think how really important it is for the whole world to like and respect the President of the United States."

A union member, leaning against the workbench in his garage: "Average hourly wages are up sixteen dollars a week, and more people are working. Also, Ike's got the peace. I'm voting for President Eisenhower again."

A cabdriver taking his dog out for a walk at night past the White House: "A neighbor of mine lives there, yep, Dwight D. Eisenhower, a man with the most important job in the world. . . . [W]hile I'm thinking of him, I've got a feeling he's thinking of me, and my future, and my family's future. In times like these, so full of peril, and problems, I'll be honest with you, I need him. Don't you? Come on, Prince. Come on, boy, it's time we went home."

As for Stevenson, who also ran again in 1956, he did appear in a few ads, but employed announcers for many more, showing pictures of Eisenhower and Nixon, and introducing, however gently, the scourge of negative campaign ads. One of them, called "How's that Again, General?," featured Estes Kefauver saying, "The general's promise to bring down prices was another broken promise. . . . The general promised a change for the better, and we got shortchanged for the worst. Think it through."

Another ad, called simply "Nixon?" and featuring a very unflattering picture of the Vice President, played on people's fears, which had only increased after four years and an Eisenhower heart attack, about the chief executive's age and health. "Nervous about Nixon?" said the announcer. "President Nixon? Vote Democratic, the party for you, not just the few."

Once again the advertising seemed to play a minor role, if any, in the outcome of the election.

ROSSER REEVES was proud of his work in the 1952 presidential campaign. "Is there anything wrong with a twenty-minute speech?" he once asked a reporter. "Or a ten-minute speech? Or a five-minute speech?" When the reporter said no, Rosser said, "Then what's wrong with a one-minute speech or a fifteen-second speech?" He went on: "Do you remember that old radio speech of Franklin Roosevelt—his first acceptance speech? And the phrase about the only thing we have to fear is fear itself? . . . that's a fifteen-second spot." And another example: "Do you remember the speech that Churchill gave at Westminster College in Fulton, Missouri? What did he say there? . . . That an iron curtain had descended on Europe. . . . That was a fifteen-second spot from Churchill, just like the one during the war about 'never have so many owed so much to so few.'" Reeves never stopped thinking in terms of slogans.

But his was a minority voice. Not to mention a self-serving one. More common among perceptive observers was the view that political ads in the fifties, regardless of who won the races, made political discourse as simple as the advertising slogans they now emulated, and that it might remain simple-minded, and in fact get even simpler and thus more inaccurate, evermore.

The ads had made candidates more conscious of their performance skills than they had been before, and also made them more conscious of what they said in other public forums, which turned out to be an enormous, and unexpected, burden.

When a presidential candidate's speeches were heard only locally—one night in Cleveland, the next in Detroit, the following in Milwaukee—he could make essentially the same remarks every day without boring the audience or leading reporters to accuse him of a paucity of ideas. But now things had changed. Now, thanks to television, everything the candidate said, no matter where it was said, was national, and this meant that he constantly needed new ideas, or at least new phrases to express his old ideas; he needed new opening lines, new ways to organize his thoughts, new topics to inject into his discussions, rousing new perorations, more frequent changes of wardrobe, different kinds of venues in which to appear.

"With its constant demand for freshness," wrote journalist Robert Bendiner, "TV poses for politicians the same problem it poses for the entertainer. It consumes material at a prohibitive rate. If it were ever to replace the traditional forms of campaigning, a candidate would either require a regiment of speech writers or he would have to limit his campaign to something like a month—which might be a good idea at that."

Since then, of course, campaigns have only lengthened and speech writers are hired by the army, not the regiment. Politicians have become better performers than they used to be, usually going through some sort of media training, the equivalent of acting classes, before their parties send them out to the stump or the studio. Unlike Eisenhower and Stevenson, they do not complain; this kind of thing is now as much a part of politics as kissing a baby.

The journalists that cover both the officeholders and the candidates have encouraged the intrusion of show business into politics by accepting the standards of the former as part of the fabric of the latter, so much so that they often discuss the men and women they cover in terms of their charisma rather than their deeds.

Read the reviews of any State of the Union address, for example, and you will find that the President seemed to be more assertive than he has been in the past; or that he carried himself with a greater sense of dignity than he used to; or that he appeared smoother, more confident, in his delivery; or that he commanded the rostrum with an unusual amount of poise; or that he gave the impression that he was finally growing into his role as commander in chief; or perhaps that he displayed moments of hesitation, even nervousness, delivering his lines as if his heart were not really in them, as if events or opponents had put him on the defensive.

And, oh yes, he also gave his positions on some of the issues.

Political reporters have become show-biz critics. The politicians are the acts they review. And it all began in 1952, when, for the first time, the values of television came into conflict with those of governance, the former winning decisively and becoming so ascendant in the years following that there is no longer any argument about the priorities of a campaign for public office. Commercials first, positions later.

Chapter 11

The Mystic Knights of the Sea

TWENTY-TWO "Eisenhower Answers America" ads. Twenty-one white men and women asking the questions. One white man replying. And one black man, a single minority in a cast of twenty-three, noting that the Democrats were telling him he never had it so good.

In his case, though, the Democrats do not seem to be exaggerating. The man looks free from want: young, handsome, his hair cropped short and his mustache neatly trimmed. He wears a sport coat with a plaid shirt underneath. He appears on camera for only a few seconds, less than most of the whites in the "Eisenhower Answers America" ads, but he speaks his line without a slur or drawl or grammatical misstep. Reeves had chosen him to make an impression, not serve as a stereotype.

In 1956, the Eisenhower campaign gave even more time to a black, this time a woman, in one of its ads. She was older than the man from four years earlier, her hair neatly arranged, and she wore what seemed to be an expensive white suit. She sat at a small table with a phone on it. She, too, was well-spoken. "I'm Lena Washington, a mother," she began, chin up, erect in her chair. "I'm voting for Ike because I think he can bring us lasting peace.

He stopped Communist aggression in Indochina, Iran, and right here in America. And Guatemala. Ike ended the Korean War, too. That's why I like Ike, and he'll get my vote."

It is ironic that in the vacuous setting of the political campaign ad, fifties television provided two American blacks with more distinguished roles than it did for most others of their race who appeared on television more often, in more visible formats, and for far longer periods of time.

It is no less ironic that, as blacks seldom rose above the status of plantation darkie on television, they were beginning to make modest gains in the society at large. After World War II, their unemployment rate began to drop, and continued to drop for several years. Some blacks were given more responsible positions and higher salaries than they had been able to achieve before the war. It was, thought a number of employers, only fair. If the black man was required to join his white brethren in risking his life against the Axis powers, he should again be able to join them on the assembly line or in the office when the fighting was over.

Of course, not all employers thought in terms of racial justice. The drop in the black unemployment rate was a small one, the salary increases also small. But they were the first tangible, and most widespread, gains that blacks had ever made in the American workplace. In fact, as the scholar Thomas Sowell points out, from the early 1950s to 1964, the percentage of black Americans living in poverty, or dependent on the government to raise their heads above it, was less than it would be in the first decade after President Johnson declared poverty a target of legislative warfare.

On American television, however, it was a different story. The sponsors of the shows, who continued to make the decisions for the medium throughout the fifties and even later, remained as squeamish as ever about offending racists.

SO SQUEAMISH were they, in fact, that on many an occasion they refused to let blacks be seen at all. When Reginald Rose wrote a script for *Studio One* about a black family moving into a neighborhood in which they were not wanted, he was told the premise was unacceptable. But it happens all the time in real life, Rose said. It will not happen in TV life, he was told. As Erik Barnouw writes, "The black family would have to be changed to 'something else.' A Negro as beleaguered protagonist of a television drama was declared unthinkable." So, of course, was a drama about a white family moving into a neighborhood where *they* were not wanted, which would have been acceptable to network executives but not to common sense. Rose gave up on the idea. His friends told him the time was not yet right. He wondered whether it ever would be.

Later in the decade, a series named *Riverboat* made its debut on NBC. Described as "a floating *Wagon Train*," it was based loosely on Mark Twain's book *Life on the Mississippi*. But too loosely; the writers were told not to include blacks in any of the scenes, either in speaking roles or otherwise. They were not to be photographed, not even in the background, and not to be the subjects of discussion. The explanation: there were some people in the South who might be offended by the presence of blacks in a venue where they lived in abundance both in Twain's book and in the world outside the book, both at the time the story was set and three-quarters of a century later. Of course, the sensibilities of some people in the North might be equally disturbed. Racists here, racists there, racists, racists everywhere.

One can only imagine what Twain's reaction would have been to an all-white series about a riverboat paddling up and down the Mississippi. He might have suggested another series about life in New York's turn-of-the-century slums without immigrants, or a series about the Wild West without Native Americans, or about the California mining camps without Asians. He might have suggested a series about television executives with the courage to acknowledge reality.

Remarkably, he did not have to go so far as to suggest a production of *The Adventures of Huckleberry Finn* without the Negro slave Jim. *It had already happened!* In 1954, CBS lopped old Jim from the cast of Twain's classic, the program "thus eviscerating the revolutionary soul of the book—Huck and Jim seeking freedom together." Even given the era, it was one of the most offensively spineless acts in the history of the medium. Far better not to have aired such a version of *Huckleberry Finn* at all.

Harold A. Carlborg, the chief censor for CBS, who presumably approved the network's treatment of the program, explained why he thought blacks as characters and race as a subject were not appropriate for dramatic television, no matter what the context or who was watching:

In the matter of segregation, it would be difficult to present a dramatization dealing with some aspects of this problem on a sponsored program, particularly at a time when the subject is considered highly inflammatory. . . . It would be impossible to maintain any balance of dramatizations highlighting one side of such a currently explosive issue as segregation in a sponsored *entertainment* program.

There was, however, the occasional exception. Sidney Poitier starred as a dockworker in "A Man Is Ten Feet Tall" on *Philco TV Playhouse* and played smaller parts in two *Ponds Theater* productions, "Fascinating Stranger" and "The Parole Chief." Ossie Davis landed the title role in Eugene O'Neill's *The Emperor Jones*, which was written for a black man (although it had been played on many stages with a black-faced white in the title role). And the *Hallmark Hall of Fame* aired two productions, in 1955 and 1957, of *The Green Pastures*, playwright Marc Connelly's retelling of the Old Testament in which all the characters are black. But those seem to be the end of the examples. There is no further record of appearances by blacks in significant roles in television drama in the entire decade.

IN INSIGNIFICANT ROLES, however, they were, if not plentiful, at least present from time to time. "Urban settings might feature a black delivery man, porter, or waiter," it has been noted, "but black professionals and businessmen were virtually non-existent. Some westerns like 'Rawhide' and 'Have Gun, Will Travel' presented a few black cowboys riding the range with their white counterparts." But they were usually well behind the herd or on the perimeter of the gathering at the campfire when the day was ending. Blacks were like the far bank of a river, like trees at the distant edge of a plain, like rock outcroppings on the horizon on a hazy day. They were there only if you noticed them.

Sometimes, though, they were a more menacing presence. In such syndicated programs as *Ramar of the Jungle; Jungle Jim;* and *Sheena, Queen of the Jungle,* they suddenly burst to the foreground, often in great numbers, wherein they formed "a sea of dark faces to carry spears and look mean until the white hero or heroine reminded them who was in charge." They did not speak lines of dialogue; they grunted. They did not express a range of human emotions; they kept grunting. There were no friendly faces among them, no welcoming gestures. It was clear that television meant the black man and the white man to be enemies by the very fact of their races. On most of these shows there was fear on the faces of the whites when they first encountered their opposites deep in the wilds; and on the faces of blacks, a look of menace so overblown as to be comical.

More commonly, though, and certainly when the location shifted to the United States, blacks were unthreatening figures, eager to be helpful to whites because of the assumption that it was their nature to be docile, their place to be subservient. It was, after all, the reason they had been transported to North America in the first place.

But there was more than one way to be a menial, and something about the way that Eddie "Rochester" Anderson did it made him the most famous black on the small screen in the fifties. Rochester was comedian Jack Benny's indispensable valet, factotum, aide-de-camp—and a perfect comic foil for the star of the show. Benny was taciturn, Rochester effusive; Benny was easily confused, Rochester unflappable; Benny spoke in measured tones, Rochester had perhaps the most identifiable voice in television, so harsh and squeaky as to seem serrated. But even in the funniest of settings, and even when he was the one who got the laugh, it was always clear that Rochester the manservant was more servant than man.

In one episode of *The Jack Benny Program*, for example, Benny and Rochester are in the dressing room, preparing for the show-within-the-show that was the program's usual format, when Benny tells Rochester he is ready to be shaved. Rochester goes through his supplies, making sure he has what he needs. "Shaving cream, brush, razor, smelling salts."

"Smelling salts?" Benny says. "What do I want with smelling salts?"

"That's for me," Rochester says. "I can't stand the sight of blood."

"Well, be careful."

"Yes, sir."

The shave completed, Benny announces he is ready to be dressed. "Rochester, hand me my shirt, will you, please?"

"Yes, sir."

"And give me my tie, too."

"Yes."

And then Benny asks for his trousers, which Rochester cannot find quickly enough. Or, as it turns out, at all.

"Well, hurry up," Benny says, "give me my pants. We haven't got too much time now."

"They're not here."

"What do you mean, they're not here? I put them right over here on that chair."

"They're not here now."

"Well, where did you take them?"

"I didn't take them anyplace."

And he didn't. It was guest star Bob Hope who had stolen Benny's pants as a joke, sneaking into the dressing room when no one was looking. But it was Rochester who bore the brunt of Benny's frustration, and the latter's tone of voice as he expressed that frustration, however humorously intended, however humorously received by the audience, was clearly abrasive. But Rochester's responses, his unwillingness to take the missing pants too seriously, or personally, has the effect of blunting Benny's anger, making it seem humorously futile.

In a comedy skit later in the same program, Benny and Hope play explorers captured by cannibals. They are a gang of blacks (some of whom may have been whites in makeup; the quality of the existing video makes it impossible to tell) singing nonsense syllables, dancing like gorillas, carrying shields and spears, and wearing loincloths and war paint and large bones in their hair.

"Booga, booga," says the chief, after Benny and Hope have been captured and placed into a large pot and a few vegetables added for seasoning. "Start a fire, start fire, booga, booga."

Clearly, Benny and Hope need help. To the audience's delight, it is provided by Dean Martin and Jerry Lewis, who make a brief, unannounced cameo and manage to rescue the two main courses of the upcoming meal. Rochester did not get to act as hero; he was done for the evening after his unsuccessful search for the trousers.

When he was on camera, though, Eddie Anderson had a knack for making his presence felt, often to the extent of stealing the scene. He played the role of Rochester in a much-less-servile manner than many another black might have played it. The words he uttered might at times have been obsequious, but there was always something brash in his manner. As Donald Bogle writes, Anderson

> knew how to make his entrance in a world in which he was the only black surrounded by whites: with head up and a bounce in his stride, he moved with confidence and a note of condescension as well. His attitude seemed to be that he had to help out these poor white folks who could not feed themselves, could not care for themselves, half the time could not think clearly for themselves either.

He, Rochester, however, knew exactly who he was and felt blessed at being so supremely self-sufficient.

Still, his was a secondary position in the household. Other blacks on TV in the fifties also worked as hired hands in white residences, especially in the sitcoms. There was Willie Best, who played Stu Erwin's handyman; Amanda Rudolph, the housekeeper for Danny Thomas and his brood of overly energetic kids; and Charlie (also Willie Best) the elevator "boy" on Gale Storm's *My Little Margie*. All of them knew their places, none seemed dissatisfied with them, and young white children like my friends and me, innocent and only half-aware of the larger world around us, children who knew few blacks ourselves, were learning a lesson by osmosis. There were no frictions in the world between the races, just divisions of labor and prestige that favored the whites and, being the natural order of things, were accepted by both races unquestioningly.

THE FIRST BLACK to star in a network television show was the long-forgotten singer Bob Howard, whose "popularity with the general public," in the view of musical scholar Colin Larkin, "came largely as a result of his following in the footsteps of Fats Waller, his lack of originality being cloaked in skilled musicianship and easygoing rapport with audiences." Howard's self-titled program ran on CBS from 1948 to 1950: five nights a week, fifteen minutes a night, then cancellation for low ratings.

Jazz pianist Hazel Scott, a Julliard-trained wonder at the keyboard, had a show of her own on the Dumont network in 1950. Three nights a week, fifteen minutes a night, then her own cancellation. A more talented performer than Howard, she might have lasted longer if she had not had the temerity to criticize both racial segregation and Senator Joe McCarthy's rabble-rousing. The former earned her the label of "troublemaker," the latter that of "Communist sympathizer." It was a devastating pair of charges back then, especially for a black woman. She continued to make records; in fact her album *Relaxed Piano Moods*, on which she was accompanied by bassist Charlie Mingus and drummer Max Roach, is still much admired by jazz aficionados today. But television was done with her, for the time being and forever.

The first program starring a black to make a lasting mark on the medium was the sitcom *Beulah*, the title role played initially by Ethel Waters, a singer and actress of great talent. She would not, however, win any beauty contests at this stage of her difficult life, nor would her successors in the role: Hattie McDaniel and Louise Beavers. In fact, none of them would have been cast if there had been a tiara in their backgrounds; there was no way fifties television was going to hire the kind of black woman who might stir forbidden passions in white male viewers, especially when that black woman actually lived in the same domicile as whites on the show.

Beulah was the program's title character, but not its only minority. She had a "scatterbrained" black girlfriend, played by Butterfly McQueen, who had made her movie debut in *Gone with the Wind*, and she had a boyfriend of color who was occasionally given a few minutes of air time, during which he usually made a buffoon of himself.

But primarily what Beulah had was a job. She served as housekeeper to a family called the Hendersons and, according to Bogle, perpetuated "a stale fantasy that, like so many past movies, incorporated blacks into the American dream: like everyone else, Beulah lived in a spotless, comfortable home, but, of course, she had to clean it and never, in anyone's wildest imagination, would she own it. The Negro had made it into the television's cultural mainstream. But only as a maid."

Bogle goes on to point out how important it was that Beulah and her employers got along so well. The show, he wrote,

> had no racial dissensions, only racial harmony and togetherness in an ordered, wonderful world. Beulah and the Hendersons had a breezy camaraderie without any cultural differences and certainly without any conflicts or disputes over such trifles as Beulah's work load, Beulah's hours, or Beulah's pay. Doing her job just because she enjoyed it, Beulah seemed to get a kick out of all them pots and pans.

Had she not, had she occasionally looked at the dirty pots and pans and muttered an expletive, or wondered why the white woman couldn't scrub the damn things for once in her life, it would have been the end of her breezy camaraderie with the Hendersons and, as a result, the end of the series.

Beulah did not last long, starting in 1950, ending in 1953. But by that time there was a very different kind of sitcom on TV, one that featured not just a single black in a leading role but a whole ensemble of them, one that was much more controversial at the time than *Beulah* and remains so to the present, even though very few people today have ever seen a single episode.

AMOS 'N' ANDY started out on radio in 1929, with white actors doing their best impersonations of black voices. It was a minstrel show for the ear, and it became an immediate hit, a phenomenon, Milton Berle-like in its effects on the behavior of listeners. The parents of young Charles Schulz, when he was *Peanuts*-age himself, took him to a movie one evening that he seemed to be enjoying. But when *Amos 'n' Andy* time approached and his parents asked him whether he wanted to go home and listen, his reply was an immediate yes. Mom and Dad, also enjoying the movie, agreed. The Schulzes marched out of the theater, accompanied by several others, and shortly afterward were surrounding their radio, turning up the volume, and laughing along with millions of their fellow Americans.

Amos 'n' Andy aired from 7to 7:15 P.M., Eastern time, on weeknights, and during those fifteen minutes

> much of America came to a halt. It was said that bars, restaurants, department stores, sometimes even movie theaters just about closed up shop to wheel out radios for their customers to hear the show. On any given night if you walked through the streets of a small town or city, it's been said you could also hear the familiar voices of Amos and Andy coming from open windows everywhere. Presidents such as Coolidge, later Truman and Eisenhower, all boasted of loving the series. In fact, when "Amos 'n' Andy" eventually went to television, both Truman and Eisenhower gave casting suggestions to the producers.

One of the early sponsors of the program was Pepsodent toothpaste. After a few weeks, it reported that sales had tripled. *Amos 'n' Andy*, the company believed, was the sole reason.

In 1939, the show went to television, but for one episode only, as a trial run for the developing technology. It still employed white actors, but they donned blackface for the occasion, and it melted and dripped in the heat of the studio lights, running down their cheeks and onto their clothes. Mercifully, no recording of this particular opus was ever made or, if it was, it has not managed to surface.

Then in 1951, with blacks finally playing blacks, CBS brought *Amos 'n' Andy* to network TV on a weekly basis. It was a popular show, but not nearly as popular as the radio version; in the 1951–52 season, it finished thirteenth in the ratings, the highest it ever climbed. It was, nonetheless, a landmark in the medium's history, a program to which people reacted more strongly than they had ever reacted to a TV show before. They were either attracted or repelled, delighted or offended; they laughed or cursed or both, and sometimes found themselves amazed by the vehemence of either reaction. *Amos 'n' Andy* was, without question, the most analyzed program of the decade.

The three main characters, Amos, Andy, and their pal Kingfish, were members of a black fraternal lodge called the Mystic Knights of the Sea, and it was there that much of the action took place. It was there that the characters involved themselves in dodging bill collectors, hustling rubes, scamming scammers, getting scammed by scammers, deceiving wives and girlfriends, and making a buck without breaking a sweat. The lodge hall was a place where con men could be con men.

Amos was not really one of them. Played by Alvin Childress, Amos was the owner of the Fresh Air Taxi Cab Company, so named because its single vehicle had no windshield. He did the best he could with it, though, never complaining, always dreaming of a second vehicle, a third, eventually a fleet. "Hard-working, mild-mannered, sensible, gentle, Amos is a family man devoted to his wife and daughter." He was also a straight man in a company of jokesters, a dreamer of few deceits. As such, he was not the source of the program's controversy and, in fact, as the televised version of the program developed, proved to be not nearly as significant a presence as his name in the title would indicate.

Andy, on the other hand, was "an engaging dunce, who's always falling in love and forever embarking on some hare-brained scheme to make a quick buck or live the good life." He was rotund, robust, often fiddling with the derby he wore, a hat that did not bestow upon him the dignity he thought it did. He contributed, thought some people, to the worst impressions that whites had about blacks, that they were lazy and duplicitous rather than diligent and trustworthy, shuckers and jivers rather than nose-to-the-grindstoners, second-class citizens who were lucky even to be up that high on the social scale.

Spencer Williams Jr. had been cast as Andy on TV. He did not understand why so many people, white and black alike, took his comic character so seriously. White folks did not get upset when Milton Berle put on a dress and winked at one of his male guest stars; they did not get upset when Red Skelton pulled his hair out over his ears like tiny wings and pretended to be the terminally inane Clem Kadiddlehopper. Why, then, should black folks, or anyone else, get upset when Andy figured out a way to try to make life a little less arduous or more lucrative for himself—especially since regular viewers of the program knew that Andy was certain to fail, and comically so? Were viewers laughing *with* Berle and Skelton, and *at* Williams? Why? It did not make sense, all the fuss, not to Williams at least.

But character number three, Kingfish, in the person of actor George Stevens, was both the real star of the show and the real agent provocateur of the intense debate about the show's depiction of blacks. Was *Amos 'n' Andy* really racist? Were blacks, as some people charged, joining forces with the bigots to make fun of other blacks and thereby setting back the cause of liberty and justice for all? Or were they just playing, making fun?

A "fiendishly outlandish" conniver and trickster, it was Kingfish to whom Andy turned when he wanted an idea or an accomplice for one of his addle-pated notions. Kingfish was always glad to see him, always agreeable though seldom sensible, always eager to help though seldom realistic; the wildly implausible ideas that the two of them came up with were never successfully executed. Even Lucy Ricardo would have found some of them far-fetched.

But although Andy kept the faith with his friend despite their weekly lack of results, continuing to believe that Kingfish's bluster was a form of self-possession and his impracticality a derivative of genius, Kingfish's wife, Sapphire, knew better. She looked at her man with the wariest of eyes and spoke to him with the sassiest of tongues. Kingfish's swagger, in the wake of one of his wife's tirades, quickly turned to blubbering.

Played by Ernestine Wade, Sapphire was one of many women on the program who showed themselves to be tough and resilient, strangers to passivity. They were "harpy battle-axes," it has been said, "yappin' and yellin' at the drop of a hat," and as such, were the polar opposites of virtually every white woman with a role on an early fifties sitcom. Also, as such, they were a source of chagrin to many, people of both races who thought that at least a few of the females on *Amos 'n' Andy* should have been a little less combative, a little more conventionally feminine. It was a time when female assertiveness in a marriage was looked on favorably by few of either gender.

But perhaps even more than the actions and motivations of the characters, what upset so many people about the program was the language. On *Amos 'n' Andy*, they spoke the kind of English that Stephen Foster had assigned them in song lyrics, a separate and unequal brand of the mother tongue that made people laugh at the same time that it fed all the worst stereotypes of racial inferiority. Again, Kingfish was the primary offender.

When Sapphire's tirades started him sniveling, he begged for forgiveness. "Oh, I's sorry, darlin'." "I din't mean nothin', honey bunch." "I'll nevah do nothin' like dat again! Cross muh heart."

When circumstances upset him or people let him down, Kingfish did not get disgusted; rather, he would say, "I'se regusted."

Telling Sapphire of his plan to make a fortune in real estate, he bragged, "Someday they gonna develop that whole era." Meaning *area*.

"Conferentially," he said, meaning *confidentially*.

"Inferated," he said, meaning *infiltrated*.

"Now ain't dat sumpin'!'," he uttered when he was even more impressed than usual by one of his brainstorms. Or, if he were even more impressed than that, he might let loose with an "ow-wah, ow-wah, ow-wah!"

But Kingfish wasn't the only offender in the cast. No one's English would have passed muster on a college entrance exam.

Andy: "I don't be thinkin' dat way, Kingfish, I don't think you should be thinkin' dat way."

And, after Andy failed in his attempt to boost Kingfish up through an open window so he could sneak into a house: "When I was alleyin', I don't think you was oopin'."

Amos: "We's gunna do it dis time, Kingfish, I know we's gunna do it. This here's a absolute can't-fail proposition."

Amos's Fresh Air Cab Company was not incorporated; it was *incorpulated*.

Sapphire: "I swear, Kingfish, you'se about the most ridiclious man I ever done come across."

When Kingfish failed to remember their wedding anniversary, Sapphire lashed out at him. "Don't nothin' ever mean' nothin' t' you?"

And Lightnin', the dim-witted janitor of the Mystic Knights of the Sea, when told by Kingfish to do an errand of some sort, would always reply with a high-pitched "yazzuh," instead of *yes, sir*.

But it was Kingfish who uttered what became the signature phrase of the series. His "Holy mackerel, Andy!," which came out "*Ho*-lee mack-ul, Andy!," was repeated by thousands of viewers, white and black, whenever they were surprised or bewildered or just unable to think of anything else to say at the moment.

DONALD BOGLE, who writes so expertly of the early black experience on television, believes *Amos 'n' Andy* was not, as so many people charged, a program in which the actors sabotaged their own cause of racial equality. Rather, he thinks that television was simply the wrong medium for entertainment of that kind. "Sadly," he concludes, "television's 'Amos 'n' Andy' was ethnic comedy yanked from its cultural context. Had the series been performed at black theaters for black audiences, no one would have thought twice about it. Because the program was aired on national 'white' television—reaching a white audience that saw many of the characters as true embodiments of the American Negro—it struck many as a distortion that historically *had* to go."

Another defense of the program, no less perceptive, comes from Harry Castleman and Walter J. Podrazik who, rather than faulting television for being the wrong venue for the program, fault viewers of both races for their misunderstanding:

> The characters and plots were totally interchangeable with scores of "white" sitcoms that both preceded postdated "Amos 'n' Andy." . . . "Amos 'n' Andy" was set up in an essentially all black world, where whites were rarely seen. If the Kingfish was outsmarted, it was by a black con artist, not a white one. There were also black lawyers and black doctors to balance off black stooges. As in any screwball comedy, the stories depended on misunderstandings and crazy antics by such tried-and-true stereotypes as a money-hungry bumbler, a slow-witted second banana, a shrewish wife, and a battle-ax mother-in-law. In "Amos 'n' Andy," these familiar comic caricatures just happened to be black.

The reference that Castleman and Podrazik make to white sitcoms that postdate *Amos 'n' Andy* is an intriguing one. Was there really any difference between Kingfish and Andy on the one hand and Jed Clampett and Daisy Moses (Granny) on the other? Between the two blacks and Archie and Edith Bunker? Between the two blacks and John Ritter and Suzanne Somers? Between the two blacks and Laverne and Shirley, Alf and his human hosts, Al and Peg Bundy, Roseanne and Dan? All had their unique traits, of course, but all were clowns of one sort or another. Yet whites, having long established their superiority in the culture, apparently found that one of the perks of such a position was to behave like social inferiors without either reprisal or microscopic, and ultimately belittling, analysis of their motives. After all, they were not really social inferiors; they were the vast majority of all that mattered in the United States.

THE NATIONAL ASSOCIATION for the Advancement of Colored People (NAACP), did not agree with any of the defenses of *Amos 'n' Andy*. At the group's 1951 convention, the program was a major topic of discussion, and, although it had its supporters among the delegates, it had far more critics, people who believed the show "depicts the Negro in a stereotyped and de-rogatory manner," and further, that "it strengthens the conclusion among uninformed or prejudiced people that Negroes and other minorities are inferior, lazy, dumb, and dishonest."

And perhaps even unpatriotic. On the first episode of the show to air on CBS, Kingfish mistakenly receives a draft notice and goes to pieces almost visibly. So terrified was he about the prospect of being a soldier, and so convinced did the military become of his ineptitude, that all branches of the service agreed to write him off as 4-F. Kingfish could not have been more relieved. But as historian Thomas Doherty pointed out, "Mocking the cour-age of African Americans in the midst of the Korean War seemed almost calculated to enrage civil rights groups."

The NAACP, perhaps the most enraged, urged its delegates not to buy Blatz Beer, which sponsored *Amos 'n' Andy*. It also urged the rest of America to stop watching the show. Neither happened, at least not immediately.

But the pressure did not let up. The NAACP was only one of many or-ganizations protesting *Amos 'n' Andy*, and the others consisted of people of both races, many income levels, many types of employment. So it was that after two years and a mere seventy-eight episodes, CBS dropped the series. *Variety* mourned its departure. The program, it said, was "one of the all time major casualties in the radio-to-video transition, of stellar proportions."

However, CBS did make the series available for syndication, where it found a large and appreciative audience for a remarkably long run of thirteen years. By the late sixties, however, the civil-rights movement had moved so deeply into the American mainstream that there was no place for a program like *Amos 'n' Andy*, whether it was misunderstood or not. If Donald Bogle was right in stating that TV was the wrong place for the show, the sixties were without question the wrong time. The Mystic Knights of the Sea belonged to an altogether different culture from the Black Panthers. With the rarest of exceptions, Kingfish and his pals and gals have not been seen on television since, and when they have it has been in the briefest of clips rather than an entire episode.

BUT MAYBE A BLACK could succeed on television in a different kind of role. Maybe if he were dignified rather than cartoonish, if he spoke like a white man and in fact hosted the kind of program that viewers had come to associate with whites, he could gain acceptance, avoid controversy—or so NBC hoped.

In 1956, the network gave silky-voiced, silky-mannered, silkily-attired Nat "King" Cole his own variety show, and in the hope of making it a hit, at least financially, most of the guests, who were either friends or admirers of Cole, agreed to appear without charging their usual fees. It was a magnanimous gesture, but it did not work. NBC might have saved money on guest fees but it lost a good deal more on commercials, as it could not find a single sponsor for the program. Corporate America should have been as ashamed of itself as it should have been for its censorship of live dramas in the decade.

In addition, some of the network affiliates, in various parts of the country, refused to carry the show. A few people, in fact, found it even more offensive than other programs featuring blacks. They were irate at the presumptuousness of Cole, sharing the stage with white performers, singing duets with them, smiling at them, and then chatting with them as if he were their equal—and the whites chatting back, showing Cole respect, even admiration.

On one or two of the programs, Cole and a white guest even made physical contact—a handshake, a tap on the shoulder, a distanced hug. What was next, televised acts of miscegenation? This kind of thing simply could not be. *The Nat "King" Cole Show* lasted little more than one season. NBC executives tried to figure out which among them could serve as sacrificial lamb for even suggesting such a program. It is not known who the unfortunate soul was.

Cole was furious. He had managed to win an audience with his records, as well as with his nightclub and concert appearances. (Although on one horrible occasion in Birmingham, Alabama, he was attacked partway through his performance by angry whites who rushed the stage.) He felt certain that, if given enough time, he would attract an audience on television. But, he said, "Madison Avenue is afraid of the dark." There was nothing he could do about it.

As previously mentioned, Ed Sullivan booked black entertainers on his variety show, but he preferred solo acts rather than groups. "Aware that many white adults considered [black rock 'n' roll singer Fats] Domino a threat," writes Domino's biographer Rick Coleman, "Sullivan hid his band behind the curtain, reducing the number of black faces." The band was similarly secreted away when Domino appeared on Perry Como's variety show.

Milton Berle, in many ways as foolish a performer as Soupy Sales, was also, undeniably, a courageous one. "I remember clashing," he wrote in his memoir about hosting the Texaco *Star Theatre*,

> with the sponsor and the advertising agency . . . over my signing the four Step Brothers for an appearance on the show. The only thing I could figure out was that there was an objection to black performers on the show, but I couldn't even find out who was objecting. "We just don't like them," I was told, but who the hell was "we"?
>
> Because I was riding high in 1950, I sent out the word: "If they don't go on, I don't go on." At ten minutes of eight—ten minutes before show time—I got permission for the Step Brothers to appear. If I broke the color-line policy or not, I don't know, but later on I had no trouble booking Bill Robinson or Lena Horne.

Steve Allen also booked Lena Horne on his program one night, and when she finished her song, Allen kissed her on the cheek. According to Allen's director, Bill Harbach, the hate mail poured in immediately. A few weeks later, the star decided to acknowledge one of the messages for all of his viewers to hear. "I want to read a letter," Allen said, sitting on a piano stool with only a minute or so of air time left, and he minced no words. "It's from a bigot. . . . 'How dare you kiss her in front of all those people, it was disgusting.'"

Allen put the letter down and, Harbach told me, "looking directly into the camera, said, 'First of all, this person didn't have the guts to sign his name. Secondly, if anyone out there happens to know who wrote this, please get him to a doctor immediately, he is a very sick person along with the rest of the people who feel this way."

The audience, Harbach was pleased to relate, "sat in stunned silence and then with a roar of applause we signed off. I said to myself, 'I'll work with this guy the rest of my life.'"

ON HIS CELEBRITY INTERVIEW PROGRAM *Person to Person*, Edward R. Murrow featured such black notables as Marian Anderson, Eartha Kitt, Louis Armstrong, and the baseball player Roy Campanella. They did not seem to cause much controversy, perhaps because Murrow had often created so much more controversy on his other show, *See It Now*. But the ratings for *Person to Person* when it featured blacks were never up to Murrow's usual levels. There was, for that reason, always grumbling or head-shaking in CBS corporate headquarters when Murrow decided to invite a minority as his guest.

One can explain, although certainly not justify, reactions like this. The attitude on television toward blacks was, after all, faithful to the attitudes prevalent in society. TV's portrayal of blacks was not flattering, was in fact more often than not insulting; that it was in most cases accurate, however, that it reflected attitudes prevalent in much of society, could not be denied.

Nor could it be denied that television was a business: not a means of educating the public, not a means of raising levels of taste and culture as early commentators had hoped it would do; it was a business, plain and simple and mundane. A business could not alienate its customers. A vast majority of TV customers wanted to watch white people on their screens. If blacks had to appear, it should be in supporting roles, the way it was in real life, and even then they should appear for short periods of time, as if they were a spice too pungent for most people's tastes in that bland decade so long ago.

But attitudes like this were changing, slowly and in some cases violently, and although the producers of entertainment programs would not acknowledge these new racial realities for many more years, there were others in television who did, men who made sure Americans knew that all black men were not like Kingfish, nor all black women like Beulah. They made sure Americans knew that the role of blacks on variety shows and sitcoms had little to do with the role of blacks in their homes, in the company of their families, and most important, in the schools they were now struggling to attend. These blacks, some of them at least, were about to bring to the small screen a kind of drama that had never been seen before, the impact of which would be more influential than anything television had yet accomplished.

Chapter 12

"The Technological Equivalent of a Crucifix"

OLIVER BROWN was tired of it. His daughter Linda, eight-years old, was even more tired—and less comprehending. To get to her all-black elementary school in Topeka, Kansas, in 1951, she had to ride a bus five miles and then walk through a railroad yard that Brown, a railroad man himself, believed was dangerous: too many cars being shuttled from one siding to another, too many unsavory characters hanging around, mischief on their minds, cheap alcohol on their breaths.

So: ten miles of bus-riding and two trips through the perils of the train yard every day, five days a week, virtually every weekday from fall to spring. And usually, because of the bus schedule, Linda Brown got to school too early, sometimes before the building was even open. "On winter mornings," writes historian Geoffrey Perrett, "she could be seen on the pavement outside, jumping up and down while she waited, trying to keep warm," a few other black children bouncing alongside her.

Oliver Brown worked hard to support his family, serving as a minister in addition to a welder for the railroad; he believed his daughter should work hard too—but to get an education, not to get *to* an education. Finally he decided that he, and she, had reached the breaking point.

He tried to enroll his daughter in an all-white school that was a ten-minute walk from his home. He was not surprised when school officials turned her down, but had already made up his mind not to listen to the refusal and lie down. He and twelve other sets of parents whose children had to make ten-mile daily round trips to the classroom joined with the Topeka branch of the NAACP and filed suit against the city Board of Education. They lost. Brown was not surprised about that, either. Perhaps not even troubled. As had been the plan all along, he and the others would continue the fight.

For three years they struggled against the ruling system of the South whose leader was the legendary Jim Crow. By that time, as Brown and his allies might have hoped from the beginning, the case had gone all the way from Northeast Kansas to the United States Supreme Court. On May 17, 1954, the court ruled. Racial segregation in the public schools violated the Fourteenth Amendment to the Constitution, said the Court, which provides that all citizens have equal protection under the law. The Court ordered schools not just in the South but throughout the country to be integrated "with all deliberate speed." Said Chief Justice Earl Warren, "To separate children in grade and high schools from others of similar age and qualifications solely because of their race generates a feeling of inferiority as to their status in the community that may affect their hearts and minds in a way unlikely ever to be undone. We conclude that in the field of public education the doctrine of 'separate but equal' has no place. Separate educational facilities are inherently unequal."

It was a big story, but the Army–McCarthy hearings were on at the time and they seemed to some bigger. The two fought for air time, fought for newspaper space. The Sunday morning public-affairs programs on the networks discussed the Supreme Court ruling at length, and many newspapers printed it under banner headlines, just as they did the day's events in McCarthy versus the armed forces.

In the South, the Supreme Court's unconscionable decision was the *only* story, a bombshell, and those who read it were livid. The papers believed that their readers would not comply with the court's ruling, and in fact published editorials urging noncompliance. In many Southern states, people formed themselves into Citizens' Councils; within a year of the Brown decision, there were said to be more than a hundred such organizations in Mississippi alone.

The term, of course, was a euphemism. A Citizens' Council was really a vigilante group, its purpose not to take the law into its own hands, but to break the law by making sure that no black children set foot into white schools. Why should they? There were already black adults in the schools. Who did the Supreme Court think tended the furnaces and mopped the floors and emptied all the wastebaskets at night? It was one of the jokes that made the rounds in various Topeka barrooms late at night. Why admit the kids? They were too young to do any chores.

But there was little humor elsewhere. Tensions in the South grew like sorghum in a warm, rainy spring. Whites who once ignored blacks on the street or in other public venues now glared at them, sometimes cursed them, on occasion even physically attacked them. How dare they try to force their children into all-white schools! How dare they challenge the existing order, which would not have existed for so long if it were not proper! How dare they insist on rights that had never been intended for them, regardless of what the old gray Northerners on the Supreme Court seemed to think!

In response, black rage began to simmer, although seldom to show itself publicly. How dare Whitey ignore the wishes of the Court! How dare he insist that the past was fated to be the future!

Then, in the summer of 1955, young Emmett Till came to the Mississippi Delta to visit his relatives.

THE ABC, CBS AND NBC evening news programs, each of them fifteen-minutes long, as they would be throughout most of the fifties, covered the trial of Till's accused murderers. It was not easy. Whites in the area resented the journalists' presence almost as much as they had resented young Till's. Some of the locals tried to intimidate reporters; others, just as threateningly, would buddy up to the journalists and take them into their confidence, maybe throw an arm around a shoulder, try to make sure the outsiders knew what kind of punk this Till kid really was. They would warn the men with pens, notebooks, and cameras to get their stories straight, not say anything that would make the local folks look bad. After all, if it hadn't been for Till showing up where he wasn't wanted and doing what he shouldn't have done, none of this would have happened, now would it?

The trial was not easy to cover for logistical reasons, either. After much searching, the networks found a field a few miles from the courthouse which was just barely long and wide enough to use as a landing strip for a tiny, two-seater aircraft. They shot their film every day, raced it out to the make-shift airport, and sent it back to New York in cans that also included a sheaf of hastily scribbled notes from the reporter. The stories would be edited and broadcast the next day, and were usually short, less than a minute. With an entire world to cover and only a quarter of an hour to do it, there was only so much time for Emmett Till.

Among viewers, in the South and elsewhere, there was little reaction. The story of Till's death was a terrible one, but it had already happened, and only the aftermath, meaning the trial, could be shown on TV. Often the courtroom footage was run silently, with the anchorman in New York simply summarizing the day's proceedings—a "voice-over," it was called. Till's murder was an important story, but it was not exciting television.

There was, however, an exciting moment when the verdict was an-nounced, a moment that would be a harbinger of things to come in the television coverage of race in the South. Reporters began asking people their reaction to the acquittal of the two men accused of the crime. One of those reporters was NBC's John Chancellor, whose primary responsibility was to provide stories for television, but was at the time filing a report for radio.

> With a tape recorder the size of a shoebox slung over his shoulder and a microphone as small as a postage stamp in his hand, he began interviewing. As he talked with a Negro woman, he saw fear flash across her face. She turned and ran. He saw a flying wedge of white toughs coming at him. Chancellor squared off against them and held up the only object he could to defend himself, an object whose power he had not, until that moment, truly fathomed. Thrusting the tiny microphone toward the men, Chancellor blurted out, "I don't care what you're going to do to me, but the whole world is go-ing to know it." The men stopped.

The microphone, Chancellor later said, was "the technological equiva-lent of a crucifix." If they had not realized it before, many white Southerners realized it now: they were acting in a way that the rest of the world would not be able to understand and therefore should not be allowed to witness. Those who already thought of journalists as enemies were coming to believe that they might be more powerful enemies than had first been assumed, an-other invading army from the North, some ninety years after the first one, with totally different but equally powerful weaponry.

AND FOR THE MOST PART, that meant television cameras. Radio was a threat to the mob—enough, perhaps, to have saved Chancellor from a severe thrashing, if not worse—but it was less of a threat than a camera. No one worried about newspaper stories. No one worried about magazines. Everyone worried, or would eventually worry, about moving pictures and accompanying audio. It was moving pictures that in fact had the power to move, but even they could not affect people, could not turn them against the racism in certain parts of the South, unless they were the right pictures, presented in the right context.

For instance, on December 1, 1955, a seamstress named Rosa Parks, exhausted after a long day at her sewing machine, after *many* long days at her sewing machine, broke the law by refusing to give up her seat to a white man on a bus in Montgomery, Alabama. It might have been a calculated act of defiance, meant to inflame; Parks had, after all, been arrested once before for protesting the treatment of blacks by civic authorities. Or it might have been a spontaneous act, one whose repercussions she did not consider, either to herself or to history. In fact, according to some sources, if a different person had been driving the bus, there is a possibility that Parks would have acceded to the white man and stood—a possibility.

But sitting behind the wheel that day was James Blake, "a vicious bigot who spat tobacco juice out of his bus window and cursed at 'nigras' just for the fun of it." Twelve years earlier, Blake had bullied Parks when she boarded his bus, probably calling her a *bitch* or a *coon*, as was his habit with black women, and demanding that she get off the bus, which she had entered through the front door, and get on again through the rear. She refused. She had told Blake on that earlier occasion there was no room to enter through the rear door; blacks were mashed against it like animals penned for slaughter. Blake looked back, saw that she was right. He allowed her to stay where she was, but fumed. Blake never forgot her uppitiness. Parks never forgot his insolence.

In fact, for the next twelve years, Parks had made it a point not to ride with Blake again. When a bus pulled up she peeked in at the driver and, if it was Blake, she simply waited for the next bus. But on the first day of December 1955, apparently too weary to pay attention, she stepped onto a bus with Blake in command, something she did not notice until she had taken her seat. "[H]er act of civil disobedience," believes historian Douglas Brinkley, "was partly the result of her personal revulsion toward one particular bus driver."

It was Blake who saw to it that the police were notified that Parks did not yield her place to the white man. Patrolmen were dispatched to one of Blake's next stops and removed Parks from her seat—hustling her off to jail, fingerprinting and then arresting her. As newspaper photographs would later show, she reacted to her humiliation—and fatigue—with great composure, her expression blank, revealing not a thing.

Other blacks, however, were enraged at the treatment of Parks. They were also enraged at the treatment of their fellow African-Americans by various city employees and decided that to complain about it, as they had done so many times for so many years, was no longer good enough. It was time for a more drastic step. They announced that henceforth they would do something different. They would do something that mattered. They would boycott the city's public transportation.

White Montgomery laughed at them. White Montgomery believed that blacks would not be able to get to their jobs, would not be able to get to their stores, would not be able to live their lives unless they forgot about their silly plan for economic reprisal and got back to the back of the buses. Newspapers announced the plans for the boycott and ridiculed it, both in their news accounts and in editorials.

But the boycotters were more resolute than even *they* had foreseen. They refused to avail themselves of public transport in Montgomery, no matter how great the inconvenience, no matter how early they had to rise to reach their destinations. They walked unwalkable distances; they piled into beat-up old cars—six, seven, sometimes eight of them. A few even rode bicycles and sometimes had to dodge objects thrown at them by angry whites who saw them pass. But they persevered, kept on pounding the pavement, kept on driving their barely drivable jalopies and on occasion, when the cars stalled, pushed them along the streets. Buses passed them, the passengers pointing and laughing; the blacks did not get on.

In fact, Montgomery blacks kept the buses in their city more than half-empty until the Supreme Court finally upheld a lower court ruling that segregated seating on public transportation was unconstitutional. The boycotters had overcome. It had taken more than a year, a painful and humiliating year; it had taken more effort and even suffering than they could have imagined at the start. But *they had overcome*. Blacks were now allowed to sit where they pleased, and would never again have to rise and move to the back to accommodate whites.

One of the leaders of the boycott was Reverend Martin Luther King Jr., and the event was his introduction to many Americans, as well as to officials of state and Federal governments. And since it inspired so many people with its courage and amazed so many others with its persistence, the boycott, more than *Brown v. Board of Education,* probably deserves to be called the beginning of the civil-rights movement in the United States, which is to say that not only was it one of the most significant stories of the decade; it was one of the most significant in the entire history of the nation.

But few people, especially outside the South, realized it at the time. One of the reasons was that television could not adequately convey the depth of feeling, the strength of commitment, that fueled the story. It certainly tried; the networks were there, at least at the start, and they did what they could. They shot weary black people traipsing back and forth along the city sidewalks; they shot white people taking up only a few of the seats on the buses that were now running at great financial loss. They recorded sound bites from the former, who were determined; and from the latter, who were derisive.

It was compelling video in its way, but only a few times. The network news programs could not show the same pictures of black walkers and barely occupied buses on every program, and from December 5, 1955, to December 21, 1956, that's all there was to see: one day looked just like the next in Montgomery. There was no violence, no shouting; there were no lines of picketers carrying placards—just an unyielding resolve on the parts of both sides that never varied, visually or any other way. And so, after a while, the cameras went away. The boycott persisted and in fact grew ever more effective with time; as a TV news event, though, it was finished.

But the network crews would return to Alabama less than a month after the boycott began, this time to Tuscaloosa, and this time for pictures a national audience would find so gripping that they would be imprinted forever on the hearts and minds of all who saw them.

IN JANUARY, 1956, twenty-six-year-old Autherine Lucy, who had already earned a bachelor's degree in English at an all-black college, was preparing to attend classes as a graduate student at the University of Alabama at Tuscaloosa, the first minority ever to be enrolled in the school. She was both elated and beaten down by her acceptance, having sent out applications for four years and having had every one of them rejected for reasons that were never more than cover stories for bigotry. But for almost as long, she had been working on her case with NAACP lawyers and other legal professionals, and finally, as another year began in the American fifties, the news came that the University of Alabama would open its doors to her.

But she was hardly welcomed by all. Members of still-thriving Citizens' Councils, as well as Ku Klux Klanners and unaffiliated racists of all stripe were irate at the university's decision, and reached the campus before Lucy did on her first day. Assuming their positions, they jeered and cursed as the object of their vitriol arrived and passed them; she, however, did not look their way. Like Rosa Parks before her, she showed no emotion. She had been expecting this kind of thing, this show of senseless animosity, and had steeled herself in advance.

After her last class, some of her fellow students joined the townsfolk outside and chanted at her as she left a classroom building. "Keep Bama white!" they hollered, and "To Hell with Autherine!" They snarled at her, made obscene gestures, twisted their faces in anger. Once again she did not look. Her eyes were on the future, although she could not have imagined at the time how distant that future would be.

Earlier in the day, others had been kinder, even accepting. At least a few of her fellow students had chatted with Lucy about the courses she was taking and her future plans, and even walked with her from one class to another. But they were wary all the while. Their hearts might have been with the young black woman, but they were not foolish enough to make displays of support outside the university buildings where they could be seen by protesters. When the school day ended, so did their proximity to Lucy.

More protesters showed up the next day. Then more on day number three. To depart safely from one of the buildings, Lucy had to be escorted to a car by university officials, and as they proceeded to the vehicle protesters threw rocks and eggs at them, shouting at them all the way, vowing that Lucy's stay on campus would be a short one and that those at the school who had made it possible would eventually pay a price for their unconscionable decision to take in a nigger.

That afternoon, a highway patrol car had to be summoned to remove Lucy from another of the buildings, and when she got inside the car the troopers told her to lie down on the backseat so she could not be seen or hit with anything. The car drove away through a crowd of hatemongers who provided a perilously narrow path.

After her fourth day as a student, Lucy's routine had been so disrupted that she had managed to attend only two-and-a-half days' worth of classes. In fact, the whole university had been disrupted: classes had to be canceled or moved to other classrooms; extracurricular activities were postponed; crowds of people who lived near the campus or in some cases came from miles away roamed the grounds, muttering to one another or to no one at all. They were clearly looking for trouble, and if they could not find it, they would make it.

Less than a week later, the university gave up. The administration decided that it could no longer offer Lucy sufficient protection or withstand the vehemence of the demonstrators, whose numbers gave no sign of shrinking and whose behavior was making it impossible for the campus to conduct business as usual. Autherine Lucy was told she had been suspended until further notice.

The TV networks were there the whole time. It was the biggest story in the young history of television news, and viewers took notice as they never had before. They saw Lucy maintain her poise under the most adverse circumstances possible. They saw the behavior of the mob, the violence of their deeds, and they heard the words, the vile, vicious epithets spewed at a young lady who struggled not to react, not to waver as she listened to them herself. They saw policemen who seemed themselves to be wavering: between protecting Lucy, which was their duty, and joining their friends and neighbors who threatened her, which, at least for some, was their obvious inclination.

As a result of the coverage, resentment began to build against the South.

But in the South, resentment was building against the networks, especially after the night that NBC's *Camel News Caravan* made a bad situation worse. The program ran some film of an ambulance stopping to pick up a victim, and John Cameron Swayze identified the scene as the University of Alabama and the battle over Lucy as the reason for the injury. He was wrong. In truth, the film had come from Montgomery, and had nothing to do with Autherine Lucy or racial violence at all. The next evening Swayze apologized on the air for his mistake. Most Southerners thought it had been made deliberately.

Their resentment would soon reach new heights. The following September, both TV reporters and segregationists would appear in even greater numbers, and in even more adversarial circumstances, at Central High

School in Little Rock, Arkansas. Autherine Lucy would be forgotten. The South would boil over.

IT HAD BEEN more than three years since *Brown v. Board of Education,* three years since Chief Justice Warren had said that separate educational facilities "are inherently unequal"—and Little Rock Central still was not integrated. That was long enough, U.S. District Judge Ronald N. Davies decided, and ruled that nine black students be admitted for the term beginning in the fall of 1957. Arkansas Governor Orval Faubus had expected the ruling but was dismayed nonetheless. It would, he knew, be the defining crisis of his political life.

Considered a moderate on racial matters, at least publicly, Faubus did not advocate laws to discriminate against blacks, did not insult them in his oratory, seldom even referred to them. But he was not moderate about being reelected. He wanted another term as his state's governor, wanted it badly, and knew he would not get it if he did not defy Judge Davies.

When Winthrop Rockefeller, son of John D. Rockefeller Jr., a future governor of the state and at the time "Arkansas's most famous citizen," pleaded with Faubus not to disobey the judge, to admit the blacks to Central High, he explained that he couldn't. "I'm sorry," he said to Rockefeller, "but I'm already committed. I'm going to run for a third term, and if I don't do this, Jim Johnson and Bruce Bennett [racists who were opposing him in the Democratic primary] will tear me to shreds."

Rockefeller told him there would be trouble. Faubus knew it. Rockefeller warned him that television news crews would cover the trouble and it would tarnish the image of the state in the eyes of the nation. It would perhaps tarnish the nation in the eyes of the world. Faubus knew that, too. Nonetheless, he called up 270 National Guardsmen and sent them to Central High School. Their orders, according to one of them: "Keep the niggers out!"

Eight of the nine students admitted to Central High were planning to journey together on the first day of classes, accompanied by a group of white and black ministers. But one student had not received word of this escort, a fifteen-year-old girl, small for her age, named Elizabeth Eckford, and she showed up by herself, before the others. She got off one of the town's buses, took a deep breath, and willed her body toward the school's main entrance. She wore a pair of stylish bobby socks and new shoes that her mother had bought for the occasion. She looked down at them as she took her first few steps.

Initially, when she saw the guardsmen ahead of her, she found their presence reassuring; she thought they were there to make sure she and the other black students would be admitted without incident. But as she got closer, as she saw the expressions on their faces and the rigidity of their posture, she started to wonder whether they were there to usher her in or keep her out. She began to walk more slowly. Why were the guardsmen looking at her like that? Where were her fellow black students? She continued to approach, but her heart was thumping like a bass drum.

"Here she comes, now get ready!" one of the soldiers said, and then another stepped forward and thrust his rifle at her. Eckford stopped, froze; suddenly terrified, she did not know what to do. What she should not do, she was certain, was look to either side and acknowledge the people who had gathered to support the guardsmen. They gave no sign of closing in on her, but according to journalists on the scene, although the girl was not crying, she had begun visibly to tremble.

Among the comments that Elizabeth Eckford heard in the next few minutes, and that were recorded by television and radio reporters and jotted down by newspapermen in their notebooks were the following. Most of them had to be censored before they were broadcast or printed.

"Go home, you burr head!"

"Go home, you bastard of a black bitch!"

"Go home before you get hurt, nigger. Why don't you go back to the goddamn jungle!"

"No nigger bitch is going to get into our school!"

And, again and again, "Lynch her, lynch her!"

But as the rancor was being spewed at the young girl, as she listened to it alone and unprotected, not all the journalists who had gathered en masse that day, expecting just such a reception for Eckford, were situated where they wanted to be.

Television news cameras raced for position, then focused on Eckford and the hostile crowd around her. But the CBS cameraman had gotten into place too late to catch on film the contorted faces and the yelling and the Confederate flag waving and the "Nigger Go Home" signs. When [CBS correspondent Robert] Schakne realized he didn't have the footage, he did something that revealed the raw immaturity of the new medium of newsgathering: he ordered up an artificial retake. He urged the crowd, which had fallen quieter, to demonstrate its anger again, this time for the cameras. "Yell again!" Schakne implored as his cameraman started filming.

In an act of unparalleled stupidity, the racists in fact yelled again. These people who had just taken a break from their cursing started up once more like actors doing a second take for their director, giving another display of the unreasoning barbarity that seemed to come so naturally to them.

After a few minutes, Eckford began to back up, slowly retreating to the bench at the bus stop, hoping she could get there safely and take the next bus home. Then she changed her mind. She did not want to wait for a bus, not in such a hostile environment. Instead, she ran across the street to a drugstore to call a cab. But the owner saw her coming. He didn't want any part of the young girl and her woes. He locked the door before she could get in. Eckford had no choice but to return to the bus stop and sit on the bench.

The crowd kept taunting her, threatening her, now beginning to move in her direction yet still giving her space. They seemed to want her gone more than they wanted to hurt her.

Schakne could not imagine what she was feeling, but wanted to know. He decided to talk to her. As Gene Roberts and Hank Klibanoff write in their history of race and the media, Schakne and his cameraman proceeded toward her and he held out his microphone and began by simply asking her name. "Eckford remained statue-like, her face unresponsive. 'Are you going to go to school here at Central High?' Eckford didn't move a muscle. The sights and sounds of the young girl, frozen in fear and under assault by a boisterous, noisy mob, were sucked into the television camera without filter. Schakne's simple questions came off as a cruel inquisition of an innocent victim."

Possibly. But however the questions came off, Schakne sympathized with the girl and was merely seeking information for his story. The real cruelty was not the reporter's; it was the mob's, and it was glaringly obvious that night when Schakne's report was the lead story on the *CBS Evening News with Walter Cronkite*.

After Schakne finished interviewing Eckford and a bus had still not appeared, *New York Times* reporter Benjamin Fine put his notebook in his pocket and walked down to the bus stop, sat next to Eckford, and draped his arm around her. He raised her chin with his hand. He said, "Don't let them see you cry." She just looked at him.

The crowd seethed, moved closer, got louder.

A few minutes later a white woman named Grace Lorch, whose husband taught at a local college for blacks, also offered comfort, taking a seat on the bench on the other side of Eckford. We do not know what she said, but it did not matter to the people surrounding the black girl and the two white adults. They had been screaming. If anything, Lorch's presence made them scream louder.

"She's scared," Grace Lorch screamed back. "She's just a little girl. . . . Six months from now you'll be ashamed at what you're doing."

They were not ashamed now. They called Lorch a nigger lover, repeated it over and over again, like a chant. "You stay away from that girl," one of them said.

John Chancellor and his NBC news crew were there too, watching it all happen, filming their own story. Years later, he talked to David Halberstam about that day, and Halberstam told Chancellor's story in his book *The Fifties:*

> [Chancellor] had watched Elizabeth Eckford's perilous journey with growing fear: one child, alone, entrapped by this mob. He was not sure she was going to make it out alive. He had wanted a story, a good story, but this was something beyond a good story, a potential tragedy so terrible that he had hoped it wasn't really happening. He was terribly frightened for her, frightened for himself, and frightened about what this told him about his country. . . . The mob gathered there in the street was uglier than anything he had ever seen before in his life. It was a mob of fellow Americans, people who under other conditions might be perfectly decent people, but there they were completely out of control. Chancellor wondered briefly where this young girl found her strength. It was almost as if he were praying: *Please stop all of this; please, there's got to be a better way.* He watched in agony and captured it all for NBC.

It was the lead story that night on NBC as well as CBS, and also on ABC, and it would continue to be covered as the standoff continued. It would be covered by more and more reporters with each passing day, as they poured into Little Rock in numbers that horrified the citizenry. The *New York*

Times, which had initially assigned only Fine to the story, flew in four more people. Other newspapers and wire services also increased their presence, doubling and trebling it—and Winthrop Rockefeller was proved right: three papers from London even sent reporters to the American South, as our national shame was reported on both sides of the Atlantic.

The TV networks kept shipping in personnel, just as the governor of Arkansas kept sending in reinforcements for the National Guard. It is thought that in the month that the story dominated the news, there were between forty and a hundred journalists in Little Rock at any given time, telling the tale of Orval Faubus's resistance to an increasingly captivated, and disgusted, television audience.

In that audience was President Eisenhower. He did not want to be. He did not want to get involved in the Central High crisis. Ambivalent on racial matters, a strong supporter of states' rights, and privately opposed to the Supreme Court's decision in *Brown v. Board of Education,* he was hoping for a solution without Federal government involvement. But as he watched the newscasts each evening and read the papers and talked to his advisers, he realized there would be no solution, no end to the embarrassment that was Little Rock, unless he acted.

Eisenhower told the television networks that he wanted some time. They were prompt to comply. Before an estimated one-hundred million viewers, with more than sixty percent of America's sets tuned to him, he announced that he had decided to send a thousand men from the 101st Airborne Division—a racially integrated group, the President emphasized—into Little Rock. As for the National Guardsmen who were already there and had been taking their orders from Faubus, they were told that they were now under federal jurisdiction and would henceforth be doing what the White House told them to do, not the governor. Overnight, they were to switch allegiance. Overnight, as some of them believed, they were to turn their backs not only on their fellow Southerners but on themselves and everything that they had grown up believing about the races. But they had their orders, their new orders; they were sworn to obey.

"On the 101st Airborne's first full day in Little Rock," it was reported, "news directors for the three networks got clearance to break into daytime programming virtually at will. CBS broke in eleven times, NBC eight times. ABC joined later in the day." What viewers saw was black children finally being admitted to Central High School, but still having to walk through a gauntlet of angry whites to do it. What viewers heard was the narration of journalists who, in the opinion of Roberts and Klibanoff, were committing the cardinal sin of losing their objectivity:

> The television coverage was provocative and in some ways confusing. There were reporters and commentators, and the line between them wasn't always clear. Night after night, words, phrasings, tones, and inflections became a concern to some television critics and certainly to the segregationists. The networks had pledged earlier in the year to keep opinion out of newscasts. The pledge seemed to dissipate at Little Rock, *The Atlanta Constitution*'s television critic wrote, where "all of the newscasters have become 'analysts' and 'commentators,' with a free rein to speak their own minds about what is right and what is wrong in the integration dispute."

It was true. Reporters in Little Rock sometimes let their opinions run freely, just as their emotions were running freely, their horror at what was happening to the black students having reached critical mass—and according to the canons of their profession, they should not have done so. They should have let the story speak for itself, Roberts and Klibanoff and other critics insisted, and in their way, they were right.

But in fact the story of Little Rock's Central High School *did* speak for itself. The overwhelming impressions left in the minds of viewers were not of the carefully chosen and often-opinionated words of reporters, but of the carelessly and spitefully uttered words of a good many citizens of Arkansas, not to mention their dreadful actions and the hateful expressions on their faces and the terror on the faces of Elizabeth Eckford and the other black children who could go to Central High School each day only because more than a hundred armed men cleared a path for them.

The behavior of reporters might not have been up to the strict ethical standards on which journalism prided itself, but it was the behavior of the people they covered that Americans and other people in other nations would remember, and that would prove so persuasively damning. It was not a shameful exhibition by journalists; it was an unavoidable display of humanity. The shameful exhibition was provided by those upon whom the cameras were focused and microphones aimed.

The 101st Airborne departed from Little Rock at the end of November 1957. The National Guardsmen remained until the end of the school year, and were in fact on duty the night of graduation, when Ernest Green, the only senior among the Little Rock nine, and as of this writing a successful investment banker in Washington, D.C., was spat on as he marched out of the auditorium carrying his diploma, wearing his cap and gown.

Sander Vanocur, who had replaced John Chancellor on the Central High story for NBC, witnessed the incident and reported it. By that time, NBC had long since become the Nigger Broadcasting Company to many, CBS, once the so-called Communist Broadcasting System, was now the Coon Broadcasting System, and ABC was christened the African Broadcasting Company.

THERE WOULD BE MUCH MORE REPORTING on the civil-rights movement in the following decade.

1961: the Freedom Riders, most of them white, rode their buses through the South and, as they approached Birmingham, Alabama, were beaten and harassed by members of the Ku Klux Klan, who had been encouraged by Birmingham's police chief, the notorious Eugene "Bull" Connor. In Anniston, Alabama, one of their buses was firebombed and burst into flames. When the Freedom Riders jumped outside to save themselves, they were viciously beaten by a waiting horde of nigger-lover haters.

1962: James Meredith became the first black student admitted to the University of Mississippi and a riot broke out the moment he appeared on campus. The governor, Ross Barnett, had been as determined to keep the university segregated as Faubus had been to keep the blacks out of Central High. As a result, NBC's Richard Valeriani filed a report that showed "billowing tear gas, smoke, fire, wounded flesh, military operations, and charred hulks of cars." Said Valeriani—yes, it was an opinion, but one that doubled as fact: "Irresponsible defiance in the governor's office was translated into violence on the campus."

1963: civil-rights leader Medgar Evers was shot to death in the driveway of his home in Jackson, Mississippi. Two-and-a-half months later, more than 200,000 people marched on Washington to protest not only Evers's death, but the unremitting acrimony in the South that had led to it. CBS covered the entire march, all three hours of it. NBC and ABC covered most of it, returning to their regular programming only rarely, and NBC's *Today* spent half-an-hour that morning discussing the march before it began.

All three networks broadcast the speech given late in the day by Reverend Martin Luther King Jr. from the steps of the Lincoln Memorial, in which he said, several times, that he had a dream, a dream of racial equality, "a dream that my four little children will one day live in a nation where they will not be judged by the color of their skin but by the content of their character."

TV ratings for the day were up more than sixty percent over those of the same time periods the previous week. And, as Gene Roberts and Hank Klibanoff point out, "A technological breakthrough greatly expanded the day's audience well beyond the nation's shores. Telstar, a communications satellite launched in July 1962, took live coverage of the march to six countries. . . . Television networks in West Germany, Japan, and France sent their own crews to Washington."

There was more to be covered, much more, including the bombing of the black church in Birmingham that killed four little girls; the strife-filled voter registration drive in Selma, Alabama; the dangerous civil-rights marches from Selma, Alabama, to Montgomery; the shooting of James Meredith; and finally, most devastatingly, the assassination of Martin Luther King, Jr. in Memphis in the early spring of 1968.

But eventually, far too late and all the more haunting because of the wasted years, there were stories of a different kind: stories of peaceful, if sometimes reluctant, integration in the schools, of blacks not only taking their places in the classroom but on athletic teams and in school bands and theatrical presentations and at social events and, as they graduated and grew older, as owners of more and more local businesses, participating fully in the lives of their communities, eventually to the extent of beginning to hold public office.

One story that did not get much coverage was perhaps the most searing example of wasted years, simultaneously sorrowful and hopeful.

1980: the University of Alabama overturns the suspension of Autherine Lucy.

1992: Lucy earns her masters degree in elementary education, forty years after she had first applied for admission. She is sixty-two years old now and "a proud sister of the Zeta Phi Beta sorority."

NBC'S VANOCUR BECAME FRIENDS with Andrew Young, a black who would eventually become a Congressman, the U.S. ambassador to the United Nations under President Jimmy Carter, and the mayor of Atlanta. In the fifties, though, he was an aide to Reverend King. One day, after it was all over in Little Rock, the black students having secured their place at Central High and the Army and National Guard having both departed, Young took Vanocur aside and said, "We used you, you know." By "we" he meant civil-rights leaders; by "you" he meant journalists. Vanocur nodded. "I know," he said.

Another civil-rights leader, Congressman John Lewis, acknowledged the role of reporters in a different manner. "If it hadn't been for the media," he insisted many years later, and in fact has repeated on a number of occasions, "the print media and television, the civil rights movement would have been like a bird without wings, a choir without a song."

Lewis was right. Ultimately, the courts and various government agencies and even the troops employed so reluctantly by the Eisenhower administration did not matter nearly as much to the cause of racial equality as the NBC, CBS and ABC evening newscasts. The reports they telecast were something that most people had never seen before: moving pictures of man's inhumanity to man at its most bilious and crazed. The stories changed opinions. They changed behavior. They changed laws.

Even among people who continued to believe in the inherent supremacy of the white race, there were now many who insisted that their beliefs were not license for the kind of mistreatment of blacks that they had witnessed night after night on TV.

In the mid-sixties, President Lyndon Johnson signed into law the most ambitious civil-rights program in our nation's history. He would not have been able to do so had it not been for the courageous television reporting in the years preceding. Robert Schakne might have staged an incident, although he was re-creating reality rather than constructing a fiction, and other reporters might have offered too many opinions from time to time, but these exceptions cannot obscure the fact that TV news has never done more of a service to the United States than it did in covering the civil-rights movement in the fifties. In the process, the medium laid the groundwork for the less racist, if still imperfect, society in which we live today.

Chapter 13

Sexless Objects

I N SOME WAYS, the entertainment shows on television treated women better than they did blacks. In some ways they treated them worse. The female struggle for equality was not as pervasive or as deeply felt in the fifties as it would be later in the century, and therefore was not as visible. It did not attract the interest of journalists, nor even of women in large numbers.

Understandably, then, it did not prick the consciences of television producers. The sitcoms showed women outranking the black servants in their households, and other blacks, like Charlie the elevator boy, who performed servile chores in other venues. But only in a few cases did producers allow women to rise all the way to the level of men as authority figures, and even in those cases they did not do so all the time; "the weaker sex" might transcend its limits, but only for a few minutes, in a few specialized situations. Then, by the end of the half-hour, the female would revert to form, the man reestablishing himself as the eminence grise of the family or workplace.

The sitcom, however, was not the worst of the problems TV created for females half-a-century and more ago.

PERHAPS THE MOST HUMILIATING kind of program in the history of the medium, at least until various kinds of talk and so-called reality shows a few decades later, was "the confessional quiz show," or "misery show." Among them was *Strike It Rich*, whose contestants were women in urgent need of money for such things as surgery or house payments or business debts, and whose host, Warren Hull, seemed so oblivious to their plight that he might have wandered into the wrong studio, expecting to call out bingo numbers in a church basement.

Hull had a lilt to his voice, a bounce to his step, a smile that must have hurt his cheeks. He never stopped grinning. Before the contestants told their tales of woe, he would give them a big box of Fab detergent and a tube of toothpaste from another sponsor, and act as if the poor people were now halfway down the road to recovery from their tribulations. Then he would urge the women to earn their merchandise by baring their souls.

Often husbands would appear on the program with their wives, but they were stoic, silent, occasionally nodding. It was the woman who explained the family's problems, she who revealed that the surgery would enable a child to regain his hearing or the house payments would keep the family off the streets or the business debts were so severe that law-enforcement authorities had threatened to confiscate what few assets they had left. It was she who could be counted on to whimper, wipe away a tear, bow her head as she sighed and covered her eyes with her hands.

Afterward, she and her husband were asked a few relatively simple questions. If they answered correctly, they won some money, although seldom all they had hoped for. If they answered incorrectly, Hull opened up "the Heart Line," meaning that viewers could reach for their telephones and call in and, if they were so inclined, pledge money to the contestants, as if they were the subjects of a telethon. The "Heart Line" seemed spontaneous. It was anything but. According to Walter Framer, producer of *Strike It Rich*,

> Calls were preset. We'd arrange with donors to phone in gifts for a particular contestant. If a widow with six children came on to explain the pressing need for a new roof for her house, we would contact ahead of time a roofer to set up a donation of his services. He got a "plug" for his company. . . . If someone told about needing a sewing machine in order to take in work as a dressmaker, a firm like

Singer might donate a machine—if it had been called in advance of the contestant's appearance.

Whatever its intentions and methods, *Strike It Rich* was controversial from the beginning. In fact, after a few weeks, the *Providence Journal Bulletin* dropped the program from its TV listings, finding it to be the kind of show that would "deliberately exploit human want and misery for commercial gain."

The authors Harry Castleman and Walter Podrazik agreed. In their opinion, *Strike It Rich*

> regularly crossed the line between entertainment and exploitation. Reacting to the absurd mechanics of the program, humorist [and creator of the *Li'l Abner* comic strip] Al Capp proposed that the show use a Misery Meter which would measure the strength of each tale of woe. The scale began with "sad," and worked its way through "depressing," "heartbreaking," "sickening," and "sickeningly heartbreaking" before reaching the ultimate: "unbearably tragic." The program was regularly criticized for its maudlin tone, but the most dramatic expression of outrage took place in the studio control room when the show's first director was ordered to broadcast a tight closeup of the legs of a cripple trying to walk. Instead, the director silently stood up, walked out of the control room, and never returned.

One of the least embarrassing moments on the program was provided by one of the few blacks ever to be chosen as a guest. Mrs. Loretta Danny kept her eyes clear and her voice under control as she told Hull why she wanted more money.

> DANNY: Well, I would like to strike it rich because I want to finish my course at Franklin School of Science and Arts.
> HULL: You're studying to be. . . .
> DANNY: I'm studying to be a medical technician.
> HULL: You're having a difficult time of it?
> DANNY: Yes, I am having a very difficult time. I have to pay someone to take care of the children while I'm at school. . . . Of course, there's food and clothing, books, supplies, laboratory fees. And I'm supposed to graduate in September.

Mrs. Danny then gave Hull a letter of recommendation that had been written by the president of the Franklin School of Science and the Arts. Hull read it aloud. Among other things, the letter referred to the woman's being a war widow. She nodded at the reference, still dry-eyed.

HULL: (reading) [The president] says that you have a fine disposition.
DANNY: (laughing) Thank you.

But many of those who hoped to strike it rich ended up being struck poorer. The program was filmed in New York. Contestants, however, came from all over the country, even though the show's executives warned them that they were responsible for their own travel expenses and lodgings. Some people didn't listen. Others didn't care. To them, a journey to New York for *Strike It Rich* was an investment, its yield far from certain but enticing enough so that they had to take the chance. It was a kind of lottery, except with better odds.

Those who did not beat them, who did not win anything except the detergent and toothpaste, sometimes found themselves stranded in New York after the show with no place to stay and not enough money to return home, much less to right the wrongs that had inspired their trek to *Strike It Rich* in the first place. Often, the Salvation Army and other charitable groups had to provide cots for a night or two and then the bus, train, or airfare so that *Strike it Rich* hopefuls could return to the lives from which they had so desperately wanted to escape. Once they departed from the studio, the producers of the program had no more interest in them—and, as far as they were concerned, no more responsibility.

FOR THE MOST PART, *Queen for a Day*, "the Cinderella show," drew its contestants from the Los Angeles area, where the program was filmed. People were able to get there cheaply and return home before nightfall, no begging necessary. The Salvation Army could tend to other matters.

Like *Strike It Rich*, *Queen for a Day* was "something of an inverted Horatio Alger syndrome: instead of boy or a girl making good, the lure of [the program] was woman making rock bottom." And, in addition to being a more extreme example of the type than *Strike It Rich*, *Queen for a Day* was the biggest hit of all the confessional quiz shows, featuring such emotionally charged tales of life gone wrong that *New York Times* television critic

Jack Gould reacted to the premiere episode of the show on NBC by asking, "What hath Sarnoff wrought?"

To which the response was: some of the highest ratings yet in the annals of daytime TV.

On each episode, four women—and women only; there were no kings for the day—were selected from the studio audience. They, too, had been "preset," which is to say, they had applied to be guests on the program and were placed in the audience by the producers. When called upon by host Jack Bailey—he of the narrow eyes, pencil-thin mustache, and less jocular manner than Warren Hull—they would tramp up to the stage and take their seats at a table, their facial expressions forlorn, their shoulders hunched forward. They looked as if they would rather be anywhere else in the world, but in fact there was nowhere else in the world they would rather have been; the *Queen for a Day* studio was the great hope for salvation. It was also, for many contestants, the last resort.

Let us run through a typical program.

Bailey calls the first woman's name and she gets up and trudges over to the host, standing next to him. He makes a little small talk; it is not his strength. Where are you from? Oh, my goodness, isn't that wonderful! What does your husband do for a living? Well, golly, it must be somethin' to be married to someone who does whatever your husband does.

Then Bailey gets to the point. He asks the woman why she would like to be queen for a day. Well, she says, I want a washing machine and two tires. Although he knows the answer in advance, Bailey seems surprised by the combination. The woman enlightens him. The washing machine, she says, will enable her to take in laundry from the neighbors so the family can make a few extra bucks, which they desperately need. The tires, she explains, will allow her husband to get to his low-paying job. Right now, the two rear tires on their jalopy are so bald that a mechanic has advised them the vehicle is too dangerous to drive.

Bailey nods in understanding. Thank you, dear, he replies, and seems genuinely to wish her well.

Cut to commercial.

Second contestant: this woman would like to have a dog, preferably a collie, and some educational toys for her five-and-a-half year old son. The boy, it seems, has developed a brain tumor; he has missed some school and has problems paying attention in class when he does attend. The woman does not tell Bailey whether the tumor is life-threatening, nor what the boy's chances are for recovery, nor why she does not want money to pay for medical bills. The dog will bring her son joy, she insists, and the toys will divert him and stimulate his mind—and that is all she cares about for now.

All the best to you, sweetheart, Bailey says, the very best!

Cut to commercial.

Third contestant: her request is for a special bed that will enable her brother, who can barely move because he was shot five times, to spend his days in a more comfortable fashion. Again, the story is not clear. Who shot him? Why? Why *five* times? Are the bullets still in him? Is he a bank robber or something like that? Bailey is not curious, or impolitic, enough to ask.

We're rootin' for ya, little lady. Yessir, we really are.

Cut to commercial.

Fourth contestant: what this woman wants is for someone to blast a hole in the ceiling of her living room. Bailey appears even more puzzled than he was by the request for the washing machine and two tires. He has heard of people wanting holes to be repaired, he tells her, but never of a person wanting one to be sliced into a perfectly good example of the plasterer's craft.

The woman is patient. She tells Bailey that there is no furnace in her house, only a single space heater which the family keeps on the first floor. But her three youngest children sleep in a bedroom on the second floor, and even with enough covers on them to squash them into immobility, they are so cold on winter nights that it is hard for them to sleep. She thinks if someone can knock a hole in the ceiling directly above the space heater, the children's problem will be solved.

Of course, what she really wants is a furnace, but she does not want to seem presumptuous.

Well, we'll keep our fingers crossed for you, darlin'.

Cut to commercial.

After which the show returns for its denouement—and as if the stories the women have just told before a national television audience were not humiliating enough, there now comes the ultimate in public self-flagellation. Bailey briefly summarizes each woman's tale of woe, and as the camera zooms in for a close-up the audience votes on the pathos of her plight by applauding; the louder the applause, the farther the needle moves to the right, like that of a speedometer in an accelerating car. It is Al Capp's facetiously suggested Misery Meter come to life, although *Queen for a Day* calls it an Audience Applause Meter and it appears in the lower right corner of the screen as the audience renders its verdict. The woman whose predicament sends the needle farthest into the Pity Zone is the winner, and in this case it is the one who wants the bed for her bullet-riddled brother.

When Bailey announces her victory, she rises from the table and proceeds toward him again, her gait unsteady, her expression disbelieving but pathetically grateful. "I now crown you Queen Clarice," he proudly announces, "Queen for a Day!" Whereupon some beautiful young women in high heels and sequined dresses glide onto the stage, squeeze a crown onto Clarice's head, and drape her in a cape with fake ermine lining. Then they lead her to a throne where Bailey plops so many roses on her lap that it ends up looking like a small, sloppily tended garden.

The woman gets more than just the bed for her brother. For herself and her family, she is awarded a dinette set, silverware, a tape recorder, a washing machine, a dryer, and a machine called a food center, which mixes, blends, juices, grinds meat, and sharpens knives. She is also given a gift certificate from the world-famous Spiegel catalogue so she can buy even more consumer goods. Clarice cannot believe it. She has gotten over the initial shock of victory and is now overcome with emotion—tears running down her face, sobs almost making her gasp: "good picture" as they call it in television.

And good business. As *Queen for a Day* producer Howard Blake would later explain, "A candidate had to want something we could plug—a stove, a carpet, a plane trip, an artificial leg, a detective agency, a year's supply of baby food." But a specially equipped bed for an ammo-riddled brother?

And the companies that provided the products were happy to do so, because as each of the products was bestowed upon the winner of a particular day's program, its manufacturer was saluted, its features were touted and its reliability praised. Meaning that, just as was the case with *Strike It Rich*'s Heart Line, the manufacturer got a free commercial by donating an item to the show, a commercial heard by audiences both in the studio and at home, audiences whose emotions were at a peak of warmth and receptiveness at the moment the pitch was being made.

There is no question that *Queen for a Day*, like *Strike It Rich*, did some good. The winners were always better off materially, at least for a certain period of time, than they had been before the show. But Jeanne Cagney, one of *Queen for a Day*'s production assistants, thought that even those who did not achieve regal status might have come out ahead. "It's a heart-warming experience," she said, ". . . but I often think of the runners-up and hope that maybe it helps them just to come on the show to tell someone about their problem."

Blacks almost never appeared on *Queen for a Day*; prejudice spared them the indignity. White women were the society's designated wallowers, and an uncommon number of them were willing to play their part.

IN OTHER KINDS OF SHOWS, the primary function of females was to serve as set design. *Wagon Train, Rawhide, Wanted: Dead or Alive,* and *Have Gun, Will Travel* were among the majority of westerns that had no females appearing in regular roles. And if a woman did play a part in a particular episode, it was inevitably a minor one. We might see her for a few seconds at the beginning, strolling down a sidewalk past the general store in her crinolines and lace. Then the star of the show would ride into town, tie up his horse, and, after dismounting, tip his hat to the woman and say, "Howdy, ma'am." She would nod back and continue on her way.

But the purpose of the scene was to demonstrate that the star had a gentle side as well as a rugged one, not to introduce the woman to the audience. Most likely, once she disappeared from view she would not be seen or referred to again that night.

Or a program might begin with a woman watching, horrified, through the window of her cabin as her husband, who was innocently tending to some chores around the farm, was slain by renegade Apaches. The cowboy hero would get wind of the incident and head out to the woman's ranch to find out exactly what had happened and to comfort the widow as best he could. Then he would ask her which way the Indians had gone and how much of a head start they had. She would tell him and he would take off in pursuit. The woman's tragedy was the focal point of the plot, but she too would probably disappear for the rest of the twenty- or fifty-plus minutes of air time.

In detective shows like *77 Sunset Strip* and *Bourbon Street Beat*, or other kinds of action series, females were often cast as comic relief in addition to scenery, virtually never in serious or thoughtful roles. In *Hawaiian Eye*, Connie Stevens played a pretty young thing named Cricket, who, as Douglas T. Miller and Marion Nowak tell us,

> helped out the men by cluttering up the action, getting in the way, and cowering. Much the same was true of the women in all these programs, from "Martin Kane, Private Eye" (1949) through "Wire Service" (1956) to "Surfside 6" (1960) and well into the seventies. The female inevitably appeared in a part that labeled her as

an auxiliary to a man: femme fatale, wife, sweetheart. But always she was no more than an excuse for the hero to swing into action. Women, that is, were simply impersonal props on this sort of show.

According to the Museum of Broadcast Communications, 68 percent of the characters who appeared in primetime dramas in 1952 were male. Two decades later, the percentage had risen to 74 percent. The percentage of men cast in the most prominent roles, of course, was even higher. Television was slow to consider a woman as anything more than one of those impersonal props; she was, at best, the helpmeet of a man whose strength and fortitude were such that he needed little in the way of assistance with the demands of the plot.

IT WAS A DIFFERENT MATTER, however, in commercials, especially commercials for household products. Here the female was ubiquitous, in almost all cases playing the part of housewife who seemed to be as happy with her station in life as she was with the product she had been hired to extol. She stood at the sink and washed the dishes, and was amazed at how easy it was to get them clean and shiny with the sponsor's new and improved detergent. She poured wax onto the kitchen floor and spread it with a sponge mop and was delighted at the sudden sparkle of her linoleum. She dropped her bread into the sponsor's toaster and marveled at how quickly and evenly browned the slices emerged, brushed her teeth with the sponsor's toothpaste and squinted at the brightness of her smile in the mirror, washed her hair with the sponsor's shampoo and shook her head in wonder at its manageability, not a tangle in sight and a sheen that matched the kitchen floor and her teeth.

What products these were! What a boon to existence to make use of them! What an honor to be the actress chosen to demonstrate them!

Such were the portrayals of American women in television ads in the fifties. Such were the portrayals of women in ads even later—creatures with no concerns beyond the domestic and no apparent goals in life other than to continue being the appendage of the lord of her particular manor. In the early seventies, an infamous series of ads for the vitamin supplement Geritol showed an older but still attractive lady pursuing a round of strenuous activities with her husband looking on ever so proudly. At the conclusion of the commercial, he puts his arm around her, smiles, and says, "My wife . . . I think I'll keep her." She smiles back, seeming to want nothing more than to be kept. It is supposed to be a touching moment.

It is television's snapshot of an ideal marriage. Even then it made molars grind from one end of the country to the other.

Women in commercials might have fared even worse off-camera than they did in front of it. In the fifties, a study by sociologist Kenneth Allan showed that 93 percent of all commercials were narrated by men, a mere 7 percent by females. Even as late as the eighties, the figures had barely changed; 91 percent of all TV advertisements employed men as off-camera announcers, although women were usually the ones seen in the ads doing something painfully mundane.

And looking painfully mundane. They were almost always attired in a manner that could not have been less flattering, shapeless dresses that ignored every curve or protrusion in the female form. Peter Pan collars around their necks, baggy blouses, skirts that almost touched the floor as they did their chores, and hairdos that framed their faces no more appealingly than a coonskin cap had framed the face of Estes Kefauver. This is not to suggest that women should have been made up as vixens in fifties commercials; merely that they should have been allowed to dress less like manikins and behave less like beasts of burden.

MOST OF ALL, what women seemed to have in common with blacks in the early days of network TV was that they showed up more often in sitcoms than in any other kind of program. They were, in other words, thought to be more suited to frivolous roles than to those that required an imposing presence. But even in such insulting roles the female characters seemed to bear a disproportionate brunt of derision.

Which leads one to conclude that *I Love Lucy* was not only the most popular sitcom of the period, but the most representative in terms of TV's attitude toward women. Lucy was constantly trying to ignore the duties that Ricky had assigned her as mistress of the household, to escape from them, to be a nightclub performer like her husband, his costar as well as his wife. But she was always doomed to fail.

Sometimes, though, it seemed as if she would succeed. For example, in the series' famous "lost pilot," long ago found, Lucy took over one night at Ricky's club, the Copa, when a clown got sick at the last minute. It could have been a disaster. It wasn't. Lucy put on the clown's costume and improvised a comedy routine as Ricky led the band—and the audience at the club loved it; to them she was the hit of the evening. They laughed, applauded; even the men under Ricky's baton, knowing that their boss had no patience for his wife's interference, could not help but enjoy themselves as they watched Lucy cavort around the stage on a bicycle small enough for a chipmunk, swapping one-liners with her husband, and usually getting the better of him. This Mrs. Ricardo had saved the show. What a performer she turned out to be!

Dissolve to a few hours later. Lucy has long since returned to their apartment. She hears the door open behind her and Ricky enters disconsolately. He plops down onto the sofa without saying a word. She sits next to him. When he finally speaks, he does not commend her for saving the show, for boosting his career, for being such a talented comedienne. He does not even utter a simple thank you. Instead, in his most disappointed tone, he says, "All I want you to do is just clean the house."

Lucy has a broom in her hand and waves it a few times as she replies. "I've been cleaning the house ever since I got home."

Ricky: "And hand me my pipe."

Lucy does so.

Ricky takes it gloomily, not lighting up.

Forcing a smile, Lucy says, "And cook for you and be the Momma for your children."

Ricky nods.

The "lost pilot" should have stayed lost.

AS THE NEXT SEVERAL YEARS' worth of programs would demonstrate, Lucy had not given up on show business. She would continue her attempts to share Ricky's spotlight. But at least for one night in particular, she understood her man's feelings and, as women were supposed to do unquestioningly in those days, yielded to them without regret.

In her own way, Gracie Allen made just as pathetic a concession on the program which she, too, shared with her real-life husband, George Burns. In one episode, George is not home from work yet, when Harry Von Zell, a neighbor and the show's announcer, drops in for a visit. He finds Gracie a nervous wreck; she has just put a dent in the car, and George does not yet know. As Von Zell enters, Gracie is standing at the sink, frantically energetic at her chore, which happens to be scrubbing dishes that are already clean.

HARRY VON ZELL: Gracie, why are you washing the dishes?
GRACIE: I haven't any dirty ones. I've been too upset to eat.

VON ZELL: (with genuine concern) You are upset.

GRACIE: Yes, but upset or not, a woman has to do her housework.

On *I Married Joan*, the sexism did not even wait for the story to unfold; it announced itself in the show's opening theme. First a finger would appear, pushing a door bell. Then, the camera cut to star Joan Davis, a dopey expression on her face, standing before the camera in a wedding dress although her nuptials were many years in the past, and looking ridiculous in the get-up. By now the theme song had begun to play, the effect of the lyrics made even more offensive to modern sensibilities by the even dopier facial expressions with which Davis accompanied them.

> *I married Joan.*
> *What a girl, what a whirl, what a life!*
> *Oh, I married Joan.*
> *What a mind, love is blind, what a wife!*
> *Giddy and gay, all day she keeps my heart laughin',*
> *Never know where her brain has flown.*
> *To each his own, can't deny that's why I married Joan.*

The twenty-first century viewer is not sure he has heard correctly. Joan's husband thinks there is something not quite right about her mind? He married her because love is blind? He never knows where her brain has flown? And this guy, her spouse, portrayed by the blusteringly stuffy Jim Backus, is a judge (in domestic court) in the series, a man of perceptiveness and gravity, a respected member of the community who earns his living by making decisions that he thinks are best for his fellow citizens?

In cases like these, television was not reflecting the attitudes already prevalent in society, but exaggerating them for what played at the time as comic effect. Few female characters on sitcoms were spared such treatment; even Our Miss Brooks was insulted about her gender, and by Philip Boynton, of all people, the Madison High School biology teacher who was the object of her persistent and obvious affections despite his obliviousness to her feelings. Where has *his* brain flown?

BOYNTON: When it comes to matters of physical bravery . . . it's
  only natural that men would rate above the weaker sex. . . .

MRS. DAVIS: (Brooks's landlady, who is eavesdropping on this telephone conversation on an extension) Fine, that's an insult to womanhood. Don't let him get away with it, Connie.

BROOKS: I can't quite understand the point you're trying to make, Mr. Boyston.

BOYNTON: It's just women can't be expected to do the same things men can do.

BROOKS: Who says they can't? . . . Are you implying that women are lacking in courage? . . .

BOYNTON: I didn't exactly say that.

BROOKS: . . . Are you hinting that all women are cowards?

Of course, later in the program Miss Brooks *does* demonstrate her courage, but with a reluctant, teeth-gnashing timidity. It is obvious that courage comes more naturally to men, whereas reluctance is the instinctive reaction of the women.

Father Knows Best, the most egregiously named of the fifties sitcoms, was also, ironically, one of the few in which mother seemed to know quite a bit herself. Margaret Anderson, played by Jane Wyatt, is in most cases as levelheaded and discerning as her husband Jim, played by Robert Young. He treats her with more respect than most TV husbands treat their wives and she deserves it; her manner is at once warm and dignified. "C'mon, woman, let's get on with the cooking," Jim says to her on one occasion, but he is teasing more than demanding.

Still, she got on with the cooking. Margaret Anderson was, after all, a fifties housewife, in the kitchen for at least part of the time in many episodes and missing almost completely from a few others. When the Andersons' son, Bud, started dating the daughter of the football coach, hoping that the coach would be more likely to choose him for the team as a result, it was father, not mother, who discussed with Bud the ethics of the situation. It was father who truly knew best. And it was father whose advice Bud was more likely to take to heart than mother.

At the time, *Father Knows Best* was considered as idyllic a portrait of family life as television had to offer, one that real-life families would do well to emulate. Many years later, though, in an era with very different sensibilities, Billy Gray, who played Bud, blasted the program for its less obvious meanings, claiming that it "did everyone a disservice. The girls were always trained to use their feminine wiles, to pretend to be helpless to attract men. The show contributed to a lot of the problems between men and women that we see today. . . . I think we were all well motivated, but what we did was run a hoax."

In *Leave It to Beaver,* perhaps the most affectionately remembered of the era's sitcoms, Barbara Billingsley, as Beaver's Mom, June, got top billing in the opening titles over Hugh Beaumont, who played Dad. Like Margaret Anderson, June Cleaver was a near-equal to her husband, Ward. When Beaver, embarrassed at his behavior in one episode and afraid of parental reprisal, climbed up a tree and refused to come down, his parents took up positions below him and encouraged him to change his mind. They did so, however, in entirely different manners.

Ward was flummoxed. He insisted that Beaver give up his perch; he huffed and puffed and virtually threatened to saw the tree down. Beaver did not budge. June took a more subtle approach, telling her son in a calm voice that he could stay up among the branches as long as he liked, but that she and Ward and their other son, Wally, were going home to dinner. They were hungry, and she was planning to cook something especially tasty. The three of them started to leave.

Beaver, apparently, hadn't thought about the matter of eating. Nor did he have to think about it for long. He quickly climbed down the tree and took his place with his family at the dinner table.

Still, there were those obligatory fifties moments, a certain level of female subservience having to be maintained: When, at another meal, Beaver would not eat his brussels sprouts despite June's importuning, she said, "Ward, tell him to eat."

Ward: "Beaver, go ahead."

Beaver: "OK, Dad." And he ate his tart green vegetables.

Father commands best.

The Donna Reed Show was another in which the wife was a figure of some standing in the family, although less so than her mate. Alex Stone, in the person of Carl Betz, was a doctor, Donna Stone but a housewife. They did not argue often, but in one of their spats, Alex said, "Why not mention the resentment of the female against even the mildest form of criticism, her tendency to fall apart in a crisis." Donna responded with equal vehemence and even more logic, but Alex had made his point and it was one of the show's, and the entire decade's, guiding sitcom principles.

ONE OF THE FEW WOMEN to work outside the home on television, in addition to Connie Brooks, was Susie McNamara, played by Ann Sothern on a program known at different times as both *The Ann Sothern Show* and *Private Secretary*. Susie was a single woman employed as the assistant to the head of a talent agency. A bright, perky, vivacious sort, her smile lit up the office. Her relationship with her boss Mr. Sands, played by Don Porter, was for the most part a good one; many was the time when a problem came up in the business that stumped Mr. Sands but was ingeniously solved by Susie. Mr. Sands always appreciated her help, but usually expressed his gratitude with a comic grumpiness.

There was no doubt, however, who ran the business. In a single episode of the program, Susie heard the following from Mr. Sands: "Get back to work." "Let's see if we can get a little work done around here for a change." And, "Susie, you've got to learn to mind your own business."

She took it well enough, her smile usually remaining in place, never seeming to be as upset as Mr. Sands, no matter what the circumstance. She probably realized that, if she had been married, she would have heard the same things, perhaps even more imperiously uttered, from her husband.

SUSIE DID NOT HAVE CHILDREN. Neither did Connie Brooks. They were, after all, unmarried. But almost every other sitcom woman was a mother, although one wonders how, since neither they nor their husbands ever mentioned or even hinted at procreation. Would Margaret Anderson throw her arms around Jim and plead for a roll in the hay? Would June Cleaver whisper to Ward that she needed him right now and it wouldn't kill Beaver to stay in the damn tree for another half-hour or so? And Gracie Allen— would she swear never to dent the car again if George would just give her a good boff? Impossible to imagine.

Bedrooms were seldom shown on the small screen at the time, and when they were, they were always furnished with twin beds a few feet apart, a nightstand between them. Throughout the entire fifties there was never so much as a single shot of a married couple in the same bed. And few were the shots of a married couple in their separate resting places. Most of the time, one was awake, probably the husband, pacing around the room in his bathrobe talking about something while the missus made such a cocoon of her covers that her pajamas were not even visible.

Lucille Ball managed to break through the prudish barriers of the time, just as she had broken through the anti-Communist barriers of the time, but only because nature had taken its course: far from the camera's prying eye, she had conjoined with her husband and gotten pregnant while *I Love Lucy* was still in production for the year.

The network, CBS, was not happy. The sponsor, Philip Morris, was embarrassed. There was no choice but to write Lucy's pregnancy into the show, tacitly admitting that she and Desi had stretched the freedoms of marriage to their limit and engaged in sexual congress.

But there *was* a choice about how to refer to the star's condition, and the writers were instructed never to use the word "pregnant." Lucy was "with child"; she was "going to have a baby"; she was "expecting"; the "stork would soon be visiting." "Pregnant," for some reason, was thought to be a word with a prurient context. Neither the network nor the advertisers were comfortable with it, although the logic is elusive, to say the least.

As the time for the stork's visit grew closer, the corporate suits became even less comfortable. CBS and Philip Morris realized that, regardless of the language they used, both Lucy and her fellow cast members would have to start commenting on her condition. She was, after all, waddling now instead of walking; she was sitting on the sofa and patting her stomach rather than riding a bike around the Copa stage. It was in August 1952, that Lucy started to bulge visibly, and that was when CBS and Philip Morris started to quake visibly.

But how were the cast members to comment? What kinds of things should they say, other than just asking Lucy how she felt in a particular episode? Was there any way to make jokes about her pregnancy, or rather her "with child-ness"? The producers of the show decided there was only one thing to do.

"To ensure the acceptability of the treatment of so delicate a subject," Castleman and Prodrazik tell us, "a priest, a rabbi, and a minister were present at these filmings to lend divine approval." *Divine approval for television scripts?* Would not the cause of salvation have been better served if the priest, rabbi and minister tended to their flocks rather than to CBS's scripts? Would not the cause of humor have been better served if the priest, rabbi, and minister went into a bar?

The baby, Desiderio Alberto Arnaz IV, was born on January 19, 1953. According to some reports, the birth got more coverage than the inauguration of President Eisenhower, which was televised the next day.

OTHER THAN THAT, the closest TV came to acknowledging that men had a lascivious side and women sometimes appealed to it was in the afternoon soap operas. The most titillating, apparently—although no traces remain of it today— seems to have been something called *Matinee Theater,* which debuted on NBC in 1955. "Sex is important to us because our audience wants it," explained executive producer Albert McCleery. "Sex is all a woman thinks about while she's sitting at home and we can give it to her."

But, even without having seen so much as a stray moment of *Matinee Theater,* I believe we can be certain that the program "gave it to her" conversationally, in dialogue between male and female characters that was suggestive more than explicit. Perhaps it was delivered with a leering expression; perhaps the expression was followed by a hug or kiss that suggested more amorous exercise might be in the offing at a later time. But we can be just as certain that a man never undid the top button of a woman's blouse, never slid his hands down her hips to the hem of her skirt and begin to tug upward, never led a woman into the forbidden sanctuary of a double bed. All of this having been said, one assumes that today *Matinee Theater* would be rated PG-13.

Still, many viewers were upset by the program, especially women who apparently did not think about sex all the time, and did not want to associate with television characters that did. One letter to *Matinee Theater* attacked it for subverting "what sense of decency and respect for virginity there is left in the world." Another accused the show of having "low moral standards," finding it "positively disgusting" at times.

The critic Gilbert Seldes agreed. *Matinee Theater* was "highly immoral." It "exploit[ed] the baser passions." It did so especially in one scene that was "as explicit physically as television dares to go."

Matinee Theater lasted for two-and-a-half years, then NBC canceled it, not just because of the protests but because the ratings, never high to begin with, had begun to sink. Other soap operas stayed on the air longer and attracted larger audiences but, at least through the fifties, were apparently less explicit in their dialogue, and more lady-like in their depictions of ladies than *Matinee Theater* had been.

AN OCCASIONAL QUIZ SHOW or game show hinted at a woman's sexual nature, as did an infrequent panel or variety show, when such large-breasted women as Faye Emerson, Ilka Chase, and Jennie Lewis, a.k.a. Dagmar, would make appearances in tight-fitting sweaters and skirts that specifically accentuated the attributes the fabrics so snugly covered. Sometimes the sweaters were low-cut; sometimes the skirts came down only to the knee. Usually these women wore the highest heels in which they could still maintain their balance.

Of the three, Dagmar seemed to be the most prominently endowed—no exact measurements are available. When she was introduced and walked across the stage at the beginning of a program, she did it slowly, as if so front-loaded that she might tip over if she moved any faster.

Occasionally the host of the show or one of the male guests would make a comment about the way Dagmar or Ilka or Faye was constructed. It would be innocent as those things went, with a sophomoric tone to it, the men winking at the camera as they uttered their remarks and the women faking a blush.

Emerson was probably television's most famous sex symbol of the fifties. After all, when starring in her own, short-lived program, she

was known less for her performance talents and intellectual endowments than for what one keen observer called her "snowy shoulders and well-rounded upper slopes in a plunging neckline gown." Highlighted by low-cut garb, Emerson's flashy trademarks caused no end of coy smirking. "As for that item the fans call Faye's 'TV neckline,' there wasn't much 'V' to it," noticed Jack O'Brian in a review of *Faye Emerson's Wonderful Town.* "More a gracefully feminine diagonal slide starting high on the left shoulder and scooting decorously down to a safe distance above the left side of her—oh, you know!"

That, however, was as far as it went at the time.

But for one female viewer it was too far—not just the rare flaunting of textile-enclosed breasts and some occasionally juvenile commenting on them by witless males, but the treatment of all women on all programs. This viewer was not, in other words, upset that women were portrayed as sex objects, but that they were portrayed as objects—virtually lacking in gender or humanity or dignity at all. She railed at the unwillingness of television to give females different kinds of roles, roles that revealed them to be as competent as men and as deserving of the same kind of employment opportunities and respect both within the family circle and outside it. She fumed at the female's constant confinement in the "comfortable concentration camp" of the home, and her apparent fulfillment at being so restricted.

In an article for *TV Guide*, the woman wrote that television dismissed the average American female as a "stupid, unattractive, insecure little household drudge who spends her martyred, mindless, boring days dreaming of love—and plotting nasty revenge against her husband."

Seldom did a lady on fifties television plot revenge. But the author of the article did exactly that; she plotted her revenge against television's treatment of her sisters and, more importantly, against the world that the medium mirrored, sometimes accurately, sometimes hyperbolically. Her language was extraordinarily blunt for the time, her commitment extraordinarily impassioned.

The author of the article was Betty Friedan, and in 1963 she published a book that not only expanded her *TV Guide* views but put them into a historical context that made them all the more vivid. She told of a problem, one that "lay buried, unspoken, for many years in the minds of American women. It was a strange stirring, a sense of dissatisfaction, a yearning."

The book would become one of biggest-selling and most influential volumes of the decade. Although what we now refer to as the Women's Movement had been gaining momentum, however slowly, before her book was published, it was *The Feminine Mystique* that truly ignited the movement, clarified its purposes, and served as the flag under which so many American women would march. It was, at least unofficially, the bible for the cause of equality for women, and Friedan became one of its most prominent leaders.

Television's role in all this, however inadvertent, however unacknowledged, was significant. If it had not been for the small screen's treatment of the American female in the fifties, the medium's portrayal of her as weepy, vacuous, inconsequential, and submissive, Betty Friedan might not have been so zealous or, ultimately, so successful in her condemnations—and the campaign she did so much to inspire might have been much delayed.

Chapter 14

The Constant Parade

ECAUSE OF THE racism and sexism in society at the time, it was inevitable that there be racism and sexism on television. Because of certain inherent features of the medium, it was inevitable that violence have a place, as well. The latter, however, as is about to be demonstrated, is a more esoteric point. Those of you who do not care for esoterica will, I hope, keep reading, as this tome will become less esoteric again in but a few paragraphs.

Among those who have analyzed the nature of TV violence are the previously-cited social critic Neil Postman and one-time broadcast journalist Steve Powers. In their 1992 book *How to Watch TV News*, they tell us that the TV screen "occupies about 15 percent of the viewer's visual field (compared to about 70 percent for the movie screen). It is not set in a darkened theater closed off from the world but in the viewer's ordinary living space. This means that visual changes must be more extreme and more dramatic to be interesting on television. A narrowing of the eyes will not do. A car crash, an earthquake, a burning factory are much better."

The unlikely named Jerry Mander, in his provocative 1978 volume called *Four Arguments for the Elimination of Television*, thinks along the same lines. But he gets even more esoteric, not considering the size of the image in his analysis of television's predisposition toward car crashes and earthquakes so much as the poor quality of the televised image, a trait much more evident in the fifties than it is today. He writes that the small screen

> is far better suited technically to expressing hate, fear, jealousy, winning, wanting and violence. These emotions suffer very little information loss when pushed through the coarse imagery of television. . . . Hate, anger, competitiveness are obvious broad-band expressions. Most of them can be well communicated solely through body movement. No detail is needed to get the point, and neither is any special talent on the part of actor or director. . . .
>
> For these technical reasons, among others . . . there is an emphasis on sports and violence in television programming, and there is great viewer interest in them.
>
> The popularity of such programming is not so much a sign that public tastes are vulgar, as they are assumed to be in many quarters. . . . as it is a sign that these programs are the ones which manage to communicate *something*, at least, through television.

Government officials more than half a century ago would not have been interested in such theorizing had it been offered at the time. They were, however, interested in the general subject of violence as a subject for storytelling and the effect it might be having on society.

By the mid-fifties, more than a dozen states had passed laws regulating the content of comic books, a decision largely inspired by the 1954 book *Seduction of the Innocent*. The author, psychiatrist Fredric Wertham, who spent seven years studying his subject, claimed that the small panels and blurred images of comics were poisoning young minds with their gory depictions of crime and rage, warfare and debauchery.

> A typical comic-book drawing shows a blonde young girl lying in bed. She says: "Then I was dreaming of murder and morphine." This is a crime-comic-book dream. Murder, crime and drug traffic are offered to children in a literature which the defenders of comic books call the modern version of the stories of the brothers

Grimm, Hans Christian Andersen or Mother Goose. But are there heroin addicts in Grimm, marihuana [sic] smokers in Andersen or dope peddlers in Mother Goose? And are there advertisements for guns and knives?

What Wertham describes is hardly a typical comic book drawing. It is unlikely that Little Lulu ever dreamed of murder, or Archie and Jughead of morphine. A lot of parents, however, agreed with Wertham's belief in the lurid content and dire influence of certain comic books. A lot of legislators listened. But it was not comic books that troubled them most.

In the fall of 1954, the United States Senate began looking into violence on television—larger panels than comic books but the same slightly fuzzy images, especially on color TVs. The Senate formed a Special Subcommittee on Juvenile Delinquency, and among the programs that came up in the testimony it heard was a TV movie for young viewers called *The River Patrol*. According to an article in the *New Republic*, the movie

opens aboard a boat, where a smuggler is strangling an accomplice with a nylon stocking. A man appears from the galley to throw a bread knife at the murderer as he's about to roll victim No. 1 overboard. The knife misses by a hair; the "heavy" pulls out his own yard-long blade and plunges it into the frustrated assassin's belly to the accompaniment of an agonizing scream. He then smacks a faithful accomplice hard in the stomach—just to let off excess energy. Before the villain is done in, he plots to toss Police Officer Robey into a bay, engages in a crate-heaving, head-clouting struggle with the good young man and at one point clumps down on his hand with a boot; Robey groans in a heart-rending close-up. He recovers sufficiently to rabbit-punch the villain into unconsciousness and so make law and order triumph once again.

And that was just the first few minutes! Among those who testified before the Senate's Special Subcommittee was Dr. Edward Podolsky, a Brooklyn physician who was one of the first to believe in, and to prescribe to patients, the healing powers of music. Conversely, he thought that violence on television was among society's more discordant activities. "Seeing constant brutality, viciousness and unsocial acts," he testified, "results in hardness, intense selfishness, even in mercilessness, proportionate to the amount of exposure and its play on the native temperament of the child. Some cease to show resentment to insults, to indignities, and even cruelty toward helpless old people, to women and other children."

It was not the first time the Federal government had addressed the issue of violence on the tube. Nor would it be the last. Congressional concern seems to have begun with the Kefauver Committee, which had looked into the causes of juvenile delinquency, wondering whether a new generation of organized criminals was being created by the same medium that was televising its hearings. It stated, in too many words, some of them awkwardly assembled, that its members "share the concern of a large segment of the thinking public for the implications of the impact of this new medium . . . upon the ethical and cultural standards of the youth of America. It has been unable to gather proof of a direct causal relationship between the viewing of acts of crime and violence and the actual performance of criminal deeds. It has not, however, found irrefutable evidence that young people may not be negatively influenced in their present-day behavior by the saturated exposure they now receive to pictures and drama based on an underlying theme of lawlessness and crime which depict human violence."

No wonder the Senators hadn't found irrefutable evidence that TV violence causes real life violence. There wasn't any, claimed television executives. To paraphrase what ABC vice president Robert H. Hinckley told the Special Subcommittee on Juvenile Delinquency in 1954: there was a lot of crime committed by teenagers in the Soviet Union and very few TVs, and a lot of TVs in America and very little crime committed by teenagers. Point made, Hinckley thought. Then he made a related point, which other broadcasters also emphasized to the Subcommittee: "broken homes and only broken homes make delinquents."

The Subcommittee did not agree. Neither, apparently, did a majority of its constituents. A Gallup Poll conducted the same year found that three out of every four American adults took issue with Hinckley, believing that "the constant parade of violence on the home screen was a major contributor to the growth of violent behavior, juvenile delinquency, and outright criminal behavior among the nation's young people."

Support for this view came from a group called the National Association for Better Radio and Television (NABRT). In 1958, its members spent a week watching TV in Los Angeles and taking notes as carefully as they could. According to a later report, the NABRT monitors saw 223 people die,

161 of them victims of murder. "There were also 192 attempted murders, 83 robberies, 15 kidnappings, 24 conspiracies to commit murder, and 49 other instances of violence including physical torture and attempted lynchings."

Two years later, the record of a week's viewing in Los Angeles is so detailed as to seem almost a parody. It included

144 murders (scenes of mass murder not tabulated), 143 attempted murders, 52 justifiable killings, 14 cases of drugging, 12 jailbreaks, 36 robberies, 6 thefts, 13 kidnappings (1 of a small boy), 6 burglaries, 7 cases of torture, 6 extortion cases, 5 blackmail, 11 planned murders, 4 attempted lynchings, 1 massacre scene with hundreds killed, 1 mass murder of homesteaders, 1 planned mass murder by arson, 3 scenes of shooting between gangland posses, many killed, 1 other mass gun battle, 1 program with over 50 women kidnapped, this one including an hour of violence, kidnapping, murder, brutal fighting. These figures do not include the innumerable prolonged and brutal fights, the threats to kill, the sluggings or the many times when characters in the crime programs manhandled the victims, the forced confessions, and dynamiting to illegally destroy.

Academics, too, expressed their misgivings about the prevalence of such images. The same people who, a few years earlier, had been upset because television did not educate, were now afraid that it was teaching the wrong lessons. One example, from Professor Paul A. Witty of Northwestern University, will suffice. "Parental disapproval [of television]," he wrote, "stems from a feeling that programs are too violent, too sensational, too stimulating, and include too many westerns. A surprising number of persons who do not yet own TV sets look upon television with something very close to terror."

SURELY SOME OF THIS was having an effect on viewers, especially those of impressionable age. If children had been inspired to buy millions of coonskin caps when they saw Davy Crockett wear one, was it not reasonable to assume that they would be inspired to commit an antisocial act or develop an antisocial outlook when they saw the bad guys on the same program act violently, or when Crockett responded to baddies with violence of his own? Would they not be similarly motivated by other shows, other displays of defiance to law and decency, and other acts of retribution? If television was influential enough to move merchandise, how could it not be influential enough to shape attitudes?

It sounds like a sensible question. It is, in fact, specious. Not all messages will be processed the same way by those who receive them even if they are delivered by the same medium, especially messages of a wildly differing nature. A variety show does not affect us the way a baseball game does. A newscast does not affect us like a cartoon, nor a cartoon like a commercial. By our very nature, we human beings are much more likely to buy a harmless product like a coonskin cap than do something harmful like punch a fellow human being in the mouth, even though, in the fifties, punches were even more prevalent on the tube than caps.

The most consistently violent shows of the decade were the westerns, which Philo T. Farnsworth had complained about several years before Professor Witty. In addition to promoting the sales of coonskin caps and lunch boxes and various other products, westerns were having "a decided effect on firearms production." So said Fred A. Roff Jr., a vice president of Colt's Patent Firearms. He went on to tell a Washington radio interviewer, as paraphrased by television producer Gary Grossman in his book *Saturday Morning TV*, "that the demand for Western-type guns had stepped up manufacturing to a modern record of ten thousand per month. Rolf estimated that by the time the average male youngster reached his teens, he had played with fifteen to twenty replica guns."

But note the use of the word "replica." American youngsters were not getting their hands on real guns and taking potshots at one another; they were buying toy guns and playing cowboys and Indians, and many of them, certainly including me, would never handle a real gun, not as children or adults, and would in fact grow up to oppose the ease with which deadly weapons could be purchased by others.

Still, those of us who spent so much time in our childhoods with plastic guns in our hands might have been harmed in other ways. So stated a number of critics in a number of forums. Those programs found most offensive by the NABRT included *Zorro*, "because of its emphasis on might-makes-right"; *The Lone Ranger* and *Rin Tin Tin* "because of their emphasis on villainy and crime"; and *Robin Hood*, because "it is difficult for young children to understand why it appears to be morally correct to rob the rich and aid the poor."

A child was believed to be more vulnerable than an adult to the messages of these shows for several reasons: "he reacts emotionally rather than intellectually to what he sees; he is easily aroused and responds fully; he does not distinguish clearly between reality and fantasy and is vague in his understanding of time, history, cause and effect; he has a limited sense of social responsibility and ethical behavior." According to another source, television was teaching children to "confuse violence with strength."

It is a point worth considering. When he is no longer in his early years, might a person become a less sensitive adult because of his youthful preoccupation with make-believe violence? Yes, he might. But another point worth considering is that a youthful preoccupation with violence may be a phase through which many children naturally pass, and that they end up better for that passage in the long run rather than worse, the passage freeing them from absorption in the matter in their later years.

Among researchers who thought so was Dr. Phillip Polatin, Assistant Clinical Professor of Psychiatry at the College of Physicians and Surgeons at Columbia University. In that lengthy series of his in the *New York Times* in 1951, cited earlier, Jack Gould summarized Polatin's views as follows: "He held that cowboy films, despite general parental disapproval, are 'an excellent outlet' for children's hostility and aggression. Critics who object to television's 'passive entertainment,' he said, should watch a group of boys popping cap pistols, yelling at villains and encouraging heroes as they sit before the screen."

I can remember even more pistol popping and yelling at villains when the shows were over and, inspired by them, my friends and I would go outside to be heroes and villains ourselves. We began almost as if we were choosing sides for a baseball game in the alley, picking our roles, the specific heroes whose parts we would assume, and usually assigning the younger children to be Indians or cattle rustlers or rogues of some other type. Then we would chase one another through the backyards and alleys that in our eyes were the Old West and fire indiscriminately.

"Gotcha!"

"Did not."

"Did so. Gotcha right in the heart."

"Oh, all right," the victim would say, and drop to the ground, writhing a few times as he pretended the life was ebbing out of him, before getting up and joining the festivities again a few minutes later, this time taking his turn at firing the shot that would fell one of the other boys.

It wasn't just hostility and aggression that we were working out, as Polatin stated; it was sheer energy. Those of us motivated by TV violence to run after one another in our own version of the cowboy and cop shows were less likely than others to fail President Kennedy's physical fitness tests in the sixties when we got to high school. In fact, that is what violence on television in the early fifties seemed like to my friends and me: exercise. Cowboys falling off horses, leaping off the roofs of saloons, being knocked off stagecoaches, and rolling over several times on the ground as we landed—it was a form of acrobatics to us, circus acts. When we tried to emulate them, we made no associations with pain or injury or death; we were too young, the violence too artificial, our minds as yet unable to grasp the real thing.

The memories of those years remain, both of the television shows and our improvised neighborhood versions of them. I still recall the acrid yet sweet smell of the caps as our guns were fired, and the frustration we felt, all too frequently, when the caps did not discharge as they were supposed to. We would keep at our games until called for dinner, at which point we would be model citizens for the rest of the day.

And, in the majority of cases, for the rest of our lives.

THE DEBATE about brutal behavior on the tube reached its peak in 1959, when ABC began broadcasting *The Untouchables*, a Prohibition-era crime drama—produced by Desilu, of all companies—with the highest death toll of any show to date. The program "had a gritty, film-noir flair," said the *New York Times*, many years later, when the series was released on DVD, "and was startling in its level of violence."

On one side were federal agents led by Eliot Ness, played by the virtually expressionless Robert Stack; on the other side, the roster included such hoodlums as Al Capone, captured in full menace by Neville Brand, "Mad Dog" Coll, Dutch Schultz, and numerous other underworld figures from Chicago and New York. The violence was more graphic on *The Untouchables* than it was on any other program of the time, but not exponentially so. TV cameras did not zoom in for close-ups of people dying, nor did they highlight bullets embedded in body parts, knives slashing skin, or blood flowing from wounds.

But there was something else different about *The Untouchables*: a harder edge to the plots, a colder tone to the dialogue, a more callous outlook about the value of human life. The westerns and cop shows *included* violence; Eliot Ness and company *were* violence.

Of course, so was criminal life in the United States in the thirties. It was a time when bootleggers would settle business disputes with submachine guns, when racketeers would punish those who had welched on a debt or an interest payment by emptying a revolver into them, when a paid assassin could be found whenever a victim was anointed. If Quinn Martin, the producer of *The Untouchables*, had "sanitized the subject matter," said one of his defenders, "he would have seriously undercut the very premise of the show and left it virtually indistinguishable from every other TV crime series. Instead, *The Untouchables* stood apart with its strong characters, good scripts, and very realistic setting."

Of course, as far as critics were concerned, this was beside the point. The program might have had a certain grisly realism to it, but was television, the entertainment medium that entered the home and drew the whole family for an audience, the proper place for such realism? Why not be realistic about lifestyles and activities that were less gruesome? Present accurate accounts of social workers helping troubled families work out their problems? Tell true-to-life stories about teachers of uncommon dedication? Relate the lives and times of clergymen trying to save souls? Why not leave the gangsters to movies, where they had already been brutalizing one another for many years, and where they were less likely to be seen by young viewers?

Martin had no patience for such questions. "I like the idea of sadism," he said on one occasion to his writers, "but I hope we can come up with another approach to it." They did. Time and again, with each program in the series, it has been noted, featuring a minimum of "two shootouts with police, a beating, and a cold-blooded murder." And usually more.

Take an episode called "The Noise of Death." It begins with Ness and a few of his agents finding a man's corpse hanging from a hook in a meat locker. He is bound by his wrists and ankles, with the rope looping up around his neck. We do not see his face, nor any kind of disfigurement; still, it is for the time a startling image. A few moments later, a woman arrives on the scene. "Don't go in, Mrs. Vitterini," says Ness to the person who is now Mr. Vitterini's widow. But she does, and as she sees her husband's body twisting slowly in the frigid air, her shriek echoes off the locker's walls and through the living rooms of America.

The Untouchables ran for only four years. "In 1963," the *New York Times* reported, "after the series came under fire from viewers weary of violence and the derogatory depiction of Italian-Americans, Mr. Stack holstered his .38."

But guns did not remain holstered for long on television, and their use would eventually be accompanied by some of the foulest language ever heard on the medium. It would take a long time for the connection to be firmly made, but to watch some episodes of *The Untouchables* today is to imagine a youthful Tony Soprano sitting avidly in front of his set, knowing his time would come, and that when it did he would not be nearly so restrained in his behavior or speech as were the television criminals of the fifties.

ONE IS REMINDED of the argument, even before the fifties, that television would be the death of the book. It wasn't, but it did inflict injury, and the book has never fully recovered, nor will it. Has televised violence, especially today's more realistic and violent brand thereof, inflicted injury of its own on society? Probably not, not on the society as a whole. But it has certainly had an effect on a number of individuals, people over the years who have been convicted of crimes and admitted that their deeds were prompted by something they saw, either on the small screen or large.

But without exception, these were people susceptible to bizarre behavior in the first place. No one has ever proved, much less seriously suggested, that an emotionally healthy person can be driven to ruthless conduct, or even a ruthless disposition, by exposure to fictional violence. We can be offended by it, but if we are, we simply reduce or eliminate our exposure to such programs; there is no reason to think that make-believe assault or homicide or sadism can make us into kinds of people we would not otherwise be.

The main contention of this book is that television's influence on America at the midway point of the twentieth century was profound, pervasive, and enduring. The main contention of this chapter, however, is that there are, after all, limits.

Chapter 15

Serving the Sky Chief

AMONG THOSE MOST TROUBLED by violence on television in the fifties were men of the cloth. They not only preached against it; sometimes they joined forces to try to persuade their local stations not to carry programs of a violent sort. They called the stations to protest and urged their parishioners to do the same. On occasion they conducted petition drives. As guests on public affairs radio programs, they inveighed against brutality on the small screen. Never were they heeded.

A man who went to weekly services at a small Catholic church in western Pennsylvania, and whose family had just bought its first TV, received a phone call a few days later from his minister. He had never called the family before, but said he wanted to congratulate them on their new purchase. After he did, he went on to make some small talk that seemed too small to be worth the effort. The man on the receiving end, although puzzled, small-talked back as best he could.

What the minister really wanted, it turned out, was to offer some viewing tips, and just before hanging up, he did. Susie McNamara was OK, he said in effect; Marshal Dillon was not.

Click.

YEARS EARLIER, in 1933, Catholics had formed something called the Legion of Decency, the purpose of which was to protest, and assign rankings to, movies with objectionable content. By the time I started going to Mass, or rather was finally old enough to understand what the priest was saying on those rare occasions when he wasn't conducting the Mass in Latin, I heard him insist that we members of the congregation state our allegiance to wholesome entertainment. He would tell us the names of new films that the Church did not want us to see, and we were to swear aloud not to see them. It was like a responsive reading.

The adults, for the most part, took the vows seriously, or seemed to, as they spoke their words loudly and enunciated so that all could understand. We children, though, would usually just move our lips without making a sound. Lip syncing. Or we might cover our mouths with our hands, clearing our throats or coughing, not even faking it. I suppose we believed that this would give us an out with our Maker if we decided to go to one of the forbidden movies. We had, after all, not technically promised to avoid them.

Once in a while the priest would slip in the name of a TV show, reminding us that Jesus was a man of peace and would be even more troubled by violent programming in the sanctity of the home than He was in the more worldly realm of a movie theater. In this case, we youngsters were even less likely to mutter assent.

By this time clergymen had joined laymen in testifying before Congress on the effects of violence on television. One of the more notable of the former was Reverend Everett C. Parker, director of the Communications Research Project of the Broadcasting and Film Commission of the National Council of the Churches of Christ in the U.S.A., a group that worked under the auspices of the Yale University Divinity School. Called before a subcommittee of the Senate Judiciary Committee, Parker told about his current project, involving TV viewers in both New Haven, Connecticut, where Yale was located, and New York City. "Throughout the broadcast day," Parker said to the lawmakers,

New York stations average six acts or threats of violence per hour and the New Haven station four. In children's drama, however, New York stations averaged eighteen violent acts or threats per hour and the New Haven station fifteen.

By this measurement children's drama is twice as violent as adult crime drama. It should be reported that most of this violence occurred in a non-humorous context rather than in a humorous context.

Parker told the senators that he was appalled by the findings. He believed they were an ominous portent. Stricter regulation of the industry, he stated, was the only answer, and that was up to the legislators, some of whom were eager to comply. Over the course of several months, a number of bills were considered in Congress; none, however, became law. The consensus seemed to be that the Federal Communications Commission had been created for the purpose of monitoring the media, and it was up to that agency, not the House or Senate, to deal with complaints.

THE CHURCH, both Protestant and Catholic, has a long history of opposing the diversions of its members, whether they involve violence or not. Over the centuries, it has either warned against or censured such activities and institutions as theater and dance and minstrelsy, chess and checkers, mahjong and crossword puzzles, and movies and radio. Against violent TV shows it had a stronger case than it did against Shakespeare or the Fox Trot.

The larger point, though, is that the Church had—and continues to have—an inborn fear of all manner of secular pastimes, those distractions from the struggles of daily life that can also be distractions from commitment to the Almighty. The Church, in other words—words seldom uttered by clergy—is afraid of losing ground to the forces of worldliness, no matter how innocent they may be.

Journalist Robert Kass apparently had something like this in mind in 1956 when, in *The Catholic World,* he railed against the men who wrote television's live dramas.

In looking over the body of work of these well paid scriptwriters, I am struck by the fact that, in several instances, they have labored so resolutely in the name of the "sick" school of drama. . . . almost exclusively concerned with psychoneurotics and deviants who suffer from assorted maladies of the soul and spirit. The popularity of the misfits both in the theatre and TV is a mystifying one and represents an unhealthy preoccupation with sex and psychoanalytic misbehavior. . . . Apparently there is no drama in sane, ordinary people any more. Mr. Chayefsky's "little" people, the misfits who inhabit the lower depths of the Bronx, Mr. Serling's twisted introverts, Mr. [Reginald] Rose's rebellious outcasts are all crowding the TV dials week after week. [Rose wrote the teleplay for *12 Angry Men*, the jury drama that also became a movie and a play.]

But by 1956, as noted earlier, Chayefsky and Serling and Rose no longer had many outlets for the kind of fare that Kass opposed, and the outlets that still existed were among television's lowest rated programs. The heyday of live drama had passed before Kass got around to criticizing it.

JOHN GREGORY MURRAY, the Archbishop of St. Paul, Minnesota, saw even more reasons to be wary of television. According to an editorial in the *Christian Century* a few years earlier, Murray "has reminded the faithful that they take on a serious moral responsibility if they admit a television set into their homes." Meaning that they must carefully control its use and not allow its excesses to disrupt the household. Meaning further that much of what television had to offer was in one way or another offensive to the teachings of the Church—with its displays not only of violence, but of sex, crime, greed, political chicanery, mindless humor and chitchat, and lack of family harmony.

It was similar to the kind of accusation that intellectuals were making against television, with men of the cloth adding an additional, and to them even more pernicious, component.

Few were the clerics who went so far as to claim that television was an implement of Satan. More commonly, they found it an example of the devilish influence of mammon. But change was soon to come. Gradually, as the fifties inched their way forward, opposition began to waver. Clerics examined the new medium more carefully and then, tentatively at first, allowed themselves to embrace it, or think about embracing it, daring to believe that if they proceeded cautiously, always keeping the Almighty's ends in mind, they might be able to utilize TV for their own purposes. And, in fact, they would.

SERMONETTE was the first television show to feature a man of God. Or rather, the first shows, plural, since each station that presented a brief theological discourse at the end of its broadcast day called upon its own community's priests, ministers, and rabbis to deliver the message. But it was not much of a forum, just two minutes or so of a holy man standing in front of a camera with either a cross or Star of David behind him. He was trying to spread the word of God, but at such an ungodly hour that no one heard it.

In fact, the little program quickly became something of a joke. Someone would make fun of another show by saying that even *Sermonette* had more viewers. Or someone would complain that he or she had had such a boring day that it would have been more fun watching *Sermonette*.

Regardless, the two minutes were an important event for television, as they introduced the medium to religion and vice versa. They demonstrated that the small screen would concede a place for worship on the air, although for the time being that place was the broadcasting equivalent of Siberia. The Church, with its foot now in the door, was encouraged to think it might find other outlets for itself on TV, preferably when more people were awake and watching and receptive to its message. The Founding Fathers believed in the separation of church and state. No one ever said anything about separating church and tube.

That, at least, was the opinion of, among others, a publication called *Catholic World*.

> The impact of television on American life will depend on those who control this inanimate device. How will it form the attitudes of Americans toward the great facts: the existence of God and of the moral law, the dignity of the person and the solidarity of nations? If organizations and individuals who love the things of the spirit get behind television, it can become an immense force for good. But if we abandon it to the low tastes of advertisers and entertainers, it will become a vulgarizing force. As for the Church, how long, O Lord, how long shall we neglect this amazing medium for preaching Christ in the living rooms of America?

Not long at all. As the fifties began, the Catholic Broadcasters Association (CBA) was already in existence, its goal "to acquaint American Catholics with the potentialities of TV." The CBA expressed its appreciation to local stations for *Sermonette*, often holding banquets to present the stations with plaques and certificates of gratitude, and featuring a speaker who encouraged the stations, as well as the networks, to devote more hours to the nutrition of the soul. There were not enough shows that dramatized the stories of the Bible, the speaker might say, or that illustrated the role of faith in the lives of ordinary people when extraordinary events beset them, or that provided analysis of current affairs in a religious framework, or that simply presented the word of God at length—a sermon without the diminutive ending.

In the sixties, when there were a number of such programs on the air nationally, the CBA would begin to present an annual award called the Gabriel to recognize the best of them, those productions that "uplift and nourish the human spirit."

Catholicism, some people thought, was of all religions the best suited to TV. Even other Christians had to admit it. "The Roman Catholic Church," stated an article from a Protestant source, "with its pageantry and color, will have an appeal in television which the Protestant Churches lack. Thus, following the recent telecast of the Christmas Eve Midnight Mass in Chicago, it was discovered that a very large percentage of Protestant owners of sets had watched the proceedings." Other cities televised Mass too, not only on Christmas Eve but also on Good Friday and Easter, and perhaps other days of special holy import.

There were enough Masses on television, in fact, to provoke a reaction from the Vatican. In January 1954, Church officials warned that, although watching a service on TV was "laudable," it was not enough. The Church was worried because, as the *New York Times* put it, "[r]egular television broadcasts [of Masses] began in Italy this month. In the past, Vatican authorities have told Roman Catholics that hearing Mass by radio does not fulfill the church's requirements for attendance." In other words, a Catholic had to show up in the pew, not just on the sofa.

TV SHOWS OF A RELIGIOUS NATURE that were not Masses, shows the networks began to present in the fifties, did not fulfill the Church's attendance requirements either. Nonetheless, the Vatican seemed pleased with them. So did the hierarchies of other denominations. For the most part, television had not given into the pleas of those who wanted instructional programs on the air; it was proving more receptive to the desires of clergymen.

The first faith-based program of note, which actually made its debut in 1948, was CBS's *Lamp unto My Feet*, the title taken from Psalm 119, line

105, in the King James version of the Bible: "The word is a lamp unto my feet, and a light onto my path." It was an obscure phrase for most people at the time, and the show was a difficult one to categorize. Sometimes it provided religious instruction for children, but in a more entertaining manner than they were used to—Sunday school except with cartoons to make a point clearer or more memorable. At other times it brought noted actors into the studio to read from biblical texts. And at still other times it assembled a panel of experts to discuss difficult passages from the Bible and their relevance to everyday life. On one occasion *Lamp unto My Feet* ignored church doctrine altogether, devoting the entire thirty minutes to folksinger Pete Seeger, who simply sang his songs of freedom and love, and made small talk to the camera at the Shaker Museum in Old Chatham, New York.

Lamp unto My Feet was a hodgepodge. It was also a hit, lasting for more than thirty years, starting on the air in the Truman presidency and holding its place on Sunday mornings almost until Ronald Reagan began to campaign against Jimmy Carter.

CBS tried a similar approach with *Look Up and Live*, which was as eclectic as *Lamp unto My Feet* and even more ecumenical. The program was produced by the Protestant National Council of Churches one week, the National Council of Catholic Men the next, and the New York Board of Rabbis the week after that.

One of its episodes was a condensed version of Nathaniel Hawthorne's *The Scarlet Letter*, with a young Leslie Nielsen, in his pre-goofball days, as the tortured Reverend Dimmesdale. Another was a tutorial on gospel music hosted by Mahalia Jackson, who not only sang her songs to the glory of the Lord but explained the roots and meanings of her selections. Yet another episode, dismissed by some for its artiness and praised by others for its cultural merit, was a dance drama, set to religious music. "Among the sources of the scenario," *America* magazine pointed out, "were St. Paul and other scriptural writers, St. Bernard of Clairvaux and Pope Pius XI's Encyclical on Christian Marriage. The program's basic message was a conception of marriage as a living daily ritual expressing the love of God for His Creation and the love of Christ for the Church."

A show of a different sort was *Crossroads,* an anthology series that premiered on ABC in the fall of 1953 and ran for three years. Like the secular anthology series of the decade, *Crossroads* featured a different cast and story every week, although nothing of a controversial nature.

All episodes, however, dealt with the same theme: a man of God who found his faith while put to an unexpected test. A tale called "The Riot" told of a priest who unwittingly got involved in a jailbreak. "Johnakunga— Called John," was based on the true exploits of a missionary who tried to make Christians of a tribe of Indians who did not want to be converted. Still another presentation of *Crosssroads*

> concerns a young minister who is duped into letting a con artist become a church fundraiser. The man absconds with the money but is caught and sent to jail. The minister later supports him at his unsuccessful parole hearing. Though the church elders reprimand him, he argues for the Christian principle of forgiveness. Later the minister learns that the man has had a religious conversion. Despite his qualms that it might be a ruse, he again speaks for him at a parole hearing, this time successfully. The one-time conman's conversion turns out to be genuine, and the minister's faith and charity are redeemed.

THE FIFTIES was also the decade in which Billy Graham began to appear on television with his crusades, which were basically a series of conventional church services, consisting of songs and Bible readings and a sermon, held in venues larger than churches—tents, arenas, convention centers, the Grand Canyon. All right, *not* the Grand Canyon, but at the height of his career, he could have come remarkably close to filling it. Graham was a handsome man, wavy-haired and earnest, a charismatic speaker who was all the more appealing because of the slight Southern twang to his delivery. He appealed to millions of viewers, regardless of their particular faiths. There had never been anyone like him. He did not spend as much time urging people to send in their hard-earned money as some later TV evangelists did; rather, his emphasis was on the Holy Spirit, the joys and contentment it could bring to those who accepted its benevolent aura. Even to those not of religious inclination, Graham seemed a man worth listening to, a man who could be trusted, and in fact he would in time become a spiritual confidant to several American Presidents, which would in turn make him seem all the more worthy of being a spiritual confidant to millions of everyday Americans.

Graham grew up on a dairy farm in North Carolina, but never considered a vocation other than the ministry. Born into the Associate Reformed

Presbyterian Church, he became a Southern Baptist at a revival meeting at the age of sixteen. While still in seminary, he began to preach on the radio in a small town in Illinois. At first only a few people listened, but his audience grew quickly in both size and devotion. There was something about so young a man speaking with such clarity and fervor that made people want to tune in.

After a few years, Graham set out for other venues, and before long his prominence was such that television cameras were joining worshippers in welcoming him at his various stops, most of which were initially in the South but soon ranged from one end of the country to the other.

Eventually, Graham was preaching in such prestigious venues as Madison Square Garden, where he set up shop for a few nights in 1957. In the audience one of those nights was a reporter from *Variety*, who proclaimed Graham's cast of singers and fellow clerics a "surefire click," and Graham himself "tremendous box office." The cameras that awaited him there belonged to ABC, meaning that he was seen all across America, and *Time* reported that "Trendex awarded him an 8.1 rating, highest ever registered by [ABC] for the crucial time slot opposite TV Titans," such as Jackie Gleason and Perry Como. Como, in fact, praised Graham for his zeal and eloquence. Gleason had no comment.

Soon, Graham was presiding over what

amounted to a vast privately ordered society of [his] own, complete unto itself—his own communications network, with his weekly *Hour of Decision* broadcasts carried on some 900 stations around the world, his crusades televised three or four times a year over 310 metropolitan areas holding 90 percent of the potential audience, "about the exposure General Mills achieves for Wheaties," as one B[illy] G[raham] E[vangelistic] A[ssociation] official declares.

Graham remained humble, both publicly and in private, during the years of his ascendancy, but he never really got used to television. In fact, he often confessed to associates that he was a nervous wreck before he stepped in front of a camera, a nervousness that never showed but that he would never conquer. He did not complain *too* much, though; an agitated state backstage, he believed, was a small price to pay for so effective a means of communication. He was delighted with the contribution TV made to his mission. It was "the greatest medium to get the message across," he said, "and serves to break down public indifference to the church."

SO PLEASED WERE RELIGIOUS LEADERS at the inroads they were making into television, and therefore into the society at large, that, in addition to urging the networks to develop even more programs, some denominations began to encourage broadcast training in seminaries. Introductory Biblical Hebrew was mandatory in most such institutions, but how about Making the Camera Your Friend? Introduction to Prophetic Literature was a must for a religious curriculum, but How to Modulate Your Voice for the Microphone was gaining ground.

Said the *Christian Century*, "We simply cannot assume that a man who is an acceptable preacher is *ipso facto* a good broadcaster. A man without special training has no more business at a microphone than a man without driving lessons has at the wheel of an automobile—in fact, less. We are in great need of ministers who understand the demands of these mass media and can then go on to use them imaginatively and creatively."

Although not a minister, there was one servant of the Lord who did not need training. Actually, he had had some training of a sort, but the results were not promising. While studying for the priesthood, he had joined his college debate team, but did not start out well. In fact, his coach had told him that he was the team's worst performer, a criticism that probably wounded him more than he let on.

In time, though, that would change. In time the young man would become not only competent in the art of oral presentation, but masterful, much more than any of his fellow debaters. He would become, in fact, the most dynamic and revered spokesman for the word of God ever to appear regularly on the small screen. Perhaps it was he rather than Ed Sullivan *or* Estes Kefauver who truly deserves to be called the least likely star of the era.

YET THERE MUST HAVE BEEN TIMES when he thought he had displeased his Maker. There must have been times when he thought the Lord had not exhausted his punishments on Job, that He had saved a few final penalties for him. But why? He had overcome his initial ineptitude in debate at St. Viator College in Illinois and gone on to win awards for his oratory. After that, he had been the most conscientious of students at Saint Paul Seminary in Minnesota. Upon graduation he had distinguished himself as the host of a religious radio program in Detroit, the show proving successful enough that it was eventually syndicated to more than 100 stations across the country. A few years later, he was rewarded with his own TV show on the Dumont network.

But the radio program, called *The Catholic Hour*, had been on opposite *Amos 'n' Andy*. Who knows how many stations would have carried it at a different time? And the TV show, called *Life Is Worth Living*, was scheduled to compete with Milton Berle on Tuesday nights at 8! What were the odds that this priest, who had tried to match jokes with theology back in Detroit, could do it again now? Berle was already known far and wide as "Mister Television." Sheen, known neither far *nor* wide, had just been appointed archbishop of the Roman Catholic Diocese of New York. Maybe the Lord should have thought this through more clearly. Maybe He should have taken a look at the TV listings before slotting Sheen onto the national television schedule.

Berle was gracious in his public comments about the new show opposite him. His sponsor, Texaco, made a premium brand of gasoline called Sky Chief; Berle joked that he and the archbishop both worked for the same boss. Berle was known as "Uncle Miltie." He referred to his competitor as "Uncle Fultie." It was the kind of magnanimity one can afford when one feels totally unthreatened.

Sheen's program made its debut on the small screen in 1952, and it lasted for five years. Although he never beat Berle in the ratings, he usually finished a strong—and surprising—second. Some weeks, more than twenty-million people watched him. There were days, Sheen claimed, although it hardly seems possible, that he received as many as twenty-five-thousand pieces of mail.

He remembered one letter in particular. It came from an aspiring actor who had become such a fan that he asked for permission to adopt the archbishop's name for his own. Permission granted—and young Martin Sheen, already being talked about as a new James Dean or Marlon Brando, had been, in a manner of speaking, born again.

Another missive came from President Eisenhower, who said that, riding in his limousine the previous night, "I was told that as I was passing through the streets of New York you stopped at a street corner to greet me. I failed to see you, but I do assure you that I am more than complimented by your friendly thoughtfulness.

"I would have valued the opportunity to have stopped my car, however briefly, to chat for a moment."

The mail brought more than mere correspondence. Some people, Sheen said, "even sent in their old gold jewelry. Students sacrificed their high school or college rings and sent the equivalent to the missions. In one telecast I said I liked chocolate cookies. The following week we could hardly get in the door of the office, which was blocked with boxes of chocolate cookies."

There were times, Sheen said, when he would "ask my listeners for a dime for the poor of the world," but he usually got more than that, much more, as coins and bills and checks came flooding in. On one occasion, he "opened a yellow envelope and $10,000 in cash fell out. Scrawled in pencil was a note: 'I don't need this any more. God told me to give it to the poor.'"

The amount was atypical, perhaps the largest single donation Sheen ever received. But over the years his audience sent in millions of dollars, all of which was forwarded to a Catholic missionary group called the Society for the Propagation of the Faith. Sheen also donated the entire paycheck he received for *Life Is Worth Living* to the Society. First from Dumont, and later from ABC, which took over the program, Sheen received the staggering total for the time of $26,000 per episode. He lived on his salary as an archbishop, to which he continued to devote as much time as he could. He told people his compensation from the Church was more than enough for his needs.

His concerns, after all, were spiritual, not material. "Television," he would one day write in the autobiography, "is like the New Testament, for the Word is seen as it becomes flesh and dwells among us."

IN THE LAST YEAR OR SO of Sheen's run, Berle's show began to sink in the ratings. First it was moved to a different time period and then, to the shock of the substantial number of viewers who still remained addicted to him, to whom Tuesday at eight was a sacred time, Uncle Miltie was canceled. Now the competition for *Life Is Worth Living* was *I Love Lucy*, of all things!

Again, the archbishop finished a strong second. Again it was a startling response for an offering of its type. The Lord, Sheen must eventually have concluded, demonstrated a knack for TV programming no less than He did for salvation.

LIFE IS WORTH LIVING displayed none of the pomp that was supposed to make the Catholic Church so telegenic—except, perhaps, for the appearance of its star. Sheen attired himself in a snug-fitting black cassock with a rich purple cape called a *ferriola* over his shoulders. It flowed down his back and trailed elegantly behind him. Around his neck was a large gold cross on a thick chain.

But it was not his raiment that made Sheen so magnetic a presence. In part it was his voice, a baritone both rich and commanding. It was said he would have made a fine Shakespearean actor had he not become a priest. In larger part, though, it was his eyes, which seemed to be as dark as his cassock and gave the impression that he was looking into the very soul of the viewer. They were science-fiction eyes, the kind of eyes that shot out rays; those within range were powerless to resist. I remember watching several of Sheen's programs with my parents as a nine- or ten-year-old, feeling virtuous just for tuning in. But feeling more than that: if the man had asked me to recite the Legion of Decency vow, I would have opened the windows and shouted it through the neighborhood. I would have sworn off Davy Crockett if he had told me to. Fortunately, he made no such demands.

The program was simple in format. It began with an off-camera announcer providing an introduction. "Admiral," he said, referring to the appliance manufacturer, "takes pride in presenting His Excellency, Bishop Fulton J. Sheen, in *Life Is Worth Living*, a program devoted to the everyday problems of all of us." At which point the camera would pan slowly across a set designed to look like a study, past a bookcase and a sofa, toward a door through which the archbishop entered. The studio audience applauded. Sheen smiled graciously, but there were no waves, no show-business mannerisms, no promises of a "really big show."

He glided over to center stage and, as the applause trickled out, positioned himself before a blackboard. Several times in each program he would write notes on it with a piece of chalk, as if he were teaching a class. Almost always the first thing he wrote, at the top of the slate in the center, were the initials *JMJ*. It was a habit he had gotten into long before, when, in seminary, he taught an occasional class. The letters stood for Jesus, Mary and Joseph, and he was calling on them to bless his endeavor.

The chalk and blackboard were the only props Sheen ever used. The latter, he said, "was on a swivel so that after writing on one side it could be turned over. I created the illusion that an 'angel,' who was one of the stagehands, would wash one side of the board as I moved away from one of the cameras' range. When the board was clean I would perhaps use the blackboard again but always attributing its cleanliness to the angel, who became nationally famous."

The purpose of *Life Is Worth Living*, Sheen once said, "was to draw Americans together by drawing them to God. And fittingly, therefore, democracy would be a theme that could very well be emphasized."

And emphasized it was. What made the archbishop unique for his time was that he was a political figure as well as a religious one, and if he considered himself a teacher of Catholicism he was, in the political realm, a student of Eisenhower's Secretary of State John Foster Dulles, the coldest of cold warriors. He was not, however, a McCarthyite. He did not believe that the Soviets had infiltrated the inner workings of the United States, certainly not to the extent that a takeover was imminent.

But he did believe the Soviets were a threat to our country, not just because Communists were a godless people, but because, in this case, they were a belligerent one and could attack the United States at any time. "Fellow citizens," he said on one program, "be not deceived. Remember, when Russia talks peace, it is a tactic, and a preparation for war. . . . A peace overture of Russia will be the beginning of another Pearl Harbor."

Consider Sheen's reply to the letter from Eisenhower, when the President had failed to stop for him.

> In America, when the President passes a friend on the street and fails, through no fault of his own, to salute him, he writes a personal letter of greeting. This is Democracy!
>
> In Russia, when the Dictator passes a friend without salutation, it means he is marked for liquidation. That is communism!
>
> Frankly, Mr. President, I am glad you missed me! The greeting would have lasted a second, your letter will last a lifetime.
>
> God Love You!

SHEEN COULD NOT BE on the air today. If somehow he were, he would be a figure of unabating controversy. Those who disagreed with his religion would demand equal time for their own faiths. Those who disagreed with his politics would rail at the injustice of such a one-sided presentation in so complicated a world. Those who disagreed with the notion of religion and politics being combined as Sheen did, regardless of his specific message, would consider legal action against him on a charge of unconstitutionality. Few would find network television an appropriate venue for what the archbishop chose to say.

In the fifties, though, he was simply the host of a television show, and TV columnists commented less on the politics of his faith than the seriousness of his subject matter. They found it commendable that so substantive a program as *Life Is Worth Living* could hold its own against Berle and Ball, two of the most popular entertainers of all time. Sheen, apparently, could not create an uproar no matter what topic he chose. And, in retrospect, it seems that he tried to create an uproar almost every Tuesday night.

"Abortion is wrong," he told viewers at the beginning of one program. "Why? Because if there's a soul, there is a person. Is unmerciful killing wrong? Yes. Why? Because the person has certain inalienable gifts, inherent gifts that inhere in the soul from God."

Yet there were no protests about statements like this, no picket lines around the studio calling for Sheen's dismissal, no demands for a spokesman to rebut him. *Of course* a Roman Catholic prelate would oppose abortion. Those in Sheen's audience who took issue with him about a woman's right to choose simply found that particular episode of *Life Is Worth Living* less to his or her liking than others, enough so, perhaps, that they turned their dials to see what Uncle Miltie was up to. And those who disagreed with Sheen on both this and other matters were probably not watching to begin with.

It was that simple. The average American had not yet gotten into the habit of being contentious about television, still so grateful for the existence of such a marvel that he or she accepted whatever content it chose to provide. Or, when the content was not to one's liking, it was rejected without fanfare.

Regardless of his subject, it bears repeating again that Sheen was the most gifted of orators. His old college-debate coach, since deceased, must have been looking down on him from heavenly realms, shaking his head and smiling. The program that opened with the comments on abortion ended as follows: "If you wish to keep your perfume, you must keep your flowers. If you wish to keep your forests, you must keep your trees. And if you wish to keep your rights as Americans, you must keep your God!"

A flourishing sweep of the arm at this point, and as the archbishop bowed, the studio audience applauded, just as they had he was introduced.

Sheen was not always so serious, however. He ended another of his shows by telling of a speech he was scheduled to give one night at Town Hall in Philadelphia. Because the weather was pleasant and he had time to spare, he had decided to walk to the site from his hotel rather than take a cab. But after a few blocks he realized he was lost.

"I stopped a group of boys and I asked them the way to Town Hall, and they told me. And they said, 'Who are you?' And I said, 'I'm Father Sheen.' 'What are you going to do there?' I said, 'give a talk.' 'On what?' I didn't want to tell the boys that I was talking on my usually dry subject . . . so I simplified it and said, 'Boys, I'm going to talk about Heaven and how to get there. Would you like to come and find out?' They said, 'You don't even know the way to Town Hall.'"

It got a laugh worthy of Berle.

In 1952, the first year *Life Is Worth Living* was on the air, Sheen won an Emmy as Most Outstanding Television Personality, beating out Ball, Arthur Godfrey, Edward R. Murrow, and Jimmy Durante. Nineteen-fifty-two was also the year Kefauver was presented with an Emmy for his hearings, making for the strangest of nights at the awards ceremony—a preacher and a politician winning awards for their performances on a medium dominated by show biz.

In his acceptance speech, Sheen was typically generous. "I feel it is time to pay tribute to my four writers," he said, and proudly named them. "Matthew, Mark, Luke, and John."

But, in truth, there was a fifth writer, and he was the one who deserved most of the credit for the success of Sheen's program. His material might have been based on the Gospels but, with the exception of an occasional quote, the words were those of the archbishop, and given the fact that he was speaking to a large audience of different faiths rather than a gathering of Catholics at Mass, he tried to make his views as ecumenical as possible. He spent about thirty hours preparing for each week's presentation.

> A day or two before the actual broadcast I would "try out" my comprehension of the subject by giving the talk in Italian to an Italian professor who was a friend of mine and also in French to a member of the staff who spoke French fluently. I did this not because of great expertise in either language but because I was forced to think out the idea in another tongue and I knew that would help me clarify the subject in my mind.

But Sheen *kept* the subject in his mind. He might have been the fifth writer but, unlike the other four, he did not commit anything to paper. He did not use what he dismissed as "idiot cards," did not rely on notes, did not receive cues from an associate in the wings—and the teleprompter had not yet been invented. *Time* magazine found it hard to believe that Sheen could fill half-an-hour of air time like this, and sent a reporter to the set to watch him one night, to look for tricks.

But, except for the angel at the blackboard, there were none. When he began to speak, he simply beamed those eyes of his into the camera and the camera beamed them across America and Sheen spoke from the heart about what he believed to be the needs of the inner being. Matthew, Mark, Luke, and John were not really his partners; they were his inspiration.

AT THE SAME TIME that Archbishop Sheen was using the electronic pulpit to opine on issues of the day, another clergyman, the Pentecostalist Oral Roberts, was using it to cure the physical ills of the day. Or claiming to—just as he claimed that he had been cured himself, a faith healer supposedly having rid his body of tuberculosis when he was a teenager.

The audiences for the two men could not have been more different. There were exceptions, of course, but for the most part Sheen tended to attract well-educated people to his program, often college graduates, whereas the Roberts following included men and women of lesser acuity. Sheen's viewers were interested in current events, Roberts's in the life after this life. Sheen appealed to urban viewers of means, Roberts to rural viewers of lesser means. Between the two of them, Sheen and Roberts provided fifties television with the two extremes of religious experience, and both, for a time, presided over highly rated programs in their time periods.

THE EARLY DAYS of Oral Roberts were not promising, and not just because of his tuberculosis. Roberts's parents were so poor that they could not send him off to school in new clothes or buy him new toys to play with when he finished his homework. Nor could they afford a doctor to help him with either his TB or his stuttering problem which, after several years of hard work, he was able to overcome himself.

A determined young man, he worked at a number of jobs to put himself through college. But he was directionless, unable to see a path worth the taking. Until, that is, sitting in a college classroom one day, he claimed that the Word of God interrupted the prattling of his instructor. "Son," the holy voice told him, "don't be like other men. Don't be like any denomination. Be like Jesus, and heal the people as He did."

Not long afterward he did just that. He bid good-bye to his parents and friends, telling them he had important work to do, and became an itinerant preacher. He would stop in any town, no matter how small, and at any place of worship, no matter how ramshackle. He would beg the pastor to share his Sunday service with him and the pastor often agreed, knowing his congregation would enjoy the presence of a "guest star," especially one with powers beyond those of mortal man.

When Roberts was introduced, usually near the conclusion of the service, he would walk onto the altar, sit on a chair, and bid the infirm to approach him, one at a time. He would lay his hands on them, on their foreheads and cheeks, on their shoulders and forearms, on any malfunctioning part of their bodies—and he would beseech the Almighty to transmit medicinal miracles through him from the empyrean. Many people thought he did, and his reputation began to grow. Soon he was not pleading with local clergymen to share their pulpits with him; *they* were begging *him*, and his name would appear on the message boards in front of churches all week, excitement building for his Sunday presence, hope soaring for those severely under the weather.

ROBERTS FIRST CAME to national attention in 1951, when *Life* magazine profiled him in an article whose headline proclaimed that ORAL ROBERTS "HEALS" THE MULTITUDE. The particular multitude that *Life* covered had assembled in Atlanta, and it was as raucous as it was reverent. *Life* told its readers that "the crowds gasped, murmured 'Praise the Lord,' and eyewitnesses reported that a man with an injured back leaned down and touched the floor, a deaf woman heard some whispers and a palsied man held his hand out steady."

But in the four pages that *Life* devoted to Roberts, there was but a half-page of text and fully a dozen photos, one of them taking an entire page: a woman named Lizzie Mae Stevens down on her knees, her eyes closed, squeezing her hands together above her head, in the middle of a deeply felt righteous writhe. "Violent prayer," the magazine called it, although it was clearly a violence that had grown out of ecstasy, not anger.

Another photo showed some of the assembled throng in the tent that had been set up for the night's service. The remaining ten captured the star of the show—Oral Roberts himself, romping across the stage, seeming to be possessed of divine energy; Oral Roberts sitting peaceably in his chair, reaching out his hands to ailing worshipers. Caption of one photo: "WITH GOITER: Mrs. Roy Stevenson leans back for Roberts to hold hand on her neck. . . . Swelling did not appear to lessen." Caption of another photo: "WITH STIFF THUMB: Mrs. H. E. Thompson is suffering from a nerve injury. Roberts examines it carefully, then prays for it. She was able to wiggle it."

But just as pictures often overwhelm language on television, so did they overwhelm it in *Life*'s account of Roberts. Few people paid attention to the fact that the word "heal" had been placed in quotation marks in the headline of the article, indicating a certain degree of skepticism. Few paid attention to the fact that Mrs. Stevenson's goiter seemed the same size post-treatment as it did pre-treatment. What mattered was impression of the photos, the action and sense of purpose they conveyed, and the fact that a magazine as prestigious as *Life* had devoted so much space to them.

Roberts—or Brother Roberts, as he preferred to be known—was quick to capitalize on the publicity. Instead of continuing to travel to various churches and other gathering places around the country to treat the afflicted, he would now bid the afflicted to come to him. He settled down in a church of his own in Tulsa, Oklahoma, and, after a while, began a weekly series of TV broadcasts, buying time on various stations around the country and using it, in the manner of the present-day infomercial, to sell his product: his divinely bestowed healing powers. No one had ever done anything like this before. He did not know how he would be received.

As it turned out, he was received like exactly what he claimed to be—a man of God sharing a body and a mission with a man of medicine. His program, almost always broadcast on Sunday morning, "caused a sensation!" he later wrote.

People had never had a live healing crusade service coming right into their front rooms via TV. Millions of people in America and Canada had a front-row seat to see and hear a man, who despite all his faults and shortcomings, was really called of God. They could see the expressions on our faces, hear distinctly every word of my preaching and teaching, and literally see the healings. Hearing and seeing what was happening sharply divided the nation between those who believed and those who did not.

Among those on the negative side of the divide, in addition to people who doubted his healing gifts, were people who wearied of Roberts's constant pleas for money. On every show, more than once, he asked his viewers to send him "generous letters" so he could continue with his work. Those who did had their names filed away so that Roberts could send them requests for more generous letters in the future. Some viewers did not mind. Others wondered what the preacher's priorities truly were.

A TYPICAL ROBERTS SERVICE consisted of two parts: the sermon, which was always as lengthy as it was fiery, and then something "quite different from any other TV presentation," the treatment of the ailing. The *New York Times*'s Jack Gould, watching one episode at home with notepad in hand, reported on the exhibition before him.

> The climactic moment of the program was the case of a small boy who suffered from double club feet.
> The youngster was held in the arms of a woman relative and, before Brother Roberts invoked his power of faith, the youngster exclaimed with the help of some coaching, "Boy, am I a lucky duck?" He said he was going to be made well, he said.
> Brother Roberts took the boy in his lap. As he placed his hands vigorously on the boy's feet he stressed that "the ligaments had been cut." Under such circumstances, Brother Roberts added, only a miracle, nothing else, could enable the boy to walk. "Lord, when I put this child down, he's got to walk," he said. The boy scampered off the stage.

It does not get any more impressive than that, thought most of those in attendance. It does not get any more phony than that, thought the *Times*'s Gould, who had long since made up his mind about Roberts's priorities, and proceeded to excoriate television for its complicity in what he believed to be the preacher's fraudulence. "To allow the enormously influential medium of television to be used week after week to show undocumented 'miracles' with all their implied aspersions on the competency of medicine, seems contrary to the spirit, if not the letter, of the industry's code governing mature and responsible broadcasting. . . .

"If Brother Roberts wishes to exploit hysteria and ignorance by putting up his hands and yelling 'Heal,' that is his affair. But it hardly seems in the public interest, convenience and necessity, for the TV industry to go along with him."

But go along with him it did, to Roberts's enormous profit. "By the midfifties," historian J. Ronald Oakley tells us, "he had a 280-acre ranch near Texas, a twelve-passenger plane, a runway for his plane on his farm, an overseas ministry, a television and radio show airing on 400 stations, and $53 million in annual revenues."

Yet all was not as it seemed in the glittering realm of Brother Roberts. His opponents were growing in both number and fervency as his ministry grew in acreage and possessions. Like Gould, mainstream Protestant clergymen were dubious of his ability to cure the incurable, even though Roberts insisted he was merely God's conduit, and they were further upset by the flamboyance of his lifestyle.

The American Medical Association (AMA) went further. It thought Roberts a dangerous impostor, accusing him of misleading the vulnerable and doing more harm than good, and evidence was now accumulating to support the AMA's charges. A diabetic woman in Detroit went to see Roberts and told him of her plight. He laid on his hands and uttered a brief prayer. He told her she was cured. She went back home, stopped taking her insulin, and died. So did a woman who had supposedly had her cancer exorcised by Roberts. Neither had wanted to be dispatched to the life after this life quite as soon as they were.

And an increasing number of people informed reporters that although the evangelist had brought them relief, it had been only temporary, which reinforced the notion of many critics that Roberts relied more on the power of suggestion and the optimism of his patients than he did the wondrousness of the Lord.

Many people, however, continued to believe, and almost 1,500 of them heeded Roberts's command and wrote letters of complaint to Gould for the apostasy of his article. Some of them damned him, some promised prayer on his behalf so that he would escape damnation. It was like McCarthyites lambasting Murrow all over again. But, as in that previous case, the number of men and women willing to take up the defendant's cause was beginning to shrink, as was the number of TV stations willing to carry Roberts's program. There had simply been too much criticism from too many reliable sources. In retrospect, it seems remarkable that Roberts's influence diminished as slowly as it did.

ORAL ROBERTS DIED AT THE AGE OF 91, spending his final years in Newport Beach, California, supporting himself on a reported $83,505 a year from the ministry he created and adding significantly to that sum with the returns from his many investments. In 1963, he founded Oral Roberts University in Tulsa and, after serving as its president for many years, gave up the office and turned to a life of even greater luxury than he had known before, flying by private jet to his second home on an exclusive Florida golf course to play a few rounds each weekend. He also gave up his television ministry, with both ventures passing to his son Richard, also a clergyman and healer, and no less fiery than his father.

But in 2007, even though he was approaching his ninetieth birthday, Roberts returned to take partial control of ORU affairs after Richard was charged with misappropriating funds. He denied having done so, but the evidence against him seems undeniable. Father told son to take a little time off, let the heat die down, invite the healing grace of the Almighty to work its wonders.

Richard did, telling people God wanted him to depart. Then he came back, telling people God wanted him to return. As of January 2010, Richard was still appearing on television, the Roberts family now having accomplished the remarkable feat of passing the half-century mark on the small screen. Richard and his wife Lindsay host a daily program called *The Hour of Healing*. It is produced by Golden Eagle Broadcasting, headquartered on the ORU campus, and Golden Eagle syndicates it throughout the country. Few cable services carry it, though, and far fewer people watch the program than watched his father in his heyday.

On each episode, Richard and Lindsay ask their viewers to write in and "plant a seed," a euphemism for continuing to send money. They don't get as much of that as they used to either, and there is no way of knowing how much of the money they receive these days, if any, goes to jet fuel.

Chapter 16

The Black Sox of the Airwaves

I N 1919, the Chicago White Sox won 88 games and lost 52, the best record in the American League. As a result, they would play the National League's best team, the Cincinnati Reds, in the World Series that fall.

Most people who followed baseball gave the edge to the White Sox. They had better pitchers, including Eddie Cicotte, who won 29 games during the regular season and lost only 7, in the process compiling an almost invisible earned run average of 1.82. And the Sox had better hitters, including the legendary "Shoeless" Joe Jackson, whose 1919 batting average was .351. In the early wagering, to no one's surprise, most of the money was placed on Chicago.

Yet as the opening game of the Series approached, things began to change. All of a sudden a number of bettors were casting their lot with Cincinnati, and it was not the usual practice of a few high-rollers deciding at the last minute to take a chance on an underdog. There were more people than usual involved in the late wagering, more than a paltry sum of money switching allegiances. It was as if the gamblers knew something that the average fan did not. In fact, they did.

The idea to fix the 1919 Series seems to have originated with White Sox first baseman "Chick" Gandil, a one-time boxer, one-time boilermaker, and a baseball player who, like many players of the time, felt underpaid and underappreciated. Gandil arranged to meet with a friend of his named "Sport" Sullivan, a man of dubious reputation and high contacts in low places. One of those contacts was the notorious gangster Arnold Rothstein, known to some as "The Big Bankroll." Rothstein agreed to put up the money to alter the Series outcome. It would be up to Gandil to talk his teammates into accepting it.

One of the first he approached was Jackson. Gandil knew that Jackson had received $5,000 from gamblers before the Series even began, and was therefore, presumably, already in on the deceit. What Gandil did not know was that Jackson had made several attempts to give the money back later. Why he took it in the first place no one can say. But Jackson's batting average for the Series was .375 and he made no errors in the field. He certainly does not seem to have been in on the chicanery. In fact, when accused, Jackson swore he had played the games honestly, and he repeated the claim, never wavering, for the rest of his life. "I'm about to face the greatest umpire of all," he said shortly before he died, "and He knows I am innocent."

About several of Gandil's other teammates, however, the great umpire knew differently. Seven of the White Sox went along with the plan to rig the games, including Cicotte, whose second pitch of the first game hit the Reds' leadoff batter in the ribs, sending him to first base and putting Rothstein and his fellow investors at their immediate ease.

Cincinnati won the best-of-nine Series 5 games to 3.

What made the White Sox decide to trespass on the most fundamental canon of athletic endeavor? By today's standards at least, baseball players *were* underpaid in those days. Almost all of them had full-time jobs in the off-season and still found themselves scrounging at times, living no-frills lives from paycheck to paycheck even though, in the spring and summer, they were the idols, or at least the preoccupation, of countless fans. The extra money they would make for winning the World Series was a pittance compared to what the gamblers would give them for throwing it.

In addition, the Sox were united in their hatred of owner Charles Comiskey, whom they believed was even stingier than the average owner, not to mention more cantankerous and unreliable. Losing the Series would serve Comiskey right, several of the White Sox thought. In fact, even if they *didn't* get paid for going into the tank, it might be worth it just to give the old man a comeuppance.

Rumors that Chicago was taking a dive started while the games were still being played. They continued through the winter of 1919–20, picking up steam as the weather began to turn, and becoming the talk of baseball when spring training began the next season. At about the same time, they also became the talk of law enforcement officials, and in September 1920, a grand jury was convened to look into the matter.

Some of the players confessed their misdeeds, both orally and on paper, as soon as they were accused. But then they changed their minds; they had *not* deliberately allowed Cincinnati to win the Series, they now declared, and when authorities tried to confront them with their signed admissions of guilt, it seems the papers had mysteriously disappeared. No one was sure what happened to them, either then or since. Signed confessions gone, oral confessions repudiated—the grand jury had no choice but to acquit all eight of the accused players.

Officials of major league baseball, however, were not bound by legalities. They could do whatever they wanted, and for the integrity of their game, they banned the players for life. Soon the whole White Sox team, innocent and guilty alike, was known as the Black Sox, a name that still lives in infamy ninety years later.

It was the most famous scandal in the history of American sport. A number of books have been written about it and one of them, the authoritative *Eight Men Out* by Eliot Asinof, was made into a movie. In another movie, *Field of Dreams*, "Shoeless" Joe and some of the other Black Sox magically reappear, long after their deaths, through the high stalks of a cornfield in Iowa. Next to the field, the character played by Kevin Costner, a farmer, has built a baseball diamond, and the Sox descend on it from the afterlife to play again, to redeem themselves, in their own eyes if not in the history books. And in an earlier movie, *The Godfather, Part II*, one of the hoodlums says, "I've loved baseball ever since Arnold Rothstein fixed the World Series in 1919."

But for fans at the time, the 1919 Series was the most disillusioning of experiences. And not just for the fans. As Asinof writes, if a bit overheatedly,

> the American people were at first shocked, then sickened. There was hardly a major newspaper that did not cry out its condemnation and despair . . . but the scandal was a betrayal of more than a set of

ball games, even more than of the sport itself. It was a crushing blow at American pride. The year before, America had won the war in the image of nobility and humanity. "Saving Europe from the Hun" was a sacrificial act. Our pride in victory was the essence of American pride in itself. Baseball was a manifestation of the greatest of America at play. It was our national game; its stars were national heroes, revered by kids and adults alike. In the public mind, the image was pure and patriotic.

Now, suddenly, that pride had been shattered. The National Pastime was nothing more than another show of corruption. . . .

There is no way to gauge the extent of the damage on the American psyche. It is impossible to add up bitterness like a batting average. How great was the layer of cynicism that settled over the nation?

The lesson, if overstated, is clear. Americans took their games seriously. They wanted to trust them, to know that the winners won fairly and the losers lost honestly, and that the fairness and honesty of the game were symbols of justice in the larger society.

ALMOST FOUR DECADES LATER, it seemed that TV quiz shows, with *The $64,000 Question* leading the way, were becoming as much a national pastime as baseball. Jack Gould, for one, was not surprised. "The game of finding out who knows the answers," he wrote, "has been a flourishing social institution ever since Eve made Adam guess in which hand she held the apple. Television merely improved upon its economic features."

There were more quiz shows on the air in the late fifties than there had ever been before, including *Name that Tune*, on which a Marine and future astronaut named John Glenn won $15,000 for correctly identifying twenty-five songs after hearing only a few notes of each. During the summer of 1958, ten new quiz shows made their debuts, all the networks wanting to get in on the mania, hoping their payoffs would far exceed those of the contestants.

But it was too much of a good thing. With so many programs on the air that were so similar in format, viewers became saturated and their interest began to wane. "[Movie actress] Loretta Young's anthology series defeated *The $64,000 Challenge*," it was reported. "A mediocre Western, *The Californians*, nosed out *The $64,000 Question*. Ancient reruns of *I Love Lucy* beat new episodes of *Twenty-One*. *Dotto*, a smash hit on CBS in the daytime, flopped in a nighttime version on NBC."

But in 1958 *Dotto* had more problems than just low ratings.

In the spring of the year, a man named Ed Hilgemeier, who hoped to be an actor one day but was having more luck finding part-time work as a butler, decided he had to do something about the depleted state of his finances. A fan of *Dotto*, he thought he would give the show a try. He applied to be a contestant, which meant that, if chosen, he would attempt to fill in a connect-the-dots puzzle by answering questions; each correct answer provided another line between the dots.

Hilgemeier was chosen, but as a standby, which meant that he would go on only if one of the other contestants couldn't make it, or, more likely, if one contestant trounced a competitor so badly and quickly that there was extra time available on one of the programs.

Hilgemeier, like other standbys, was assigned a particular day, and that day only, to show up at the studio and wait in the wings. When it came, he planted himself offstage, hoping for his chance to go on. But things did not look good. Marie Winn, the reigning champion of *Dotto*, was on the air answering every question correctly and would probably continue to do so for the rest of the program. Her foe, however, seemed up to the challenge, answering his own questions and prolonging the contest. Hilgemeier sighed and looked at the clock. The minutes were flying by. He could close his eyes and see himself back in his butler's uniform, his bank account containing the same meager sum that it did now.

Then, eyes open, he looked down at the floor. He saw a notebook. He picked it up, began to leaf through it. What he found stunned him. In the notebook were the questions that had just been asked of Marie Winn. Following each was the answer. At first, Hilgemeier did not know what to make of it. Who had dropped the notebook? Who had looked at it prior to its being dropped? Suddenly he understood. The questions and answers were Winn's, in her own handwriting, and the reason she was so confident and accurate onstage was that she had been provided with a script of a sort beforehand.

Hilgemeier couldn't believe it. The fix, he realized, was in. He slipped the notebook into his pocket.

As he feared, he did not get on the air that evening, and after pondering what to do for the next few days, he told the producers of *Dotto* about his discovery. He was not, apparently, trying to extort them, but just to play it safe the producers assumed the worst and decided to buy the notebook back from him. With it, implicitly, would come Hilgemeier's silence about the notebook's existence. The bribe was $1,500.

It was more money than Hilgemeier had ever seen before, and he took it eagerly. But he was still not satisfied. After a few days, he decided to punish the producers, filing a complaint about *Dotto* with the New York District Attorney's office. He also let the show's sponsor, Colgate toothpaste, know of the fraud. Perhaps Hilgemeier had decided that he could have made a lot more than $1,500 had he actually been a contestant. Perhaps he decided he could have made a lot more than $1,500 had he put a higher price tag on the notebook.

By this time, CBS had found out about the notebook and, after a few meetings, both among their own executives and with officials of Colgate, decided to cancel the show. The action was taken so quickly that there wasn't even time to send out a press release.

To most viewers it came as a jolt. In the week or two following the cancellation there were whispers about irregularities of some sort, but nothing specific and nothing that could be proved. TV columnists wrote about *Dotto*'s demise but not much; many of them knew of Hilgemeier and the notebook, and a few of them alluded to it in print, but for the most part they treated it as an aberration. Surely *Dotto* hadn't been a crooked show, at least not for its entire run. After all, no criminal charges had been brought against anyone, and there was no reason to think that other quiz shows were doing anything deceptive. Perhaps *Dotto* wasn't, either. Perhaps there was even an explanation for the notebook other than deceit. Case closed—for the time being.

But it was a short time. Within weeks newspapers would be so full of stories about the dishonesty of quiz shows that they might have been a matter of national security.

CHARLES VAN DOREN was an engaging young man, to say the least. Thirty years old, the son of Pulitzer Prize–winning poet Mark Van Doren and nephew of Pulitzer Prize–winning biographer Carl Van Doren, Charles was an instructor at Columbia University. He was "shy, gentle, somewhat self-deprecating, like a young, more intellectual Jimmy Stewart." Tall and lanky like Stewart, with a shock of sandy hair that seemed constantly on the verge of unruliness, he was "smart enough to win yet modest enough to seem just a little uneasy with his success."

The success came at the end of November, 1956 when Van Doren began to appear on the quiz show *Twenty-One* which, at least for the past few weeks, had not been doing well in the ratings. The main reason, the producers believed, was that the audience did not care for the show's current champion, Herbert Stempel. "A complacent, arrogant contestant," says Thomas A. DeLong in his book *Quiz Craze: America's Infatuation with Game Shows*, "[Stempel] struck viewers as the know-it-all 'heavy,' while readily winning $48,000 in a half-dozen broadcasts."

Van Doren, the anti–Stempel, was booked on the show immediately after the producers met him. He took his place in a soundproof, glassed-in booth and defeated Stempel, in his own booth, handily. Unlike *The $64,000 Question*, *Twenty-One* was a program that did not allow contestants to choose the subjects on which they would be interrogated; they were, instead, required to show their expertise on whatever topics the writers came up with—and Van Doren did, revealing his knowledge of such unrelated fields as George Washington's military career and musical comedies, the paintings of Leonardo da Vinci and bodies of water, and anatomy and European monarchs. "One January night," he said, "I was asked to give the nicknames of several Second World War airplanes and in February I was asked to name the seven Prime Ministers of Britain between the world wars. A critic later wrote that mine 'was a remarkable and seductive performance.'"

So much so that Van Doren eclipsed Dr. Joyce Brothers to become the most popular quiz show contestant ever. Or so it seemed to the critics and columnists who paid attention to such things. A large part of Van Doren's appeal, in his own words, written more than half a century later, more wistful than arrogant, was that he appeared the "the very image of a young man that parents would like their son to be."

In other words, he was not only the anti–Stempel; he was the anti–Elvis. Presley had made the first of three appearances on Ed Sullivan's show by now, and those who were put off by his sultriness were charmed by Van Doren's wholesomeness. When Presley talked on TV, he sounded like the truck driver he had once been. When Van Doren talked, he sounded like the academic he currently was—"the ideal teacher," he wrote, "which is to say patient, thoughtful, trustworthy, caring."

Van Doren received as many as 500 letters a week, some of them proposing marriage. His phone rang so frequently that he had to get an unlisted number. He was on the cover of *Time*. He received an offer to star in a movie for $50,000, but turned it down. And, most important to the producers of *Twenty-One*, the episode of the show on which Van Doren defeated Stempel without so much as a moment's indecision, became the first program in a regularly scheduled TV series ever to pull in more viewers than *I Love Lucy*.

By the time Van Doren dispatched a number of opponents and found himself facing Vivienne Nearing, he had won $138,000. Nearing, a lawyer "with a hard-candy smile," was the wife of one of Van Doren's previous victims, one of ten in his ten weeks on the program. Mrs. Nearing, she said, was out for revenge.

But she did not get it, not at first. On February 25, 1958, the two contestants tied. It was the first time that had ever happened on *Twenty-One*. The suspense built. The press coverage approached overload. The program beat *Lucy* by an even bigger margin.

The next week Van Doren and Nearing tied again. No one could believe it. What were the odds? The American heartbeat skipped like a badly tuned engine.

The week after that it skipped even more, as the combatants tied for the third time. What was going on here? You can't make this kind of thing up. Or can you?

As the hour approached for Van Doren–Nearing IV, a neighbor of the Burnses who had watched their three previous encounters told my mother she would not be turning her set on for this one. The suspense was too great, she said; she couldn't bear to watch. She would call us as soon as the show was over to find out who had won. She hoped, of course, it was young Charles.

It was not. Van Doren provided the most unsatisfactory climax possible for such an epic duel, failing to name the king of Belgium on the first question of the night. It seemed one of the easiest questions he had yet been asked. But he missed it. Duel over. Van Doren vanquished. Something like twenty-five minutes of air time were still left on the program. Mrs. Vivienne Nearing had restored her family's good name "and *Twenty-One*," it was accurately observed, "had to face its real test: Could it survive without Charles Van Doren, America's favorite egghead?"

The immediate answer seemed to be no. On the night of Van Doren's defeat, *Twenty-One* finished eight-and-a-half points ahead of *Lucy* in the ratings, the worst defeat Lucille Ball had ever suffered in Hooper numbers. Seven days later, on the first show in more than three months without the Columbia instructor as a contestant, *Twenty-One* lost to *I Love Lucy* by nine points, a seventeen-and-a-half point swing in a mere seven days.

Van Doren, however, started out surviving very nicely without *Twenty-One*. He had won more money in fourteen weeks than he would have earned teaching in a decade, if not a lifetime. And even more was on the way. He signed a five-year contract with NBC for a reported $10,000 annually to join the cast of *Today*, on which manners and breeding would make him the anti–J. Fred Muggs. NBC radio also chipped in, paying him an unknown amount to be a regular panelist on the high-brow talk program *Conversation*.

When *Dotto* was canceled in the spring of 1958 amid rumors of impropriety, Van Doren paid no attention. As far as he was concerned, the world of quiz shows was behind him now, and he was living a kind of life he had never imagined for himself. What he had done to ensure the financial underpinnings of that life was something he preferred not to think about. Others, however, could not get it out of their minds.

SUMMER, 1958: Herbert Stempel was fuming, hotter than the weather. He was tired of seeing Charles Van Doren on television, tired of hearing him on the radio, tired of seeing his name in print. He had had quite enough of Van Doren glorification. He knew the saint to be a sinner, the genius to be a mere actor, and it was time, he told his wife, that others knew it as well. She tried to talk him out of a public statement; they were, after all, $48,000 richer than they would have been without *Twenty-One*. But he would not be dissuaded. The money had been spent. They should be richer still.

Stempel went to the newspapers with his charge that the show was a sham. He said he had been ordered to lose by the producers and that Van Doren had been programmed to win by having been given answers to every question he was asked. Stempel had to admit, however, that he had previously been programmed himself. In fact, according to Van Doren, Stempel had been programmed to an almost laughable degree.

He was to pat his brow (it was hot in those glass booths) but not rub it, to avoid smearing his makeup. In addition, he was instructed to get a Marines-type 'whitewall' haircut, to wear an ill-fitting suit (it had belonged to his deceased father-in-law), and to describe himself as a penurious student at City College. In fact, he was a Marines veteran married to a woman of some means who once appeared on the set wearing a Persian-lamb coat and was quickly spirited away so that she wouldn't blow his cover.

Stempel was also told to wear a six-dollar wrist watch that 'ticked away like an alarm clock,' as he later testified, and was audible when he stood sweating in the booth.

Stempel's complaint, in other words, although he did not look at it this way, was not that the game was fixed, but that he had not been allowed to cheat for as many weeks, and to as great a financial advantage, as Van Doren had. He also stated that, had he not been forced to a give an incorrect response when he knew the right one, neither Van Doren nor anyone else would have had a chance against him. He was smart enough, in other words, to have defeated Van Doren—and Nearing, if it came to that—without the producers' illicit assistance.

The story detonated in the press. Stempel was not just attacking one of America's favorite forms of entertainment, but "one of America's new folk heroes."

Van Doren, filling in for Garroway as the *Today* host that week, responded to Stempel on the air. He was "sad and shocked," he said. "[I]t's enough to shake your faith in human nature . . . I myself was never given any answers or told any questions beforehand, and, as far as I know, none of the contestants received any coaching of this sort . . . the television quiz show in this country has become an institution. A quiz show is fundamentally a matching of wits and it is an American tradition to do this. I, for one, think it's a good tradition."

But soon others besides Stempel were speaking out about the tradition, and like him finding it not so good. Among them was a *Dotto* contestant who said she had been given "indirect help anyone but an idiot could follow." She was joined by a *$64,000 Challenge* competitor who said he had been fed his lines a few days before the show aired. And another *Twenty-One* contestant, James E. Snodgrass, declared that he too had been provided with answers in advance.

Unlike the others, however, Snodgrass had proof; he had made a copy of the answers and sent them to himself via registered mail. He handed over the envelope to the New York District Attorney, dated several days before he appeared on the program. The D.A. opened the envelope before an office full of witnesses. The evidence lay on his desk before them all, irrefutable.

Even celebrities confessed to having been manipulated, albeit to their own advantage, on quiz shows. Patty Duke, a thirteen-year-old actress who would in a few years win an Academy Award for playing Helen Keller in the movie version of *The Miracle Worker*, admitted that she had been coached for *The $64,000 Challenge;* and Latin bandleader Xavier Cugar said the same thing had happened to him on the same program. Neither thought anything of it at the time. They were both in show business, after all; to them *Twenty-One* was just another gig with a script, and they were pleased to play the role of winner.

At this point, if not even before, the networks panicked. By September 1958, four of the top quiz shows of recent years had been canceled, including *The $64,000 Challenge*. A month later *Twenty-One* was gone, having dropped from sixth place in the ratings to the mid-thirties in the wake of Van Doren's departure and Stempel's charges. By now, Van Doren would later admit, he was more worried than he had ever been in his life.

One of the main reasons was that a grand jury had begun looking into the operations of quiz shows. Van Doren and other contestants, not to mention the men who managed the quiz shows, feared the worst, but after hearing more than 100 hours of testimony from more than 200 witnesses, the grand jury handed down only one indictment. Albert Freedman, the producer of *Twenty-One*, was charged with lying when he said that neither he nor anyone who worked for him ever supplied answers to those who appeared on the program.

He could have gone to prison. Instead, he went to Mexico. First, though, he had to make a deal with authorities; in return for confessing his program's duplicity, he was allowed his freedom south of the border.

SINCE THERE WAS NO POINT in denials anymore, the producers of quiz shows turned to the next best thing: excuses. One member of a quiz show staff said, "You cannot ask random questions of people and have a show. You simply have failure, failure, failure, and that does not make entertainment." Dan Enright, who helped to create *Tic Tac Dough*, admitted that the nighttime version of his program was fixed, by his reckoning, seventy-five percent of the time. He did not bother fixing the daytime version of the show, he told the House Subcommittee on Legislative Oversight, which had control over the FCC, because not as many people were watching in the afternoon; the ratings weren't so important.

Then he went on. "Deception is not necessarily bad," he said to the congressmen. "It's practiced in everyday life . . . it should be measured in terms of the hurt it inflicted on people." And Enright believed that quiz shows inflicted hurt on no one. The contestants on *Tic Tac Dough* went home with either money or prizes, and those who viewed the show in their homes were fascinated by the proceedings.

Bud Granoff, producer of ABC's *Treasure Hunt*: "The questions are the unimportant part of the show, worth only $50. We often ask a contestant the same question he has already answered correctly in his pre-show interview."

And Albert Freedman of *Twenty-One*, before donning his sombrero and departing, said:

> In the field of TV programming, saturated with murder and violence, it is my opinion that the quiz shows, as entertainment, were a breath of fresh air. . . . it is about time the television industry stopped apologizing for its existence and began to fight back. It should insist that programming be recognized and judged as entertainment and entertainment only.

It was as if Eddie Cicotte had said the 1919 World Series should have been judged as entertainment and entertainment only.

Freedman believed that what ultimately led to the demise of quiz shows was that, in their heyday they "were too successful. The stakes were too high, and the quiz winners fused themselves into the home life and the hopes and aspirations of the viewers."

In the view of Hal March, the host of *The $64,000 Question*, which was never accused of impropriety, the shows were not only too successful but ubiquitous. "It got to the point," he said, "where there were just too many quiz programs. Ratings began to drop and some producers turned to rigging to make sure the shows kept their audiences. They just couldn't afford to lose sponsors."

Eventually, President Eisenhower ordered his Attorney General to look into quiz shows, and Justice Department officials began to investigate. Eisenhower's Secretary of State, Christian Herter, was paraphrased by author Walter Karp as asking, "What kind of country had America become? What kind of people were we producing?"

And the political scientist Hans Morgenthau, finding Van Doren's performance "a great event in the history of America," described him as having been "formed by a world which condones the betrayal of truth for the sake of wealth and power." Those who did not condemn Van Doren, Morgenthau went on, were guilty "of a moral obtuseness which signifies the beginning of the end of civilized society."

But by then most of the big money programs were off the air, or soon would be. As for those that remained, they were being policed as carefully as a Communist rally in front of a factory owner's mansion. As a result, neither the White House nor the Congressional Subcommittee on Legislative Oversight ever took any action.

THESE DAYS, it is hard to imagine the impact that quiz-show cheating once had on the country, the kind of apocalyptic rhetoric it inspired—these days when scandals are more scandalous than they used to be, hypocrisy more expected, dishonesty a more common practice not only in television but in politics and commerce and dealings among hedge fund managers and their greed-besotted clients. It is for this reason that *Quiz Show,* director Robert Redford's superb 1994 film about the Van Doren charade, did not resonate with audiences as much as it would have a few decades earlier, when Americans had not yet been presented with so much cause for cynicism in the public sphere.

But Van Doren was one of the early instigators of our cynicism, and he paid dearly for it, passing in little more than a moment from icon to object of scorn, from a person who had won a lot of money to a person who had lost almost everything else.

He had insisted on his innocence for almost three years—to friends, family, coworkers, his own lawyer, Congress, a grand jury, even swearing under oath to the latter that he had not been given answers. He was, thus, guilty of "second degree perjury, a misdemeanor," and by the time he finally admitted it, he was also admitting that his life had been shattered both by the lie he had lived initially and his continued repetition of it. "I would give almost anything I have to reverse the course of my life in the last three years," he eventually said. "I was involved, deeply involved, in a deception. . . . I was almost able to convince myself that it did not matter what I was doing because it was having such a good effect on the national attitude toward teachers, education, and the intellectual life."

Almost, but not quite. When he was asked about his relationship with Freedman, Van Doren said the producer did more than just furnish answers.

He "instructed me how to answer the questions, to pause before certain of the answers, to skip certain parts and return to them, to hesitate to build up suspense, and so forth. . . . He gave me a script to memorize and before the program he took back the script and rehearsed me in my part."

Ironically, Freedman's script did not include the name of the king of Belgium. When Van Doren said he didn't know it, he was, for a change, answering honestly.

It was, by the way, Baudouin I.

Van Doren either resigned from or was forced to quit the Columbia faculty. NBC dropped him from both *Today* and *Conversation*. He disappeared from public view as suddenly as he had appeared, and sometimes even hid himself from private peeks; there were friends he did not want to see anymore, others who did not want to see him. For a time he became an editor for Praeger, a small book publisher in New York, but New York was not the place for him to be at this time in his life.

He moved to Chicago, where he worked with a friend of his father, the philosopher Mortimer Adler, on the *Encyclopaedia Britannica*. It was, he later said, "the time when I fell down, face down in the mud, and [Adler] picked me up, brushed me off, and gave me a job." Van Doren also edited several volumes of collected essays and aphorisms, including *The Great Treasury of Western Thought* and *The Joy of Reading*.

Occasionally he was asked to go on television to promote the books. He always refused. Says David Halberstam, "He was aware that if he made a book tour, he was not likely to be asked about the history of Western thought, or about the relative influence of Plato, Aristotle, and St. Thomas Aquinas on our lives, but rather about Freedman [and] Enright." Van Doren would not talk about *them* to anyone.

BOB HOPE, however, knew good material when he found it, and the quiz show scandal was good material. "How d' do, ladies and gentlemen," he said in the opening monologue of one of his TV shows. "This is Bob Hope (I think that's my real name) coming to you for the Buick Co. (that can be proved) over the NBC network (which can also be verified) . . . let's see Congress fool around with that. Let me be the first to wish you an honest Christmas and an unrigged New Year. . . .

"The type of show I do is called 'entertainment' except in Washington, where it's called 'evidence.'. . . I understand they're gonna subpoena Mother

Goose. They just found out that little Bo Peep was a sheep rustler and the Three Blind Mice had 20-20 vision. . . .

"From now on, shows will have to be just what they say they are—*Wagon Train* will have to take place on a wagon, *River Boat* on a river, and *Naked City* will have to go off the air."

AND WITH THAT came the end of an era, not with a bang but with a punch line. Or, to put it in different terms, it was the end of a decade, "a troubled decade," according to the *New York Times*, of which the quiz-show scandals were "the final phoniness." Television was nothing when the fifties started, everything when they ended; nowhere when they started, everywhere when the sixties made their entrance. But with time and circumstance Americans had lost not only their initial enthusiasm for the medium; we had lost our belief in its veracity and good intentions, and for most of us, neither quality would be fully restored.

Still, television would remain the most persuasive of cultural forces for the rest of the century and into the next one. It would continue to be the most powerful of forums for the sale of people, products, and ideas, however superficial and unnecessary most would be. It would continue to affect our daily routines, our attitudes, our behavior, our beliefs, our priorities, our political processes, our use of language, our taste in music and fashion, our notions of child-rearing, our definitions of morality, our choice of heroes and villains, our sense of right and wrong. The Internet still lurked, was still considered a threatening presence, had in fact become a general presence. But although many in television panicked, as was their way; although they laid off humans and cut back budgets, the small screen remained as powerful and profitable a medium as ever.

Even the most optimistic of the medium's founding fathers could not have imagined how powerful their legacy would be. One, in particular, was positively dumbfounded.

Epilogue

The Man with a Secret

'VE GOT A SECRET was a game show, not a quiz show. That is to say, its prizes were pocket change, and it did not require the kind of knowledge necessary for *The $64,000 Question* or *Twenty-One*. It did not, in fact, require knowledge at all, except of one's own life. A panel of four famous people sat behind a desk and took turns asking questions of a guest who had done something notable or unusual or just plain ridiculous. The panelists tried to find out what that something was; the guest hoped to stump them. Garry Moore, crew-cut and wholesome and a little too glib, was the host of the program and sat next to the guest at another desk, keeping order and prompting the guest when he or she was not sure how to respond to a panelist's query. There was a celebrity visitor at the end of the program, and the panelists were blindfolded as they tried to guess his or her identity.

Usually the noncelebrity guests were introduced by name; they were almost always someone of whom the panel had not heard. But one day in July, 1957, a man who could not be called a celebrity, at least not any longer, appeared on the show and was identified as Dr. X. His face was not familiar to anyone; the panelists did not have to hide their eyes. It was possible, however, that his name might register with a panel member, and if it did his secret would be revealed as well.

Dr. X was tall, bespectacled, and lean, so lean that his shirt collar seemed a size too big for his neck. His hair, a little curly, was combed back from his forehead, the hairline receding on the sides. It might have been Charles Van Doren thirty years later.

"Now, Doctor," said Moore, "if you will whisper your secret to me we'll show it at the same time to the folks out there."

Dr. X leaned into Moore, held a hand over Moore's ear, and pretended to tell the host what he already knew. At the same time his secret was flashed on the screen for the home audience. Those in the studio were able to see it on monitors, and when they did they clapped their hands appreciatively. The secret was that Dr. X. had invented electronic television. His name—and it was just as likely *not* to register with a panelist—was Philo T. Farnsworth.

The first to question Dr. X was from Bill Cullen, who was well-known by virtue of his being the host of other game shows. He asked whether the secret involved some kind of object. Farnsworth said yes. Cullen followed up. "Is this some kind of machine that might be painful when it is used?"

"Yes," he said. "Sometimes it's most painful."

Chuckles all around at this. There was something about the way Dr. X had given his response, at once sorrowful and bemused.

The questioning went on for several more minutes, Dr. X providing his answers in a stumbling, awkward manner; he was clearly not comfortable in front of a camera. But since the panelists did not seem to be getting close to learning his secret, their enquiries leading nowhere; and since the program was running out of time, Moore cut the interrogation short and announced he was awarding Dr. X the maximum in prize money. Then he revealed both the man's identity and his accomplishment.

The audience applauded again and this time the panel joined in.

When the applause died down, Henry Morgan, a humorist who appeared not only on *I've Got a Secret* but on a number of other shows as well, wondered about something. "Doctor, truthfully," he said, "are you sorry?"

"No," Farnsworth said, "no."

But Moore jumped in and said, "I asked him the same question and he said 'sometimes.'"

A few moments later, with the program about to end, Moore shook Farnsworth's hand and expressed to him "our eternal gratitude. I'd be out of work if it weren't for you."

Farnsworth smiled uncertainly. Then he stood and walked past the panelists' desk, shaking hands with each and shambling off the stage with his prizes: eighty dollars in cash and a carton of the sponsor's product, Winston cigarettes. It was impossible to tell whether his apparent confusion was the result of the experience he had just been through, or his ever-growing uncertainty about the fate of his baby, the image dissector, the machine of which he was the *real* father, in the decades ahead.

Notes

INTRODUCTION: PHILO T. FARNSWORTH'S DISCONTENT

2 "I have my periods": quoted in Gray, p. 204.
3 "see by electricity": quoted in http://www.fcc.gov/omd/history/tv/1880-1929/html.
3 "An eminent scientist": quoted in ibid.
3 "television [is] on the way": quoted in Greenfield, *Television*, p. 32.
3 "At an age," Carskadon, T. R., "Phil, the Inventor": *Collier's*, October 3, 1936, p. 19.
4 "found the study-hall blackboard," Wilson, Mitchell, "The Strange Birth of Television": *Reader's Digest*, February 1953, pp. 19–20.
5 "I asked Phil": Everson, pp. 38–39.
6 "was that the smoker": ibid., p. 12.
6 "It is a matter": quoted in *New York Times*, April 8, 1927, p. 20.
7 "went over very well": ibid., p. 1.
7 "Far-Off Speakers," and other headlines: ibid., pp. 1 and 20.
9 "This is a beautiful instrument": quoted in Schwartz, p. 208.
10 "he wouldn't even allow": quoted in Stashower, p. 252.
11 "There's nothing on it worthwhile": quoted in http://inventors.about.com/library/inventors/blfarnsworth.htm.

CHAPTER 1: DAMNING THE "TIIEENK"

15 "Da svitch": quoted in Schwartz, p. 293.
15 "I hate what they've done": quoted in en.wikipedia.org/wiki/Vladimir_Zworykin.
16 "We're in the same position": quoted in Boddy, p. 239.
16 "The instrument can teach": quoted in Corwin, p. 52.
16 "billion dollar blunder," and "is being murdered": Cousins, Norman, *Saturday Review*, December 24, 1949, p. 20.
17 "a medium of entertainment": quoted in Shulman and Youman, p. 8.
17 "It is hard to tell": quoted in Ritchie, p. 23.
18 "a vast wasteland": http://en.wikipedia.org/wiki/Wasteland_Speech.
18 "The horrible prospect": quoted in Smith, Jack, *Los Angeles Times*, September 14, 1988, p. 1, section 5.

18 "[T]elevision's perfect": quoted in Corwin, pp. 197–98.

18 "Thus being seduced": quoted in David, p. 117.

19 "watching television": Ansolabehere and Iyengar, p. 102.

20 "Adults spend": *Time*, February 13, 1950, p. 44.

21 "I have frequently": quoted in "Books and TV," *Publishers' Weekly*, June 17, 1950, p. 2638.

21 "It would be": quoted in "Television and Education," *Commonweal*, January 18, 1952, p. 366.

22 "the nodding heads," and "of 562 students": "TV and the Kids," *Newsweek*, December 26, 1949, p. 36.

22 "The children are tired": quoted in Shayon, p. 20.

23 "No more television": Wilson, p. 66.

23 "There are some things": quoted in Greenfield, *No Peace*, p. 108.

24 "More likely causes," and "negligible": Gould, Jack. *New York Times*, June 28, 1951, p. 18.

24 "To put it another way," "What TV Is Doing to America": *U.S. News & World Report*, September 2, 1955, p. 39.

25 "There is something": quoted in "Book and TV," *Publishers' Weekly*, June 17, 1950, p. 2639.

25 "TV as novelty": ibid., p. 18.

26 "between 1640 and 1700": Postman, *Amusing*, p. 31.

26 "as high as 62 percent": ibid., p. 32.

26 "Even in the back-country counties": Ellis, p. 80.

27 "The only thing that boomed": Smith, p. 301.

27 "Higher literacy proficiencies": and following quote are contained in an e-mail received by the author on December 19, 2006 from Marsha L. Tait, senior vice president, ProLiteracy Worldwide, Syracuse, New York.

27 "Use of television," and "[i]mproved vocabularies": ibid., June 29, 1951, p. 27.

28 "62 representatives": *New Republic*, January 22, 1951, p. 22.

28 "Several officials": *New York Times*, June 30, 1951, p. 19.

30 "93,000 pupils," "How TV Is Used in Education and Religion,": *U.S. News & World Report*, September 2, 1955, p. 42.

30 "will watch the first": *Life*, June 6, 1949, p. 74.

31 "might well rank": Altschuler and Grossvogel, p. 18.

CHAPTER 2: THE NEW AMERICAN FAMILY

34 "Make sure": quoted in http:/www.quotationspage.com/quotes/Dorothy_Sarnoff.

35 "Firemen not only trip": *Time*, June 19, 1950, p. 69.

36 "just love it": quoted in ibid., p. 69.

37 "No doubt your invention": Philo T. Farnsworth Papers, Special Collections, Manuscripts Division, Marriott Library, University of Utah, Box 21, Fd. 7.

37 "They used to come up to me": author interview with Win Fanning. January 14, 1980.

38 "One day": quoted in Schwartz, p. 291.

38 "Weather reports": "Effect of TV on Farm Life": *U.S. News & World Report*, September 2, 1955, p. 48.

39 "Hospitals have found": "What TV Is Doing for Shut-ins": ibid., p. 48.

39 "is 15 per cent more": "What TV Is Doing to America": *U.S. News & World Report*, September 2, 1955, p. 37.
39 "The busy Mrs. America": Marling, p. 235.
40 "The freezing process": Mouchard, Andre, "Frozen in Time, Fifty Years Ago, the TV Dinner Appeared and Changed the Way America Thinks about the Family Meal," *Orange County Register*, June 20, 2003, online version (unpaginated).
40 "dietary loss": Oakley, p. 107.
40 "inducted," and "solidifying the TV Dinner's role": http://www.Swansonmeals .com/50th/fun_facts/1986.html.
40 "Perfect for TV dining": quoted in Marling, p. 189.
40 "joined a whole family": ibid., p. 190.
41 "TV Time Popcorn's": ibid., p. 236.
42 "loud-mouthed": Barclay, Dorothy, "A Decade Since 'Howdy-Doody,'" *New York Times* magazine, September 21, 1958, p. 63.
43 "matronly schoolmistress": Marschall, *Golden Age*, p. 120.
43 "the most persuasive apologist": Marling, p. 185.
43 "'The novel says'": quoted in ibid., p. 185–86.
44 "Television is keeping families together": quoted in *Time*, February 13, 1950, p. 44.
44 "something we can share," and "saved our marriage," and "until we got": quoted in Oakley, p. 119.
44 "God knows": quoted in "TV Newspaper," *Time*, September 15, 1952, p. 104.
44 "seemed to show": *Time*, June 19, 1950.
45 "A number of parents," Usher, Ann, "TV . . . Good or Bad for Your Children?": *Better Homes and Gardens*, October 1955, pp. 208–9.
45 "is the shortest cut": quoted in "TV and Children," *Newsweek*, March 5, 1951, p. 54.
45 "that could be responsible": Stewart, R. W., *Variety*, December 31, 1947, p. 64.
46 "What's your name, Sonny?": quoted in Gould, Jack, *New York Times*, May 14, 1950, p. 193.
46 "I know more about Lucy's relationship": Mitz, p. 1.
46 "With television": quoted in Boddy, p. 21.
47 "create[d] the illusion": Schickel, pp. 9–10.
48 "the tone of the relationship": ibid., p. 25.
49 "When newscaster Stan Chambers": Ritchie, p. 85.
49 "The Brown Derby": "The New Hollywood," *Time*, May 13, 1957, p. 44.
51 "allowed the family to escape": Marling, p. 97.

CHAPTER 3: THE HULA HOOP AND THE BOMB

53 "was so complete": Burns, p. 184.
55 "one set [in the studio] was a cabinetmaker's shop": quoted in Manchester, Harland, "TV Will Change You," *Nation's Business*, June, 1949, p. 74.
56 "You've worked hard": Wilson, p. 64.
57 "a kind of spoil of war": Greenfield, *No Peace*, p. 106.
62 "a period of general prosperity": *New York Times*, August 19, 1956.
62 "In the beginning": quoted in Castleman and Podrazik, p. 50.

CHAPTER 4: INVISIBLE DOUGHNUTS AND COONSKIN CAPS

65 "for humanizing the American teacher": quoted in http://en.wikipedia.org//wiki/ Eve-Arden.

66 "chocolate cookies," and "casting steel ingots," and "the brand,": quoted in http:// en.wikipedia.org/wiki/Bob_and_Ray.

66–67 "dropped just a few inches," and "all gone," and "to fool the neighbors," and "just right for people," and "We make this offer," and "Just write in": quoted in "TV Viewers—Easy to Satisfy," *TV Guide*, October 23, 1954, pp. 22–23.

68 "Neither Bean nor Blue Angel": ibid., p. 22.

69 "Hey, kids": Sales, p. 136.

70 "knew I was fooling," and "but except": ibid., p. 137.

70 "I was very depressed": ibid., pp. 138–39.

72 "The viewer watches commercials": quoted in Boddy, p. 156.

72 "Lucky Strike cigarettes": Greenfield, *Television*, p. 175.

72 "the Water Commissioner": Goldman, p. 265.

73 "While ad spending in general": Miller and Nowak, p. 342.

74 "named the cestus": *New York Times*, December 7, 1955, p. 79.

75 "Let your moderation": quoted in Halberstam, p. 646.

75 "[a] convention of wholesale druggists": Barnouw, *Empire*, p. 57.

75 "the greatest name": quoted in Halberstam, p. 645.

75 "Some Revlon products," ibid., p. 645.

76 "had to put on": quoted in Whiteside, Thomas, "Onward and Upward with the Arts," *New Yorker*, June 3, 1950, p. 83.

77 "her behind-the-scenes aspirations": Marling, p. 148.

77 "a model who opened": Greenfield, *Television*, p. 175.

79 "a superb show": quoted in Dallek, p. 335.

80 "Mary Jane Higby": Ritchie, p. 116.

80 "automatically and arbitrarily": quoted in Boddy, p. 201.

80 "[A]n automobile manufacturer": quoted in ibid., p. 246.

82 "[W]e get paid": quoted in ibid., p. 198.

84 "Several 'Southern White Citizens Councils": Pondillo, Bob. *Television Quarterly*, Spring 2002, pp. 39–40.

84 "The southern location": Barnow, *Image Empire*, p. 36.

85 "I was destroyed": quoted in Boddy, p. 201.

85 "Another incident": Barnouw, *Image Empire*, p. 36.

86 "has elected to avoid": quoted in ibid., p. 199.

86 "feeling that eating": quoted in ibid., p. 199.

86 "material that may give offense," and "could in any way further": quoted in Greenfield, *Television*, p. 134.

86 "the tremendous and unprecedented increase": quoted in Burns, p. 207.

87 "When a guest": ibid., p. 211.

87 "no one was to be given": quoted in ibid.

87 "short, silky and nasal": Marschall, *Golden Age*, p. 147.

87 "Sit back": quoted in Doherty, p. 67.

89 "an average New York tenement house": Atkinson, J. Brooks, "On a Sidewalk of New York," *New York Times*, January 11, 1929, p. 20.

89 "Foremost among these objections": quoted in *Theatre Arts*, November 1959, p. 95.

89 "A scene in which": Twitchell, *Culture*, p. 219.

91 "Over and over": quoted in Grossman, p. 15.
92 "a dirty, lazy": Oakley, p. 262.
92 "When he claimed": "Crockett and Circulation," *Newsweek*, July 18, 1955, p. 60.
94 "I was in third grade": quoted in Jones, p. 44.
94 "Don't tell me": and following, quoted in Michaelis, p. 337.
94 "The wholesale price": ibid., p. 45.

CHAPTER 5: "REALLY BIG SHOWS"

97 "Writers and producers": Marschall, *Golden Age*, p. 66.
97 "If you study": Van Horne, Harriett, "The Living Theatre on Television," *Theatre Arts*, September 1951, p. 52.
98 "in the spring twilight," and "the sky green": Shaw, p. 2.
99 "107 actors": Greenfield, *Television*, p. 130.
99 "The final dramatic scene": quoted in ibid., p. 131.
100 "You remember how things were?": Miller, J. P., Days of Wine and Roses, "Golden Age of Television," October 2, 1958, original live broadcast on Rhino Home Video, transcribed by the author.
101 "In the 1950's": author correspondence with Paul Newman, August 1, 2007.
101 "the intangible magic": Greenfield, *Television*, p. 132.
101 "to catch the glowing": quoted in ibid., p. 132.
104 "The first show": Hart, p. 145.
105 "I was just tizzin'": "The Lost Pilot," *I Love Lucy*, season 1, vol. 1, Paramount Pictures (DVD), transcribed by the author.
105 "milder set of adventures": Marschall, *Golden Age*, p. 50.
106 "Right here, tonight on our stage": quoted in Marschall, *History*, p. 29.
107 "As a former newsman": ibid., pp. 151–52.
107 "I was booked": quoted in Greenfield, *Television*, p. 66.
108 "Ed Sullivan will be around": quoted in Oakley, p. 100.
110 "wandered the West": quoted in www.fiftiesweb.com/tv/cheyenne.htm.

CHAPTER 6: THE COMPETITION

114 "depth interviews": quoted in Manchester, Harland, "TV Will Change You," *Nation's Business*, June, 1949, p. 41
114 "movie attendance": ibid., p. 41.
114 "which, if true": Gould, Jack, "What Is Television Doing to Us?" *New York Times* magazine, June 12, 1949, p. 7.
114 "Among TV set owners": *Time*, February 13, 1950, p. 44.
116 "took her bourbon": McMurtry, p. 50.
116 "weekly attendance in movie theaters": "What TV Is Doing to America," *U.S. News & World Report*, September 2, 1955, p. 43.
116 "Output of major feature films": ibid., p. 43.
116 "Movie theaters could not run": Greenfield, *No Peace*, p. 111.
117 "I'm not an actor": quoted in http://en.wikipedia.org/wiki/Victor_Mature.
118 "In July 1956": Boddy, p. 138.
118 "originally including a 10-minute segment": Marschall, *History*, p. 76

119 "43 per cent": "What TV Is Doing to America," *U.S. News & World Report*, September 2, 1955, p. 43.

119 "A single Hollywood TV show": "The New Hollywood," *Time*, May 13, 1957, p. 44.

119 "When you take into consideration": "What TV Is Doing to the Movie Industry," *U.S. News & World Report*, February 7, 1958, p. 88.

122 "Television reception": quoted in Boddy, pp. 19–20.

123 "Even without the coming": Allen, p. 238.

124 "Before buying a TV set": "What TV Is Doing to America," *U.S. News & World Report*, September 2, 1955, p. 44.

125 "Many rural areas": Manchester, Harland, "TV Will Change You," *Nation's Business*, June, 1949, p. 42.

128 "While home": Gould, Jack, "What Is Television Doing to Us?," *New York Times* magazine, June 12, 1949, p. 27–28.

128 "all forms of dining out": Manchester, Harland, "TV Will Change You," *Nation's Business*, June, 1949, p. 41.

128 "that they go": *Time*, February 13, 1950, p. 44.

CHAPTER 7: THE FIRST SENATOR

135 "Gloria Swanson's 'Sunset Boulevard,'" and, "Noel Coward battling flu": Sullivan, Ed, "Little Old New York," *Daily News*, September 24, 1950.

135 "consider the charm technique": ibid., September 17, 1950.

136 "came off as a sort of": Halberstam, p. 191.

136 "intelligent, shrewd," and "Words escaped him": ibid, p. 188.

137 "cunning": quoted in Gorman, p. 47.

137 "the most American": quoted in ibid., pp. 48–49.

138 "matter is too big": quoted in ibid., p. 74.

139 "they had to be more careful": Fontenay, p. 180.

139 "turned out to be": Halberstam, p. 190.

140 "I didn't know": quoted in Gorman, p. 87.

140 "as 'insurance'": http://en.wikipedia.org/wiki/Joe_Adonis.

140 "I'm gonna refuse," and "I heard it": quoted in Doherty, p. 116.

141 "You bastards": quoted in McCullough, p. 864.

141 "the prime minister": quoted in Solberg," p. 199.

141 "Mr. Costello": quoted in Halberstam, p. 192.

141 "TV's First Headless Star": Gould, Jack, "Costello TV's First Headless Star; Only His Hands Entertain Audience," *New York Times*, March 14, 1951, p. 1.

142 "Practically nothing," and "Nothing": quoted in Goldman, p. 192.

142 "a raspy baritone," and "seemed to emanate": English, p. 85.

142 "acute laryngo-tracheitis": quoted in Hagerty, James A., "Costello Defies Senators, Walks out of Hearing Here; Faces Arrest on Contempt," *New York Times*, March 16, 1951, p. 25.

142 "KEFAUVER: You refuse": quoted in Manchester, pp. 600–601.

143 "With staggering impact": quoted in McCullough, p. 865.

143 "The committee proposed": Fox, p. 303.

144 "Organized criminal gangs," Kefauver Committee Report, p. 174.

144 "the principal support": ibid., p. 175.

144 "Nearly every section": ibid., p. 170.
144 "set up a special rackets squad": Fox, p. 304.
145 "that a violent, subversive": Sage, p. 323.
146 "The twelve months": Gorman, p. 91.
147 "Ten Percent Off": quoted in Goldman, p. 194.
147 "The week of March 12, 1951": "Who's a Liar?," *Life*, April 2, 1951, p. 22.
147 "electric irons burned": Solberg, p. 198.
147 "One day": Shayon, Robert Lewis, "TV and Radio: Campaigning before the Cameras," *Saturday Review of Literature*, October 6, 1951, p. 37.
148 "*Confidential*'s success": Thumim, ed., p. 122.
148 "smudged the screen": Fontenay, p. 182.
148 "bringing the workings": quoted in Halberstam, p. 194.
149 "I did my best": quoted in Gorman, p. 94.
149 "all of our great men": quoted in Gorman, p. 49.
150 "the first big broadcast": "Who's a Liar?", *Life*, April 2, 1951, p. 22.
150 "the public hearing": Gould, Jack, "The Crime Hearings: Television Provides Both a Lively Show And a Notable Public Service," *New York Times*, March 18, 1951, p. 13.

CHAPTER 8: THE SECOND SENATOR

151 "In their drearier stretches": Bendiner, Robert, "How Much Has TV Changed Campaigning?," *New York Times* magazine, November 2, 1952, p. 13.
152 "that being telegenic": Marschall, *History*, p. 1986.
153 "to supplement the salaries": Ambrose, p. 284.
154 "You folks know the work": quoted in Nixon, pp. 83–84.
156 "Of what avail": quoted in http://en.Wikipedia.org/wiki/Richard_Nixon.
156 "You've been taking": quoted in Nixon, p. 99.
157 "There has just been a meeting," and, "It's kind of late," and, "I've got another suggestion," and, "Just tell them": quoted in Morris, pp. 822–23.
158 "There had been": ibid., p. 825.
159 "a GI bedroom den": quoted in ibid., p. 826.
159 "then stand next to it": ibid., p. 826.
159 "I just don't think," and, "Of course you can": quoted in ibid., p. 827.
159 "My fellow Americans," and other excerpts from speech: quoted in http://www.historyplace.com/speeches/nixon-checkers.htm.
160 "Why do we have to tell people": quoted in Aitken, p. 215.
160 "a descent into the corniness": ibid., p. 215.
162 "may aspire to the grace": quoted in Halberstam, p. 241.
162 "What a scenario!": Castleman and Podrazik, p. 73.
162 "I have seen": quoted in Halberstam, p. 241.
162 "Almost $60,000": Oakley, p. 137.
162 "From all across the country": ibid., p. 137.
163 "You're my boy": quoted in Oakley, p. 137.
163 "For the first time": author correspondence with Monica Crowley via e-mail, May 16, 2007.
163 "TV is apt to change," Gelernter, pp. 166–67.

CHAPTER 9: THE THIRD SENATOR

166 "While I cannot": quoted in Barnouw, *Golden Web*, p. 267.
167 "set off the most shocking panic": quoted in Boddy, p. 99.
167–69 *"Lillian Hellman,"* and following quotes: *Red Channels: The Report of Communist Influence in Radio and Television.* American Business Consultants, 1950.
169 "Where there's red smoke": quoted in Barnouw, p. 265.
170 "refused to look for Reds": Alwood, pp. 63–64.
170 "Pal, you're dead": quoted in Barnouw, p. 268.
171 "But Mrs. McCullough": quoted in ibid, p. 269.
172 "may detect a note": *New Republic*, January 21, 1952, p. 8.
174 "my favorite redhead": quoted in Doherty, p. 56.
174 "dangerous problems," and "doing his best": quoted in Merritt, p. 383.
174 "twenty years of treason," and other excerpts: from *See It Now*, transcript at www.honors.umd.edu/HONR269J/archive/Murrow540309.html.
178 "Chicago Bishop Bernard Sheil's speech": Fried, p. 139.
179 "You know, it's interesting": "McCarthy Years (DVD)," *Edward R. Murrow Collection*, docurama, distributed by New Video, 2005, transcribed by author.
179 "He proved again": ibid.
179 "A hazel-eyed dynamo": quoted in von Hoffman, p. 238.
179 "the golden boy": quoted in Doherty, p. 224.
180 "wreck the Army": quoted in www.mindcontrolforums.com/news/john-adams-dies.htm.
180 "Unlike other recruits": Manchester, pp. 706–7.
181 "conservative suit," and "He appeared at times": Cook, p. 489.
181 "CBS, fearful of losing revenue": Jacoby, p. 12.
182 "Now, while you have an audience": quoted in Manchester, p. 711.
183 "WELCH: Mr. Cohn," and other excerpts: from Army-McCarthy hearings, transcript at historymatters.gmu.edu/d/6444.
185 "went on to a career": Marschall, *Golden Age*, p. 153.
186 "What did I do?": quoted in ibid., p. 716.
187 "hepatitis, acute, cause unknown": quoted in Reeves, p. 671.
187 "unequivocably": ibid., p. 672.
187 "MURDERED!": *Manchester* (New Hampshire) *Union Leader* (City Edition), May 3, 1957, p. 3.

CHAPTER 10: ADVERTISING FOR PRESIDENT

190 "Television personalities": Crosby, John, "Television's Future Effect on Politicians," *Reader's Digest*, January, 1951, p. 5.
191 "reassure, entertain, or educate": http://en.wikipedia.org/wiki/Rosser_Reeves.
191 "melt in your mouth": quoted in ibid.
191 "the pain reliever": quoted in Fox, p. 192.
191 "grating and annoying": http://en.wikipedia.org/wiki/Rosser_Reeves.
191 "All the tars": quoted in Halberstam, p. 503.
192 "The narrator informs us": Shapiro, pp. 83–84.
195 "Eisenhower Answers the Nation!," and later excerpts: from 1952 Eisenhower ads and Stevenson ads, transcribed by author at Livingroomcandidate.movingimage.us.
192 "hell of a way": quoted in Twitchell, *Adcult*, p. 37.

193 "real people in their own clothes": quoted in Halberstam, p. 230.
193 "To think that an old soldier": quoted in ibid., p. 230.
194 "The man is very good": quoted in Fox, p. 310.
195 "the commercials showed": author correspondence with David Schwartz, Curator, Museum of the Moving Image, New York, via e-mail, May 30, 2007.
196 "Eisenhower hits the spot": quoted in Halberstam, p. 231.
197 "This is the worst thing": quoted in ibid., p. 232.
197 "On the few occasions": McKeever, p. 185.
197 "Suppose that every Monday evening": quoted in ibid., p. 445.
198 "You get the audience": quoted in Halberstam, p. 229.
200 "should probably be given": "How Much Has TV Changed Campaigning?," Bendiner, Robert, *New York Times* magazine, November 2, 1952, p. 71.
200 "To be happy," and other excerpts: from 1956 Eisenhower and Stevenson ads, transcribed by author at Livingroom candidate. movingimage.us.
201 "Is there anything wrong?": quoted in Halbstam, p. 231.
201 "Do you remember?": quoted in ibid., p. 232.
202 "With its constant demand": "How Much Has TV Changed Campaigning?," Bendiner, Robert, *New York Times* magazine, November 2, 1952, p. 71.

CHAPTER 11: THE MYSTIC KNIGHTS OF THE SEA

205 "The black family": Barnouw, *Empire*, p. 34.
206 "thus eviscerating": Coleman, p. 116.
206 "In the matter of segregation": quoted in Boddy, p. 202.
207 "Urban settings": Lichter, Lichter, and Rothman, p. 338.
207 "a sea of dark faces": Bogle, p. 238.
208 "Shaving cream, brush, razor": *The Jack Benny Comedy Hour*, Goodtimes Movie Classics, on Goodtimes Home Video, transcribed by the author.
209 "knew how to make": Bogle, p. 239
210 "popularity with the general public": Larkin, p. 2614.
211 "scatterbrained": Wilson, Guittierez, and Chao, p. 160.
211 "a stale fantasy," and "'had no racial dissensions": ibid., p. 236.
212 "much of America came to a halt": ibid., p. 250.
213 "Hard-working, mild-mannered": ibid., p. 252.
213 "an engaging dunce": ibid., p. 252.
214 "fiendishly outlandish": ibid, p. 252.
214 "harpy battle-axes": ibid., p. 253.
215 "Oh, I's sorry," and other quotes from *Amos 'n' Andy*: *The Amos 'n' Andy Show*, Platinum Edition, Education 200 (DVD), transcribed by the author.
216 "Sadly, television's 'Amos 'n' Andy": ibid., pp. 253–54.
216 "The characters and plots": Castleman and Podrazik, p. 59.
217 "depicts the Negro": quoted in ibid., p. 59.
217 "Mocking the courage": Doherty, p. 77.
217 "one of the all time": ibid., p. 80.
219 "Madison Avenue is afraid": quoted in Coleman, p. 168.
219 "Aware that many white adults": ibid., p. 138.
219 "I remember clashing": Berle, p. 293.
219 "I want to read a letter," and "sat in stunned silence": author correspondence with Bill Harbach, via e-mail, May 29, 2007.

CHAPTER 12: "THE TECHNOLOGICAL EQUIVALENT OF A CRUCIFIX"

222 "On winter mornings": Perrett, p. 367.
223 "with all deliberate speed": www.ourdocuments.gov/doc.php?flash=true&doc=87.
223 "To separate children": quoted in Solberg, p. 297.
225 "With a tape recorder," and, "the technological equivalent": quoted in Roberts and Klibanoff, p. 155.
226 "a vicious bigot": Brinkley, p. 58.
226 "bitch," and, "coon": quoted in ibid., p. 58.
226 "[H]er act of civil disobedience": ibid., p. 59.
229 "Keep Bama white," and, "To Hell with Autherine": quoted in ibid., p. 130.
231 "Arkansas's most famous citizen": Manchester, p. 800.
231 "I'm sorry": quoted in ibid., p. 800.
231 "Keep the niggers out!": quoted in Halberstam, p. 674.
232 "Here she comes now": quoted in Jacoway, p. 4.
232 "Go home, you burr head!": quoted in Manchester, p. 801.
232 "Go home, you bastard": quoted in Halberstam, p. 675.
232 "Go home before you get hurt": quoted in Jacoway, p. 4
232 "No nigger bitch," and, "Lynch her": quoted in Halberstam, p. 675.
232 "Television news cameras": Roberts and Klibanoff, p. 160.
233 "Eckford remained statue-like": ibid., p. 161.
234 "Don't let them": quoted in ibid., p. 161.
234 "She's scared": quoted in Jacoway, pp. 5–6.
234 "You stay away": quoted in Roberts and Klibanoff, p. 161.
234 "[Chancellor] had watched": Halberstam, p. 676.
235 "On the 101st Airborne's first full day": Roberts and Klibanoff, p. 180.
236 "The television coverage": ibid., p. 182.
237 "billowing tear gas": ibid., p. 299.
237 "Irresponsible defiance": quoted in ibid, p. 299.
238 "a dream that": quoted in http://en.wikipedia.org/wiki/I_Have_a_Dream.
238 "A technological breakthrough": Roberts and Klibanoff, p. 347.
239 "We used you": author interview with Sander Vanocur, via telephone, January 4, 2007.
239 "If it hadn't been for the media": quoted in ibid., p. 407.

CHAPTER 13: SEXLESS OBJECTS

241 "confessional quiz show," and "misery show": quoted in Cassidy, Marsha F., *LookSmart Ltd.*, summer 2001, www.findarticles.com/p/articles/mi_m2342/is_2_35/ai_97074190/print, p. 1.
241 "Calls were preset": quoted in DeLong, p. 154.
242 "deliberately exploit human want": quoted in ibid., p. 151.
242 "regularly crossed the line": Castleman and Podrazik, p. 60.
242 "DANNY: Well, I would like," and "HULL: (reading) He says": quoted in Cassidy, Marsha F., *LookSmart Ltd.*, summer 2001, www.findarticles.com/p/articles/mi_m2342/is_2_35/ai_97074190/ print, pp. 3–4.
243 "the Cinderella show": Paley Center for Media, program A-570, transcribed by the author.
243 "something of an inverted": http://en.wikipedia.org/wiki/Queen_for_a_Day.

244 "What hath Sarnoff wrought?": quoted in Cassidy, Marsha F., *Look Smart Ltd.*, www. findarticles.com/p/articles/mi_m2342/is_2_35/ai_97074190/print, p. 5.

246 "I now crown you": ibid.

246 "It's a heart-warming experience": quoted in DeLong, p. 103.

247 "helped out the men": Miller and Nowak, p. 360.

248 "My wife": quoted in http://en.wikipedia.org/wiki/Geritol.

250 "All I want you to do": *I Love Lucy*, season 1, vol. 1, Paramount Pictures (DVD), transcribed by the author.

250 "Harry Von Zell": quoted in Thumim, ed., p. 60.

251 "I Married Joan": *TV's Lost Shows: Family & Comedy*, Diamond Entertainment (DVD), transcribed by the author.

251 "Boynton: When it comes": ibid., transcribed by the author.

252 "C'mon, woman": Paley Center for Media, program A-577, transcribed by the author.

252 "did everyone a disservice": quoted in http://en.wikipedia.org/wiki/Father_Knows _Best.

253 "Ward, tell him to eat": Paley Center for Media, program A-575, transcribed by the author.

254 "Get back to work": Paley Center for Media, program A-581, transcribed by the author.

255 "To ensure the acceptability": Castleman and Podrazik, p. 75.

256 "Sex is important": quoted in Thumim, ed., p. 131.

256 "what sense of decency," and "low moral standards": quoted in ibid., p. 131.

256 "highly immoral," and "exploit[ed] the baser passions," and "as explicit physically": quoted in ibid., p. 141.

257 "was known less": quoted in Doherty, p. 64.

258 "stupid, unattractive, insecure": quoted in www.museum.tv/archives/etv/G/ htmlG/genderandte/genderandte.htm.

258 "comfortable concentration camp": quoted in Thumim, ed., p. 35.

258 "lay buried, unspoken": Friedan, p. 15.

CHAPTER 14: THE CONSTANT PARADE

259 "occupies about 15 percent": Postman and Powers, p. 108.

260 "is far better suited": Mander, pp. 269–70.

260 "A typical comic-book drawing": Wertham, p. 84.

261 "opens aboard a boat": Goodman, Walter, "Bang-Bang! You're Dead!," *New Republic*, November 1, 1954, p. 12.

261 "Seeing constant brutality": quoted in ibid., p. 12.

262 "share the concern": quoted in "What TV Is Doing to America," *U.S. News & World Report*, September 2, 1955, pp. 37–38.

262 "broken homes": Goodman, Walter, "Bang-Bang! You're Dead!," p. 13.

262 "the constant parade": Oakley, p. 107.

263 "There were also": Barclay, Dorothy, "A Decade Since Howdy-Doody," *New York Times* magazine, September 21, 1958, p. 63.

263 "144 murders": quoted in Barnouw, *Empire*, p. 154.

263 "Parental disapproval": quoted in Shayon, p. 19.

264 "a decided effect": quoted in Grossman, p. 25.

264 "that the demand": ibid., p. 25.

264 "because of its emphasis," and "because of their emphasis": Barclay, Dorothy, "A Decade Since Howdy-Doody," *New York Times* magazine, September 21, 1958, p. 63.

264 "it is difficult": quoted in ibid., p. 63.

265 "he reacts emotionally": ibid., p. 63.

265 "confuse violence with strength": quoted in Gould, Jack, *New York Times*, June 29, 1951, p. 27.

265 "He held that": ibid., p. 27.

266 "had a gritty, film-noir flair": *New York Times*, May 27, 2007.

267 "sanitized the subject matter": Castleman and Podrazik, p. 133.

267 "I like the idea": quoted in Miller and Nowak, p. 347.

267 "two shootouts": Lichter, Lichter, and Rothman, p. 282.

267 "Don't go in": "The Noise of Death," *The Untouchables: The Collector's Edition* (videotape), Columbia House Company, transcribed by the author.

267 "In 1963": *New York Times*, May 27, 2007.

CHAPTER 15: SERVING THE SKY CHIEF

270 "Throughout the broadcast day": quoted in "Crime Found Rife in Children's TV," *New York Times*, June 6, 1954, p. 48.

271 "In looking over": quoted in Boddy, p. 190.

272 "has reminded the faithful": *Christian Century*, December 26, 1951.

273 "The Impact of television": "I Believe in Television," *Catholic World*, March, 1950, p. 405.

273 "to acquaint American Catholics": ibid., p. 403.

274 "uplift and nourish": quoted in http://marquette.edu/library/collections/archives/Special_Collections/ARTS,_ENTERTAIN-MENT,_AND,_MEDIA.html.

274 "The Roman Catholic Church": quoted in ibid., p. 403.

274 "laudable": quoted in *New York Times*, January 8, 1954, p. 3.

274 "[r]egular television broadcasts": ibid., p. 3.

275 "Among the sources": *America*, November 3, 1956, p. 139.

276 "concerns a young minister": quoted in Lichter, Lichter, and Rothman, p. 390.

277 "surefire click," and, "tremendous box office": quoted in "Great Medium for Messages," *Time*, June 15, 1957, p. 61.

277 "Trendex awarded him": ibid., p. 61.

277 "amounted to a vast": Frady, pp. 271–72.

277 "the greatest medium": quoted in "Great Medium for Messages," *Time*, June 15, 1957, p. 61.

278 "We simply cannot assume": Stevenson, Dwight E., "Pulpit, Mike and Camera," *Christian Century*, April 24, 1957, p. 518.

279 "I was told that": quoted in ibid., p. 68.

280 "even sent in their old gold jewelry": ibid., p. 66.

280 "ask my listeners": ibid., p. 66.

280 "opened a yellow envelope": ibid., p. 66.

280 "Television is like the New Testament": Sheen, p. 63.

281 "Admiral takes pride": Museum of Television & Radio, program A-583, transcribed by the author.

281 "was on a swivel": Sheen, p. 68.

282 "was to draw Americans": Museum of Television & Radio, program A-582, transcribed by the author.

282 "Fellow citizens": quoted in Oakley, p. 323.

282 "In America": Sheen, p. 69.

283 "Abortion is wrong," and, "If you wish": Museum of Television & Radio, program A-583, transcribed by the author.

284 "I stopped a group": Museum of Television & Radio, program A-582, transcribed by the author.

284 "I feel it is time": quoted in http://en.wikipedia.org/wiki/Fulton_J._Sheen.

284 "A day or two": Sheen, p. 70.

285 "idiot cards": ibid., p. 68.

286 "Son, don't be like other men": quoted in Roberts, p. 67.

286 "Oral Roberts 'Heals,'" and "In Atlanta": "A New Revivalist, *Life*," May 7, 1951, p. 73.

286 "Violent prayer," and "WITH GOITER," and "WITH STIFF THUMB": ibid., p. 76.

287 "caused a sensation": Roberts, pp. 142–43.

288 "generous letters": quoted in Gould, Jack, "On Faith Healing: Preachers Timely TV Miracles Raise Question of Stations' Standards," *New York Times*, February 19, 1956, section 2, p. 11.

288 "quite different from": ibid., p. 11.

288 "The climactic moment": ibid., p. 11.

288 "To allow the enormously influential": ibid., p. 11.

289 "By the midfifties": Oakley, p. 322.

CHAPTER 16: THE BLACK SOX OF THE AIRWAVES

292 "The Big Bankroll": quoted in Asinof, p. 24.

292 "I'm about to face": quoted in http://en.wikipedia.org/wiki/Black_Sox_scandal.

293 "I've loved baseball": quoted in ibid.

293 "the American people": Asinof, p. 197.

294 "The game of finding out": Gould, Jack, "Rise and Fall of the Quiz Empire," *New York Times* magazine, September 28, 1958, p. 12.

294 "[Movie actress] Loretta Young's anthology series": Castleman and Podrazik, p. 125.

296 "shy, gentle," and, "smart enough to win": Halberstam, pp. 651–52.

297 "A complacent, arrogant contestant": DeLong, p. 213.

297 "One January night": Van Doren, Charles. "All the Answers," *New Yorker*, July 28, 2008, p. 64.

297 "the very image": ibid., p. 63.

297 "the ideal teacher": ibid., p. 63.

298 "with a hard-candy smile": quoted in http://jcgi.pathfinder.com/time/magazine/article/0,9171,824734,00.html.

298 "and *Twenty-One* had to face," Castleman and Podrazik, p. 115.

299 "He was to pat his brow": Van Doren, Charles. "All the Answers," *New Yorker*, July 28, 2008, p. 64.

300 "one of America's new folk heroes": ibid., p. 125.

300 "sad and shocked": quoted in ibid., p. 125.

300 "indirect help": quoted in ibid., p. 125.

301 "You cannot ask random questions": quoted in Halberstam, p. 649.

302 "Deception is not": quoted in Castleman and Podrazik, p. 133.

302 "The questions": "Are TV Quiz Shows Fixed?," *Look*, August 20, 1957, p. 46.

302 "In the field of TV programming": quoted in Castleman and Podrazik, p. 135.

302 "were too successful": quoted in ibid., p. 135.

302 "It got to the point": quoted in ibid., p. 134.

302 "What kind of country": Karp, Walter, "The Quiz Show Scandal," *American Heritage*, May/June, 1989, p. 88.

302 "a great event," "formed by a world," and "of a moral obtuseness": quoted in ibid., p. 88.

303 "second-degree perjury": Van Doren, Charles. "All the Answers," *New Yorker*, July 28, 2008, p. 67.

303 "I would give almost anything": quoted in Castleman and Podrazik, p. 134.

303 "I was involved": quoted in Oakley, p. 411.

304 "instructed me how": quoted in Castleman and Podrazik, p. 134.

304 "the time when I fell down": quoted by Beam, Alex. "After 49 Years, Van Doren Opens Up," *Boston Globe*, July 19, 2008, p. E8.

304 "He was aware": quoted in Halberstam, p. 666.

304 "How d' do": quoted in *Television,* December 1959, p. 43.

305 "a troubled decade": quoted in Boddy, p. 220.

EPILOGUE: THE MAN WITH A SECRET

307 "Now, Doctor, if you will whisper," and other quotes: from I've Got a Secret, http://farnovision.com/farno_videos.html, transcribed by the author.

Bibliography

The primary sources for this book, other than the author himself and his acquaintances, as mentioned in the Note to the Reader at the beginning of the volume, were the journalism of the era. They were newspaper and magazine articles written in the fifties in which reporters analyzed television's effect on the culture, interviewed experts and others on their feelings about TV and the ways it was changing lives, and surveyed Americans on the subject and, as best they could, put the responses into context. The periodicals I consulted, representing a wide range of interest and points of view, are listed below. References to the specific issues cited, their dates and pages, are included in the notes.

NEWSPAPERS

Boston Globe
Los Angeles Times
Manchester (New Hampshire) *Union Leader*
Daily News
New York Post
New York Times
Orange County (California) *Register*

Pittsburgh Post-Gazette
Providence (Rhode Island) *Journal Bulletin*
Salt Lake City (Utah) *Tribune*
Tulsa (Oklahoma) *Daily World*
Variety

MAGAZINES

America
American Heritage
Atlantic Monthly
Better Homes and Gardens
Business Week
Catholic World
Christian Century
Collier's
Commonweal

Coronet
Library Journal
Life
Look
Nation's Business
New Republic
New York Times magazine
New Yorker
Newsweek

Publishers Weekly	*Television Quarterly*
Reader's Digest	*Theatre Arts*
Saturday Review	*Time*
Saturday Review of Literature	*Today's Health*
Television Magazine	*TV Guide*

BOOKS

Some of the volumes that follow provided quotes for the text, others much-needed background information. A few were especially important, such as Donald Bogle's *Blacks in American Films and Television: An Encyclopedia*, an invaluable source for chapter11; and Gene Roberts's and Hank Kilbanoff's *The Race Beat: The Press, the Civil Rights Struggle, and the Awakening of a Nation*, the definitive text on the material covered in chapter12. David Halberstam's well-researched 733 pages on *The Fifties* were helpful in a number of ways, as was the encyclopedic *Watching TV: Four Decades of American Television*, by Harry Castleman and Walter J. Podrazik; and Jeff Greenfield's similarly comprehensive, and in places compellingly quirky, *Television: The First Fifty Years*.

The primary difference between my book and the preceding is that I have been more concerned with the effects of the medium on society, the contributions it made to the fifties being the kind of decade it was and thus leading to the values of the half-century after that, than I have been on the development of the technology itself. *Invasion of the Mind Snatchers* is, in other words, a work of social history, not electronic history.

Aitken, Jonathan. *Nixon: A Life*. Washington, DC: Regnery, 1993.

Allen, Fred. *Treadmill to Oblivion*. Boston: Little, Brown, 1954.

Altschuler, Glenn C., and David I. Grossvogel. *Changing Channels: America in TV Guide*. Urbana: University of Illinois Press, 1992.

Ambrose, Stephen E. *Eisenhower: Volume Two, The President*. New York: Simon and Schuster, 1984.

———. *Nixon: The Education of a Politician, 1913–1962*. New York: Simon and Schuster, 1987.

Ansolabehere, Stephen and Shanto Iyengar. *Going Negative: How Political Advertisements Shrink and Polarize the Electorate*. New York: Free Press, 1995.

Asinof, Eliot. *Eight Men Out: The Black Sox and the 1919 World Series*. New York: Henry Holt and Company, 1987.

Barnouw, Eric. *The Golden Web: A History of Broadcasting in the United States, Volume 2—1933–1953*. New York: Oxford University Press, 1968.

———. *The Image Empire: A History of Broadcasting in the United States, Volume 3—from 1953*. New York: Oxford University Press, 1970.

Berle, Milton, with Haskel Frankel. *Milton Berle: An Autobiography*. New York: Delacorte Press, 1974.

Boddy, William. *Fifties Television: The Industry and Its Critics*. Urbana: University of Illinois Press, 1990.

Bogle, Donald. *Blacks in American Films and Television: An Encyclopedia*.New York: Garland Publishing, 1988.

Brinkley, Douglas. *Rosa Parks: A Penguin Life*. New York: Viking, 2000.

Brooks, John. *The Great Leap: The Past Twenty-five Years in America*. New York: Harper and Row, 1966.

Bryson, Bill. *Made in America: An Informal History of the English Language in the United States*. New York: William Morrow, 1994.

Burns, Eric. *The Smoke of the Gods: A Social History of Tobacco*. Philadelphia: Temple University Press, 2006.

Castleman, Harry, and Walter J. Podrazik. *Watching TV: Four Decades of American Television*. New York: McGraw–Hill, 1982.

Coleman, Rick. *Fats Domino and the Lost Dawn of Rock 'n' Roll*. New York: Da Capo, 2006

Cook, Fred J. *The Nightmare Decade: The Life and Times of Senator Joe McCarthy*. New York: Random House, 1971.

Corwin, Norman. *Trivializing America*. Secaucus: Lyle Stuart, 1983.

Creminds, Lawrence A. *Popular Education and Its Discontents*. New York: Harper and Row, 1990.

Dallek, Robert. *An Unfinished Life: John F. Kennedy, 1917–1963*. Boston: Little, Brown, 2003.

Davis, Stephen. *Say Kids! What Time Is It?: Notes from the Peanut Gallery*. Boston: Little, Brown, 1987.

DeLong, Thomas A. *Quiz Craze: America's Infatuation with Game Shows*. New York: Praeger, 1991.

Diggins, John Patrick. *The Proud Decades: America in War and Peace, 1941-1960*. New York: W. W. Norton, 1988.

Doherty, Thomas. *Cold War, Cool Medium: Television, McCarthyism, and American Culture*. New York: Columbia University Press, 2003.

Ellis, Joseph J. *After the Revolution: Profiles of Early American Culture*. New York: W. W. Norton, 1979

English, T.J. *Havana Nocturne: How the Mob Owned Cuba . . . And then Lost It to the Revolution*. New York: William Morrow, 2008.

Everson, George. *The Story of Television: The Life of Philo T. Farnsworth*. New York: W. W. Norton, 1949.

Fisher, Marc. *Something in the Air: Radio, Rock, and the Revolution that Shaped a Generation*. New York: Random House, 2007.

Fontenay, Charles L. *Estes Kefauver: A Biography*. Knoxville: The University of Tennessee Press, 1980.

Fox, Stephen. *Blood and Power: Organized Crime in Twentieth-century America*. New York: William Morrow, 1989.

Frady, Marshall. *Billy Graham: A Parable of American Righteousness*. Boston: Little, Brown, 1979.

Fried, Richard M. *Nightmare in Red: The McCarthy Era in Perspective*. New York: Oxford University Press, 1990.

Friedan, Betty. *The Feminine Mystique*. New York: W. W. Norton, 1963.

Gabler, Neal. *Walt Disney: The Triumph of the American Imagination*. New York: Knopf, 2006.

Gage, Beverly. *The Day Wall Street Exploded: A Story of America in Its First Wave of Terror*. New York: Oxford University Press, 2009.

Gelernter, David. *1939: The Lost World of the Fair.* New York: Free Press, 1995.

Goldman, Eric F. *The Crucial Decade: America, 1945–1955.* New York: Knopf, 1959.

Gorman, Joseph Bruce. *Kefauver: A Political Biography.* New York: Oxford University Press, 1971.

Gray, Charlotte. *Reluctant Genius: Alexander Graham Bell and the Passion for Invention.* New York: Arcade, 2006.

Greenfield, Jeff. *No Peace, No Place: Excavations along the Generational Fault.* Garden City, New York: Doubleday, 1973.

———. *Television: The First Fifty Years.* New York: Harry N. Abrams, 1977.

Grossman, Gary H. *Saturday Morning TV.* New York: Dell, 1981.

Halberstam, David. *The Fifties.* New York: Villard, 1993.

Hart, Jeffrey. *When the Going Was Good: American Life in the Fifties.* New York: Crown, 1982.

Healy, Jane M. *Endangered Minds: Why Our Children Don't Think.* New York: Simon and Schuster, 1990.

Hofer, Dr. Stephen F., managing editor. *TV Guide: The Official Collectors Guide.* Braintree, MA: Bangzoom Publishers, 2006.

Horsfield, Peter G. *Religious Television.* New York: Longman, 1984.

Jacoby, Susan. *The Age of American Unreason.* New York: Pantheon, 2008.

Jacoway, Elizabeth. *Turn Away Thy Son: Little Rock, the Crisis that Shocked the Nation.* New York: Free Press, 2007.

Jones, Landon Y. *Great Expectations: America and the Baby Boom Generation.* New York: Coward, McCann and Geoghegan, 1980.

Lackmann, Ron. *The Encyclopedia of American Television: Broadcast Programming Post–World War II to 2000.* New York: Facts on File, 2003.

Larkin, Colin, ed. *The Encyclopedia of Popular Music*, third edition. London: Muze, 1998.

Lichter, S. Robert, Linda S. Lichter, and Stanley Rothman. *Prime Time: How TV Portrays American Culture.* Washington, DC: Regnery, 1994.

McCullough, David. *Truman.* New York: Simon and Schuster, 1992.

McKeever, Porter. *Adlai Stevenson, His Life and Legacy: A Biography.* New York: William Morrow, 1989.

McMurtry, Larry. *The Last Picture Show.* New York: Book-of-the-Month Club, 1990.

Maguire, James. *Impresario: The Life and Times of Ed Sullivan.* New York: Billboard, 2006.

Manchester, William. *The Glory and the Dream: A Narrative History of America, 1932–1972.* Boston: Little, Brown and Company, 1974.

Mander, Jerry. *Four Arguments for the Elimination of Television.* New York: William Morrow, 1978.

Marling, Karal Ann. *As Seen on TV: The Visual Culture of Everyday Life in the 1950s.* Cambridge: Harvard University Press, 1994.

Marschall, Rick. *The Golden Age of Television.* New York: Exeter, 1987.

———. *The History of Television.* New York: Gallery, 1986.

Merritt, Jeffrey D. *Day by Day: The Fifties.* New York: Facts on File, 1979.

Michaelis, David. *Schulz and Peanuts.* New York: HarperCollins, 2007.

Miller, Douglas T., and Marion Nowak. *The Fifties: The Way We Really Were*. Garden City: Doubleday, 1977.

Mitz, Rick. *The Great TV Sitcom Book, Expanded Edition*. New York: Perigree, 1983.

Morris, Roger. *Richard Milhous Nixon: The Rise of an American Politician*. New York: Henry Holt, 1990.

Nixon, Richard M. *Six Crises*. Garden City: Doubleday, 1962.

Oakley, J. Ronald. *God's Country: America in the Fifties*. New York: Dembner, 1986.

O'Neill, William L. *American High: The Years of Confidence, 1945–1960*. New York: Free Press, 1986.

Patterson, James T. *Brown v. Board of Education: A Civil Rights Milestone and Its Troubled Legacy*. Oxford: Oxford University Press, 2001.

———. *Grand Expectations: The United States, 1945–1974*. New York: Oxford University Press, 1996.

Perrett, Geoffrey. *A Dream of Greatness: The American People, 1945–1963*. New York: Coward, McGann and Geoghegan, 1979.

Postman, Neil. *Amusing Ourselves to Death: Public Discourse in the Age of Show Business*. New York: Viking, 1985.

———. *Teaching as a Conserving Activity*. New York: Delacorte, 1979.

——— and Steve Powers. *How to Watch TV News*. New York: Penguin, 1992.

Reeves, Thomas C. *The Life and Times of Joe McCarthy: A Biography*. New York: Stein and Day, 1982.

Reppetto, Thomas. *American Mafia: A History of Its Rise to Power*. New York: Henry Holt, 2004.

Ritchie: Michael. *Please Stand By: A Prehistory of Television*. Woodstock, New York: Overlook, 1994.

Roberts, Gene and Hank Klibanoff. *The Race Beat: The Press, the Civil Rights Struggle, and the Awakening of a Nation*. New York: Knopf, 2006.

Roberts, Oral. *Expect A Miracle: My Life and Ministry: Oral Robert, An Autobiography*. Nashville: Thomas Nelson, 1995.

Sales, Soupy, with Charles Salzberg. *Soupy Sez: My Zany Life and Times*.New York: M. Evans, 2001

Schickel, Richard. *Intimate Strangers: The Culture of Celebrity*. Garden City: Doubleday, 1985.

Schwartz, Evan I. *The Last Lone Inventor: A Tale of Genius, Deceit, and the Birth of Television*. New York: HarperCollins, 2002.

Seldes, Gilbert. *The Great Audience*. Westport, CT: Greenwood, 1970.

Shapiro, Ben. *Project President: Bad Hair and Botox on the Road to the White House*. Nashville: Thomas Nelson, 2008.

Shaw, Irwin. *Short Stories: Five Decades*. New York: Delacorte, 1978.

Shayon, Robert Lewis. *Television and Our Children*. New York: Longmans, Green, 1951.

Sheen, Fulton J. *Treasure in Clay: The Autobiography of Fulton J. Sheen*. Garden City: Doubleday, 1980.

Shulman, Arthur, and Roger Youman. *How Sweet It Was*. New York: Bonanza, 1966.

Siepmann, Charles A. *Radio, Television and Society*. New York: Oxford University Press, 1950.

Slater, Robert. *This . . . is CBS: A Chronicle of 60 Years.* Englewood Cliffs: Prentice–Hall, 1988.

Smith, Page. *Redeeming the Time: A People's History of the 1920s and the New Deal.* New York: McGraw–Hill, 1987.

Solberg, Carl. *Riding High: America in the Cold War.* New York: Mason and Lipscomb, 1973.

Sowell, Thomas. *The Vision of the Anointed: Self-congratulation as a Basis for Social Policy.* New York: BasicBooks, 1995.

Stashower, Daniel. *The Boy Genius and the Mogul: The Untold Story of Television.* New York: Broadway Books, 2002.

Stephens, Mitchell. *A History of News: From the Drum to the Satellite.* New York: Viking, 1988.

Streitmatter, Rodger. *Sex Sells! The Media's Journey from Represssion to Obsession.* New York: Westview, 2004.

Sykes, Charles J. *Dumbing Down Our Kids: Why American Children Feel Good about Themselves but Can't Read, Write or Add.* New York: St. Martin's, 1995.

Terrace, Vincent. *The Complete Encyclopedia of Television Programs, 1947–1979*, volume 1, A–L, second edition. New York: A. S. Barnes, 1979.

Thumin, Janet. *Small Screens, Big Ideas: Television in the 1950s.* London: I. B. Tauris, 2002.

Twitchell, James B. *Adcult USA: The Triumph of Advertising in American Culture.* New York: Columbia University Press, 1996.

———. *Carnival Culture: The Trashing of Taste in America.* New York: Columbia University Press, 1992.

von Hoffman, Nicholas. *Citizen Cohn: The Life and Times of Roy Cohn.* New York: Doubleday, 1988.

Wendt, Gerald. *Science for the World of Tomorrow.* New York: W. W. Norton, 1939.

Wertham, Fredric, M.D. *Seduction of the Innocent.* New York: Rinehart and Company, 1954.

Wilson, Clint C. II, Felix Guitierrez, and Lena M. Chao. *Racism, Sexism, and the Media: The Rise of Class Communication in Multicultural America.* Thousand Oaks: Sage, 2003.

Wilson, Sloan. *The Man in the Gray Flannel Suit.* New York: Thunder's Mouth, 2002.

OTHER SOURCES

Kefauver Committee Report on Organized Crime. New York: Didier, 1951.

The Philo T. Farnsworth Papers, Marriott Library, University of Utah.

Red Channels: The Report of Communist Influence in Radio and Television. New York: American Business Consultants, 1950.

Various videos, DVDs, and Web sites, cited in notes.

Acknowledgments

Once again, I am indebted to the reference staff of the Westport Public Library, led by the indefatigable Debbie Celia, for assistance on a book of mine. If Debbie ever decides to go into a different line of work, I'll have to switch vocations, too. My debt extends to virtually the entire staff, although I would like to single out Susan Madeo and Lynn Hudock for their procurement of interlibrary loans, of which I needed many, some of them more than once.

On second thought, perhaps the word *debt* is misleading. It suggests services having been rendered for which I will eventually provide compensation. I won't. Try though I might, I'll never be able to adequately repay my local librarians for their kindness and competence. The preceding sentence, by the way, includes the first conscious use of a split infinitive in all the books I've ever written. I seem to be getting less pedantic in my older years. My wife, more than anyone else, will be pleased.

My appreciation also goes to Eileen Reddy of the Manchester, New Hampshire Public Library and *Newsday* columnist Ellis Henican, whom I am pleased to call friend.

Various people provided information that only they could provide, and it was indispensable to my efforts. Among others, they were Marsha Tait, Senior Vice President of ProLiteracy Worldwide; and the guardians of the Philo T. Farnsworth Papers at the University of Utah Marriott Library.

I also express my gratitude to Ms. Tait for allowing me to interview her for this volume. Other interviewees, who responded either by letter, e-mail or in person, include my neighbor, the late actor Paul Newman; Win Fanning, the late radio-TV editor of the *Pittsburgh Post–Gazette*; former NBC newsman Sander Vanocur; Monica Crowley, the editorial adviser and research consultant to Richard Nixon in his post-presidential years; another neighbor, Bill Harbach, a long-time NBC director; and David Schwartz, chief curator of the Museum of the Moving Image in New York.

For a number of reasons, my own ineptitude among them, final production of this book was more of a trial than it should have been. Matthew Laughlin and Paul Kobelski saved me with a series of last-second heroics. Thank you, gentlemen, and thanks to Charles Ault at Temple, himself a last-second savior.

Also at Temple, and also recipients of my gratitude, are the tireless and caring Gary Kramer, the cool, calm, and resourceful Ann-Marie Anderson, and the diligent and level-headed Micah Kleit.

My neighbor, Miggs Burroughs, deserves some adjectives as well. Living at least part-time in the digital world while I continue to long for quill pens and parchment, Miggs prepared the photos for this volume. I appreciate the superb job he did, especially with Ed Sullivan, whose visage, like his personality, proved especially difficult.

Invasion of the Mind Snatchers is, of course, a history. Thanks to the preceding individuals, it is as fresh and relevant a version of the past as I am able to provide.

Index